Did growing literacy in the later medieval period foster popular heresy, or did heresy provide a crucial stimulus to the spread of literacy? Such questions were posed in the polemic of the time – heretics were *laici illiterati* but were at the same time possessors of dangerous books which their opponents sought to destroy, and among them were preachers whose skills in dialectic and in exegesis threatened orthodoxy – and have challenged the investigators of heresy and literacy ever since. This collaborative volume, written by a group of established scholars from Britain, continental Europe and the United States, considers the importance of the written word among the main pre-Lutheran popular heresies in a wide range of European countries, and explores the extent to which heretics' familiarity with books paralleled or exceeded that of their orthodox contemporaries.

CAMBRIDGE STUDIES IN MEDIEVAL
LITERATURE 23
Heresy and Literacy, 1000–1530

CAMBRIDGE STUDIES IN MEDIEVAL LITERATURE 23

General Editor: Professor Alastair Minnis, Professor of Medieval Literature,
University of York

Editorial Board
Professor Piero Boitani (Professor of English, Rome)
Professor Patrick Boyde, FBA (Serena Professor of Italian, Cambridge)
Professor John Burrow, FBA (Winterstoke Professor of English, Bristol)
Professor Alan Deyermond, FBA (Professor of Hispanic Studies, London)
Professor Peter Dronke, FBA (Professor of Medieval Latin Literature, Cambridge)
Dr Tony Hunt (St Peter's College, Oxford)
Professor Nigel Palmer (Professor of German Medieval and Linguistic Studies, Oxford)
Professor Winthrop Wetherbee (Professor of English, Cornell)

This series of critical books seeks to cover the whole area of literature written in the major medieval languages – the main European vernaculars, and medieval Latin and Greek – during the period *c.* 1100–*c.* 1500. Its chief aim is to publish and stimulate fresh scholarship and criticism on medieval literature, special emphasis being placed on understanding major works of poetry, prose and drama in relation to the contemporary culture and learning which fostered them.

Titles published
Dante's Inferno: *Difficulty and dead poetry,* by Robin Kirkpatrick
Dante and Difference: Writing in the Commedia, by Jeremy Tambling
Troubadours and Irony, by Simon Gaunt
Piers Plowman *and the New Anticlericalism,* by Wendy Scase
The Cantar de mio Cid: *Poetic creation in its economic and social contexts,* by John Duggan
The Medieval Greek Romance, by Roderick Beaton
Reformist Apocalypticism and Piers Plowman, by Kathryn Kerby-Fulton
Dante and the Medieval Other World, by Alison Morgan
The Theatre of Medieval Europe: New research in early drama, edited by Eckehard Simon
The Book of Memory: A study of memory in medieval culture, by Mary J. Carruthers
Rhetoric, Hermeneutics and Translation in the Middle Ages: Academic traditions and vernacular texts, by Rita Copeland
The Arthurian Romances of Chrétien de Troyes: Once and future fictions, by Donald Maddox
Richard Rolle and the Invention of Authority, by Nicholas Watson
Dreaming in the Middle Ages, by Steven F. Kruger
Chaucer and the Tradition of the "Roman Antique", by Barbara Nolan
The Romance of the Rose *and its Medieval Readers: Interpretation, reception, manuscript transmission,* by Sylvia Huot
Women and Literature in Britain, 1150–1500, edited by Carol M. Meale
Ideas and Forms of Tragedy from Aristotle to the Middle Ages, by Henry Ansgar Kelly
The Making of Textual Culture: Grammatica *and Literary Theory 350–1100* by Martin Irvine
Narrative, Authority and Power: The medieval exemplum and the Chaucerian tradition, by Larry Scanlon
Medieval Dutch Literature in its European Context, edited by Erik Kooper
Dante and the Mystical Tradition: Bernard of Clairvaux in the Commedia, by Stephen Botterill
Heresy and Literacy, 1000–1530, edited by Peter Biller and Anne Hudson

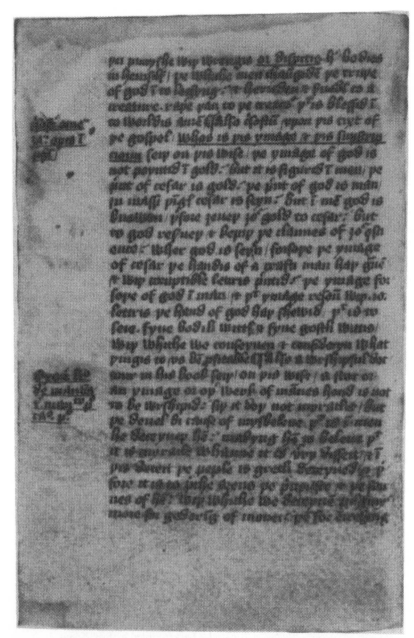

English text discussing the legitimacy of images, quoting amongst other authorities a 'wrshipful doctour in his book', amplified in the side-note 'Oxon' libro de mandatis mandato primo capitulo primo' – this is Wyclif's Latin *De mandatis*. Oxford, Bodleian Library Ms. Eng.th.f.39, fol. 7v. (With permission of the Bodleian Library.)

HERESY AND LITERACY,
1000–1530

EDITED BY

PETER BILLER
University of York

AND

ANNE HUDSON
University of Oxford

CAMBRIDGE
UNIVERSITY PRESS

Published by the Press Syndicate of the University of Cambridge
The Pitt Building, Trumpington Street, Cambridge CB2 1RP
40 West 20th Street, New York, NY 10011-4211, USA
10 Stamford Road, Oakleigh, Melbourne 3166, Australia

First published 1994
First paperback edition 1996

A catalogue record for this book is available from the British Library

Library of Congress cataloguing in publication data
Heresy and literacy, 1000–1530 / edited by Peter Biller and Anne
Hudson.
p.   cm. – (Cambridge studies in medieval literature; 23)
Includes bibliographical references.
ISBN 0 521 41979 4 (hardback)
1. Heresies, Christian – History – Middle ages, 600–1500.
2. Literacy – Europe – History. 3. Europe – Church history – Middle
Ages, 600–1500. 4. Europe – Social conditions – To 1492. 1. Biller,
Peter. II. Hudson, Anne, 1938–. III. Series.
BT1319.H47   1994
273'.6 – dc20   93–27475 CIP

ISBN 0 521 41979 4 hardback
ISBN 0 521 57576 1 paperback

Transferred to digital printing 2004

Contents

Illustrations

Acknowledgements

The editors of any collaborative volume must owe an incalculable debt to their contributors. Our gratitude to the thirteen contributors to the present volume is no less sincere for being traditional and for being briefly expressed. All have been remarkably patient with editorial queries and doubts, with requests for urgent response, and, in the case of those whose chapters were translated from their native language, with enquiries about intended meaning. It would be invidious to mention any by name, but we are especially indebted to one contributor who undertook to fill a gap at short notice. We were particularly glad to meet all our contributors (apart from one unfortunately prevented by illness from attending), and a number of other eminent scholars (two of whom, Michael Clanchy and Malcolm Lambert, are repeatedly cited in the chapters here), at a conference on the subject of the book at Lady Margaret Hall Oxford in July 1992. The conference gave the opportunity for discussion of views, for comparisons between heresies and their contexts, and for the elucidation of disagreements; we think the written words that follow are the better for the oral conversations that occurred then. It was particularly pleasing to be able to welcome visitors from Czechoslovakia and Russia, and we regretted the absence of one scholar from Bulgaria who had hoped to attend.

Warm thanks are due to the Cultural Department of the French Embassy for financial help towards the travel and translation expenses for three French contributors here, and to the British Academy for funds to enable Professors Gurevich and Šmahel to travel to the conference. The wise advice and encouragement of Professor Barrie Dobson and of Professor Michael Wilks gave us cheer at difficult moments. We are grateful to the institutions acknowledged elsewhere for supplying photographs, and are particularly indebted to Professor Paolini for his help in obtaining

plate 6. We are indebted to Dr Frances Andrews for help with the translation of the text of Professor Paolini's chapter, and to Dr Douglas Galbraith for translations of those of Dr Brenon and Professor Paravy. We are grateful to the officers of Cambridge University Press, especially Dr Katharina Brett, Miss Joanna West and Mr Kevin Taylor, for their advice and admonitions over many months, and to the copy-editor, Jenny Potts, for her meticulous attention to our text.

Collaborative editorship is a taxing process, especially when a considerable number of contributors from many countries is involved and the editors work some 200 miles apart. We have both been amazed by the ease and good humour of the whole process. If neither of us would willingly begin another such enterprise in the near future, this by no means detracts from our gratitude to each other.

PB, AH

Contributors

GABRIEL AUDISIO Professor of History, Centre des Lettres et Sciences Humaines, University of Provence (Aix–Marseille)

PETER BILLER Senior Lecturer in History, University of York

ANNE BRENON Directrice, Centre Nationale des Etudes Cathares/ Centre René Nelli, Villegly

AARON GUREVICH Professor, Institute for General History of the Academy of Sciences, Moscow

BERNARD HAMILTON Professor of History, University of Nottingham

GENEVIÈVE HASENOHR Professor, University of Paris–Sorbonne, Paris IV

ANNE HUDSON Professor of Medieval English, University of Oxford

ROBERT E. LERNER Professor of History, Northwestern University

R. I. MOORE Professor of Medieval History, University of Newcastle upon Tyne

LORENZO PAOLINI Professor, Dipartimento di Paleografia e Medievistica, University of Bologna

PIERETTE PARAVY Professor, Department of History, University of Grenoble

ALEXANDER PATSCHOVSKY Professor, Philosophische Fakultät, Fachgruppe Geschichte, University of Konstanz

BOB SCRIBNER Fellow of Clare College Cambridge

FRANTIŠEK ŠMAHEL Director, Historical Section of the Czech Academy, Prague

R. N. SWANSON Senior Lecturer in History, University of Birmingham

Abbreviations

Note: whilst this work was in the final stages of preparation, important revised editions of two books frequently cited here, Clanchy and Lambert, were published; they are noted below. Since, however, the chapters in which they are mentioned were written with knowledge only of the first editions of each, all references have been left to these. The only exception to this is the use by Hamilton, chapter 3, of the second edition of Lambert.

AASS	*Acta Sanctorum*, ed. J. Bolland and G. Herschen (Antwerp, 1643ff.)
ABAW	*Abhandlungen der bayerischen Akademie der Wissenschaften* (Munich, 1835ff.)
AD	Archives départementales
AE	Archives d'Etat
AFP	*Archivum Fratrum Praedicatorum* (Rome, 1931ff.)
AKuG	*Archiv für Kulturgeschichte* (Berlin and Leipzig, 1903ff.)
Alain	Alain de Lille, *De fide catholica*, *PL* 210.305–430
ALKG	*Archiv für Literatur- und Kirchengeschichte des Mittelalters*, ed. H. Denifle and F. Ehrle, 7 vols. (Berlin and Freiburg, 1885–1900)
Amati	*Processus contra Valdenses in Lombardia superiori anno 1387*, ed. G. Amati, *Archivio Storico Italiano* 37 (1865), 3–52, and 39 (1865), 3–61
Anselm of Alessandria	A. Dondaine, 'La hiérarchie cathare en Italie: II, Le Tractatus de hereticis d'Anselme d'Alexandrie O.P.', *AFP* 20 (1950), 234–324

ARG	*Archiv für Reformationsgeschichte* (Berlin, Leipzig and Gütersloh, 1903ff.)
ATV	*Antichi Testi Valdesi*, ed. A. D. Checchini, general eds. E. Balmas and L. B. Cedrini (Turin, 1979ff.)
Audisio	G. Audisio, *Les Vaudois du Luberon. Une minorité en Provence (1460–1560)*, Association d'Etudes Vaudoises et Historiques du Luberon (Gap, 1984)
Balmas and Dal Corso	E. Balmas and M. Dal Corso, *I manoscritti valdesi di Ginevra* (Turin, 1977)
BIHR	*Bulletin of the Institute of Historical Research* (London, 1923ff.)
Biller, 'Aspects'	P. P. A. Biller, 'Aspects of the Waldenses in the 14th century' (unpubd D.Phil. thesis, Oxford, 1974)
Biller, 'Construction'	P. P. A. Biller, 'Medieval Waldensians' construction of the past', *Proceedings of the Huguenot Society* 25 (1989), 39–54
Biller, 'Oral and written'	P. P. A. Biller, 'The oral and the written: the case of the Alpine Waldensians', *Bulletin of the Society for Renaissance Studies* 4 (1986), 19–28
Biller, 'Topos'	P. P. A. Biller, 'The topos and reality of the heretic as illiteratus', in D. Harmening (ed.), *Religiöse Laienbildung und Ketzerabwehr im Mittelalter*, Quellen und Forschungen zur europäischen Ethnologie 17 (forthcoming)
BISI	*Bollettino dell'Istituto Storico Italiano per il Medio Evo (e Archivio muratoriano)* (Rome, 1866ff.)
BM	Bibliothèque Municipale
Borst	A. Borst, *Die Katharer, MGH Schriften* 12 (Stuttgart, 1953)
BSSV	*Bulletin de la Société d'Histoire Vaudoise* (Torre Pellice, 1884–1933), *Bollettino della Società di [Storia Valdese (1934–5)] Studi Valdesi* (1935ff.)

CaF	*Cahiers de Fanjeaux* (Toulouse, 1966ff.)
Cambridge UL	University Library, Cambridge
CCCM	*Corpus Christianorum Continuatio Medievalis* (Turnhout, 1971ff.)
CCSL	*Corpus Christianorum Series Latina* (Turnhout, 1952ff.)
CFVA	*Le Confessioni di Fede dei Valdesi Riformati*, ed. V. Vinay, Collana della Facoltà Valdese di Teologia, 12 (Turin, 1975)
Chevalier	J. Chevalier, *Mémoire historique sur les hérésies en Dauphiné avant le XVIe siècle accompagné de documents inédits sur les sorciers et les vaudois* (Valence, 1890)
Clanchy	M. T. Clanchy, *From Memory to Written Record. England 1066–1307* (London, 1979; 2nd edn, Oxford, 1993)
Clement. 1.1.1	*Clementinarum* liber 1, titulus 1, canon 1
Cod. 1.1.1	*Codex Justinianus* liber 1, titulus 1, lex 1
CYS	*Canterbury and York Society* (London, 1907ff.)
d'Ablis	*L'Inquisiteur Geoffroy d'Ablis et les Cathares du comt de Foix (1308–1309)*, ed. A. Pales-Gobilliard, Sources d'Histoire Médiévale Publiées par l'Institut de Recherche et d'Histoire des Textes (Paris, 1984)
d'Avray	D. L. d'Avray, *The Preaching of the Friars: Sermons Diffused from Paris before 1300* (Oxford, 1985)
Decr. D. 1 c. 1	*Decretum Gratiani* Distinctio 1, canon 1
Decr. 11 C. 1 q. 1 c. 1	*Decretum Gratiani* 11 Causa 1, questio 1, canon 1
Decr. 111 *de Cons.* D. 1 c. 1	*Decreti tertia, pars de Consecratione* Distinctio 1, canon 1
Decret. 1.1.1	*Decretales Gregorii IX* liber 1, titulus 1, canon 1
De heresi catharorum	A. Dondaine, 'La hiérarchie cathare en Italie: 1, Le *De heresi catharorum*', *AFP* 19 (1949), 280–312
Dig. 1.1.1	*Digestum* liber 1, titulus 1, fragmentum 1

Doat	*see* Paris BN
Döllinger	I. von Döllinger, *Beiträge zur Sektengeschichte des Mittelalters*, 2 vols. (Munich, 1890)
Douais	C. Douais (ed.), *Documents pour servir à l'histoire de l'Inquisition de Languedoc*, 2 vols. (Paris, 1900)
DSP	*Dictionnaire de spiritualité, ascétique et mystique*, ed. M. Villier (Paris, 1932ff.)
Dublin TCL	Trinity College Library, Dublin
Durand, *Liber antiheresis*	*Der Liber Antiheresis des Durandus von Osca*, ed. Selge, vol. II
Durand, *Liber contra Manicheos*	*Une somme anti-cathare. Le 'Liber contra Manicheos' de Durand de Huesca*, ed. C. Thouzellier, Spicilegium Sacrum Lovaniense, Etudes et Documents, 32 (Louvain, 1964)
Duvernoy, *La Religion*	J. Duvernoy, *Le Catharisme: la religion des cathares* (Toulouse, 1976)
Duvernoy, *L'Histoire*	J. Duvernoy, *Le Catharisme: l'histoire des cathares* (Toulouse, 1979)
EFV	*Enchiridion Fontium Valdensium*, ed. G. Gonnet, vol. I [only vol. published, covering 1179–1218], Collana della Facoltà Valdese di Teologia, 4 (Torre Pellice, 1958)
EHR	*English Historical Review* (London, 1886ff.)
Emden, *Cambridge*	A. B. Emden, *A Biographical Register of the University of Cambridge to A.D. 1500* (Cambridge, 1963)
Emden, *Oxford*	A. B. Emden, *A Biographical Register of the University of Oxford to A.D. 1500*, 3 vols. (Oxford, 1957–9)
Fournier	*Le Registre d'Inquisition de Jacques Fournier, évêque de Pamiers (1318–25)*, ed. J. Duvernoy, 3 vols., Bibliothèque Méridionale, ser. 2, 41 (Toulouse, 1965), and additional *Corrections* (Toulouse, 1972)

Fredericq	*Corpus documentorum inquisitionis haereticae pravitatis Neerlandicae*, ed. P. Fredericq, 5 vols. (Ghent, 1889–1906)
Friedberg	*Corpus iuris canonici*, ed. E. Friedberg, 2 vols. (Leipzig, 1879)
Geneva BPUL	Bibliothèque Publique et Universitaire, Geneva
Glorieux	Jean Gerson, *Oeuvres complètes. Introduction, textes et notes*, ed. P. J. Glorieux, 10 vols. (Paris and Tournoi, 1960–73)
Gonnet and Molnar	G. Gonnet and A. Molnar, *Les Vaudois au moyen âge* (Turin, 1974)
Goody	Jack Goody (ed.), *Literacy in Traditional Societies* (Cambridge, 1968)
Grundmann, *Ausgewählte Aufsätze*	see *MGH Schriften* 25/1–3 (1976)
Grundmann, *Bewegungen*	*Religiöse Bewegungen im Mittelalter* (Berlin, 1935; 2nd edn, Hildesheim, 1961)
Grundmann, 'Litteratus'	H. Grundmann, 'Litteratus–illitteratus. Der Wandel einer Bildungsnorm vom Altertum zum Mittelalter', *AKuG* 40 (1958), 1–65
Gui, *Manuel*	Bernard Gui, *Manuel de l'inquisiteur*, ed. C. Douais, 2 vols., Les Classiques de l'Histoire de France au Moyen Age, 8–9 (Paris, 1926)
Gui, *Practica*	*Practica inquisitionis heretice pravitatis auctore Bernardo Guidonis ordinis Fratrum Predicatorum*, ed. C. Douais (Paris, 1886)
Guiraud	J. Guiraud, *Histoire de l'inquisition au moyen âge*, 2 vols. (Paris, 1935–8)
Head and Landes	Thomas Head and Richard Landes (eds.), *The Peace of God: Social Violence and Religious Response in France around the Year 1000* (Ithaca and London, 1992)
Heresis	*Heresis. Revue d'hérésiologie médiévale* (Villegly, 1983ff.)
Hudson	A. Hudson, *The Premature Reformation. Wycliffite Texts and Lollard History* (Oxford, 1988)

Ilarino	Ilarino da Milano, *Eresie medioevali* (Rimini, 1983)
ISIME	Istituto Storico Italiano per il Medio Evo
JEH	*Journal of Ecclesiastical History* (Cambridge, 1950ff.)
Kurze	*Quellen zur Ketzergeschichte Brandenburgs und Pommerns*, ed. D. Kurze, Veröffentlichungen der historischen Kommission zu Berlin, 45, Quellenwerke, 6 (Berlin and New York, 1975)
Lambert	M. Lambert, *Medieval Heresy: Popular Movements from Bogomil to Hus* (London, 1977); 2nd edn with subtitle *Popular Movements from the Gregorian Reform to the Reformation* (Oxford, 1992)
Leff	G. Leff, *Heresy in the Later Middle Ages* 2 vols. (Manchester, 1967)
Lerner	R. E. Lerner, *The Heresy of the Free Spirit in the Later Middle Ages* (Berkeley and London, 1972)
Limborch	*Liber sententiarum inquisitionis Tholosanae ab anno Christi MCCCVII ad annum MCCCXXIII*, ed. P. van Limborch (Amsterdam, 1692)
Livre des deux principes	*Livre des deux principes*, ed. C. Thouzellier, Sources Chrétiennes, 198 (Paris, 1973)
Livre secret	*Le Livre secret des Cathares. Interrogatio Iohannis. Apocryphe d'origine bogomile*, ed. E. Bozóky (Paris, 1980)
London BL	British Library, London
Manselli, 'Enrico'	R. Manselli, 'Il monaco Enrico e la sua eresia', *BISI* 65 (1953), 41–63
Manselli, *L'eresia*	R. Manselli, *L'eresia del male* (Naples, 1963)
Manselli, *Studi*	R. Manselli, *Studi sulle eresie del secolo xii*, ISIME, Studi Storici, 5, 2nd edn (Rome, 1975)
Marx	J. Marx, *L'Inquisition en Dauphiné. Etudes sur le développement et la répression de l'hérésie et de la sorcellerie du XIVe siècle au début du règne de François Ier*, Bibliothèque de

Marx (*cont.*)	l'Ecole des Hautes Etudes, 206 (Paris, 1914)
MBVP	*Maxima Bibliotheca Veterum Patrum*, ed. M. de La Bigne, 28 vols. (Lyons and Geneva, 1677–1707)
McKitterick	Rosamund McKitterick (ed.), *The Uses of Literacy in Early Medieval Europe* (Cambridge, 1990)
MEFR	*Mélanges d'Archéologie et d'Histoire, Ecole Française de Rome* (Paris, 1881ff.)
Merlo	G. G. Merlo, *Eretici e inquisitori nella società piemontese del trecento* (Turin, 1977)
MGH	*Monumenta Germaniae historica*
Ep	*Epistolae selectae* (Berlin, 1887ff.)
Schriften	*Schriften der MGH* (Stuttgart, 1938ff.)
SS	*Scriptores in folio*, 30 vols. (Hanover, 1824–1924)
Moneta	Moneta of Cremona, *Adversus Catharos et Valdenses Libri Quinque*, ed. T. A. Ricchini (Rome, 1743)
Montet	E. Montet, *Histoire littéraire des vaudois du Piémont* (Paris, 1885)
Moore, *Birth*	R. I. Moore, *The Birth of Popular Heresy* (London, 1975)
Moore, *Origins*	R. I. Moore, *The Origins of European Dissent*, 2nd edn (Oxford, 1987)
Paolini	*Acta S. Officii Bononie ab anno 1291 ad annum 1310*, ed. L. Paolini and R. Orioli, 2 vols. + 1 index vol., ISIME, Fonti per la Storia d'Italia, 106 (Rome, 1982)
Paris BN	Bibliothèque Nationale, Paris
Doat	Collection Doat
Patschovsky, *Passauer Anonymus*	A. Patschovsky, *Der Passauer Anonymus. Ein Sammelwerk der Ketzer, Juden, Antichrist aus der Mitte des XIII. Jahrhunderts, MGH Schriften*, 22 (Stuttgart, 1968)
Patschovsky, *Quellen*	*Quellen zur böhmischen Inquisition im 14. Jahrhundert, MGH, Quellen zur Geistesgeschichte des Mittelalters*, 11 (Munich, 1985)

Patschovsky and Selge	*Quellen zur Geschichte der Waldenser*, ed. A. Patschovsky and K. V. Selge, Texte zur Kirchen- und Theologiegeschichte, 18 (Gütersloh, 1973)
PG	*Patrologia Graeca*, ed. J. P. Migne, 161 vols. (Paris, 1857–66)
PL	*Patrologia cursus completus series latina*, ed. J. P. Migne, 221 vols. (Paris, 1844–64)
Potthast	*Regesta pontificum Romanorum inde ab anno post Christum natum 1198 ad annum 1304*, ed. A. Potthast, 2 vols. (Berlin, 1874–5; repr. Graz, 1957)
Prague Met. Kap.	Knihovna Metropolitní Kapituli, Prague
Prague Univ. Knih.	Universitní Knihovna, Prague
RBPH	*Revue Belge de Philologie et d'Histoire* (Brussels, 1922ff.)
RHE	*Revue d'histoire ecclésiastique* (Louvain, 1900ff.)
RHGF	*Recueil des Historiens des Gaules et de la France*, ed. M. Bouquet *et al.*, 24 vols. (Paris, 1738–1904)
RIS	*Rerum italicarum scriptores*, ed. L. A. Muratori, 25 vols. (Milan, 1723–51); new edn. ed. G. Carducci and V. Fiorine, 35 vols. in 109 fasc. (Città di Castello and Bologna, 1900ff.)
Rituel cathare	*Rituel cathare*, ed. C. Thouzellier, Sources Chrétiennes, 236 (Paris, 1977)
Rodulfus	*Rodulfus Glaber Opera*, ed. John France, Neithard Bulst and Paul Reynolds (Oxford, 1989)
Rottenwöhrer	G. Rottenwöhrer, *Der Katharismus* (Bad Honnef, 1982)
RS	*Rerum Brittanicarum medii aevi scriptores*, 99 vols. (London, 1858–1911) = *Rolls Series*
RTAM	*Recherches de théologie ancienne et médiévale* (Louvain, 1929ff.)
Sacconi	Rainier Sacconi, *Summa de Catharis et Pauperibus de Lugduno*, ed. F. Sanjek, *AFP* 44 (1974), 31–60

SCH	*Studies in Church History* (London and Oxford, 1964ff.)
Selge	K.-V. Selge, *Die ersten Waldenser*, 2 vols., Arbeiten zur Kirchengeschichte, 37 (Berlin, 1967)
Sext I.I.I	*Sexti Decretales* liber I, titulus I, canon I
Seyssel	Claude de Seyssel, *Adversus errores et sectam Waldensium disputationes perquam eruditae ac piae* (Paris, 1520)
SM	*Studi Medievali*, ser. 1 (Turin, 1904–13), n.s. (1928–50), ser. 3 (Spoleto, 1960ff.)
STC	*A Short-Title Catalogue of Books Printed in England, Scotland and Ireland and of English Books Printed Abroad 1475–1640*, ed. A. W. Pollard and D. R. Redgrave, revd W. A. Jackson, F. S. Ferguson, K. Panzer and P. R. Rider, 3 vols. (London, 1976–91)
Stephen of Bourbon	*Anecdotes historiques, légendes et apologues tirés du recueil inédit d'Etienne de Bourbon, Dominicain du XIIIe siècle*, ed. A. Lecoy de la Marche (Paris, 1877)
Stock	B. Stock, *The Implications of Literacy. Written Language and Models of Interpretation in the Eleventh and Twelfth Centuries* (Princeton, N.J., 1983)
Thouzellier, *Catharisme*	C. Thouzellier, *Catharisme et valdéisme en Languedoc à la fin du XIIe et au début du XIIIe siècle. Politique pontificale-controverses*, 2nd edn (Louvain and Paris, 1969)
Thouzellier, *Hérésie*	C. Thouzellier, *Hérésie et hérétiques. Vaudois, Cathares, Patarins, Albigeois*, Storia e Letteratura, Raccolta di Studi e Testi, 116 (Rome, 1969)
Traité cathare	*Un traité cathare inédit du début du XIIIe siècle, d'après le 'Liber contra Manicheos' de Durand de Huesca*, Bibliothèque de la *RHE*, 37 (Louvain and Paris, 1961)
Trefnant reg.	*Registrum Johannis Trefnant*, ed. W. W. Capes (*CYS* 1916)
TRHS	*Transactions of the Royal Historical Society* (London, 1971ff.)

Vienna ÖNB	Österreichische Nationalbibliothek, Vienna
Vinay	V. Vinay, *Le confessioni di fede dei Valdesi Riformati con documenti del dialogo fra 'prima' e 'seconda' Riforma*, Collana della Facoltà Valdese di Teologia, 12 (Turin, 1975)
Wakefield and Evans	*Heresies of the High Middle Ages*, ed. W. L. Wakefield and A. P. Evans, Records of Civilization, Sources and Studies, 81 (New York, 1969)
Wilkins	*Concilia Magnae Britanniae et Hiberniae A.D. 446–1717*, ed. D. Wilkins, 4 vols. (London, 1737)
Zanella	G. Zanella, 'L'eresia catara fra XIII e XIV secolo: in margine al disagio di una storiografia', *BISI*, 88 (1970), 239–58.

Since the publication of *Heresy and Literacy, 1000–1530* a number of important studies of the topics covered in it have appeared. The following are particularly relevant:

S. McSheffrey, 'Literacy and the Gender Gap in the Late Middle Ages: Women and Reading in Lollard Communities', and P. Biller, 'Women and Texts in Languedocian Catharism', in L. Smith and J. H. M. Taylor (eds.), *Women, the Book and the Godly* (Cambridge, 1995), pp. 157–70 and 171–82.

S. McSheffrey, *Gender and Heresy: Women and Men in Lollard Communities 1420–1530* (Philadelphia, 1995).

P. Paravy, *De la chretienté romaine à la réforme en Dauphiné. Évêques, fidèles et déviants (vers 1340–vers 1530)*, 2 vols. Collection de l'École Française de Rome 183 (Rome, 1993); see in particular ch. 21 'La bibliothèque vaudoise', vol. 2 pp. 1085–1149.

F. Šmahel, *Husitska Revoluce*, 4 vols. (Prague, 1993).

H. L. Spencer, *English Preaching in the Late Middle Ages* (Oxford, 1993).

PB, AH

CHAPTER I

Heresy and literacy: earlier history of the theme

Peter Biller

The title of the present book pays respect to tradition, *c.* 1000 as a conventional starting-point in the history of medieval heresy, and *c.* 1530, the beginnings of Waldensian adhesion to Reform, as its conventional end; the chapters are not straitjacketed by those precise years, but go back into the early middle ages and reach well into the sixteenth century. This book does not address the literacy and heresy of the individual academic theologian: his literacy is self-evident. Rather it deals with literacy and 'popular' heresy.

Heresy and the question of the 'literate', 'illiterate' and 'education' (*litteratus, illitteratus, litteratura*): whatever these were in historical reality in the middle ages, they have also constituted a *theme*, in the western medieval Church, in Catholic–Protestant polemical historiography, and in twentieth-century heresiology. Sketched in the following is this earlier awareness and discussion of the theme, leading up to this book's account of it: an overture.

I MEDIEVAL

In the middle ages the early evidence is the *topos* of the heretic as illiterate, whose repetitive and ubiquitous presence implies the theme's existence in the consciousness of various writers. The theme is implicit in all of the Church's later action against vernacular texts. It is explicit by the later twelfth century in extended direct discussions of lack of literacy and heretics' unfittedness to preach, and by the mid-thirteenth century in brief historical schemas of learning in the Church and heresy. It achieves its most precise literary expression in the early fourteenth century, in delicate delineations of heretical 'textual communities'.

Our understanding of the presence of the theme in texts of this period needs to take into account broad changes in the education

and culture of the Church's writers, broad changes in the dimensions of heresy and its audience, and a general bifurcation of the
areas in which awareness of the theme was expressed. Firstly,
because of the educational and intellectual developments of the
central middle ages there is a gulf between the Church's writers of
just after 1000 and those of 1200. Just after the millennium there are
writers stimulated, to some degree, by intellectual currents from
Cluniac monasticism, but broadly speaking belonging to an earlier
and thinner culture, and, more deeply, members of what Morris has
described as the predominantly 'cultic' Church of this time. By 1200
there is Morris's 'pastoral' Church.[1] In it there has been the development of cathedral and then university learning and the rise of
academic theology, the appearance and from now on residence on
the European scene of university masters, and their part grip on
high office in the Church. These later writers are showing a rapidly
growing capacity to describe and analyse faiths and cults, a development partly forced on by grappling with Judaism, Islam, Catharism
and Waldensianism, and, in the mid-thirteenth century, the 'religion' of the Mongols. In the earliest accounts of heresy in the eleventh
century a monk with (comparatively) slight resources can do little
better than look up St Augustine's *On Heresies*, and produces thin
and unsystematised description. By *c.* 1200 an academic's (Alain de
Lille's) account of Judaism, Islam, Catharism and Waldensianism is
still 'comparative faiths', but is laying the ground for 'comparative
religion' ('religion' in the modern sense of 'religious entity', rather
than the medieval sense of 'religious order'). By the early fourteenth
century an inquisitor's account of a sect is not only widely based on
deposition and literary evidence, but its systematic thematic
approach – the history of a sect, its articles of belief, its way of life, its
mode of evangelising – implies a yet higher stage in capacity to
describe and analyse a 'religious' entity.[2]

Secondly, there were large changes in the dimensions of heresy.
Whether fragmentary (*c.* 1000 – *c.* 1050), silent (*c.* 1050 – *c.* 1100) or
mere prolegomena (*c.* 1100 – *c.* 1150), as modern textbooks have it,
it was heresy of the later twelfth and first half of the thirteenth
century which was itself massive and provoked a massive reaction of
the Church, in crusade, foundation of the Dominican Order and
(later) the inquisition, the coming into existence of the literary genre

---

[1] C. Morris, *The Papal Monarchy. The Western Church from 1050 to 1250* (Oxford, 1989),
p. 580.
[2] P. P. A. Biller, 'Words and the medieval notion of "religion"', *JEH* 36 (1985), 353–69.

of anti-heresy polemic, and counter-reform: in Pullan's usefully provocative formulation, a twelfth- and thirteenth-century 'proto-reformation' and 'counter-reformation'.[3] At the centre were Waldensianism and Catharism: and therefore more focussed attention and reaction to what lay at the heart of these movements in terms of texts, reliance on memory and reading, and education. With counter-measures and counter-reform there came bifurcation of the areas in which one finds the theme of heresy and literacy present: on the one hand, directly present in anti-heresy polemic and descriptions of heresy; on the other hand, indirectly present in counter-measures and counter-reform where these focussed on the literacy of the orthodox clergy.

(a) Early dominance of the 'topos' of 'illiterate' heretic

By the mid-thirteenth century writers were to have at their disposal some heretical texts, much deposition evidence, discussions with heretics, and the Church's accumulated experience of heresy. So much less was available to earlier writers. When dealing with heresy and the literate or illiterate, their thesaurus of words and concepts came partly from scripture, partly from patristic writings, partly from inherited and contemporary Latin usage. Hints from scripture suggested cunning in a heresiarch, his vulpine or fox-like nature, the sheep-like simplicity of his followers, and the presence of women (pejoratively *mulierculae* (little women)) among them.[4] Where these might seem easily usable, other texts and traditions may have caused hesitation or embarrassment. One was the tradition about apostles and learning which went back to Acts 4:13: John and Peter as *sine litteris, et idiotae* (unlettered and idiots); in the formulation of Caesarius of Arles, Christ chose as apostles *piscatores sine litteris* (unlettered fishermen).[5] The suspectness of learning and holy simplicity were commonplace themes in subsequent monastic discussion. Much of what was most evident in the most prominent early father, St Augustine, was also not apposite: his emphasis, in his *On Heresies*, on heresy originating in philosophic speculation, and in particular his emphasis on bookishness in his description of the Manichees. These were ignored – deliberately?

Prominent in the Latin of these writers were the words and

---

[3] B. Pullan, *A History of Early Renaissance Italy* (London, 1973), p. 67.
[4] Judges 15:4–5, Song of Songs 2:15, Matt. 7:15; 2 Tim. 3:6.
[5] Caesarius of Arles, Sermo 1.20, ed. G. Morin (*CCSL*, 103, 1953), p. 16.

concepts *litteratus* and *illitteratus* (literate, illiterate). The growth of vernacular literature and of lay people who could read was soon to begin a slow erosion in the meanings of these terms, but in the eleventh century they still designated, as Grundmann showed in 1958,[6] two 'education-worlds': 'literate', the education-world of Latin and the cleric, and the norm of reading and writing; 'illiterate', the education-world of the vernacular and the lay person (of any estate), and the norm of not reading and writing. When reading these words it is important to remember both the original distance from the modern meanings of the two words and the gradual changes which were about to occur.

In the earliest period then, in the eleventh century, the first *topos* to emerge was that of the heretic as illiterate,[7] that is to say, outside the Latin 'education-world', when heresy was contrasted with the literate Church. This was complementary to the *internal* picture of teacher and taught inside a sect, when a sect was being looked at in its own right. Then, internally, in a sect, there were the masters or teachers, who were cunning and clever; and there were the simple or stupid people they seduced. Where agency of the devil was emphasised, teachers' cunning could acquire diabolic assistance, enabling an adept, for example, to become learned in letters in a matter of days.[8]

Where, however, the sect was compared to the Church, there was the simple counterposing of the illiterates of the sect and the literate men of the Church: to be found universally in chronicles, canon law, inquisitors' treatises, polemics, this flourished for a long time. It acquired a stock theme (earliest with Guibert de Nogent, *c.* 1115):[9] exemplification through an example of mistranslation of a brief passage in the Vulgate, showing simultaneously lack of Latin and stupidity.

By the late twelfth century, in the writings by Bernard of Fontcaude and Alain de Lille against preaching by the Waldensians, the theme of heresy and literacy or illiteracy is explored extensively. Before parading his ripostes, Bernard reports the Waldensians' arguments – St Gregory's *Dialogues* preserve the memory of laymen who preached, the first apostles were 'unlettered idiots' (again Acts 4:13), they were lay and preached, we should imitate their acts.[10]

---

[6] Grundmann, 'Litteratus'.

[7] There is fuller citation of evidence on this in Biller, 'Topos'.

[8] Wakefield and Evans, p. 139; on this text, which is now known to date back at least to the early eleventh century, Moore, ch. 2 below, n. 5.

[9] See, below, Moore ch. 2, p. 23, and Patschovsky, ch. 7, p. 132.

[10] Bernard of Fontcaude, *Adversus Valdensium sectam* 4.15, *PL* 204.809.

Alain takes up the point more forcefully in extended discussion of the inappropriateness of a non-literate teaching what he cannot understand.[11] Meanings of the key-words overlap in these texts: layman/illiterate' (= not belonging to the Latin education-world), 'layman' (= not in orders) and 'illiterate' (= not educated, not able to understand).

The *topos* was to have a later history, and a persistence throughout the middle ages. With the appearance of extensive polemical refutations, from the later twelfth century, there was to be a lexical development: a widening of the thesaurus of words meaning 'stupid' which were used about parchment/paper opponents. More significant was to be the widening of 'literate : illiterate' in the mid-thirteenth century by the Anonymous of Passau. In his powerfully polarised features of 'Church : Heresy' the theme was linked to numbers, rank, power and sex. 'A multitude of believers [proves our faith], for every kind of man has our faith: philosophers, the literate [*or* educated], and Princes; but only a few have the faith of the heretics, and these are only the poor, workmen, women, and idiots [= the illiterate]' ('Multitudo credencium, quia omne genus hominum habet fidem nostram: philosophorum, litteratorum, principum. Sed hereticorum pauci et hoc tantum pauperes et opifices, mulieres et ydiote').[12]

(b) The crisis of c. 1200: grappling with literacy among heretical preachers

The *topos* of heretic as illiterate persists – one finds as ever, for example, a Prussian inquisitor and polemicist writing in 1395, 'O vos illiterati haeretici' (Oh, you illiterate heretics).[13] But it was no longer centre-stage. The massive growth of heresy in the later twelfth century was making the Church think why heresy had such an appeal. A lack of educated preachers was decried in a crescendo of voices from St Bernard ('Who will give me "literate" pastors?')[14] onwards through the twelfth century. There followed fundamental

---

[11] Alain, 2.1–4, 377–82.

[12] Patschovsky, *Passauer Anonymus*, p. 109.

[13] Peter Zwicker in his *Cum dormirent homines*; see Patschovsky below, ch. 7, n. 49, and P. P. A. Biller, 'Les vaudois dans les territoires de langue allemande vers la fin du XIVᵉ siècle: le regard d'un inquisiteur', *Heresis* 13/14 (1989), p. 215.

[14] R. Ladner, 'L'Ordo Praedicatorum avant l'ordre des prêcheurs', in P. Mandonnet, *Saint Dominique. L'idée, l'homme et l'œuvre*, ed. M.-H. Vicaire and R. Ladner (Paris, 1938), vol. II, pp. 11–68 for the following general picture, and vol. II, p. 17 and n. 27 for St Bernard; d'Avray, ch. 1, gives a more modern account of the general background.

legislation in 1179 and 1215 for the provision of diocesan education of the clergy and the institution of preachers, and the emergence of the concept and then the existence of an 'Order of Preachers', precisely dedicated to a preaching efficiently based on a highly functional education system and the use of practical 'how to do it' pocket-manuals. In the decades around 1200 papal bulls, legislation, treatises of reform (most notably in Jacques de Vitry's account of the western Church) and sermons contain countless allusions to and discussions of preaching and instruction, literacy/illiteracy of preachers (including the persistent but minor theme of the holy 'illiterate' preacher, following the early illiterate fishermen). These commonplaces in the history of the twelfth- and thirteenth-century Latin Church are repeated here as a reminder that such thought spelled out, and repressive measures and counter-reform implied, awareness of the same range of reasons: lack of 'literacy' in the Church's preachers when compared to the preaching of skilled heretical preachers, the expectations of their audience and (more particularly) the question of the use of vernacular texts. Present throughout implicitly, and sometimes explicitly, was the theme of heresy and literacy/illiteracy. By the mid-thirteenth century descriptions of heresy assume this backcloth, and when they turn to literacy/illiteracy and heresy they concentrate on particulars.

Detailed quotation and discussion of these later texts appear elsewhere in this book (see especially Patschovsky, Biller, Paolini and Lerner). Here one should note some salient features. The Cathars appear as very learned: for example, in Alain de Lille's presentation of southern French Cathars, who use alongside authorities arguments (*rationes*) which depend on scholastic logic,[15] or in Yvo of Narbonne's letter, where Italian Cathars send adepts to the University of Paris.[16] The Waldensians are painted with various shades by Stephen of Bourbon and the Anonymous of Passau. These include use of the vernacular, degrees of literacy, relationship between texts, literacy and the extensive use of memorisation; the latter present in more stereotypical form in the treatise by the (Pseudo-)David of Augsburg.[17] Writers now display much sophistication on these themes.[18] In the mid-thirteenth century Stephen of

---

[15] Biller, ch. 4 below, n. 114.   [16] Paolini, ch. 5 below, n. 59.
[17] For this use of memory, see Biller, 'Construction', pp. 44–7.
[18] Patschovsky, ch. 7 below, emphasises more the element of caricature.

Plate 1   Scene from the life of St Dominic, when, during debate with Cathars,
books are put to ordeal by fire, in which the Cathar book is consumed but St
Dominic's book escapes unharmed. Relief work by Nicola Pisano (*c.* 1264–7) on the
tomb of St Dominic, Church of St Dominic, Bologna. (With permission of the
Convento Patriarcale S. Domenico, Bologna.)

Bourbon and the Anonymous of Passau seem to be essaying a historical presentation of degrees of learning in the Church and heresy, comparing *c.* 1200 with the mid-thirteenth century: *then* many learned heretics but few in the Church, by implication as opposed to now.[19] In the early fourteenth century, in the set-piece systematic descriptions of sects in his inquisitor's handbook, Gui delicately discriminates (with an accuracy which is not at issue here): literate, not literate, or a mixture; use of texts; vernacular of Latin; modes of their use. One example is his description of the dissemination of books and pamphlets of Olivi, records of Olivi in different sorts of texts, specification of Latin and vernacular, followers living in villages and gathering to listen to readings in the vernacular (see plate 9).[20] To the modern reader it uncannily calls to mind the most sophisticated modern analysis of heresy and literacy (discussed below) and its 'textual communities'.

Broader stereotypes came to be established in art during the thirteenth century. The Church's crisis around 1200 achieved general representation through the iconography of one scene in the lives of St Dominic and St Francis. St John Lateran – and, more widely, the Church – topples down while a pope (Innocent III) sleeps within and dreams; St Dominic (or St Francis) rushes along to prop up the Church. One regularly represented scene from St Dominic's life was rooted, historically, in one of the formal debates between Cathars and Catholics in southern France, where there were exchanges of schedules or little books containing arguments and counter-arguments.[21] Two little books are thrown on to a fire: the heretic's book is consumed, while St Dominic's leaps out miraculously (see plate 1).[22] Elsewhere, a confuted heretic came to be represented as someone tearing up a book.[23] Commonplaces for the later middle ages were thus provided, both of the crisis of *c.* 1200 and one of its elements: heresy with a book, a peril vanquished by St

---

[19] Biller, ch. 4 below, nn. 87, 122.   [20] Lerner, ch. 11 below, nn. 5 and 54.

[21] Biller, ch. 4 below, n. 72.

[22] G. Kaftal, *Iconography of the Saints in Tuscan Painting* (Florence, 1952), col. 311 and fig. 358; the earliest pictorial representation known to me is the relief work of the Arca di S. Domenico, Bologna (*c.* 1264–7). The falling church: cols. 313–14, 389, 391–2, and G. Kaftal, *Iconography of the Saints in Central and South Italian Schools of Painting* (Florence, 1965), cols. 357, 473–4.

[23] In the 'Mission of the preachers in the Church' fresco by Andrea Bonaiuti in the Spanish Chapel, Santa Maria Novella, Florence (between 1366 and 1368). For an example of earlier heretics represented thus (*c.* 1400), J. and P. Courcelle, *Iconographie de Saint Augustin. Les cycles du XIVe siècle* (Paris, 1965), p. 98 (and fig. 107).

Dominic with a book. The heretic's book has already vanished or is being destroyed, while the Church triumphs through the continuing visibility of its book.

(c) Heretics' views

Heretics' own commonplaces were close parallels of the two discussed above: first, heretic as illiterate opposed to the literate Church; second, a view of the heresy and Church in which both had literacy and books, but each was characterised differently.

The *topos* of heretic : illiterate was appropriated by heretics and turned round, in their version of the tradition of the unlettered early apostles. This is implicit in an address by an early thirteenth-century French Cathar to the Catholic clergy: 'O insensati litterati' (Oh, you insensate literate (*or* learned) men!).[24] It is explicit in a letter by Italian Waldensians of *c.* 1367 in which the Waldensians write extensively about themselves as the unlettered, using the phrase of Caesarius of Arles ('unlettered fishermen') quoted above; unlettered, and also weak in worldly terms, following the early apostles.[25] Irony: the Cathar was writing a treatise in elegant and learned Latin, the Waldensians a letter in flowery and quite learned Latin! The opposed literacy of the Church was rationalised: 'Although chaplains and religious understand the scriptures and the law of God, they do not want to reveal [them] clearly to the people, the better to rule over them' (Capellani & religiosi licet intelligant scripturas & legem Dei nolunt revelare clare populo, ut ex hoc melius dominentur in populo).[26] The Waldensian follower attesting this in 1311 recalls the Anonymous of Passau linking literacy with the powerful.

In a rather different context the encounter of 'oral' peasants with the learned apparatus of inquisitors, handbooks, leading questions and written process produced an uneven sharper expression, proverbially expressed. As one follower of the Cathars said to another, who was about to be interrogated, 'bouem rapit homo per cornu et rusticum per ling[u]am' (A man takes an ox by a horn and a peasant by his tongue).[27] One particular example of 'us' and 'them'

---

[24] Biller, ch. 4 below, n. 107.   [25] Biller, 'Aspects', pp. 278–80.
[26] Limborch, p. 377.
[27] Doat 25, fol. 296v. Compare J. W. Hassell, *Middle French Proverbs, Sentences, and Proverbial Phrases* (Toronto, 1982), p. 55, no. B118.

is momentarily glimpsed here in 'peasant' minds as 'literate' versus 'oral'.

The second theme looms larger – heretics' own use of books, the enormous implications of their use of the vernacular, their own literacy. One example of their rare general presentations of this comes from Waldensian preaching remembered in Piedmont. In this, the apostles split into two groups. The smaller and weaker group, four apostles, had Christ's books (i.e. the Gospels), and people understood their singing (i.e. preaching – because in the vernacular, or unglossed?), while the larger and stronger group, eight apostles, had other books, and no-one understood their singing. The larger group took the marketplace (openness), and drove the smaller group into secrecy.[28] Here the view of Waldensian/Church contrasts (small : large, weak : powerful, secrecy : publicness) had been added to contrasts in the books possessed and their use: Christ's books : other books, comprehensible : incomprehensible. We have only the final result of a contemporary contrast perceived and thought about so deeply and for such a long time that eventually it had acquired its own historical myth, its historical warranty, in a projection back to apostolic times.

2 CONFESSIONAL POLEMICAL HISTORIOGRAPHY: PROTESTANT HISTORY

Confessional polemical history dominated heresiology between the sixteenth and early eighteenth centuries, and continued to supply the biggest stimulus to the public's interest in medieval heresy till well into the twentieth century. Here only one strand appears, Protestant history, and only one representative of that strand, Flacius Illyricus, who was, after Bale,[29] its most important begetter. His *Catalogue of Witnesses to the Truth (Catalogus Testium Veritatis)* laid down the fundamental lines of interpretation, a continuity of witnesses between the early Church and Luther, and provided basic material for later historians through its editions of important medieval texts on heresy. Although the ancient theme of the fittedness of

---

[28] Merlo, p. 220, and for discussion Merlo, pp. 22–4, and Biller, 'Construction', p. 50.
[29] On Bale's contribution, see L. Fairfield, *John Bale, Mythmaker for the Reformation* (West Lafayette, 1976).

the illiterate Peter for preaching re-appears,[30] illiteracy is not prominent. His interpretive scheme pushed Flacius to look among heretics for a continuity of at least 'some teachers and followers' (*doctores et auditores*) who opposed the Roman Church 'in word and writing' (*voce et scriptis*). 'Wherever there will have been a more right-thinking teacher there will also have been many listeners ... [also some who] through fear did not dare to write anything, or if they did write something ... it will have perished' ('ubi unus doctor rectus sentiens fuerit, ibi quoque plurimos auditores ... vel metu scribere ... ausi sint, vel etiam si quid scripserunt ... perierit').[31] In his presentation of the central middle ages his counterposing of apostles of Satan in the Roman Church and heretics as Protestant witnesses continues the *topos* of excessive learning in the Church, where two of Satan's apostles, Peter Lombard and Gratian, collect and distort sentences of the fathers.[32] Set against these are the heretics, giving only scripture, and Valdes providing it in the vernacular. Running through the (self-evident) themes of excess learning against *sola scriptura*, however, is a simple emphasis on praise of medieval heretics: and where this involves learning, praise of their learning. Thus Valdes becomes a 'learned man' (*homo doctus*),[33] there is zeal for learning and teaching, Waldensians have teachers (*praeceptores*) in Lombardy, 'learned and subtle teachers' (*doctos ac subtiles doctores*), 'schools or Academies' (*scholae seu Academiae*),[34] and the (eventual) printing of their dialect bible is done 'elegantly' (*eleganter*).[35]

Flacius was read by most significant later Protestant historians of heresy, well into the nineteenth century. While his *Catalogue of Witnesses* may have bequeathed to them some simplification of the theme it also gave them an edition of the Anonymous of Passau.[36] This was proportionately very large in the *Catalogue of Witnesses* (texts about other heresies had much less space), and there was therein a double significance. Flacius encouraged later historians to make Waldensians prominent in the picture of medieval 'heretical' Protestants. Since the themes of heretics' literacy, illiteracy, use of

---

[30] M. Flacius (Illyricus), *Catalogus Testium Veritatis* (1st edn, Basel, 1556; cited here from Strasbourg, 1562 edn), p. 1.

[31] Flacius, *Catalogus*, preface.   [32] Flacius, *Catalogus*, p. 414.

[33] Flacius, *Catalogus*, p. 414.

[34] Flacius, *Catalogus*, p. 430.   [35] Flacius, *Catalogus*, p. 427.

[36] Flacius, *Catalogus*, pp. 431–44.

memory and use of the vernacular are so prominent in the Anonymous, Flacius also encouraged later historians to recall or develop
these themes.

3 MODERN

'Libres penseurs ... théologiens philosophes' (Free thinkers ...
philosopher–theologians): the vocabulary used about heretical
preachers by the mid nineteenth-century Lutheran heresiologist
from Strasbourg, Schmidt,[37] betrays the way one later current of
thought imposed its concepts on 'literate' medieval heretical
preachers. This is only one example among many. A full investigation of the later masks worn by these preachers could start with
the use of Borst's 1953 history of the post-medieval study of medieval
heresy[38] as a basic guide to a researcher who would ask of each later
school, 'How did it present heresy from the point of view of literacy?'
This is not attempted in this sketch, partly because the research has
not been done, and partly because the centuries-long dominance of
the main lines of Protestant historiography renders it of less general
significance: it would be an interesting footnote.

The final area to be sketched is this: the beginnings and expansion
of modern interest in heresy and literacy, divided here into (a)
particular scholarly developments ((i) texts, (ii) interpretive scholarship), (b) more general intellectual movements.

(a) Scholarship

(i) Texts
Modern expansion of interest in heresy and literacy rests in the first
instance on developments in pure scholarship. Where earlier historians could find no writings of heretics, because they had perished,
or paid little attention to those which survived, the mid- and later
twentieth century has seen an extraordinary expansion in the
volume of texts written by heretics which are now paraded for study.
The Dominican Dondaine's discoveries included a mid-thirteenth-
century Italian Cathar treatise, Valdes's profession of faith and two

---

[37] C. Schmidt, *Histoire et doctrine des Cathares* (Paris and Geneva, 1848–9), vol. I, p. ii.
[38] Borst, pp. 27–58, to which would be added the accounts of historiography in *CaF* 14 (1979)
and in the book ed. by Merlo cited in n. 59 below.

anti-Cathar Waldensian treatises, in one of which were the extensive remains of an early thirteenth-century French Cathar treatise; and he also rehabilitated a seventeenth-century copy, long thought a forgery, of a Cathar administrative document.[39] From Selge and Thouzellier came meticulous studies and editions of some of these.[40] Another Dominican, Kaeppeli, accounted for the relation between the Waldensian *Liber electorum* (see plates 7 and 8) and a group of mid-fourteenth-century letters by Waldensians and ex-Waldensians, which were later edited in an unpublished thesis by Biller.[41] From Venckeleer came the identification of a Cathar gloss on the *Pater Noster*.[42] From the Rouses there has just come the identification of another text by the Waldensian Durand of Huesca.[43]

Other landmarks have been the editing and study of the writings of the Waldensians and Lollards in the later middle ages. The modern begetter of Lollard study, McFarlane, had mourned the paucity of sources: but did not use the extensive writings of the Lollards.[44] Since the early 1970s these have been subjected to searching textual and historical scrutiny by Hudson,[45] edited (by Hudson, and also Gradon),[46] and, finally, they have been used, together with all the traditional historical material, principally trial data, as the basis for a major re-interpretation inside Hudson's large and new general account of Lollardy.[47] Lollardy has been more firmly tied to its Oxford source; it has more spine; the roles of the production and dissemination of books, teaching, and literacy are now at the centre of the picture.

[39] On Dondaine's discoveries see Y. Dossat, 'La découverte des textes cathares: le père Antoine Dondaine,', *CaF* 14 (1979) 343–59, and 'Introduction' in A. Dondaine, *Les Hérésies et l'inquisition XIIe–XIIIe siècles*, ed. Y. Dossat (London, 1990), pp. vii–x; Selge, vol. II, pp. ix–x.

[40] Durand, *Liber antiheresis* and *Liber contra Manicheos; Livre des deux principes*. From Thouzellier also the edn of the *Rituel cathare*.

[41] T. Kaeppeli and A. Zaninovic, 'Traités anti-vaudois dans le manuscrit 30 de la Bibliothèque des Dominicains de Dubrovnik-Raguse', *AFP* 24 (1954) 297–325; ed. in Biller, 'Aspects', pp. 264–353; apart from Oxford, copies of this are at the Centre National des Etudes Cathares, Villegly, and the Società di Studi Valdesi, Torre Pellice.

[42] Brenon, ch. 8 below, n. 16.   [43] Patschovsky, ch. 7 below, n. 25.

[44] Hudson, p. 2.

[45] Studies from 1971 to 1984 are listed in Hudson, pp. 531–2. The most important other studies came from M. Aston, collected in her *Lollards and Reformers. Images and Literacy in Late Medieval Religion* (London, 1984); see the listing of these and further bibliography in Hudson, p. 527.

[46] A. Hudson (ed.), *Selections from English Wycliffite Writings*, (Cambridge, 1978); A. Hudson and P. Gradon (ed.), *English Wycliffite Sermons*, 3 vols. (Oxford, 1983–90; Gradon edited vol. II).

[47] Hudson.

At around the same time there were taking place two notable initiatives in the parallel field of Waldensian alpine dialect literature, under the direction of a Milan scholar, Balmas.[48] One was a suggestion for ʿinterpretation. Where earlier scholarship had struggled to identify what was Waldensian, relegating some works in the dialect manuscripts as Catholic or Catholic imitations, Balmas's team pointed out that it was naive to think that the Waldensian preachers, clerical and living when they did, could be anything but part of later medieval clerical culture. But – and this is the point – they *chose* what they wanted from this culture. The scholar's task, therefore, is the careful study of the contours of this choice (as well, of course, of original work).[49] The other initiative was a grand plan to edit the texts, manuscript by manuscript, in a series entitled *Antichi Testi Valdesi*. This would present texts as they appear in one particular manuscript, with philological apparatus, glossaries and bibliographies of earlier studies, but without identification of quotations (other than scriptural) or sources.[50]

The picture is not all bright. After the quick appearance of two volumes of texts (1979, 1984) there has been nothing.[51] Further, Balmas and his team are editors and philologists, who do not use historians' evidence (trial material), and the historians of this area have tended to make little use of the manuscript books:[52] a contrast with the fusion recently achieved in the Lollard field.

These are qualifications to a larger picture, in which the main theme is massive expansion in the availability of texts *by* heretics, and therefore a greater role played by this evidence in accounts of heresy. This has stimulated greater and deeper investigation of those themes which have never been entirely absent, such as literacy, heretical composition, culture, schooling and modes of dissemination.

(ii) Interpretive scholarship: Grundmann, Stock

The most significant mid-twentieth century advances in interpretive scholarship came from Grundmann. Three points and dates stand

---

[48] For the following, see Biller, 'Oral and written', 19–28.

[49] Their studies were collected in E. Balmas (ed.), *Nuove ricerche di letteratura occitanica* (Turin, 1983).

[50] See *ATV* I, pp. iii–viii, and the (varying) advertised details of the project at the beginnings of the two published vols.

[51] Dr Claudio Papini, director of the series' publishing house, Editrice Claudiana, Turin, has informed me that the project is at a standstill (September 1992).

[52] Recent exceptions are G. G. Merlo, *Val Pragelato 1488* (Torre Pellice, 1988), pp. 48–52, and Paravy, ch. 9 below.

out. Grundmann's work on the *topos* of the heretic (1927) drew attention to the element of the heretic as stupid and illiterate.[53] His showing of the religious movements (whether orthodox or heretical) of the twelfth and thirteenth centuries as generically similar phenomena (1935) opened the way for the investigation of parallels, significant also in this field.[54] Since Grundmann anyone who reads, for example, a monograph by d'Avray on mendicants carrying their little *vade-mecum* books on their journeys to preach and hear confessions[55] will juxtapose these with Cathar perfects and Waldensian brothers journeying to visit their followers with their little *vade-mecum* books. Finally Grundmann's article on the words 'literate' and 'illiterate' (1958),[56] carefully showed their various medieval connotations, and thus laid the foundations for modern study of what they designated. Since Grundmann there have been some local contributions, in particular Mundy's studies of literacy and Catharism in the Toulousain,[57] and one major monograph from Stock (1983). Stock brought to bear on early medieval heresy the concerns of modern anthropological and sociological study of the function of orality and literacy in a society. In the eleventh century the relations between oral and literate cultures in western Europe were changing, and with them modes of thought. For Stock the early heresies were a by-product of this seismic shift.[58] From this time Stock's book has provided much of the themes and vocabulary (e.g. 'textual communities') of debate.

(b) Historiographic and wider intellectual trends

Why should the theme of heresy and literacy so predominate now? A firm answer may eventually come from a later intellectual historian: what follows is speculation.

If one uses the image of concentric circles for the intellectual background, then a remote outer circle is the stimulus to historical questions provided by the contemporary technological revolution in

---

[53] H. Grundmann, 'Der Typus des Ketzers in mittelalterlicher Anschauungen', reprinted in his *Ausgewählte Aufsätze* 1 (= *MGH Schriften* 25.1), p. 316 and n. 9.

[54] Grundmann, *Bewegungen*.

[55] D'Avray, pp. 45, 51 and n. 2, 56–62; see Brenon, chapter 8 below, for dimensions of Waldensian books, and compare Biller, ch. 4 below and, his nn. 75–81 on Cathar books.

[56] Grundmann, 'Litteratus'.   [57] Biller, ch. 4, n. 3.

[58] Stock, pp. 88–151, 231–3, 235, and (on Valdes) his *Listening for the Text. On the Uses of the Past* (Baltimore and London, 1990), ch. 1.

communications, fairly remote circles are modern French philosophy and literary theory, and (perilously) nearer circles are the explosion in almost all areas of the humanities of books riddled with vogue words such as *Orality* and *Textuality*, usually with capital initial letters. Among the inner circles are the developments in heresy scholarship which have just been sketched; and also historiography.

Though never uniform, the map of the historiography of heresy in the English-speaking world in the 1950s and 1960s showed some prominent features.[59] The Columbia school of heresiology, founded and led by A. P. Evans, followed – and continues to follow – a concern to set heresy in a material, concrete, tangible world. More radically, there was in this period a vogue for investigating (sometimes only to criticise) Marxist accounts of heresy; and then a decline by the early 1970s. What was to fill the vacuum left by this decline and the lack of a fundamental interpretive crux in the Columbia school? Now, the early and mid-1970s saw the publication of N. Cohn's *Europe's Inner Demons* (London, 1975), R. I. Moore's *The Origins of European Dissent* (London, 1977) and R. E. Lerner's *The Heresy of the Free Spirit in the Later Middle Ages* (Berkeley, Los Angeles and London, 1972). Some common concerns can be seen. Grundmann's article on the *topos* of the heretic influenced all three in their concern to whittle away what could be regarded as true in reports of heresy. Grundmann's article on the problems of using trial evidence based on leading questions[60] influenced two of them – Moore's book, pre-inquisition, was too early for this to be relevant. These books pursued different theses: the demonisation of medieval heretics as a prelude to the witch-fantasy (Cohn), the unreliability of clerical sources on heresy between *c.* 1000 and *c.* 1200 (Moore, in part), and the sect of the Free Spirit as a fantasy, a product of the *topos* allied to the use of leading questions and torture (Lerner). However, they showed a common drift in their concern, broadly, with knowledge, and, more narrowly, the distorted *image* of a phenomenon, the independent tradition of images in a textual tradition. They can be seen as precursors. And they have

---

[59] An account of this is given in P. P. A. Biller, 'La storiografia intorno all'eresia medievale negli Stati Uniti e in Gran Bretagna (1945–92)', in G. G. Merlo (ed.), *Eretici ed eresie medievali nella storiografia contemporanea* (Torre Pellice, 1994), 39–63.

[60] H. Grundmann, 'Ketzerverhöre des Spätmittelalters als quellenkritisches Problem', repr. in his *Ausgewählte Aufsätze* I (= *MGH Schriften* 25.1), pp. 364–416.

direct heirs in those whose use of the later themes of 'popular' and 'elite culture' includes the desire to demonstrate the remoteness of images or heretics independently transmitted in Latin texts in 'elite culture'.

Meanwhile there was the spread in general in European historiography of this theme of 'popular' and 'elite cultures'. Its ramifications were various. The journal *Annales* promoted 'popular culture' as a theme for study. There was a Russian interest in dialectical opposition between the two cultures which went back to the much earlier literary theory writings of Bakhtin. Meanwhile, in Italy, Gramsci had proposed that rule by the 'elite' over lower ('subaltern') groups was maintained by the latter's acceptance of the former's culture, something which was facilitated by 'elite culture' 'recuperating' elements of 'popular culture' into itself in order to be more persuasive. The dichotomous view of the two cultures was attested most among Italian, French and Russian medieval or early modern studies (e.g. Ginzburg, Schmitt, Gurevich),[61] most influentially by Ginzburg.

Now, there has been a long tradition of putting masks onto medieval heretics – Flacius gave them Protestant masks, Engels revolutionary, Rosenberg Nazi,[62] Koch feminist[63] – and by the 1970s their latest, 'popular cultural', mask was taking shape. First in modern heresiology (1977) was a subtle study in which Merlo used the vocabulary and concerns of this approach in his investigation of heresy in the valleys and mountains of fourteenth-century Piedmont. Second (1984) came a study of the same area in the fifteenth and sixteenth centuries by Cameron.[64] This put forward a more black-and-white model in which heretics were exponents of 'popular culture' (rural, oral, proverbial), misunderstood by 'elite culture'

[61] C. Ginzburg, *The Cheese and the Worms. The Cosmos of a Sixteenth-century Miller*, 1st edn, 1976, transl. J. Tedeschi and A. Tedeschi (London and Henley, 1980), pp. xiii–xxiv; J.-C. Schmitt, *The Holy Greyhound. Guinefort, Healer of Children since the Thirteenth Century*, 1st edn, 1979, transl. M. Thom (Cambridge and Paris, 1983), pp. 1, 7–8, 176–8; A. I. Gurevich, *Medieval Popular Culture: Problems of Belief and Perception*, transl. J. M. Bak and P. A. Hollingsworth (Cambridge and Paris, 1988), pp. xiii–xx.

[62] On Engels and Rosenberg, R. Manselli, 'Les approches matérialistes de l'histoire du Catharisme', and J.-L. Biget, 'Mythographie du Catharisme (1870–1960)', *CaF* 14 (1979), 230 and 314–15.

[63] G. Koch, *Frauenfrage und Ketzertum im Mittelalter*, Forschungen zur mittelalterlichen Geschichte 9 (Berlin, 1962).

[64] Merlo; E. Cameron, *The Reformation of the Heretics. The Waldenses of the Alps* (Oxford, 1984), on which see J.-P. Gilmont, 'Les Vaudois des Alpes: mythes et réalités', *RHE* 83 (1988), 74.

(medieval inquisitors and, later, Geneva-trained pastors). Here heretics' literacy and books were prominent through their absence, since the book's thesis rested in part on arguments for their exclusion.

Finally, there has been the coming-together of the English-writing academic world and European heresy scholarship. The impulse towards *heresy* and *literacy* may be strongest in one area. The suggestion for this book came from a British university press in 1990, and it has been pursued and edited by two British scholars. Perhaps not just a single accident? A British scholar (Clanchy) put the England of the middle ages on the vanguard of medieval literacy studies in 1979; in English, from a North American scholar (Stock), there has come the most intellectually problematic of all works on heresy and literacy; and it is English heresy which has seen the largest and most significant advance in the understanding of a medieval heresy through closer examination of the writings, schools and modes of instruction of a set of heretics (Hudson's work on Lollardy). At the same time, currently, heresy scholarship in general in Germany, central Europe, France and Italy is enjoying a golden period. A number of great heresy scholars represented in this volume are at the height of their careers, and in the case of eastern Europeans there has been the happy recent opening up of possibilities for work and collaboration through the fall of the iron curtain. Czech, French, German, Italian and Russian scholars have come together with American and English scholars, in this book, to speak on heresy and literacy: with diverse voices. They are in a tradition which goes back to just after the year 1000.

CHAPTER 2

Literacy and the making of heresy, c. 1000 – c. 1150

R. I. Moore

> The writing down of some of the main elements in the cultural
> tradition in Greece brought about an awareness of two things:
> of the past as different from the present; and of the inherent
> inconsistencies in the picture of life as it was inherited by the
> individual [with] the cultural tradition in its recorded form.[1]

What Goody and Watt describe as the consequences of the appearance of literacy in classical Greece are also fundamental to the
religious reform movement of eleventh-century western Europe,
whose manifold expressions included the first assertions of popular
heresy since antiquity. Hardly a source or a secondary account of
that period fails to remind us that 'reform' meant first and foremost
a drive to recover the ancient purity and vigour of the early Church,
as revealed by the lives and writings of its Fathers, and through
them the spirit of the gospels and apostles. If ever a movement was
inspired by books (irrespective of its origins in radically changing
social relations) it was this one. Anxious that monastic communities
were failing to live in strict observance of the Rule of St Benedict,
the spiritually ambitious left to live in the forests and on the moun-
tainsides, emulating the heroes of the *vitae patrum*. Leo IX and his
successors on the throne of St Peter appealed continually to the
writings and pronouncements of their founding fathers to give form
and legitimacy to their revolutionary claim to authority over the
western Church and its ministers and members, and their antago-
nists replied in kind. Bernard of Chartres's famous image of the
scholars as dwarfs on the shoulders of giants[2] asserted that the

An earlier version of this paper was delivered at the annual meeting of the Medieval Academy
of America at Columbus, Ohio, in March 1992. I wish to express my gratitude to the Medieval
Academy, the organiser of the session, Richard Landes, and many participants in the meeting.
[1] Jack Goody and Ian Watt, 'The consequences of literacy; in Goody, pp. 27–68, p. 56.
[2] In John of Salisbury, *Metalogicon*, ed. C. C. J. Webb, (Oxford, 1929), p. 136; cf. Stock,
pp. 517–21.

present was different from the past – and implied that the future
would be different again, since by virtue of their elevated position
the dwarfs could see a little further. The much humbler people who
were arraigned as heretics before the Christmas synod of bishop
Gerard of Cambrai at Arras in 1024–5 replied serenely 'Lex et
disciplina nostra, quam a magistro accepimus, nec evangelicis
decretis nec apostolicis sanctionibus contrarie videbitur, si quis eam
diligenter velit intueri'[3] (The teaching and rule that we have
learned from our master will be seen to contravene neither the
precepts of the gospels nor those of the apostles by anybody who is
prepared to examine them carefully). They spoke for their age in
measuring their belief and conduct against the text, confident that
virtue and orthodoxy consisted in stripping away the encrustations
and deformations of tradition which literacy alone (though in their
case indirectly) enabled them to recognise as departures from the
historically authenticated canon upon which they took their stand.

The literacy of the eleventh century was the restricted literacy of
all traditional societies, and had its usual corollaries – the mystifi-
cation of the book, the social and political aggrandisement of those
who had access to it, the consequent extension and reinforcement of
social hierarchy, the identification of orthodoxy with privilege and
illiteracy with unfreedom, and the elaboration of a concept of heresy
to police the frontier between them.[4] Guy Lobrichon has recently
discovered a new text, in an early eleventh-century manuscript from
St Germain at Auxerre, of the letter in which a monk named
Heribert describes *quamplurimi heretici* (numerous heretics) who had
appeared in the Périgord.[5] They would not eat meat, drink wine or
accept money, despised the mass and hated the cross. They also
possessed distinctly sinister capacities. Heribert had been present
when 'ferreis compedibus victi fuerunt missi in tonnam uinariam,
fundum patentem habens, sursum clausum, deorsum custodibus
adhibitis. In crastinum non solum sint inuenti sed nec semita eorum
est inventa usquequo se representaverunt' (they were loaded with
chains and put in a great wine-barrel. It had an open bottom, its top
was shut, and guards had been set over it. In the morning they were

---

[3] *Acta synodi atrebatensis, PL* 142, col. 1272.
[4] Goody, pp. 11–20; cf. Patrick Wormald, 'The uses of literacy in Anglo-Saxon England and
its neighbours', *TRHS* 5/27 (1977), 95–114.
[5] Guy Lobrichon, 'The chiaroscuro of heresy in early eleventh-century Aquitaine. A letter
from Auxerre', in Head and Landes, pp. 80–103.

gone, and furthermore they left no tracks until their next appearance). Heribert's letter has long been well known, but had been associated with a much later date. Lobrichon's revision, however, is not merely chronological. He argues powerfully that 'Heribert' was not describing real heretics at all; the letter was part of a debate within the Cluniac order, and satirises certain internal critics of the dramatic developments of the liturgy, and of the organisation of the abbey's estates and relations with other Cluniac houses, which were taking place under the 'imperial' abbacy of Odilo.[6]

This conclusion does not remove the Heribert letter from the list of sources for the birth of popular heresy. It only transfers it from the history of those who deliberately and publicly repudiated Catholic teaching and authority to that of the apprehensions and expectations about heresy and heretics which were entertained by Catholics themselves. Those expectations were largely formed and nourished by the warnings of the scriptures and the fathers, but were expressed in response to contemporary anxieties and experiences, which sometimes but by no means always included encounters with real dissenters. The relationship between these two histories, logically and in fact quite distinct from one another, of heresy and the apprehension of heresy, is casual, fluctuating and often non-existent. The value of Heribert's letter is not that it tells us what any real heretics were like, but that it shows what they were expected to be like, just at the moment when dissent was in fact taking shape among the people of northern Europe for the first time.

According to Heribert, 'nemo namque tam rusticus se cum eis iungit, qui non infra octo dies sit sapiens, litteris verbis et exemplis, ut nec superari a quoquam ulterius ullomodo possit' (no one, no matter how rustic, adheres to their sect who does not become, within eight days, wise in letters, writing and action, so that no one can overcome him in any way). In this he anticipated the complaint of bishop Roger of Châlons-sur-Marne, *c.* 1043, about some people discovered in his diocese. 'Si quos vero idiotas et infacundos huius erroris sectatoribus adiungi contingeret, statim eruditissimis etiam catholicis facundiores fieri asseverabat'[7] (He asserted that if simple, uneducated people happened to become followers of this heresy they

---

[6] See also J. Iogna-Prat, *Agni immaculati: recherches sur les sources hagiographiques relatives à saint Maieul de Cluny (954–994)* (Paris, 1988); Barbara Rosenwein, *To be the Neighbor of St Peter* (Ithaca and London, 1989).

[7] Anselm of Liège, *Gesta episcoporum Leodicensis*, ed. R. Koepke, *MGH SS* vii, 226.

immediately become more eloquent than the most learned Catholics). The same nervousness is represented by the shadowy figures to whom the spread of heresy was sometimes attributed – the Italian Gundolfo, who (according to Gerard of Cambrai) was quoted as their leader by the men examined at Arras in 1024–5, or the woman, also Italian, whom Radulfus Glaber credited with the seduction of the clerks burned at Orléans in 1022.[8] Radulfus is also our source for the sad story of Leutard of Vertus, who some years earlier discarded his wife, attacked his parish church and embarked on a career of heretical preaching until he was exposed as a charlatan by the bishop and threw himself into a well in despair at the loss of his following. Radulfus lays heavy emphasis both on Leutard's madness (*vesania, insaniens*) and on his fraudulent claim to familiarity with scripture.[9] Although he does not overtly make a causal connection between the two, his story may remind us of the man whom Esther Goody encountered in Bole (northern Nigeria), whose madness was thought to be the result of his reading certain parts of the Koran without taking the appropriate precautions.[10]

The combination of anxiety that heresy would result from unauthorised access to the scriptures with nervousness of the magical properties associated with books and their use is nowadays seen to be connected with restricted literacy, and particularly with the desire to sustain the restriction.[11] Even though (as seems probable) the actual diffusion of literacy in most or all of its forms was increasing during the eleventh and twelfth centuries, the principle of restriction was articulated far more clearly, and asserted far more aggressively, than formerly. In the ninth century the famous requirement of the *admonitio generalis* that education should be available to the children of the unfree (though subsequently restricted to prospective monks), echoed in Theodulf of Orléans's insistence that priests should hold schools *per villas et vicos* (in every farm and district) confirms that there was no sharply delineated conceptual boundary between the literate and the illiterate, or any sense that literacy was inappropriate or undesirable in the poor or unfree.[12] By the twelfth century, when western Europe was changing from a warrior into a clerical society, the enormous power represented by the ability to read and

---

[8] *PL* 142, col. 1271; Rodulfus, p. 138.

[9] Rodulfus, pp. 88–91.   [10] Goody, p. 13.   [11] Goody, pp. 11–20, 199–241.

[12] Rosamond McKitterick, *The Carolingians and the Written Word* (Cambridge, 1989), p. 220; P. Riché, *Daily Life in the World of Charlemagne* (Liverpool, 1978), p. 199.

write made literacy – Latin literacy, that is – not only an invaluable personal asset but an increasingly visible social marker. It was coming to be regarded, with celibacy, as a defining attribute of the clerical class which provided not only spiritual but administrative and governmental services and leadership, at a time when the power and status associated with those functions was growing rapidly.[13] Since at the same time the perfection and promulgation of the seigneurial ban scored a universal division sharp and deep across Western society, subsuming the manifold gradations of freedom and obligation among the *pauperes* of the Carolingian world into a single servile class, it was bound to follow that literacy would be associated not only with clerisy but also with freedom.

Nervousness of heresy tended to exaggerate its power and sophistication. The rustics who questioned the necessity of church marriage, or the capacity of their priest to absolve in others the sins of which he had so manifestly failed to purge himself, were quickly discovered on interrogation to have been infected by the emissaries of a hidden but universal sect which preached a sophisticated doctrine of theological dualism. Clement of Bucy, near Soissons, revealed under interrogation by Guibert of Nogent in 1115 that he thought that *beati eritis* in the Sermon on the Mount meant 'blessed are the heretics', but the sect to which he belonged 'certe cum per latinem conspersi sint orbem' (are undoubtedly dispersed throughout the Latin world). Guibert knew how to account for that: 'si relegas   haereses ab Augustino digestas, nulli magis quam manichaeorum reperies convenire'[14] (if you look up the heresies summarised by Augustine you will find that this resembles none more than that of the Manichees).

Guibert was rather ahead of his time. In general the myth of the medieval manichee was a creation of the period after the middle of the twelfth century.[15] Until then those who encountered dissent usually accounted for it by postulating sources external to their own communities, but did not generalise whatever contamination they identified into an elaborate or universal stereotype. If, in the manner of Mary Douglas, we see this sensitivity to contamination as

[13] Clanchy, pp. 175–201; Alexander Murray, *Reason and Society in the Middle Ages* (Oxford, 1978), pp. 112–30, 213–44.

[14] Guibert de Nogent, *Autobiographie*, iii.17, ed. E.-R. Labande (Paris, 1981), pp. 428–30.

[15] Moore, *Origins*, pp. 243–6.

an indication of insecurity about social boundaries,[16] it would follow that, while such insecurities were certainly rife in the earlier period, the new social order which they sought to protect was not yet clearly envisaged as a coherent and overarching whole, as it came to be by the end of the twelfth century.[17] As society began to settle into a regular and clearly articulated hierarchy premised on absolute and unbridgeable distinctions between servile and free, clerical and lay, male and female, heir and younger son, the divisions between those organising categories, crevices vulnerable to penetration by contaminating agents of one sort or another, themselves assumed a regular and articulate form, like the lines of mortar in a well-built wall. The Bogomil church, with its hierarchically organised missionaries, its elaborate mythology and theology, its deacons (of both sexes), bishops and pope, as they came to be imagined in the thirteenth-century West, was in that sense a conceptual counterpart of the society of the three orders. The parts (the Black Pope excepted) were real enough, but their sum was far less than the constructed whole.[18]

How the concept of literacy, no less than the fact, became in this period the great instrument of the power and influence of the *clerici* who appropriated it as a possession and prerogative of their class has been clearly established by the work of Clanchy, Murray, Stock and others. The equation of illiteracy with the notions of paganism, rusticity and heresy itself served to discredit popular acclaim, as opposed to clerical authority, in other contexts besides the imputation of heresy, including, for example, the veneration of relics and trial by ordeal.[19] Thus heretics were effectively characterised in terms of the two great axes of the social revolution of the eleventh century, as those who lacked both freedom and learning, the defining attributes of legitimate secular and spiritual power, and who challenged the moral basis upon which that power was founded.

---

[16] Mary Douglas, *Purity and Danger* (London, 1966), applied to Guibert by R. I. Moore, 'Guibert of Nogent and his world', in H. Mayr-Harting and R. I. Moore (eds.), *Essays in Medieval History Presented to R. H. C. Davis* (London, 1985), pp. 107–17.

[17] Georges Duby, *The Three Orders* (Chicago, 1980), pp. 271–353.

[18] Cf. the famous comment of Dondaine, *De heresi catharorum* pp. 292–3: 'l'on parle du catharisme comme d'*une* réligion ... C'est là une erreur historique grave. Il y a eu *des sectes* dualistes, aussi bien en Orient qu'en Lombardie' (people speak of Catharism as *a* religion ... That is a serious historical error. There were *dualist sects*, as much in the East as in Lombardy).

[19] Stock, pp. 244–52; Robert Bartlett, *Trial by Fire and Water* (Oxford, 1986), p. 86.

Conversely, the same process helped, much more broadly, to establish a sense of solidarity and community among the clerks themselves, and to associate them firmly with the ranks of privilege, in contradistinction from the despised and terrifying world of the ignorant and brutish peasantry.

Popular heresy in the eleventh and twelfth centuries was in this sense a social construction. That it was also a great deal more is most obviously attested by its capacity to rally people to ways of life and courses of action which were different from those they would otherwise have followed, and often exposed them to real danger and hardship. As Eberwin of Steinfeld reported to St Bernard, of the first Cathars detected in the west and burned at Bonn in 1143, 'Quod magis mirabile est, ipsi tormentum ignis non solum cum patientia, sed etiam cum laetitia introierunt et sustinuerunt'[20] (The amazing thing was that they entered and endured the torment of the flames not merely courageously but joyfully). In the preceding decades Catholic observers had often been shocked by what crowds might do under the inspiration of heretical preachers, when Tanchelm of Antwerp had mocked the figure of the Virgin, for example, and his follower Manasses expelled the priest from St Peter at Ghent and taken over the church, when Henry of Lausanne had precipitated an insurrection against the clergy of Le Mans, after which he apparently controlled the city for several weeks, or when Peter of Bruys presided over the burning of crosses and the destruction of holy images.[21]

Both the sneers of the clerks and the obduracy of the heretics illustrate Brian Stock's invaluable insight that literacy in this period not only marked communities, but made them. The clerical elite which was now in the process of formation (or, as it preferred to say, re-formation) and the groups which gathered around preachers and leaders like Leutard, Henry or the early Cathars, are equally examples of Stock's 'textual communities', for whom allegiance and association founded on kin or lordship, locality or vocation, were expressed in or superseded by those based on common loyalty to a particular body of texts as mediated by a particular leader.[22] They

---

[20] *PL* 182, col. 677.
[21] R. I. Moore, 'New sects and secret meetings: association and authority in the eleventh and twelfth centuries', *SCH* 25 (1986), 47–68.
[22] Stock, pp. 88–92.

differed, however, in another and fundamental respect. The Europe created in the eleventh and twelfth centuries conforms very closely (even though it did not constitute a single polity) to Ernest Gellner's model of what he calls the complex agro-literate society, in which a very large number of producing communities, relatively undifferentiated in their internal structure and generally communicating with one another only at the level of local exchange, are dominated by an elite which is sharply differentiated internally (the three orders again) but owes its unity to a cosmopolitan high culture which it shares and monopolises, and through which it exercises its hegemony.[23] It will be convenient to refer to these respectively as the 'small' (or 'little') and the 'great' communities. Some of the connotations of Redfield's terminology are unacceptable,[24] but the terms themselves describe better than any alternative Gellner's essential contrast between the everyday social homegeneity and cultural particularity of the one, and the necessary commitment to cultural universality and social differentiation of the other.

The people examined at Arras in 1024–5, possibly weavers but more probably peasants (though seemingly prosperous enough to foreswear the use of domestic servants[25]), belonged among the producers, whose values they articulated clearly when they told bishop Gerard of Cambrai that the tenor of their teaching was 'mundum relinquere, carnem a concupiscentiis frenare, de laboribus manuum suarum victum parare, nulli laesionem quaerere, charitatem cunctis quos zelus huius nostri propositi teneat, exhibere'[26] (to abandon the world, to restrain the appetites of the flesh, to prepare our food by the labour of our own hands, to do no injury to any one, to extend charity to every one of our own faith).

The 'textual community' of the clerks who confronted them, by contrast, was nothing less than the high culture itself, and Gerard was one of its most articulate spokesmen in his time, as he demonstrated in an elaborate and wide-ranging response which paid very little attention to what had actually been said by the defendants. His

---

[23] Ernest Gellner, *Nations and Nationalism* (Oxford, 1983), pp. 8–13.
[24] Cf. Goody, pp. 6–9.
[25] Neither I nor, so far as I know, anyone else had previously noticed this implication of these people's insistence on preparing their food with their own hands; despite the concurrence of Wakefield and Evans, p. 84, I cannot defend my previous translation of *parare* as 'earn' (*Birth*, p. 17). None the less, the reference to the *supplicia* (torture) to which they were subjected before the hearing clearly implies that they were unfree.
[26] *PL* 142, col. 1272.

concern was rather to defend the external forms and rituals of the traditional church against the intellectually innovative and socially destabilising tendencies within the ranks of the elite which were represented by neoplatonist theologians, Clunaic monks and the Peace movement.[27]

Gerard's fears that Cluny and the Peace of God constituted a threat to social hierarchy turned out to be the opposite of the truth. In that respect he made the same mistake as the free tenants and small landholders who flocked to the relics at the great peace rallies in Aquitaine and the Auvergne of the 990s. They answered the summons to defend the *pauperes* – that is, the monks – against the depredations of the universally reviled *milites* (warriors), only to find that the purpose of the canons which they swore on these occasions to uphold was not to overturn the seigneurial regime which was being constructed through the privatisation and extension of the powers of the ban to support castle-building, forced labour services and a vast range of new pecuniary exactions, but to ensure that control over it remained in the hands of the churches themselves and those laymen whom they recognised as legitimate.[28]

I have suggested elsewhere[29] that the bitter accusations of a popular heresy in the 1020s which Richard Landes has so skilfully set in context in his examination of the writings of Adémar of Chabannes arose from mutual disillusionment between Church and people upon the realisation of that contradiction. Landes has shown how in the space of a few years Adémar, who had been an enthusiastic advocate, even architect, of the alliance between Church and people, became an embittered fanatic.[30] Disillusionment was completed by the humiliation which he endured in public debate at the hands of a wandering monk named Benedict of Chiusa, in 1029. Adémar had devoted his energies and writings for thirty years to establishing the apostolicity of St Martial of Limoges and building up popular support for his cult. To the vociferous delight of the assembled populace Benedict denounced it all as mere cover for the greed of the monks, and Adémar's life's work collapsed around his

---

[27] Moore, *Origins*, pp. 12–16; Duby, *Three Orders*, pp. 28–43.

[28] R. I. Moore, 'The peace of God and the social revolution', in Head and Landes, pp. 308–26.

[29] R. I. Moore, 'Heresy, repression and social change in the age of Gregorian reform', in S. L. Waugh and P. D. Diehl (eds.), *Medieval Christendom and its Discontents* (Cambridge, 1996), pp. 19–46.

[30] Richard Landes, 'The dynamics of heresy and reform in Limoges: a study of popular participation in the peace of God', in Head and Landes, pp. 184–218.

ears. In a subsequent rewriting of his history he uncoupled from a description of a tragedy that took place in 1018 (when the newly enlarged shrine of St Martial collapsed and some fifty people were trampled to death) the famous paragraph which announced the appearance of popular heresy in Aquitaine: 'Paulo post exorti sunt per Aquitaniam Manichaei, seducentes plebem'[31] (Soon after Manichees appeared in Aquitaine, leading the people astray). Instead of appearing as in some degree a response to this tragedy, popular hostility to clerical authority and avarice thus became the fortuitous consequence of contamination from without.

In that context we may see not only that the 'Manichees' were Adémar's rationalisation of the disenchantment between Church and people which succeeded the initial rapture of the peace movement, but also that here in Aquitaine, as in Champagne where Leutard had inveighed against tithes, and as at the synod of Arras, the expression of sentiments which churchmen construed as heresy stood for the assertion of the values and interests of the little community against the great. There was a contradiction in the ethos of 'reform' which long remained unresolved. It had to appeal, both for spiritual respectability and intellectual coherence, to a universal ideal derived from the neoplatonist spirituality of the late Carolingian schools and given programmatic form and European-wide circulation by the Gregorian papacy and its agents, and for practical support in local conflicts to popular indignation arising from grievances which, though doubtless very widely shared, were none the less to each community peculiarly its own – demands for tithes and payments for services, the unfitness of priests and so on. It was one of the fruits of the victory which had been largely secured by the first decades of the twelfth century that this contradiction could increasingly be resolved by designating as heretics those whose professed loyalties remained with the small community. The point is illustrated by the life and teaching of Henry of Lausanne,[32] not only the best-documented, but the most articulate and successful dissenting preacher of the age.

Henry enters the record in 1116 when, having been admitted to preach in Le Mans during Lent, the vigour of his assault on the misdeeds of the cathedral clergy precipitated a popular rising. When

---

[31] Adémar of Chabannes, *Historiarum libri iii*, ed. G. Waitz, *MGH SS* IV, 138.
[32] There is even less justification for calling him 'of Lausanne' than 'the monk' – the authority is Bernard in each case – but if it is untrue, the implications are much less misleading.

bishop Hildebert returned from the Easter synod at Rome he was able to expel Henry only with great difficulty.[33] This looks very much like a spiritual equivalent of the process of disillusionment over the wealth of the church which had taken place in Aquitaine a hundred years earlier. That Henry approached Hildebert, before his departure, for permission to preach in the city – not the action of a heretic – and that it was granted, suggests that neither initially saw the other as an antagonist. For twenty years and more itinerant preachers had toured this rather backward region denouncing a conspicuously unreformed clergy. Hildebert had long supported one of the fieriest, Robert of Arbrissel, founder of Fontevrault, who had died in the previous year. To each man, in other words, the other initially appeared to be on the same side. Both were 'reformers', for whom the clergy of Le Mans (one of whom was nicknamed William Qui-non-bibit-aquam – who-doesn't-drink-water) represented the self-evident source of present evil as plainly as the *milites* of late tenth-century Aquitaine had done in their time. It was the intensity of the reaction to Henry's sermons which brought them to the parting of the ways, forcing each of them to stare down the barrel, as it were, at the prospect of popular insurrection and the overthrow of clerical authority.

The ancient choice which confronted them, between the light of conscience and the voice of authority, also had profound social implications. Hildebert of Lavardin, classicist, poet and ecclesiastical statesman, represented to perfection a new and cosmopolitan clerical elite which was defined by ordination, but distinguished and united by its common Latin culture. The story of his journey to Rome and return in the nick of time to save his flock from the wolf which had been devouring its souls in his absence underlines not only the ultimate source of Hildebert's authority but his citizenship of the wider world by which the reforms he was introducing in Le Mans were inspired. Henry was as fitting a spokesman for the little community as Hildebert was for the great. He possessed a formidably articulate and consistent theology, characterised by stark individualism and uncompromising rejection of large and abstract structures of authority in favour of those firmly rooted in the community itself. He denounced clerical vice and

---

[33] *Gesta domini Hildeberti episcopi* in *Actus pontificum Cenomannis in urbe degentium*, ed. G. Busson and A. Ledru, *Archives historiques du Maine*, vol. II (Le Mans, 1901), pp. 407–15; Moore, *Origins*, pp. 83–90.

avarice, and repudiated most sources of clerical income and power. He denied the authority of the Fathers to interpret the scriptures and insisted on his own right to do so. He maintained that marriage was entirely a matter for those concerned and not a sacrament of the church. He advocated the baptism of adults, not of infants, and confession in public before the community, not in private to priests. In short, the faith he preached plainly affirmed the values of a world in which small groups of men and women stood together as equals, dependent on each other, suspicious of outsiders, and hostile to every external claim upon their obedience, allegiance or wealth.[34]

Henry's impact on the people of Le Mans was not transient. 'Eos enim Henricus sic sibi illexerat', concludes the hostile chronicler, 'quod vix adhuc memoria illius et dilectio a cordibus eorum deleri valeat vel depelli'[35] (They had become so devoted to Henry that even now his memory can scarcely be expunged, or their love for him destroyed or driven from their hearts). For another thirty years he ranged across southwestern France, reducing it, according to Bernard of Clairvaux, to a land where 'Basilicae sine plebibus, plebes sine sacerdotibus, sacerdotes sine debita reverentia sunt ... moriuntur homines in peccatis suis ... parvuli Christianorum baptismi negatur gratia' (Churches are without people, people without priests, priests without the deference due to them ... men dying in their sins and children denied the grace of baptism). 'O infelicissimum populum!', Bernard continues, expressing with his own eloquence exactly the point I have been making so laboriously, 'Ad vocem unius haeretici siluerunt in eo omnes propheticae et apostolicae voces, quae de convocanda in una Christi fide e cunctis nationibus Ecclesia, uno veritatis spiritu cecinerunt' (Unhappy people! At the voice of one heretic you close your ears to all the prophets and apostles who with one spirit of truth have brought together the Church out of all nations to one faith in Christ).[36]

Henry is described by Bernard, in that same letter, as litteratus.[37] It is plainly no accident that we find this alternative cosmology most clearly articulated by the only dissenting leader of our period of

---

[34] Manselli, 'Enrico', pp. 41–63 (Engl. trans. Moore, Birth, pp. 46–60); for fuller discussion, Moore, Origins, pp. 96–101.

[35] Gesta domini Hildeberti, ed. Busson and Ledru, pp. 414–15.

[36] Ep. ccxli, PL 182, col. 434.

[37] PL 182, col. 435.

whom it can be asserted with some confidence that he possessed a significant level of literacy. His capacity for abstract thought, and the acumen with which he handled himself in the debate with the monk William from which our knowledge of his teaching derives, would be hard to account for otherwise. Peter the Venerable read a book of which. Henry was said to be the author, presumably the same one to which William refers during the debate: 'De ecclesiis vero, quas in primo capituli posuisti dicis quod non sunt lignee vel lapidee faciende' (In your first chapter you say that churches should not be made either of wood or of stone), etc.[38]

Predictably, most (but not all) of the other dissenting and enthusiastic movements of the period are described as being founded or spoken for by disillusioned clerks or priests, who presumably possessed at least a measure of pragmatic literacy. Nevertheless, it would be quite wrong to describe the formation of these movements, the formulation of their ideas, and their capacity to attract support, entirely in terms of the impact of literacy (or even the semi-literacy of the ordinary priest or choir monk) on a non-literate population. That would be to overlook the enormous influence of literate usages, especially in law and government, on the habits of thought and social action of those affected by them, even when they are not literate themselves – of what is called, logically if in some degree misleadingly, passive literacy. The point is very simply made if, returning to Stock's conception of the textual community, we ask upon what conditions it is likely that a text will gain such authority as Stock describes, obviously correctly, among those who cannot read it. The circumstances which assist a new religious leader to gain influence in any small community – social dislocation, exceptional need for impartial mediation, loss of trust by former leaders and so forth – are quite familiar and have been exhaustively applied to the religious movements of the eleventh century.[39] But nothing in the theory of the holy man requires him to display, in addition to sanctity of character, the ability convincingly to claim textual authority for his prescriptions.

---

[38] *Petri Venerabilis contra Petrobusianos hereticos*, ed. J. V. Fearns, *CCCM* 10, p. 5; Manselli, 'Enrico', p. 61.

[39] Peter Brown, 'The rise and function of the holy man in late antiquity', *Journal of Roman Studies* 61 (1971), 80–101; Janet L. Nelson, 'Society, theodicy and the origins of heresy', *SCH* 9 (1972), 65–77; T. Asad, 'Medieval heresy; an anthropological view', *Social History* 11 (1986), 354–62; Moore, *Origins*, pp. 270–77.

It is unnecessary to labour the extent to which, in Nelson's words, 'a crucial feature of the cultural context of Carolingian literacy was the church's commitment to the practice of the written word'.[40] It is perhaps not so readily appreciated, as she shows with great learning and subtlety, quite how widely and for what a variety of purposes writing and written instruments were used in Carolingian government, not only in the royal household but everywhere that imperial authority aspired to reach. Consequently, the Carolingian world experienced some aspects of the transition 'from memory to written record' which Clanchy explored so brilliantly in Anglo-Norman and Angevin England. The subjects of Charles the Bald were accustomed not only to seeing written inscriptions and hearing bibles and service books read (or at least recited) in their churches, but in their workaday lives to swearing fidelity to written affirmations, seeing law preserved in and pronounced from written texts, having their dues and obligations recorded (and thereby limited) in written surveys, and title to land and the perquisites associated with it in written diplomas. All of these documents would be produced, read out and if necessary translated on the appropriate public occasions. In short, the conditions existed for a high degree of passive literacy. People were accustomed to hearing, understanding and acknowledging the authority of the written word – and also, therefore, had a clear view of the conditions in which it ought be heard and understood, and on which it might be accepted as authoritative.

Once again the synod of Arras illustrates these points almost to perfection. When bishop Gerard had completed his long rebuttal of errors they had not professed, they were required to subscribe a confession of faith. 'Haec quae Latina oratione dicebantur, non satis intelligere poterant' (they did not fully understand it because it was in Latin), it was translated into the vernacular, they swore that they accepted its tenets, and 'ad confirmandum suae fidei testamentum, unusquisque eorum in modum crucis hujusmodi [cross in the text] quemdam characterem conscripsit' (to confirm this attestation of their faith each of them inscribed a mark in the shape of the cross, like this).[41] The procedure is exactly that by which they would have witnessed a charter, or seen one witnessed.[42]

---

[40] Janet L. Nelson, 'Literacy in Carolingian government', in McKitterick pp. 258–96, at p. 265. See also Mitchell and McKitterick in that volume, pp. 186–225, 297–318.

[41] *Acta synodi Atrebatensis, PL* 142, col. 1312.

[42] Clanchy, pp. 159–66, 202–14, 246–7.

In associating the extent of passive literacy with the emergence of popular heresy at the time when Carolingian authority was in the last stages of its disintegration we may particularly note two further points in Nelson's discussion. First, she specifically includes among those in whom a high degree of passive literacy might be expected 'the mass of free or freedmen landholders'[43] – just the people whose late tenth- and early eleventh-century descendants were finding their freedom subverted and their lands commandeered in the process of seigneurialisation against which the earliest dissent was directed. Second, in discussing regional variations in the ways in which written texts and instruments were used, and hence the likely extent of passive literacy, she shows that it was not confined to Romance speakers, and that the crucial variables were whether the region in question had been part of the Roman Empire, or strongly influenced by it, and how long christianity had been established there.[44] The earliest foyers of popular heresy – Aquitaine and the Auvergne, the Rhineland and the Low Countries – score high on both tests.

The rapidly rising level, use and prestige of literacy in the eleventh- and twelfth-century West benefited those who commanded it in all the expected ways, including that of defining their status and extending their power through the elaboration of a concept of heresy and the means of enforcing it both intellectually and practically. But as its uses became increasingly general, and the habits of mind it stimulated spread to those who were not themselves literate, literacy also began to empower those over whom its power was exercised. The reading and translation of the confession at Arras provides a direct insight into the connection between passive literacy and the creation of textual communities by the formally illiterate. It may even suggest that if active literacy was a condition of the making of heresy, understood as the creation among the elite of a conception of enforced orthodoxy, so-called passive literacy was equally a condition of popular receptivity to the active dissemination of heretical teaching.

However, literacy was not new in the eleventh century, and nor was its association with power. On the other hand neither the fear nor the reality of popular heresy seems to have been a significant

---

presence in the Carolingian world. Accusations were occasionally exchanged among scholars and ecclesiastical politicians, arising from much the same mixture of intellectual ferment and personal intrigue that characterised academic disputes in the eleventh and twelfth centuries, or the twentieth. There is little to suggest that they were turned outwards from such circles before the eleventh century, to be used as a means of asserting social distance or direct power over the *pauperes*, or conversely that frustrated, or disillusioned or rebellious groups among the *pauperes* expressed their grievances or aspirations through the medium of religious dissent.

It is clearly hard to think of heresy or dissent as in any simple sense a consequence of the spread of literacy, active or passive, if one was new in the eleventh century and the other was not. The case of England will make the point. There is neither space nor need to reopen here the old (and logically unanswerable) question why there was no popular heresy in early medieval England. The solution probably lies largely in the firmness of secular administrative control exerted over that much-governed country throughout the relevant period. Additionally, many of the functions which might have been served by religious dissent in the most critical decades, the later eleventh and first half of the twelfth centuries, were catered for by English-speaking hermits who were allowed to exercise a good deal of influence by the conquerors in a mutually convenient accommodation which it would have suited neither side to jeopardise by excessive zeal in matters of doctrine.[45]

The English hermits do not falsify the thesis that active literacy assisted the promulgation of heresy as an instrument for the fortification and aggrandisement of the large community, while passive literacy made possible the articulation of dissent in the small. They simply remind us that neither did so exclusively. Just as the imputation of heresy was only one of many through which the clerks of the twelfth century asserted themselves, along with Judaism, leprosy, sodomy and others,[46] the articulation of dissent was only one of the ways in which the *pauperes* could attempt to proclaim their solidarity, or to establish the means of mutual support, the expression of shared values and the pursuit of common goals.

[45] Henry Mayr-Harting, 'Functions of a twelfth-century recluse', *History* 60 (1975), 337–52.
[46] R. I. Moore, *The Formation of a Persecuting Society: Power and Deviance in Western Europe, 950–1250* (Oxford, 1987).

If literacy helped indispensably to sharpen and define the frontier between the 'great' and the 'little' communities after the millennium, it also represented a vehicle by which that frontier might be crossed – or breached. In that ambiguity lies the dilemma of the literate. However necessary it may be to insist on the harshness with which the new social order was ordained and imposed, no Catholic prelate could turn his back on the spiritual condition of the *pauperes* without making a nonsense of his office and faith. Nor did most of them do so. We need not make heavy weather of the elementary assertion that the Western Church throughout our period was an evangelical Church, and took its pastoral responsibilities seriously. However patchy and imperfect the results, its commitment to the principle that its teachings and services should be available in good condition to the whole people was the chief engine of both the Carolingian and the Gregorian reforms. The problem of mediation between the great and little communities could not be left to historians. It was a central preoccupation of ecclesiastical policy.

The solution which proved successful turned out to be one which in some ways resembled the heretic and his following, and was most directly in competition with him – the parish. On the face of it this may seem paradoxical. A great deal of what Henry of Lausanne opposed (and in this he was untypical only in the coherence of his thought) was directly, though neither exclusively nor necessarily, associated with the dissemination of the parish system – the payment of tithe and for church buildings, the sacramental view of marriage, insistence on infant baptism and on confession to priests, and so on. To that extent the growth of popular heresy in the twelfth century and beyond was increasingly a reaction against the success of reform.[47] But it had not been so from the outset. There is a good deal to suggest that at an earlier period the parish had often been seen as the expression of the community itself, rather than of the bishop's authority over it. The early dissemination of the parish system in much of northern and western Europe was closely associated with the extension of cultivation and the formation of new communities that went with it.[48] The reformers of the eleventh century and the middling and humble people who on so many occasions supported

---

[47] Moore, *Origins*, pp. 73–81, 89–90.
[48] Robert Fossier, *Enfance de l'Europe, Xe–XIIe siècles* (Paris, 1982), pp. 345–58, 499–500; Leopold Génicot, *Rural Communities in the Medieval West* (Baltimore, 1990), pp. 90–107.

them indispensably had a common enemy in the system of pro-
prietorship which converted the Church, its priests and its services
into sources of seigneurial revenue. The canons of the Peace Councils are more than sufficient witness that popular enthusiasm was
readily available to secure the improvement of the services offered
by local churches, including the maintenance of fabric and the
support of the priest, on what was seen as the necessary condition of
independence from lay control.[49] What was obnoxious about paying
for the services of the priest, now and later, was not necessarily the
payments themselves – after all, the priest had to live – so much as
their appropriation by the lord, which not only increased the burden
but, like clerical marriage, diminished the quality of the service.
There are indications that an early effect of the success of the reform
movements, and probably still more of the extension of cultivation
in areas where those who could supply the labour found themselves
to a degree in a sellers' market, was to give parishioners a good deal
of freedom in the management of parochial affairs, and the parish
itself a correspondingly high degree of identification with its
community.[50]

The period of liberty (or anarchy, as it is more usually described
in the context, to which it belongs, of Georges Duby's characterisation of this period as an age of disorder between two ages of order)
was, of course, short-lived. The control which had once been exercised by unreformed laymen was slowly but (on the whole) surely
reasserted by reformed bishops. Once again, the parish priest might
find himself caught in the middle, in danger of wandering into
heresy as a result of identifying too closely with his flock. Albero of
Mercke, near Cologne, lost his benefice in the 1160s for denying the
validity of the mass of tainted priests, yet the implication of his
position also was to reject what his bishop maintained, the authority
and ascendancy of the great community over the little.[51] Lambert le
Bègue's criticism of the laxity of his fellow priests in the diocese of
Liège in the 1160s led to his dismissal and imprisonment on charges
of heresy, yet it is quite clear that the real cause of his troubles was

[49] R. I. Moore, 'Family, community and cult on the eve of the Gregorian reform', *TRHS* 5/30
(1980), 49–70.
[50] Robert Fossier, *Chartes de coutume en Picardie (XIe–XIIe siècles)* (Paris, 1974), pp. 67–154;
P. Duparc, 'Les cimetières, séjours des vivants *(XIe–XIIe siècles)*', *Bulletin philologique et
historique* (1964) (Paris, 1969), 483–504; Susan Reynolds, *Kingdoms and Communities in
Western Europe 900–1300* (Oxford, 1984), pp. 77–100.
[51] Moore, *Origins*, pp. 187–9.

too close an identification with his parishioners – including, to return to the question of literacy, making a vernacular translation of the Acts for use at private prayer meetings. It is notable that one of the accusations against Lambert, though he vehemently denied it, was that the most devout of his followers absented themselves from mass.[52]

Another indication that there was more in common than has always been noticed between the priest and the heretic, and between the parish and the sect, is the similarity of treatment accorded to them in the following century, under the provisions of Lateran IV. The determination of an Eudes of Rouen or a Robert Grosseteste to eradicate ignorance and corruption among his parish priests was not much more different in spirit than were the inquests they conducted in method from those which a Peter Martyr or a Jacques Fournier brought to the pursuit of heresy. One aspect of it is that, just as in the eleventh century literacy in the wrong places was *ipso facto* ground for suspicion, so in the thirteenth the priest's fitness to represent the great community to the little was seen to require that he should be literate. It was necessarily so, for the parish too was in its way a textual community, and in that capacity its institutionalisation under regular auspices represented, among other things, acceptance that a society with the high level of 'passive' literacy which we have identified as a condition for the successful dissemination of popular heresy required religious services appropriate to its skills and expectations. That, after all, was what the heretics had set out to offer.

---

[52] Frédéricq, 2, 9–36, trans. in part Moore, *Birth*, pp. 101–11. For discussion, J. B. Russell, *Dissent and Reform in the Early Middle Ages* (Berkeley, 1965), pp. 90–6; Moore, *Origins*, pp. 191–4.

CHAPTER 3

Wisdom from the East: the reception by the Cathars of Eastern dualist texts

Bernard Hamilton

Explicit secretum hereticorum de Concorresio portatum de Bulgaria Nazario suo episcopo plenum erroribus.[1]

No reputable scholar now doubts that Catharism was an offshoot of medieval eastern dualism, though it was clearly not a simple transplant but developed its own distinctive form. The Bogomils, whom the Cathars most resembled in their lifestyle and beliefs, do not seem to have had any writings of their own when they first appeared in tenth-century Bulgaria. The priest Cosmas described them as members of a rustic, pietist movement, who held dualist beliefs which they expressed in folkloristic terms. Their only book was the New Testament, which they read in the same text as the Orthodox, although they interpreted it in a heterodox way: 'Although they carry the Holy Gospel in their hands, they interpret it falsely and thus seduce men'.[2]

The older dualist church of the Paulicians, also found in the tenth-century Balkans, did have a literature of its own. While basing their teachings on the New Testament alone,[3] its members also circulated works composed by their own leaders.[4] But although the Paulicians may indirectly have influenced the development of Cath-

---

[1] 'Here endeth the secret book of the heretics of Concorrezo, brought from Bulgaria by their bishop Nazarius [and] full of errors' (*Livre secret*, p. 86). Malcolm Lambert has drawn my attention to Duvernoy's assertion that this passage should be translated 'was brought from Bulgaria to their bishop Nazarius', *La Religion*, p. 35 n. 47. This view is not convincing because Sacconi relates that Nazarius has received his teaching from the bishop of Bulgaria and his Elder Son, Sacconi, p. 58. See p. 55 below.

[2] *Le Traité contre les Bogomiles de Cosmas le Prêtre, traduction et étude*, H-C. Puech and A. Vaillant (Paris, 1945), p. 76.

[3] They may have used a slightly different canon. Peter of Sicily, *Historia Manichaeorum qui et Pauliciani dicuntur*, c.42, ed. Ch. Astruc, W. Carus-Wolska, J. Gouillard, P. Lemerle, D. Papachryssanthou and P. Paramelle, *Les Sources grecques pour l'histoire des Pauliciens d'Asie Mineure*, Travaux et Mémoires (Paris, 1970), vol. IV, p. 21.

[4] *Historia Manichaeorum*, c.43, pp. 21–3.

arism in the twelfth century,[5] there is no evidence that they penetrated the West before then.

Although most recent scholarship is sceptical about the influence of Bogomilism on Western heretical movements in the eleventh century[6] the question seems to me to be by no means closed. If one looks for evidence of fully fledged Bogomilism as described by twelfth-century Byzantine writers among the alleged 'Manichees' in western Europe in the years before 1050 it will not, of course, be found, because it did not exist in the East either. But the 'new Manichees' in the West were very like the Bogomilism which was evolving in the Balkans at that time. Critics of the Bogomil hypothesis draw attention to the fact that Western sources emphasise the ascetic lifestyle of the new heretics while saying nothing about their dualist beliefs; but a similar observation has been made about primitive Bogomils by Sir Dmitri Obolensky: 'the exposition of the doctrinal errors of the heretics forms a comparatively small part of the *Sermon* of Cosmas, which is concerned above all with the moral and social aspects of the heresy'.[7]

The development of a new heresy in Bulgaria in the second half of the tenth century, followed by isolated outbreaks of heresy in parts of western Europe which share many of the characteristics of the Balkan movement, is strong presumptive evidence that the two developments were linked. The opponents of this view claim that the link is missing, because there is no evidence of Bogomil preachers in the West at that time, but it seems possible that the link is being sought in the wrong place. It is known from the writings of Euthymius of Acmonia that at precisely the point when 'Manichee' outbreaks are reported in the West, Bogomilism was spreading into the Greek-speaking lands of Byzantium, and was taking root in some monasteries there, including Euthymius's own community of the Periblepton in Constantinople.[8] What one should perhaps be looking for in western Europe is a correlation between the places where outbreaks of heresy occurred and those which Orthodox monks are known to have visited. Certainly there was no shortage of Orthodox monks perambulating the shrines of the West at that time,

---

[5] B. Hamilton, 'The origins of the dualist church of Drugunthia', *Eastern Churches Review*, 6 (1974), 115–24.

[6] For example, Moore, *Origins*, pp. 23–45; M. Lambert, *Medieval Heresy*, 2nd edn (Oxford, 1992), pp. xii–xiii.

[7] D. Obolensky, *The Bogomils: a Study in Balkan Neo-Manichaeism* (Cambridge, 1948) p. 126.

[8] Euthymius of Acmonia, *Liber invectivus contra haeresim … haereticorum qui Phundagiatae dicuntur*, *PG*, 131, 48–57.

some of whom settled there permanently,[9] and there may have been Bogomils among them. That this was sometimes the case is suggested by a passage in the *Life* of St Simeon the Hermit of Padolirone near Mantua. Simeon was an Armenian who came to Rome in the reign of pope Benedict VIII (1012–24).[10] When he performed his devotions in the Lateran basilica he was attacked by bystanders who alleged that he was a heretic, but the pope, who had him examined by an Armenian bishop, pronounced Simeon's faith orthodox.[11] Yet the fact that this misunderstanding occurred at all suggests that some of the eastern monks who visited the West in the early eleventh century were men of heterodox views.

But if Balkan dualism did enter the West at that time it would seem to have come with no books except the New Testament. Accounts of groups which might have been influenced by dualist preachers from the East bear this out. The heretics of Monforte arrested by bishop Aribert of Milan in *c.* 1028,[12] and the followers of Gundulfo, an Italian, interrogated by Gerard of Cambrai at about the same time, both claimed parts of the bible as their sole authority.[13]

It seems improbable that either the French or the Italian groups had a vernacular version of the New Testament. The earliest partial translations of the bible into French date from the twelfth century, and into Italian from the thirteenth century, and even then only certain books were translated. It would be straining credulity to suppose that small, isolated, dissenting groups had been able to undertake major literary work of that kind a century in advance of the rest of their societies.[14] It seems likely therefore that if the missionaries were Bogomils they used a Greek or Old Slavonic text of the New Testament and paraphrased it for their followers, and

[9] B. Hamilton and P. A. McNulty, '*Orientale Lumen et Magistra Latinitas*: Greek influences on Western monasticism (900–1100)', *Le Millénaire du Mont Athos, 963–1963, Etudes et mélanges* (Chevetogne, 1963), vol. I, pp. 181–216.

[10] He is said to have come to Rome in the pontificate of an unnumbered pope Benedict whom the Bollandists identified with Benedict VII (974–83), but since the *Life* places Simeon's stay in the West in the reign of Arsenius, Armenian bishop of Jerusalem 1006–38, the reference would seem to be to Benedict VIII (1012–24). *De S. Simeone monacho et eremita, AASS, Jul.*, VI, 324.

[11] *De S. Simeone*, c.II, 327.

[12] *Landulphi senioris Mediolanensis historiae libri quatuor*, II, 27, ed. A. Cutolo, *RIS*, new edn, IV(2), 69.

[13] *Acta Synodi Atrebatensi*, Fredericq, I, 2–5.

[14] C. A. Robson, 'Vernacular scriptures in France', K. Foster, 'Vernacular scriptures in Italy', *Cambridge History of the Bible* (1969), vol. II, pp. 436–65.

that if they were western Europeans they paraphrased the Vulgate. But if Bogomil missions were responsible for some of the outbreaks of heresy reported in western Europe in the first half of the eleventh century, they failed to take root. Between 1051[15] and 1114 there are no reports of heresy in the West which could be considered dualist.[16]

But during the eleventh century Bogomilism spread into the Greek-speaking lands of the Byzantine Empire, where it became far more intellectually sophisticated. This is known from the treatise of Euthymius of Acmonia written *c.* 1050, and from book xxvii of the *Dogmatic Panoply* written in the early twelfth century by Euthymius Zigabenus, the private theologian of the emperor Alexius I Comnenus (1081–1118).[17] Both sources relate that the Bogomils had a service book, which seems to have been in use by the first quarter of the eleventh century.[18] The Byzantine Bogomils were developing their own theological literature. Euthymius Zigabenus cited passages from a Bogomil commentary on St Matthew's Gospel written in Greek.[19] Moreover, by the early twelfth century the Bogomils of Constantinople had extended their canon of scripture to include the Psalter and the Prophets.[20]

Between 1018 and 1186 the peoples of Thrace, Greece and Bulgaria formed part of a single state. Greek was the official language of the Byzantine Empire, but many people in the Balkans and even in mainland Greece were Slav speakers, and the Orthodox Church encouraged the use of a vernacular liturgy among them. In the ninth century Sts. Constantine and Methodius had translated the bible and the service books of the Orthodox Church into Old Slavonic, and their disciple, St Clement, founded a school of translators in the monastery of Ochrida in Macedonia. In this way the religious literature of the Greek Orthodox Church began to be rendered into Old Slavonic.[21]

---

[15] In 1051 Henry III hanged heretics at Goslar possibly for believing in the transmigration of souls; *Herigeri et Anselmi Gesta episcoporum jeodiensium*, ii, 64, ed. R. Koepke, *MGH SS*, vii, p. 228; Lambert, *Medieval Heresy*, p. 27.

[16] For the case of Clement of Bucy in 1114 see n. 36 below.

[17] Euthymius of Acmonia's letter about Bogomilism is ed. G. Ficker, *Die Phundagiagiten: ein Beitrag zur Ketzergeschichte des byzantinischen Mittelalters* (Leipzig, 1908); see also the *Liber invectivus*. Euthymius Zigabenus, *Panoplia dogmatica*, PG, 130, cols. 1289–1332.

[18] Euthymius of Acmonia, ed. Ficker, p. 77; Euthymius Zigabenus, *Panoplia dogmatica*, xxvii, 16, *PG*, 130, 1312–13.

[19] *Panoplia dogmatica*, xxvii, 27–52, *PG*, 130, 1321–32.

[20] *Panoplia dogmatica*, xxvii, 1, *PG*, 130, 1292.

[21] J. M. Hussey, *The Orthodox Church in the Byzantine Empire* (Oxford, 1986), pp. 90–101; A. P. Vlasto, *The Entry of the Slavs into Christendom* (Cambridge, 1970), pp. 159–79.

Thus the Slav-speaking Bogomils would have had no need to translate the New Testament into the vernacular because a good, modern translation already existed. They may, however, have needed to translate the Bogomil service-book. The origins of this work are obscure and I have discussed them elsewhere.[22] It appears to have been transmitted to the Bogomils through Paulician converts, although it is not known in what language it was read by Paulicians in the Balkans. It was in use among Greek-speaking Bogomils in the first quarter of the eleventh century who may have commissioned a translation direct from an Armenian original, or from a translation into Old Slavonic made by the Paulicians. By the twelfth century both the Greek-speaking and Slav-speaking Bogomils had an identical form of service-book, although the precise wording of their liturgies may have differed. This is known because Cathars, some of whom were evangelised from Bulgaria, others from Constantinople, all shared an identical form of public worship.[23]

It is universally agreed that Catharism was present in western Europe from 1143, when a Cathar bishop and his companion were brought to trial at Cologne. These men were conscious of their eastern roots, although they themselves may not have been of eastern origin. Eberwin of Steinfeld, who conducted the trial, reports their claim that: 'hanc haeresim usque ad haec tempora occultatam fuisse a temporibus martyrum, et permansisse in Graecia et quibusdam aliis terris' (this heresy had been hidden from the time of the martyrs to the present day and had survived in Greece and certain other countries).[24] This group had evidently been living in Cologne for a while before they were arrested. Some light is shed on their origins by St Hildegard of Bingen, a friend of St Elizabeth of Schönau, whose brother Egbert led the campaign against the renewed outbreak of Catharism at Cologne in 1163.[25] In July 1163 Hildegard wrote an account of a vision she had just had about the Cathars. She saw them in an apocalyptic context as one of the consequences for the inhabitants of the earth of the unleashing of the devil, whom she describes as 'antiquus serpens cum phylacteriis

---

[22] B. Hamilton, 'The Cathars and the seven churches of Asia', in J. D. Howard-Johnstone (ed.), *Byzantium and the West c. 850 – c. 1200* (Amsterdam, 1988), pp. 291–5.

[23] Hamilton, 'Origins of the dualist church', pp. 115–24.

[24] Appendix to the Letters of St Bernard, no. CDXXXII, *PL*, 182, 679.

[25] *Sanctae Elizabeth Vita, partim ab ipsamet dictata, partim ab Eckberto fratre scripta, PL*, 195, 120–4.

vestimentorum', (the old serpent with phylacteries [amulets] on his vestments), which perhaps reflects the imagery of her vision. The sequence of future events in the Apocalypse of St John is not easy to determine, but Hildegard seems to have interpreted it in this way: after the devil had been released from the bottomless pit,[26] the four angels who had held back the four winds at the corners of the earth 'until the servants of God had been sealed',[27] unleashed them, causing evils to sweep across the world.

Hildegard gave very precise dates for those two events. Of the release of the devil she says: 'Sed tamen sexaginta anni sunt atque viginti et quatuor menses, quod antiquus serpens cum phylacteriis vestimentorum populos deludere coepit' (But sixty years and twenty and four months have passed since the ancient serpent wearing clothes decked with amulets began to lead the people astray). The year reckoning could be taken to mean either sixty-two years ago, which is how it is understood by her editor,[28] or eighty years (60 + 20) and four months ago. If the first interpretation is correct then the year in question would be 1101, whereas if the second interpretation is correct, then the passage must refer to 1083. The four months, since Hildegard was writing in July, would relate to the beginning of the christian year on Lady Day, 25 March. Of the second event, the spreading of error through the release of the four winds, she writes: 'Nam viginti et tres anni ac quatuor menses sunt, quod a perversis operibus hominum, quod ab ore nigrae bestiae efflantur, quatuor venti per quatuor angelos angulorum in magnam ruinam moti sunt (For twenty-three years and four months have passed since through the wicked works of men which are blown out from the mouth of the black beast, the four winds have been set in motion by the four angels of [the earth's] corners, causing great destruction).[29] This would give a very precise date, the beginning (in March) of 1140. It seems quite reasonable to suppose that the first appearance of Catharism in the Rhineland, which culminated in the trial of 1143, did occur at about that time, and that Hildegard is retailing information which in her day was common knowledge. But the earlier date is more problematic. If it relates to 1083, it could refer to the capture of St Peter's basilica in Rome by Henry IV,

---

[26] Rev., 9:11. Phylacteries: see Matt. 23:5.   [27] Rev. 7:1–3.
[28] St Hildegard, Ep. x, *De Catharis*, ed. J. B. Pitra, *Analecta sacra*, 8 vols. (Paris 1876–82), vol. viii, p. 349, n. 4.
[29] *Analecta sacra*, p. 349.

which ultimately resulted in the flight of Gregory VII and the enthronement of the antipope Clement III.[30] Such a date might have seemed of apocalyptic significance to Hildegard because it witnessed the beginning of a conflict between pope and emperor which had continued intermittently for much of her lifetime. The date 1101 would have had a different kind of significance, since it marked the defeat of the new crusade sent to reinforce the christians who had remained in the Holy Land after the capture of Jerusalem in 1099.[31] If Hildegard was referring to the origins of Catharism, such a date might be more persuasive for the following reasons.

I doubt whether anybody would wish to claim that all Cathars throughout the West derived from the congregation whose leaders were brought to trial at Cologne in 1143. All the evidence suggests that Catharism entered the West by a variety of routes and that the process took quite a long time. One of the few opponents of the movement who was at all interested in its history was the inquisitor Anselm of Alessandria, who wrote in c. 1270. He tells this story: there were originally three dualist bishops in the East, in Drugunthia, Bulgaria and Philadelphia; then Greeks from Constantinople learned this faith in Bulgaria and set up a Bishop of the Greeks in Constantinople.

Postea francigene iverunt Constantinopolim ut subiugarent terram et invenerunt istam sectam, et multiplicati fecerunt episcopum, qui dicitur episcopus latinorum. [Next the bishopric of Bosnia was set up.] Postea francigene, qui iverant Constantinopolim, redierunt ad propria et predicaverunt, et multiplicati constituerunt episcopum Francie.[32] (Afterwards Frenchmen went to Constantinople to conquer land and discovered that sect and, having increased in numbers, they appointed a bishop who is called the bishop of the Latins ... Afterwards the Frenchmen who had gone to Constantinople returned to their own land and preached and, having increased in numbers, appointed a bishop of France.)

He goes on to relate that the *provinciales*, taught by preachers from France, set up four bishoprics, and how, much later, a French notary came to Lombardy and converted Mark, the first Lombard Cathar Bishop. Since Anselm dates Mark's conversion to Catharism

---

[30] F. Gregorovius, *History of the City of Rome in the Middle Ages*, transl. A. Hamilton (London, 1896), vol. IV (I), pp. 229–31.

[31] S. Runciman, *A History of the Crusades* (Cambridge, 1952), vol. II, pp. 18–31.

[32] Anselm of Alessandria, cap. I, p. 308.

to *c.* 1174,[33] the other events he records must be earlier. His reference to Frenchmen going to Constantinople 'to conquer the land' is usually taken to refer to the Second Crusade,[34] but there is no cogent reason for thinking this. Indeed, it could apply equally well to the First Crusade, for that had been launched partly to reconquer Asia Minor from the Turks.[35]

If this reading of the passage in Anselm is correct it would accord well with the information given by St Hildegard: that the significant date for the beginning of Catharism was the aftermath of the First Crusade. Certainly in the next fifty years Cathars begin to be recorded in many different parts of the West. 'Manichees' were reported at Soissons in *c.* 1114, although not all modern scholars would agree with Guibert of Nogent, who examined them, that they were dualists.[36] Cathars were present in the Toulousain, perhaps as early as 1145,[37] certainly by 1165 when they had their headquarters at Lombers near Albi.[38] By that time they had also established congregations in parts of northern France and the Low Countries, and had spread to Italy.[39]

Although the Bogomils who sent missions to western Europe in the first half of the twelfth century were an ethnic mixture of Byzantine Greeks and Bulgars, they were united in a common faith. But later in the century a schism occurred among them about the validity of the sacrament of salvation. This schism divided those Bogomils who were absolute dualists from those who retained the moderate dualist faith first taught by *pop* Bogomil. In broad terms, the Greek-speaking Bogomils in the churches of Constantinople and Dragovitsa (or Drugunthia) were absolute dualists, while the Slav-speaking Bogomils of Bulgaria and Bosnia (and perhaps also the

---

[33] 'Isti portaverunt heresim in Lonbardiam(sic) a Neapoli: Marchus, Iohannes Iudeus, Ioseph et Aldricus, circa tempus quo currebat Mclxxiiii' (These men brought heresy to Lombardy from Naples: Mark, John the Jew, Joseph and Aldricus, in about the year 1174). Anselm of Alessandria, cap. 13, p. 319.

[34] An opinion first suggested, I think, by C. Thouzellier, 'Hérésie et croisade au xɪɪe siècle', in Thouzellier, *Hérésie*, p. 24.

[35] Urban II's letter to Flanders, ed. H. Hagenmeyer, *Die Kreuzzugsbriefe aus den Jahren 1088–1100* (Innsbruck, 1901), pp. 136–7.

[36] Guibert of Nogent, *Histoire de sa vie*, ɪɪɪ, 17, ed. E-R. Labande (Paris, 1981), pp. 428–34.

[37] If the *Arriani* mentioned by Geoffrey of Auxerre were Cathars. M. Roquebert, *L'Epopée cathare. I, 1198–1212: L'invasion* (Toulouse, 1970), pp. 57–8. For a more cautious view, R. I. Moore, 'St. Bernard's Mission to the Languedoc in 1145', *BIHR* 47 (1974), 1–4.

[38] *Ex Actis Concilii Lumbariensis, RHGF*, vol. xɪv, pp. 431–4.

[39] Duvernoy, *L'Histoire*, pp. 107–12, 119–21, 129–30, 137, 165–71.

church of the Milingoi) remained moderate dualists.[40] In *c.* 1170
Nicetas, who to judge from his name and from what is known of his
teaching was bishop of the Greeks of Constantinople, that is of the
Byzantine Bogomil Church, came to the West and presided over a
council of all the French and Lombard Cathar leaders at Saint-Félix
in Languedoc.[41] For a time he succeeded in uniting all the western
Cathars in the absolute dualist *ordo*, but a division arose when a rival
mission was sent to the West by the Bulgarian Bogomils. Consequently, whereas the Cathars of Languedoc remained true to
Nicetas's teaching and held the absolute dualist faith, as did the
church of Desenzano in Italy,[42] the rest of the Cathars returned to
moderate dualism either in its Bulgarian or in its Bosnian form.[43]
This is of relevance in the present discussion, because from *c.* 1180
different Cathar churches in the West preserved links with different
Bogomil churches in the East.

It is clear from the descriptions given by their opponents and from
Inquisition records that all Cathars used a form of the same Ritual,
which would seem to have come from the Balkans, where its adoption had antedated the schism of *pop* Nicetas's day. The earliest
evidence for its use in the West comes from a sermon of Egbert of
Schönau about the Cathar community of Cologne in 1163: 'Statui-
tur in medio infelix ille qui baptizandus sive catharizandus est. Et
assistit ei archicatharus, tenens in manu libellum deputatum ad
officium hoc' (That wretch who is to be baptised, or rather to be
catharised, is stood in the middle. And the chief Cathar ministers to
him, holding in his hand the book appointed for this purpose).[44]
Egbert later says that at the point of initiation the book is placed on
the candidate's head.[45] This would mean that it included at least the
text of a Gospel, and perhaps the whole of the New Testament. It is
possible that the Cathars customarily bound their Ritual into copies
of the New Testament, as is the case with the only surviving
example, the Lyons manuscript.[46]

[40] B. Hamilton, 'The Cathar Council of Saint-Félix reconsidered', *AFP* 48, (1978), 38–9.
[41] Hamilton, 'Cathar Council', pp. 23–53; D. Obolensky, 'Papa Nicetas: a Byzantine dualist
    in the land of the Cathars', *Okeanos: Essays Presented to Ihor Ševčenko, Harvard Ukrainian
    Studies*, 7 (1983), 489–500.
[42] Called the Albanenses by Sacconi.   [43] Sacconi, p. 59.
[44] Egbert of Schönau, *Sermones contra Catharos*, VIII, ii, *PL*, 195, 51.
[45] 'Quem imponens vertici ejus dicit benedictiones' (Placing it on his head he pronounces the
    blessings); *Sermones*, VIII, ii, *PL*, 195, 51.
[46] L. Clédat, *Le Nouveau Testament traduit au XIIIe siècle en langue provençale, suivi d'un Rituel
    Cathare* (Paris, 1887).

Plate 2 The beginning of the Cathar ritual, in Occitan (with some Latin), in a manuscript, possibly written between *c.* 1250 and *c.* 1280, which also contains the New Testament in Occitan. Though other texts written or used by the Cathars are known, this is the only surviving book which one can assume was itself once in the hands of Cathars in Languedoc and was used by them. Lyons, Bibliothèque Municipale, Ms. P.A.36, fol. 236r. (With permission of the Bibliothèque Municipale de Lyon.)

The Cathar Ritual must once have existed in a very large number of copies, but only two are known to us. An incomplete Latin text, dating from *c.* 1235–50 and written in Italy;[47] and the complete text in a Provençal version, contained in a manuscript written in the second half of the thirteenth century.[48] There are enough references in Catholic polemical writings and in inquisition depositions to show that these two examples are not eccentric but conform to the normal pattern of Cathar worship. The relationship between the Latin and Provençal Rituals was for a long time obscured by a too ready acceptance of Borst's opinion that the Latin text had been translated from Provençal.[49] As M. Roy Harris has shown, there is no evidence whatever to support this view.[50] But there is strong presumptive evidence that the Provençal Ritual had been translated from Latin, for the common forms of prayers used by the Cathars, including the Lord's Prayer and the prologue to St John's Gospel, which make up the opening section of the Ritual (see plate 2), are all in Latin, and are always cited in Latin when they occur in other, vernacular, parts of the text. It is normal practice for translated liturgies to retain certain well-known responses in the original tongue,[51] and it is reasonable to suppose that this custom was followed when the Occitan translation of the Cathar Ritual was made. The Latin Ritual of Florence and the Ritual of Lyons are not identical texts, and it is likely that they both ultimately derive from a common Latin archetype which was adapted to the use of different Cathar churches.[52]

Christine Thouzellier, who edited the Latin Ritual, while recognising common features between the descriptions of Bogomil worship in Eastern sources and the ceremonies of the Cathar Rituals, was nevertheless reluctant to assign an Eastern origin to the latter.[53] Duvernoy pointed out quite rightly that the only part of the Ritual which she was able directly to trace to a Western source is the gloss on the Lord's Prayer, but that this is the only part of the text

---

[47] *Rituel cathare.*   [48] Clédat, *Le Nouveau Testament*, pp. ix–xxvi.   [49] Borst, p. 280.

[50] M. R. Harris, 'Prolegomènes à l'histoire textuelle du Rituel cathare occitan', *Heresis* 6 (1986), 7.

[51] For example, the Coptic liturgy translated from the Greek still preserves some Greek forms. F. E. Brightman and C. E. Hammond (eds.), *Liturgies Eastern and Western* (Oxford, 1896, repr. 1965), pp. 144–88.

[52] The differences are clearly set out in the tables annexed to *Rituel cathare.*

[53] *Rituel cathare*, pp. 182–4.

which may be extemporised by the officiant.[54] The differences
which she cites between the Bogomil and the Cathar rites of initiation are not significant,[55] whereas the parallels are so close that
filiation seems certain. No full text of the Bogomil Ritual is known,
but a mid-fifteenth century Bosnian manuscript made for Radoslav
'the Christian' (the name normally applied to Bosnian Bogomils[56])
contains an Old Slavonic version of the opening section of the
Provençal Ritual, which it resembles very closely. The editors of the
Radoslav manuscript argued from calligraphic evidence that it was
copied from an archetype perhaps dating from the twelfth
century.[57] It would appear therefore that the Radoslav manuscript
preserves a part of the Bogomil Ritual, and that that Ritual was
translated in its entirety into Latin in the twelfth century for the use
of Western converts. It would also seem likely that the two surviving
Western texts both derive from this original translation, one
remaining in Latin, the other preserving some Latin forms. This
would imply that the standard practice of the early Cathars had
been to conduct public worship in Latin (a usage preserved in the
thirteenth century by the Cathars of north and central Italy, where
Latin may still have been comprehensible as an archaic form of the
vernacular), and that the Cathars of Languedoc were the innovators
in adopting a vernacular liturgy.

Consideration of the text of the bible used by the Cathars presents
a different range of problems. Only one copy of the Cathar New
Testament is known, the Occitan translation in Ms. PA 36 of the
Bibliothèque Municipale of Lyons, and that was only identified
because the text of the Cathar Ritual was bound in with it.[58] In
addition there are numerous scriptural texts cited by Cathar writers,
chiefly in Latin, but sometimes in Provençal. Despite the importance of the Lyons text, no critical edition of it has yet been made.
Christine Thouzellier asserted that it was a translation from the
Latin of BN Ms. Lat. 342,[59] but M. R. Harris has demonstrated that
this was not so, even though the two texts are closely related. He

---

[54] Duvernoy, *La Religion*, unnumbered pages at the end of the work, 'Addition au chapitre: "Le baptême"'.

[55] Duvernoy, *La Religion*, 'Addition à la "Conclusion"'.

[56] Duvernoy, *L'Histoire*, pp. 47–76, especially pp. 69–70.

[57] The Slav text with a French translation may be found in the tables at the end of *Rituel cathare*. Thouzellier discusses the date of this manuscript with full bibliography, pp. 63–70.

[58] Ed. Clédat, *Le Nouveau Testament*.   [59] *Rituel cathare*, p. 29.

argues that the New Testament passages cited in other Cathar works, written independently of the Lyons manuscript, need to be collated to establish whether there were specific Cathar readings which diverged from the normal Vulgate tradition and were consistent throughout all the Cathar churches, an objective he describes as trying to discover whether the Cathars had an 'Authorised Version' of the bible.[60] If Duvernoy is right in his contention that some of the variants in the Lyons New Testament derive from the Greek manuscript tradition and are not found in any of the main Western Vulgate families,[61] this would suggest that the Cathars derived their text of the bible, as well as their interpretation of it, from the Bogomils.

The New Testament of Lyons contains the apocryphal Pauline Epistle to the Laodiceans. M. R. Harris has edited this, and points out that although this is the only known Occitan translation, the Epistle is found in a number of Latin and vernacular manuscripts of the Vulgate New Testament, in some of which it is placed immediately after the Epistle to the Colossians as it is in the Lyons manuscript. It is not heretical in content, being merely a catena of Pauline writings, and its use by the Cathars is not in itself a sign of heterodoxy.[62] Nevertheless, the comment of a late-eleventh- or early-twelfth-century writer, in a *scholion* on Peter of Sicily's account of the Paulicians, is worth noting: 'the Paulicians ... of the present day only recognize the four Gospels ... and the fifteen Epistles of St Paul, because they also have an Epistle to the Laodiceans'.[63] The Lyons manuscript is a product of Occitan Catharism, which was of the absolute dualist school, and it was the absolute dualists among the Cathars who had indirect links with Paulicianism.[64] It is therefore possible that the decision to include the additional Epistle was a sign of that influence, even though the text itself, as Harris has shown, was of Western provenance.

No text of the Cathar Old Testament has yet been identified, although it is known that the absolute dualists among them accepted

---

[60] Harris, 'Prolegomènes', p. 11.

[61] J. Duvernoy, 'A Propos de l'article de Marvin Roy Harris', *Heresis* 6 (1986), 14.

[62] M. R. Harris, 'The Occitan Epistle to the Laodiceans: towards an edition of Ms. PA 36', in A. Cornagliotti *et al.* (eds.), *Miscellanea di Studi Romanzi offerta a Giuliano Gasca Queirazza*, 2 vols. (Alessandria, 1988), vol. I, pp. 428–46.

[63] P. Lemerle, 'L'histoire des Pauliciens d'Asie Mineure d'après les sources grecques', *Travaux et mémoires* 5 (1973), 132.

[64] Hamilton, 'Origins of the dualist church', pp. 115–24.

as canonical the non-historical books, unlike the moderate dualists who would only accept the New Testament.[65] In origin this had not been a doctrinal division: the Byzantine Bogomils of the early twelfth century were moderate dualists, yet they had a scriptural canon which included substantial parts of the Old Testament.[66] This canon was adopted in a modified form by the absolute dualists among the Cathars. There are quite numerous quotations from the Old Testament in Cathar writings, and a study of these might prove worthwhile, because if a pattern of variants from the Vulgate text could be established this might make it easier to identify a Cathar text of the Old Testament, which would comprise the Psalms, the Wisdom Literature and the Prophets only.

It would not have been necessary for the Cathars to make a complete translation of their canonical scriptures from Greek into Latin, since the version they used was not significantly different from that used by all other Christians.[67] What distinguished it from the Vulgate used by Catholics were a small but significant number of variants. It is possible that further research into the Cathar use of scripture will show that there was a 'standard' Cathar text which resulted from the collation of the Vulgate with manuscripts deriving from the Septuagint tradition to produce a series of readings, like the 'manichaean' punctuation of John 1:3,[68] which were more susceptible of a dualist interpretation than the received text. A faint memory of such a process may be preserved in the gloss on the Lord's Prayer in the Cathar Ritual of Florence: '"Quoniam tuum est regnum" – hoc verbum dicitur esse in libris grecis vel hebraicis' ('For thine is the kingdom' – this phrase is said to be in the Greek and Hebrew texts).[69] If this interpretation is correct, then the Occitan version of the New Testament would have been made from the 'standard' Cathar Latin text. It is possible, as M. R. Harris has suggested, that the Cathars may not have made this translation *de novo* but have

---

[65] Sacconi, pp. 51–2, 58.

[66] Euthymius Zigabenus, *Panoplia dogmatica*, xxvii, i, *PG*, 130, 1292.

[67] Euthymius Zigabenus says that the text of the Gospel book belonging to the Bogomil leader Basil did not in any way differ from that used by the Orthodox Church; *Panoplia dogmatica*, xxvii, 20, *PG*, 130, 1317.

[68] 'Omnia per ipsum facta sunt et sine ipso factum est nichil. Quod factum est in ipso vita erat' (All things were made by Him and without Him nothing was made. That which was made in Him was life), Lyons Ritual, in Clédat, *Le Nouveau Testament*, p. 470. Augustine condemned this as a Manichaean reading, *In Johannis evangelio*, i, i, 16, *PL*, 35, 1387.

[69] *Rituel cathare*, p. 21.

used an existing vernacular translation.[70] That could also have been collated with their 'standard' Latin text, although this cannot be known for certain until a critical edition of the New Testament of Lyons has been produced. The fact that the *incipits* of books in the New Testament of Lyons are in Latin suggests that the Cathars for whom it was made were accustomed to reading a Latin text of scripture.

All the Cathars appear to have read the apocryphal work known as *The Vision of Isaiah*. The original was a Greek Gnostic text perhaps dating from the first century AD, which is preserved in its entirety only in an Ethiopic translation. Part of the Greek text was translated into Latin in the late fifth or sixth centuries.[71] During the central middle ages a new version was made for Bogomil use, and changes were introduced in the text at places where it did not agree with Bogomil beliefs.[72] It is possible, and some scholars think likely, that this adaptation was the work of the Byzantine Bogomils and was written in Greek.[73] If so, the Greek text has not survived and the Bogomil recension is known only in an Old Slavonic version, the earliest manuscript of which dates from the late twelfth century,[74] and in a new Latin translation, which has been preserved only in a printed version made in 1522 from an unknown manuscript. It is often assumed that the Latin translation was made from Old Slavonic, but it could equally well have been made from Greek, had there been a Greek text of the dualist version.[75] Its use among the Cathars is first attested by Durand of Huesca, writing against the absolute dualist southern French Cathars in 1222–3,[76] while in *c.* 1240, the Dominican Moneta of Cremona observed that the moder-

---

[70] Harris, 'The Occitan Epistle to the Laodiceans', p. 435.

[71] *Codex rescriptus* of the Acts of Chalcedon, *Vat. Lat.* 5750; R. H. Charles, *The Ascension of Isaiah* (London, 1900), pp. xviii, 87–92, 102–8.

[72] E. Turdeanu, 'Apocryphes bogomiles et apocryphes pseudo-bogomiles', *Revue de l'histoire des religions* 138 (1950), 213–18.

[73] This was the opinion of Charles, *Ascension*, pp. xviii–xxxiii, and of E. Tisserant, *Ascension d'Isaiae*, (Paris, 1909), pp. 37–8.

[74] Text in J. Ivanov, *Livres et légendes bogomiles*, transl. M. Ribeyrol (Paris, 1976), pp. 136–48.

[75] I have not been able to see a copy of the 1522 text by Antonius de Fantis, printed at Venice, and have used the reprint of it by A. Dillmann, *Ascensio Isaiae Aethiopice et Latine cum ... additis versionum Latinarum reliquiis* (Leipzig, 1877), pp. 76–83. For the view that the text was translated directly from Greek see E. Turdeanu, 'La Vision d'Isaie. Tradition orthodoxe et tradition hérétique', in I. E. Anastasiou (ed.), *Kyrillos kai Methodios* (Thessalonika, 1966–8), vol. II, p. 318. The case for a translation into Latin from Old Slavonic is made by Ivanov, *Livres*, pp. 153–60.

[76] Durand, *Liber contra Manicheos*, pp. 256–7, 287–8.

ate dualists of Lombardy held that the Prophets were evil, except for Isaiah 'cujus dicunt esse quemdam libellum, in quo habetur quod spiritus Isaiae raptus a corpore usque ad septimum caelum ductus est' (to whom they attribute a certain book, in which it is recounted that the spirit of Isaiah, being drawn out of his body, was taken up to the seventh heaven).[77] In the late thirteenth century the Cathar author of the Occitan gloss on the Lord's Prayer cited a passage from the *Vision* to illustrate his argument: 'aisicom lo angel ensegna a Ysaya profeta, e dis a luy en la soa vision: "Aici ja no es trhon ni li angel senestre mas de la vertu del seten cel an ordenament; acqui ont es lo ric fill de Dio, e tuit li cel"' (as the angel taught Isaiah the prophet and said to him in his vision: 'Here there is no Throne, nor Angels of the Left, but they are governed by the Virtue of the Seventh Heaven, where the mighty Son of God dwells, and [so are] all the heavens').[78] The fact that all Cathar churches received this book suggests that it was part of their early inheritance from the Bogomils and that its translation antedated the schisms of the late 1170s. So far as is known, the Cathars read this text in Latin and it was never translated into the vernacular.

The Cathars in general, and the moderate dualists among them in particular, were faced with difficulties because of their rejection of the accounts of creation in the Book of Genesis. This, no doubt, made them view the *Vision of Isaiah* with sympathy because it gave the authority of a canonical figure to the exposition of a dualist cosmology. Yet there is no evidence that they considered this work equal in authority to canonical scripture. Their attitude towards apocrypha seems to have been very like that of Catholic contemporaries, who would cite, for example, the *Protevangelium* for information about the life of the Blessed Virgin, while accepting that is did not possess authority as the inspired revelation of God.

After the schism the moderate dualist Cathars of Concorezzo obtained another apocryphal book from the Bogomils, but this proved more controversial. Unlike the *Vision of Isaiah*, the *Book of St John* does not seem to derive from an early Gnostic work, but to have been written by the Bogomils and attributed to St John the Divine. It is set in the framework of the Last Supper, at which St John asks

---

[77] Moneta, II, ix, iv, p. 218.
[78] T. Venckeleer (ed.), 'Un recueil cathare: le manuscrit A.6.10. de la "Collection vaudoise" de Dublin. II: Une glose sur le Pater', *RBPH* 39 (1961), 764.

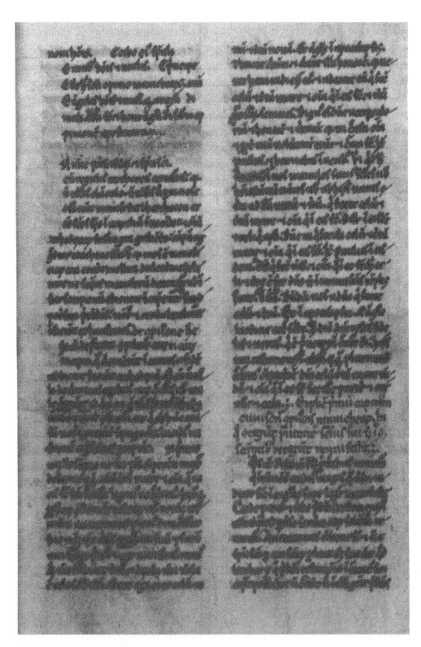

Plate 3 The beginning of an apocryphon of Bogomil origin, called the *Secretum* (Secret), which was brought from Bulgaria to the Italian Cathars in 1190. Vienna, Österreichische Nationalbibliothek Ms. Lat. 1137, fol. 158v. (With permission of the Bild-Archiv der Österreichischen Nationalbibliothek.)

the Lord to reveal to him the mysteries of the universe, and it must have fulfilled a useful function, especially for the moderate dualists, who had rejected the whole of the Old Testament and were therefore left with no coherent scriptural explanation of the nature of the creation, even though this occupied so central a place in their teaching.[79] The most recent editor of this text, Edina Bozóky, points to its strong doctrinal affinities with the Bogomilism professed by the heresiarch Basil at Constantinople in the early twelfth century as recorded by Euthymius Zigabenus, and inclines to think that the work was originally written in Greek.[80] It is difficult to be certain, because it survives only in two Latin versions: one represented by a single incomplete manuscript in Vienna (see plate 3), the other preserved in several copies which all derive from a manuscript once in the archive of the Inquisition at Carcassonne.[81]

The colophon to the Inquisition copy notes that Bishop Nazarius had brought it to the Cathar Church of Concorezzo from Bulgaria.[82] Nazarius is known from other sources. Concorezzo was the largest of the moderate dualist churches of Lombardy and derived its *Ordo* from the Bogomil Church of Bulgaria.[83] The author of the *De heresi*, writing in the early thirteenth century, names Nazarius as Elder Son of the Church of Concorezzo;[84] he had died before 1254, when Innocent IV ordered his body to be exhumed and burnt.[85] Rainier Sacconi, the convert Cathar perfect who became Inquisitor of Lombardy, writing in *c.* 1250, related how he had met Nazarius when he was a very old man, and how he asserted that Christ had an angelic nature and body received from His mother, who was an angel: 'et dixit quod habuit hunc errorem ab episcopo et filio maiore ecclesie Bulgarie iam fere elapsis annis LX' (and he said that he had been taught this error by the Bishop and Elder Son of the Church of Bulgaria almost sixty years ago).[86] This would place Nazarius's visit to Bulgaria in *c.* 1190.

Rainier does not mention *The Secret Book*, but Anselm of Alessandria, who succeeded him as inquisitor in Lombardy, recorded that through his attachment to the *Secret Book* Nazarius had caused a schism in the Church of Concorezzo, for his Elder Son Desiderius did not merely reject the book 'sed reputat illud malum' (but

---

[79] *Livre secret*, pp. 42–86.   [80] *Livre secret*, pp. 192–5.   [81] *Livre secret*, pp. 17–21.
[82] *Livre secret*, p. 86.   [83] Sacconi, pp. 50, 59.   [84] *De heresi catharorum*, p. 312.
[85] Potthast, no. 15492.
[86] Sacconi, p. 58.

considers it evil).[87] It is not possible to resolve the problem of the language in which this *Book* was written. There may have been a Byzantine Greek original from which the Old Slavonic translation was made for the Bogomils of Bulgaria, but that is not certain. It seems likely that the version which Nazarius brought back to Italy with him was in Old Slavonic. Anselm of Alessandria, who possessed one copy of this book, perhaps the lost Carcassonne manuscript, described it as being written in bad Latin.[88] This may reflect the fact that it had been translated from Old Slavonic and that it was more difficult to find experienced bilingual translators in that language than in Greek.

Desiderius of Concorezzo and his contemporary in the absolute dualist church of Desenzano, John of Lugio, were educated Cathars who were not interested in the mythology which had from the start formed an important part of the beliefs of the Bogomils. These young Italian coadjutor bishops wrote speculative works about dualist theology in the second quarter of the thirteenth century before persecution had begun in many parts of Lombardy.[89] Their existence suggests that there might be some truth in the letter attributed to Yvo of Narbonne, which claims that the Cathars of Como in *c.* 1214 had reported that the Cathar congregations of Lombardy and Tuscany sent believers to study logic and theology in the schools of Paris in order to strengthen their own faith and refute Catholic doctrine.[90] This story may merely be a piece of Catholic propaganda intended to make the Cathars appear menacing, but it is a fact that after *c.* 1200 the Cathars no longer sought to obtain theological writings from the Bogomils and developed a religious literature of their own.

---

[87] Anselm of Alessandria, cap. 1, p. 311.

[88] '*Secretum de Concorezo*. "Ego Iohannes frater vester ... etc." ... "Hoc est secretum hereticorum de Concorezo portatum de Bulgaria plenum erroribus" et etiam falsis latinis' (*The Secret of Concorezzo*. 'I John your brother ... etc.' ... 'This is the secret [book] of the heretics of Concorezzo, brought from Bulgaria [and] full or errors', and also [written in] bad Latin), Anselm of Alessandria, 319. Compare the colophon of the Carcassonne manuscript, *Livre secret*, p. 86.

[89] John of Lugio's teachings are described by Sacconi, pp. 52–7. Whether the 'quoddam volumen magnum X quaternorum' (a certain great book of ten quires) ascribed to John by Sacconi (p. 57) is the same as the *Book of the Two Principles*, or whether the latter is the work of some member of John's school, is uncertain. The teachings of Desiderius of Concorezzo are described by Anselm of Alessandria, pp. 310–12, and by Moneta of Cremona, IV, viii, i, p. 347. His work was read by St Thomas Aquinas, *Contra impugnantes Dei cultum*, c. 6, ed. P. Mandonnet, *S. Thomae Aquinatis Opuscula omnia* (Paris, 1927), vol. IV, p. 78.

[90] Matthew Paris, *Chronica majora*, ed. H. R. Luard, *RS* (London, 1877), vol. IV, p. 271.

It is possible that a great many translations of theological works were made from Greek and Old Slavonic by the Cathars and that they have not survived. I think this doubtful, because unlike the Cathars' own writings considered by Peter Biller in another chapter in this volume, there are no certain traces of such translations in the surviving sources. Scholars have looked for such materials, but have not found convincing evidence for them. Duvernoy, for example, has drawn attention to a saying attributed to the Lord in the *Gospel of the Nazarenes*, which Prepositinus of Cremona states was used by the Cathars.[91] But this is not necessarily evidence that they had a copy of the text, since the saying might have been transmitted to them orally by the Byzantine Bogomils.

Yet although the evidence suggests that a new generation of Cathar leaders tended to turn their backs on the Bogomil churches as sources of esoteric knowledge, empirical links were maintained with them throughout the thirteenth century. In 1325 Pope John XXII complained to the prince of Bosnia that 'magna haereticorum caterva de multis et variis partibus congregata ad principatum Bosnen. ... confluxit (a great crowd of heretics gathered together from many different regions has flocked to the principality of Bosnia).[92] If this report is true it would explain the sudden and apparently synchronous disappearance of organised Catharism throughout western Europe at about this time.

On a popular level 'Bulgaria' was remembered in the West as the land of marvels, from which the perfect had derived their teaching. Peter Biller has kindly drawn my attention to an inquisition deposition made between 1273–9 by Peter Perrin of Puylaurens. He had taken part in a discussion about how the weather in Languedoc was deteriorating: when the Cathar perfect were living in southern France there had been fewer storms. One person present remembered a woman saying that the perfects had a book which they would look at which enabled them to avert natural disasters of that kind, 'and this in Bulgaria'.[93]

The evidence considered in this chapter suggests that the Cathars' indebtedness to the Bogomil churches of the East in regard to books

[91] Duvernoy, *La Religion*, pp. 35–6.
[92] Ed. *Bullarium Franciscanum*, incepit J. H. Sbaralea, continuavit C. Eubel (Rome, 1898), vol. v, pp. 287–8, no. 577. Calendared, G. Mollat (ed.), *Jean XXII (1316–1324). Lettres communes, Litterae de Curia*, no. 32126 (Paris, 1909), vol. v, p. 448.
[93] Paris BN, Doat, 25 fol. 217r: *et hoc in Bulgaria*.

was very limited; that it dated chiefly from before *c.* 1170; but that nevertheless it was of great importance to the formation of Catharism. The Cathars certainly obtained their Ritual (although not the gloss on the Lord's Prayer) from the Bogomils, and the *Vision of Isaiah* came from the same source; while the argument that the Cathars collated the Vulgate text of the New Testament with a text established by the Bogomils but based on the Septuagint seems very persuasive, although in the present state of published research it must remain hypothetical.

The work of translation, I have argued, was all, in the first instance, carried out in Latin, although subsequently the Ritual and the New Testament were translated into Occitan. This ties in well with the findings about the Latinity of the Cathar perfect presented by Peter Biller in his chapter, and his observation that after the legatine council of Toulouse in 1178 the perfects were never accused of ignorance of Latin by their opponents.[94] Indeed, the evidence considered in this chapter would suggest that the Cathars initially used Latin as the language of public worship, that they read the bible in Latin, and that they translated Eastern dualist texts into Latin, and that they only used the vernacular, as the Catholic clergy at the time used it, when preaching. It was only later that the southern French Cathars adopted a vernacular liturgy and an Occitan translation of the New Testament, but there is no evidence that Cathars elsewhere ever abandoned the use of Latin as the language of worship.

So far as I am aware, little consideration has yet been given to the way in which the Cathars made translations, or, indeed, to the way in which Cathars and Bogomils communicated with each other. There were, it is true, frequent contacts between the West and the Byzantine Empire in the twelfth century, but the capacity to translate religious texts, or convey theological knowledge, requires a different kind of linguistic skill and a different range of vocabulary from that possessed by merchants or travellers. Only people resident in the Byzantine Empire for a long time were likely to develop the necessary kinds of expertise.

That some Western people living in Constantinople did become sufficiently versed in literary Greek to undertake the work of translation is known from the Latin version made in 1048–9 of the

---

[94] See p. 80.

Romance of Barlaam and Ioasaph. The preface tells us that this work was carried out 'in the translator's sixtieth year and the thirty-first of his residence [in Constantinople], through the encouragement of a certain nobleman, Leo, son of John ... [he] carefully rendered it in succinct language from the Greek tongue into graceful Latin, and where it was expedient he altered it and adapted it to the manners of our people'.[95] The text was thought to be a saint's life, although it was in reality a life of Prince Gautama, the Buddha, influenced by Asiatic Manichaeism.[96] Yet though it should in theory have proved attractive to Cathars, there is no certain proof that they read it. It was certainly read by Catholics for edification,[97] and I cite it here as an example, not of dualist literature, but of the conditions in which such translations were possible.

The evidence of Anselm of Alessandria is again important here. 'Postea francigene iverunt Constantinopolim ut subiugarent terram et invenerunt istam sectam, et multiplicati fecerunt episcopum, qui dicitur episcopus latinorum. ... Postea francigene, qui iverant Constantinopolim, redierunt ad propria et predicaverunt.'[98] What Anselm is saying is that the first Cathar, as distinct from Bogomil, church to be founded was the church of the Latins at Constantinople, whose members were expatriate westerners, and that it was that church which was responsible for the initial evangelisation of the West. This church survived and is recorded by Rainier Sacconi in his list of *c.* 1250 with a membership of fewer than fifty perfect.[99] But in the twelfth century it could have played a very significant role in the establishment of Catharism in western Europe. For if Anselm is correct, then there would have been westerners living in Constantinople in the twelfth century who were capable of translating Bogomil texts into Latin. It would make a good deal more sense of

---

[95] Ms. viii, B. 10 of the National Library of Naples, cited and translated by D. M. Lang, 'St. Euthymius the Georgian and the *Barlaam and Ioasaph* romance', *Bulletin of the School of Oriental and African Studies* 17 (1977), 308.

[96] See the introduction to the edition of the Greek text by G. R. Woodward and H. Mattingley (with new and additional introduction by D. M. Lang), *Barlaam and Ioasaph* (London 1914, repr. 1967), pp. ix–xxxii.

[97] Barlaam and Ioasaph were included in the Golden Legend of James of Voragine, and Baronius added their names to the Roman Martyrology with a feast day on 27 November. A. Butler, *The Lives of the Saints*, ed. H. Thurston and D. Attwater (London, 1937), vol. xi, pp. 321–2.

[98] See translation above, p. 44. Anselm of Alessandria, p. 308.

[99] 'Ecclesia Latinorum in Constantinopoli fere sunt L.' (There are scarcely fifty [members] of the church of the Latins in Constantinople). Sacconi, p. 50.

the origins of Catharism in the twelfth-century West to envisage that the first missions were conducted not by crusaders who had picked up some Cathar ideas while travelling through Constantinople, for their conditions of life would not have been stable enough to enable them to receive the right kind of training, nor by Greeks and Bulgars who had an imperfect command of Western vernaculars, but by members of the church of the Latins in Constantinople. Such missions would have had the opportunity to be carefully prepared, and their members would already have been using a Latin translation of the Ritual which they would have brought with them to the West. If the men who led the missions were themselves westerners who had lived for a long time in the Byzantine Empire, they would have had no difficulty in preaching their faith when they reached western Europe. They would also have been capable of undertaking a textual collation of the Vulgate with the Bogomil version of the Septuagint. This would, I suggest, help to explain the comparative ease with which Catharism spread in the West. It might also, perhaps, help to explain why Catharism became an indigenous Western movement comparatively soon.

CHAPTER 4

The Cathars of Languedoc and written materials

Peter Biller

This chapter's ultimate aim is to obtain a view of 'heresy' and 'literacy' among Cathars in Languedoc. It tries to do this by looking at their use of written materials: at night-time one sees something more clearly when looking slightly to one side of it. Trials of Cathars and their supporters (called in what follows *perfecti/perfectae* (male/female perfects) and *credens/credentes* (believer/s) contain many references to written materials, most of which have not survived. This chapter puts these references together to suggest the outlines of this lost reality, written materials and their use by the *perfecti*. Then it looks at the way this theme was seen, by *perfecti*, by *credentes* and in particular by contemporary Catholic writers. It does not discuss other ways of spreading ideas: talking about Catharism inside families, between friends and neighbours, and with one's parish priest; listening to anti-Cathar mendicant sermons, or to satirical songs; seeing abusive images of Mary and the saints, which were used by *perfecti* before 1234, as we know through an allusion by Luc de Tuy.[1]

Three points need to be remembered. First, though much about literacy and education in Languedoc in this period is in darkness – we lack a Clanchy on the theme – there are some shafts of light, from Ladurie on the confined case of Montaillou,[2] and from Mundy on the Toulousain.[3] Mundy sees an increase in formal education during

Acknowledgement is due here to Professor W. Wakefield for transcripts of some of the damaged parts of Toulouse BM Ms. 609, and to Professor John Green for help with the Occitan text cited in n. 124 below.

[1] Luc de Tuy, *De altera vita, adversus albigensium errores* 1.9, *MBVP* 25.222G–3B; see 3.12, *MBVP* 25.246C–D on use of satiric songs.

[2] E. Le Roy Ladurie, *Montaillou. Cathars and Catholic in a French Village 1294–1324*, transl. B. Bray (London, 1978), ch. 15.

[3] J. H. Mundy, 'Village, town and city in the region of Toulouse', in J. A. Raftis (ed.), *Pathways to Medieval Peasants* (Toronto, 1981), pp. 156–7, 162–3 (with much material in the notes); 'Urban society and culture: Toulouse and its region', in R. L. Benson and G. Constable (eds.), *Renaissance and Renewal in the Twelfth Century* (Oxford, 1982), pp. 234–8; *Men*

the thirteenth century. He points to the spread of parish schools and the creation of a university in Toulouse, and the evidence for the reading of vernacular literature in high-class households and the vernacular literacy of troubadours of quite humble origin. Most striking in his picture is the emergence of public scribes from about 1100. By 1200 Toulouse has between thirty and forty notaries drawing up instruments in Latin, while inquisitors' enquiries of 1245/6 show a penetration into the countryside which has already been achieved by this date, with many quite small communities having one or two notaries. There was a wide diffusion of Latin charters and texts relating to court proceedings, and Mundy suggests lay businessfolk reading quite a lot of Latin, alongside the notaries and lawyers who both read and speak it. He pens women into a category of the much less literate.

Second, although Catharism was theologically a 'heresy' to the Catholic Church, it was not structurally and socially a 'sect' but a Church. It did not spring from the Roman Church, as Waldensianism did. Ecclesially it was autonomous and highly organised, with its own clergy, its hierarchy, its diocesan boundaries, its formal meetings called 'general councils' or 'general chapters'.

Third, implanted in Languedoc (possibly already by the mid-1140s), the Cathar Church had support among the powerful and the wealthy until quite late in its history. Considerable evidence can be found in depositions about the use and movement of large sums of money in the 'Cathar economy'.[4] Cathars' considerable extensiveness among the rural nobility stands out in the depositions of the 1240s – but accidents in the survival of evidence may be producing a bias here, one which is extended in romanticising modern accounts. From some of the very late inquisitions of the mid-1280s to 1300, and Biget's studies of these, we learn more of urban Catharism.[5] For Biget, Catharism was never more than 10 per cent of the urban population. It was sharply concentrated in an urban elite of high comital and later royal officials, consular families, lawyers, notaries, doctors and merchants; he suggests that this picture should be projected back to the decades around 1200.

---

and *Women at Toulouse in the Age of the Cathars* (Toronto, 1990), pp. 2, 10, 117–18 (on illiteracy of women; see possible exception in n. 95 below).

[4] A. Roach, 'The Cathar economy', *Reading Medieval Studies* 12 (1986), 51–71.

[5] J.-L. Biget, 'Un procès d'inquisition à Albi en 1300', *CaF* 6 (1971), 273–341, and 'L'extinction du catharisme urbain; les points chauds de la répression', *CaF* 20 (1985)

The Catharism that we find is, unsurprisingly then, a written Church. Let us examine the categories of texts it used.

I TYPES OF TEXTS

(a) Finance

First are notarial documents, and the theme of finance. Living in a society of Latin charters and wills which was penetrated by a public notariate, and itself supported by the powerful and wealthy, Catharism seems to have generated and used for its own purposes instruments, almost certainly in Latin. One comes across someone procuring charters for *credentes*,[6] or a *perfectus* extracting charters from the chest of a *credens*,[7] or a *credens* going to a house of *perfecti* to get instruments necessary for him.[8] Occasionally further details allow us to discern distinct categories of document. One is that of charters relating to property: a witness in 1244 tells of the drawing up and witnessing of charters when his father granted lands *ad acapitum* (in perpetual rent) to *perfecti* living in Lauran in 1209.[9] Another is of wills. Depositions contain many references to legacies to the *perfecti*, sometimes of very large sums, and one can find reference to their writing: one witness told the inquisitor Peter Seila of his reward in goods for drawing up a will for the *perfecti*,[10] and we have the *credens* Alaman of Roaix bearing letters relating to the execution of wills.[11] The decree of the council of Béziers in 1246, which forbade notaries or scribes to draw up instruments for heretics or their supporters, was envisaging these two categories (grants, wills) when specifying the doing of this in life or death. Money-lending generated documents: a loan is recorded in the *scriptis seu memorialibus* (writings or

305–40. See also his review of Mundy's *The Repression of Catharism at Toulouse* (Toronto, 1985) in *Annales. Economies. Sociétés. Civilisations* 42 (1987) 137–40.

6 Toulouse BM 609, fol. 135r. Notable earlier investigation of the light thrown on Cathars' use of texts by references in depositions include the following: C. Douais, 'Les hérétiques du comté de Toulouse dans la première moitié du xiiie siècle d'après l'enquête de 1245', in *Compte-rendu du IIe congrès scientifique internationale des Catholiques, Paris 1891, Section 5* (Paris, 1891), pp. 158–60; Guiraud, vol. i, pp. 152ff. and ii, pp. 60, 91–4, 108, 122 n. 2, 136; Duvernoy, *La Religion*, p. 218.

7 Toulouse BM 609, fol. 34r.

8 Toulouse BM 609, fol. 239r. On such grants, in which some rights in property were not alienated, see M. Castaing-Sicard, *Les Contrats dans le très ancien droit Toulousain (Xe–XIIIe siècle)* (Toulouse, 1959), pp. 68–9.

9 Doat 23, fol. 117r–v.   10 Doat 21, fol. 206r.   11 Douais, vol. i, p. 70 n.

records) of the *perfecti*,[12] and there are letters demanding payment – an early example is the Cathar bishop Guilabert of Castres presenting one.[13] The circumstances of some other letters of the *perfecti* suggest finance as their subject.[14]

In 1293 there was a strange confession from a scribe who claimed to have found some hidden Cathar instruments, which he intended to use to extort money from descendants of the families involved. We cannot now establish what truth there was in the story (it was retracted) and in the claim that the instruments were forged (the inquisitor was sceptical about this claim). Despite this, the confession throws light on more than just the world of (possibly) blackmail, forgery and documents of *c.* 1290. For, even if only a plausible lie, it would still tell us what scribe and inquisitor in 1293 saw as *likely* in a cache of documents from the·Cathar past. And this was the cache: five wills by which *credentes*, three of whom were lords, bequeathed money to *perfecti* – a *perfectus* called Isarn had appended his seal, and among three other wills one was from a member of the high-ranking Morlane family of Carcassonne. In addition there were three *cartae debitorum* (charters of debts), detailing debts to the *perfecti* ranging from £40 to £100.[15]

(b) Church organisation

Church organisation, diocesan divisions, conciliar meetings and important business generated documents. The largest survival is a test known as the 'Acts of St Félix-de-Caraman'. Hamilton has shown that this rests on three texts no longer extant, which were once in the possession (in an archive?) of the *perfecti* of the diocese of Toulouse: an extract from a sermon; an extract from a history of Cathars; and an extract from the report of a boundary commission.[16] After deciding the limits of the Churches of Toulouse and Carcassonne this commission had instructed two named men each to

---

[12] G. W. Davis (ed.), *The Inquisition at Albi 1299-1300. Text of Register and Analysis* (New York, 1948), p. 131. Cathar finance and its documents are briefly discussed in Castaing-Sicard, *Les Contrats*, pp. 257, 276.

[13] Doat 24, fol. 87v; see Guiraud, vol. II, p. 91.

[14] For example, a letter from a *perfectus* to a man who acted as a Cathar banker in Cahors in Doat 23, fols. 216v–217r, or a letter handed over to a merchant of Albi with the request that he transact its business speedily, Davis, *Inquisition at Albi*, pp. 124, 162.

[15] Doat 26, fols. 142v–147v.

[16] B. Hamilton, 'The Cathar council of Saint-Félix reconsidered', *AFP* 48 (1978), 23–53.

make a *dictatum et Cartam* (record and charter) for each Church. One might add that formality of procedure, list of witnesses and vocabulary suggest the conjecture that we are dealing here with notaries producing formal documents. Hamilton also shows the context within which, in 1223, the bishop of Carcassone needed to have the written compilation which survives, and ordered it to be drawn up. We have further references to *perfecti* holding general councils. One attended by a *magna congregatio* (large gathering) of 600 at Mirepoix *c.*1206 was *pro quadam questione determinanda* (to determine a certain question),[17] while the *concilium generale* (general council) of Pieusse (1223) was concerned with erecting a new bishopric. Even through the informality of a witness's memory there survives formal and possibly legal terminology: Cathars of one area *petierunt et postularunt* (petitioned and requested) and *diffinitum est* (judgement was given).[18] Set beside the analogies of the treatment of diocesan questions at St Félix and what is known about the roles of notaries in Catharism, the formal vocabulary of Mirepoix suggests written proceedings, and the formal vocabulary of Pieusse written petition and judgement.

Less conjecture is needed with letters. Though no single letter survives, we have numerous references in depositions to letters sent or received by *perfecti* and carried by *credentes*. 'Did you carry a letter for them?' is an inquisitor's question.[19] Consider this miscellany. The leader of a dissident group in 1223, Bartholomew of Carcassonne, sends out letters part of whose formal Latin salutation survives;[20] a letter comes to the *perfecti* of Montségur from the bishop of *perfecti* of Cremona;[21] one *credens* who took part in *consiliis et tractatibus* (counsels and negotiations) of the Cathars bears letters;[22] another intermediary between French and Italian *perfecti* bears *litteras responsales* (letters of reply);[23] a *credens* reads out a letter in the presence of the Cathar bishop Peter Pollainh;[24] bishop Aimeri de

[17] Doat 24, fols. 240v–241r. A *concilium* was held near Belestá *c.* 1243, Toulouse BM 609, fol. 214r.

[18] Doat 23, fols. 269v–270r. Compare Paolini's comments in chapter 5 below on legal terminology used by the author of the *De heresi catharorum*.

[19] For example, in 1277: 'Interrogatus, nullam litteram ... apportavit' (Asked, [he said] he carried no letter), Doat 25, fol. 246r.

[20] Matthew Paris, *Chronica Majora*, RS 57/3, 78: 'Bartholomaeus, servus servorum sanctae fidei tali salutem' (Bartholomew, servant of the servants of the holy faith, greetings to so and so).

[21] Doat 24, fol. 171v.   [22] Limborch, p. 14.   [23] Limborch, p. 13.

[24] Doat 23, fol. 171r.

Collet sends a letter to the two deacons of a particular deanery.[25] The first salient point is the formality of these. Bartholomew's salutation and the phrase *literas responsales* suggests epistolary formality and conformity to the rules of treatises on letter-writing, something also suggested by the weighty or solemn nature of dignitaries, assemblies or the important church business which is being reported or executed. Latinity is not necessarily implied by Bartholomew's salutation (the reporter may have translated), but it would have been obvious for exchanges between *perfecti* of Lombardy and Languedoc. These latter constitute a second notable feature of Cathar letters. Long-existing relations between Cathars of the two regions were intensified by the exodus of Languedocian Cathars to Italy from the mid-thirteenth century and the exiling of their hierarchy. Two late *credentes*, one of whom confessed to three, the other to four, return journeys to Italy or Sicily bearing letters, seem to have been international postmen.[26] More frequent, of course, are deposition references to domestic 'post', *perfecti* communicating among themselves or with *credentes* by letter.[27] There is one reference to the use of the medium of a wax tablet, smuggled into jail for a deacon to inscribe on it the name of his successor.[28]

(c) Service books, scripture, theology; miscellaneous

Bernard Gui refers to two categories of Cathar books: the New Testament in the vernacular and 'books infected with errors' (i.e. works of Cathar theology), without specifying their language.[29] Surviving texts confirm these and add a third category, service books. The one manuscript book which survives in original form was written (it has been suggested on palaeographical grounds) between 1250 and 1280,[30] and it contains two categories, the New Testament and a Cathar ritual; they are, in Occitan, but with incipits, some

---

[25] Guiraud, vol. II, ch. 9. [26] The examples in nn. 22 and 23 above.

[27] Worth noting for its implications of literacy among *credentes* is one letter between the *credens* Peter of Beauville and his wife, Doat 25, fol. 312v.

[28] Doat 25, fol. 13r–v.

[29] Gui, *Practica* 5.5, p. 242. A notable earlier discussion of surviving and lost Cathar writings is in *Traité cathare*, pp. 18–21.

[30] On the Lyons manuscript, see now M. R. Harris, 'La localisation de la scripta du *Rituel cathare occitan* (Ms. Lyon. Bibl. Mun., PA 36), in P. T. Ricketts (ed.), *Actes du Premier Congrès International de l'Association Internationale d'Etudes Occitanes* (London, 1987), pp. 242–50, and the comments on this and other studies by Harris in P. Wunderli's review article in *Heresis* 10 (1988), 103–6.

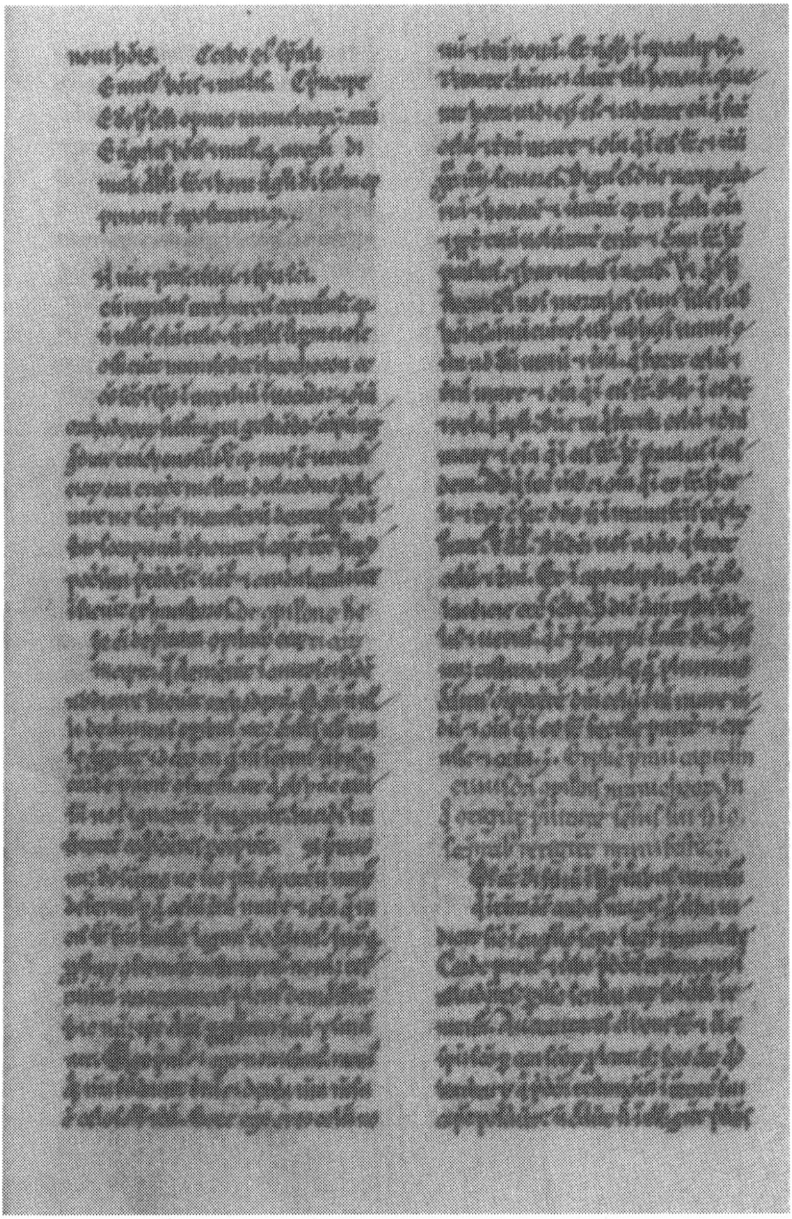

Plate 4 Part of a treatise written by the Waldensian Durand of Huesca attacking an anonymous Cathar treatise, which Durand quotes extensively, beginning in this example after the words *De compilatione hereticorum* (From the heretics' compilation) in the first column, and continuing for twenty-four lines in the second column. Much of this lost treatise can be reconstructed from these quotations. Paris, Bibliothèque Nationale Ms. Lat. 689, fol. 73v. (With permission of the Bibliothèque Nationale.)

running heads and some prayers in Latin (see plate 2). An anti-Cathar polemic written by Durand of Huesca, probably *c.* 1223–4, includes extensive extracts of a Cathar treatise of theology, and thus preserves part of one representative of Gui's second category (see plate 4).[31]

This is the tip of the iceberg. What did the submerged remainder once look like? Depositions provide some suggestions. Books contained scripture, in various forms. One man about to become a *perfectus* obtained a copy of a bible, by implication in Latin, *c.* 1209,[32] while another *perfectus* was hunting for a complete text after 1300.[33] A cache of books contained the two testaments and, separately, a *liber prophetarum* (book of the prophets).[34] There are references, widely separated in time, to the apocryphal *Vision of Isaiah*.[35] The New Testament, called the *Textus* (Text), is what is most commonly cited, sometimes with the specification of the vernacular. But one also finds parts only: a *Passio* (Passion), for example, in the vernacular.[36] The specification of use of a book by a *perfectus* who preaches the gospels and Peter and Paul might just imply the presence in the book of only some epistles, rather than the preacher's selection from the book. More surely, we can conjecture that a single quire used in giving the *consolamentum* contained only the gospel according to John.[37]

Many references to books containing theology are too brief to identify the specific texts they contained: their books *de doctrina ipsorum* (of their doctrine),[38] a book *de facto hereticorum* (on the heretics' matter),[39] a book *de fide* (about faith),[40] a book *plenum erroribus* (full of errors);[41] a book in a mixture of Latin and vernacular which was *de secta, vita, et doctrina heresis* (on the sect, life and doctrine of Catharism – in these trials 'heresy' means Catharism),[42] or a book containing *secta manicheorum et doctrina eorum* (sect of the Manichees [= Cathars] and their doctrine).[43] But other references

---

[31] *Traité cathare.*   [32] See n. 68 below.   [33] D'Ablis, p. 380.

[34] H. Blaquière and Y. Dossat, 'Les cathares au jour le jour. Confessions inédites de cathares quercynois', *CaF* 3 (1968), 263.

[35] Durand, *Liber contra Manicheos* 16, 18, pp. 256–7, 288; D'Ablis, pp. 112, 324; Fournier, vol. II, pp. 50–1, vol. III, pp. 200–2.

[36] Douais, vol. II, pp. 97, 106.   [37] Limborch, p. 113, Davis, *Inquisition at Albi*, p. 173.

[38] Limborch, p. 53; similar examples, pp. 64, 105, 110, 120.

[39] Limborch, p. 169.   [40] Fournier, vol. I, p. 280.   [41] Doat 21, fol. 229r.

[42] Fournier, vol. I, p. 285.

[43] Fournier, vol. II, p. 204.

are a little longer or more precise: *Pater Noster hereticorum scriptum* (text of the heretics' 'Our Father' – 'of the heretics' meaning with their doxology, or with their gloss?');[44] *expositio dominice orationis in Latino* (exposition of the Lord's prayer in Latin);[45] a book with *aliqui errores hereticorum* (some heretics' errors), in which one read about the invalidity of baptism;[46] *multa scripta* about God sending Lucibel to this world;[47] a book containing Cathar and Catholic arguments and counter-arguments, in the vernacular.[48] Sometimes the fact of a *book* is not spelled out, but probably implied. Thus one witness hearing *expositiones authoritatum* (expositions of authorities) from a *perfectus* was probably hearing the reading of a book containing these. This would probably have been a Cathar *summa auctoritatum* (summa of authorities) of the sort which Paolini, in chapter 5 below, conjectures was also in the hands of Italian Cathars.[49] To these deposition examples should be added what we know from literary evidence: a schedule of Cathar doctrines written in Occitan which was in the hands of *perfecti* in Toulouse in 1178;[50] the treatise partly preserved by Durand;[51] the *Perpendiculum scientiarum* (Plumbline of sciences), an anthology of dicta containing *flores* (flowers) of philosophers and *sententiae* (sayings) of saints referred to by Luc de Tuy in 1234.[52] Luc's vignette of a French Cathar writer called Arnold, who travelled into Spain and applied himself to 'sa[n]ctorum Patrum Augustini, Hieronymi, Isidori & Bernardi opuscula minora corrumpere subtrahendo vera, & adiiciendo falsa' (corrupting the minor works of the holy Fathers Augustine, Jerome, Isidore and Bernard, subtracting true things and adding false ones), tells us presumably of the composition of a Cathar book: not the *Perpendiculum?*[53]

Our authors use the plural. Durand often referred to Cathar

---

[44] Doat 21, fol. 257v.
[45] D'Ablis, p. 390; scepticism is needed about the witness's claim that this contained nothing against the faith.
[46] Limborch, p. 152.   [47] Doat 22, fol. 12r–v.
[48] Fournier, voll. II, pp. 196–7; 'rationes et contrarationes in vulgari scriptas de factis, dictis et oppinionibus hereticorum manicheorum et catholicorum, et improbabantur in dicto libro facta, dicta et oppiniones catholicorum et approbabantur facta, dicta et oppiniones manicheorum, et aliquando etiam e converso' (arguments and counter-arguments written in the vernacular about the deeds, sayings and opinions of the Manichaean heretics and the Catholics, and sometimes in the said book the deeds, sayings and opinions of the Manichees were confirmed, and sometimes the other way round).
[49] Doat 21, fol. 245r.
[50] Roger of Howden, *Gesta Henrici*, RS 49/1, p. 203, and *Chronica*, RS 51/2, p. 152.
[51] *Traité cathare*.   [52] Luc de Tuy, *De altera vita* 3.2, *MBVP* 25.241A–B.
[53] Luc de Tuy 3.17, *MBVP* 25.247H.

theological books and treatises,[54] while Gui referred to theological books. Luc de Tuy's saying that arrested *perfecti* when arrested would be carrying books like the *Perpendiculum* carries a similar implication. Possibly these uses of the plural between the 1220s and 1320s include the notion of many copies, but what the evidence paraded so far also shows is that they also denote a multiplicity of different works. Different works possessed over a long time; but composed only early? The chronology of Catholic polemic (dying away earlier in Languedoc, continuing well into mid-thirteenth century in Italy) has suggested a theological withering among Languedocian *perfecti*.[55] Certainly, the precisely identified works are early (the 1178 text, that quoted by Durand, and those referred to by Luc de Tuy), just as our evidence of high Cathar theology is early, as we shall see in the discussion of Catholic writers' image of Catharism. However, the richness of deposition references shows how much has been lost and can never be known: confident inference of a post-1230s decline is dangerous.

Finally, a few other books are found in the possession of the *perfecti* – notably a *liber medicine* (book of medicine)[56] and a book *vocatum Calendarium* (book called *Calendar*).[57] Some *perfecti* practised as physicians; the *Calendar* could have been medical, and one may be hearing here of a text which was used to help in medical work.[58]

2 TEXTS: NUMBERS, PROCUREMENT, PHYSICAL CHARACTERISTICS

Among some philological students of the Cathars' new testament one can find the argument that the Lyons manuscript was a copy of an original and the implication that copies of it were rare.[59] The sheer numbers of Languedocian Cathars, the frequency of their

---

[54] Durand, *Liber contra Manicheos*, prologue, and c. 6, 10, 12, pp. 82, 147, 183, 208. He also says 'in nonnullis hereticorum libris hunc vidimus', referring to removal of material 'de suis codicibus' (we have seen this in some books of the heretics ... [material] from their codexes), c. 1, p. 91.

[55] Intellectual weakness is the view of M.-H. Vicaire, 'Les cathares albigeois vus par les polémistes', *CaF* 3 (1968), 119.

[56] Toulouse BM 609, fol. 94r.   [57] Fournier, vol. I, pp. 315, 375.

[58] See C. H. Talbot, *Medicine in Medieval England* (London, 1967), pp. 125ff., and S. Eisner (ed.), *The Kalendarium of Nicholas of Lynn* (Athens, Ga., 1980), p. 7, on the use by doctors in medieval Europe of books with calendars.

[59] M. R. Harris, 'Prolégomènes à l'histoire textuelle du rituel cathare occitan', *Heresis* 6 (1986), 7; and the comment by P. Wunderli in his review article, *Heresis* 10 (1988), 104.

ritual need for the text, and the vast number of deposition references to the 'text' make this extraordinarily unlikely. But the order of magnitude of the numbers of copies, which once existed, is not obvious. Take first the fact that each pair of *perfecti* needed a copy of the text for administering the *consolamentum*. There were several hundred *perfecti* at any given time in the earlier period, and hundreds of occasions of the administration of the *consolamentum* are described in depositions. Take, secondly, one instance of a deacon entrusting his book to the *credentes* of a community, Cambiac, who hold a council about what to do with it,[60] and connect this with Duvernoy's conjecture of twenty-nine deaneries in the early thirteenth century.[61] Should we lean on the first cluster of data, postulating the former existence at any one (early) time of one copy of the Occitan New Testament per pair of *perfecti*: and therefore several hundred? Or construct a theory of one copy per deanery: and therefore a few dozen? And set either hypothesis beside the near complete efficiency of inquisitors in destroying all but one copy?

There are quite a large number of examples of *credentes* holding or transmitting a book belonging to a *perfectus* of no special rank. Indeed, holding such a book has become a standard inquisitor's question, becoming a possible part of the ideal type of behaviour of a *credens*. There are also books, plural. Dossat has commented on the poverty of one collection of three books, hidden in a cave.[62] Now, there are references to various particular *perfecti*, each with his books, plural. For example, one *perfectus* kept his books in Castelsarrasin,[63] another had some in Toulouse;[64] *credentes* kept the books of another *perfectus* after his death.[65] Such examples suggest that this little cache may have contained the books of one *perfectus* or pair of *perfecti*. As a Cathar central lending library it would have been remarkably thin, while as the cache of one or two *perfecti* it is unsurprising and impressive.

---

[60] Toulouse BM 609, fol. 237v; W. Wakefield, 'Heretics and inquisitors: the case of Auriac and Cambiac', *Journal of Medieval History* 12 (1986), 231, 233.

[61] Duvernoy, *L'Histoire*, pp. 347–51.

[62] Y. Dossat, 'Les cathares dans les documents de l'inquisition', *CaF* 3 (1968), 89, where the library is mentioned in connection with the author's view that there were not many manuscripts belonging to the heretics.

[63] Fournier, vol. II, p. 475.   [64] Fournier, vol. III, p. 172.

[65] Doat 23, fol. 129v. Other examples of plural books of one *perfectus*: Limborch, pp. 50, 54. One witness deposing in 1244 said that he *portabat libros eorum* (carried their books), referring to one heretic and his companions (Doat 23, fol. 341v), while another, deposing in

The depositions only provide a scatter of references to help with the question of procurement, presumably sometimes different for specifically Cathar texts, for non-Cathar texts and for documents. Part was copying, presumably sometimes by *perfecti* themselves, but also by others. A Raymond Peter *de Planis*, sentenced in the late 1240s, writes for the *perfecti* for a fee. Luc de Tuy wrote of Arnold (mentioned earlier) as a *velocissimus scriptor* (very quick scribe).[66] In 1308 we hear of negotiations about dealing with a book of Cathar theology which lacked two folios, and the restoring of these two:[67] envisaged is someone having a full text, which is to be copied. Part was buying. William Symon said that, around 1209, 'before he became a *perfectus*, the abbot of St Papoul placed a certain bible with him as a pledge for 100 Toulousan shillings, and then he [William] went off with it [to Lauran] to become a *perfectus*'.[68] About a century later quite developed book markets are implied by the *perfectus* Jacques Autier commissioning a *credens* to spend up to £20 buying a bible in Toulouse or in Montpellier.[69] A vernacular New Testament, in Bolognese script, seen in a circle *c.* 1300 which contained many lawyers, some trained in Bologna, suggests another possible source.[70] While some physical details of Cathar books are of only curious interest – a little book bound in black, another with a little linen hood[71] – one point has more significance: that some of these books were not of humble aspect, and a few may have been very costly. The Lyons manuscript has handsome and large decorated red and blue initial letters at the beginning of each gospel and epistle, while the New Testament in Bolognese script was described as *valde pulchrum* (very beautiful), praised for the beauty of its script

---

1274, recalled taunting illiterate *perfecti*, whom he saw *multos libros habebant* (had many books), asking them what they would do with them (Doat 25, fol. 161r).

66 Douais, vol. I, p. 51; Luc de Tuy, *De altera vita* 3.17 *MBVP* 25.247H.

67 Limborch, p. 169.

68 Toulouse BM 609, fol. 252v: 'antequam fieret hereticus abbas sancti papuli posuerat penes eum in pignus quendam bibliam pro c solidos tolosanos et tunc fuit factus hereticus et recessit cum ea'.

69 D'Ablis, p. 380.

70 D'Ablis, p. 380. Commentary on such Bolognese manuscripts is provided in A. Conti, *La miniatura Bolognese, scuole et botteghe 1270–1340* (Bologna, 1981), while contracts mentioning places, or persons from places, in southern France can be found in G. Orlandelli, *Il libro a Bologna dal 1300 al 1330* (Bologna, 1959), pp. 42, 72, 82, 102. Compare the comments in Balmas and Dal Corso, p. 9, on the professionalism of copying, illumination, and hence costliness of some Waldensian manuscripts.

71 Doat 25, fol. 161r: 'parvum librum coopertum corio nigro' (little book covered in black leather), Fournier, vol. II, p. 107.

and its illumination in blue and green. Hinted at, then, are piecemeal commissions for copying documents and Cathar texts, some sense, perhaps of a deposit of authentic texts to be copied, expenditure, sometimes considerable, and by 1300 (at least) the use of book markets.

Some texts were slight or small. While from early Cathar–Catholic disputes we hear of the production of presumably quite slight works called *libelli* (booklets) or *cedulae* (schedules),[72] later we hear of texts which are only one quire – the one already mentioned, used in the *consolamentum*,[73] another containing an exposition of the *Pater Noster*,[74] – and on two occasions of little books which are *sine postibus* (without boards).[75] Reasonable smallness is often implied – for example, in the description of a book being held open for reading in a hand,[76] or of a pocket for one being made out of a pair of reworked deerskin gloves.[77] There may have been a chronology here: development from small to tiny. The Lyons manuscript (from shortly after 1250?) is small but not tiny at 13.5 by 17.2 cm. The first reference to a book as little (*parvum librum*) comes in 1273/4,[78] and descriptions as really tiny after 1300: a book the length of one's hand in one description, and the length of one's palm and the width of three or four fingers in another.[79] By 1311 one has Gui interested enough to ask a *credens* whether a book he had seen had boards, and whether it was big or small,[80] possibly following information extracted by D'Ablis three years earlier about a small book without boards.[81] Two stages? The first would have been the need which the *perfecti* shared with friars; smallness for portability. The second overlapping but later need would have been tininess for the sake of secrecy.

3 TEXTS BETWEEN *PERFECTI* AND *CREDENTES*

Cathars educated. A *perfectus*, who had books, tutored three sons in a family for five years.[82] There is early reference to Cathar education

---

[72] Peter of Vaux-de-cernai, *Hystoria Albigensis*, ed. P. Guèbin and E. Lyon, 3 vols. (Paris, 1926–39), vol. I, pp. 47–9.
[73] Davis, *Inquisition at Albi*, p. 173. [74] See n. 45 above. [75] D'Ablis, p. 86.
[76] D'Ablis, p. 112, Limborch, p. 110. Sometimes, however, *in manibus* (in hands), for example Fournier, vol. III, p. 405.
[77] Limborch, p. 50.
[78] Among later references, Limborch, pp. 151, 220, Fournier, vol. I, p. 437.
[79] Fournier, vol. I, p. 341, vol. II, p. 207. [80] Limborch, p. 148.
[81] D'Ablis, p. 86.
[82] Doat 23, fol. 129v.

of the daughters of noble families.[83] But the principal area will have been training novice *perfecti*. We occasionally see such training figuring in attempts to recruit: *perfecti* said, 'docerent eum et facerent bonum clericum' (they would teach him and make him a good cleric).[84] Recruitment could be at quite a humble level, and for humble training: to one lad the *perfecti* said, 'facerent instrui ad litteras' (they would have him taught letters), while they reproved him for looking after oxen.[85] But the *perfecti* were looking also for talent, youths who were potentially great preachers or even theologians: the *perfecti* wished of one, 'quod ipse studeret in grammatica, et credebant quod ipse esset magna columna Ecclesiae id est haereticorum' (that he would study in grammar, and they believed he would be a great pillar of the Church, that is, [the Church] of the heretics).[86] Looking back from the 1260s the Anonymous of Passau described how once there had been more schools of heretics than of theologians, applying this to *Provincia* (broadly southern France, from his south German perspective?) as well as Lombardy.[87] We must remember that at the time to which the Anonymous was referring, founding the university of Toulouse had been thought of as, in part, an appropriate response to Catharism. It is plausible, then, that Cathar schools in Languedoc paralleled the Italian schools described by Paolini below, even if they were less prominent and numerous. Books must have been used in these schools, from elementary grammars to the sophisticated theological works needed to train future 'great pillars' of Catharism. But there is no direct evidence.

Much more is known about the use of books in services, and in the doctrinal instruction of *credentes*. First, central in the conferring of the *consolamentum* was a copy of the New Testament or at least the Gospel of St John, held over the recipient's head. Witnessed by many, sometimes only glimpsed through a keyhole, this is the most frequently reported use of a book: a book, known as *Textus* (the Text), entering as a ritual instrument into hundreds if not thousands of houses in Languedoc.

---

[83] See the text of Jordan of Saxony, quoted by Guiraud, vol. i, p. 250 n. 5, on daughters of nobles handed over to heretics, because of poverty, *erudiendas et nutriendas* (to be instructed and brought up).

[84] Toulouse BM 609, fol. 29r.   [85] Toulouse BM 609, fol. 42r.   [86] Doat 22, fol. 61v.

[87] Quoted in Paolini, chapter 5 below, n. 65. See n. 115 below for another reference to schools.

Secondly, among their frequent reports of *perfecti* preaching, *credentes* sometimes describe them reading a book. There is less reporting earlier and more later, especially in the circle of *credentes* around the Autier family. Discerning a broad development here is dangerous. For example, books loom very large in one early inquisition in Quercy in 1240/1,[88] much less in the enquiries of 1245/6. What survives from the latter are depositions mainly from small communities in rural areas, and also very summary depositions – over 5,000 in the surviving copy of one part of the original manuscripts! – which may simply have left less time for such details.

Among a few of the gatherings of *credentes* in small fortified villages which were large and formal and described quite fully in depositions, one detail does stand out. The later of two instances at Labécède (*c.* 1232, *c.* 1236/7) is clearest. In the hall of a knight's house the Lords of Labécède, various knights and other inhabitants, male and female, listened first to a *perfectus* preaching, then a scribe and public notary reading the passion, then the *perfectus* expounding it; the rite of adoration followed. There are clear parallels at Sorèze (*c.* 1228) and Vaudreuille (*c.* 1232), and possible parallels, with someone not a *perfectus* reading, at Gourdon, Moissac and Avignonet.[89] There are, probably, two kinds of authority and function here, those of a notary in a small community reading and guaranteeing the authenticity of texts, and those of a *perfectus* in discerning and expounding truth in a sacred text. Found in early Catharism, public ritual involving a notary was no longer possible in the more secret and circumscribed world of late Catharism when, monotonously, almost as if referring mentally to the iconography of a preaching saint, *credentes* describe how a *perfectus* sat in a room, held a book in his hand and held forth.

Gui's list of questions included asking a Cathar *credens* if he *tenuit libros hereticorum* (held the heretics' books).[90] Since this is not found in earlier question-lists, we have a circular problem when examining the greater presence of *credentes* handling books in later depositions: dependent on a greater reality? Or (only later) the ready

---

[88] See below, nn. 96–8.

[89] Labécède: Doat 23, fol. 98r; earlier Toulouse BM 609, fols. 8or, 121r, 213v. Other examples: Doat 21, fols. 187r, 201v, 301v (Moissac – the clearest example, hearing someone reading books of the *perfecti*, and then the *perfecti* expounding), Doat 25, fol. 331r–v. Similar comment in A. Brenon, *Les femmes cathares* (Paris, 1992), pp. 212–13.

[90] Gui, *Practica* 5.5, p. 243.

availability of the question? The question covered one area of activity found early as well as late: guarding, carrying and transmitting heretics' books. A council is held among *credentes* in Cambiac to decide what to do with the book of a captured deacon;[91] a woman momentarily loses the book of a *perfectus*, which she has in a bag, in the melée of a successful onslaught on a castle;[92] there are many other less dramatic examples of *perfecti* relying on *credentes* as depositaries.

It is more difficult to assess the other area covered by Gui's question, *credentes* reading these texts. Categories of literacy among the *credentes* are schematically outlined or implied by conciliar legislation and inquisitors' handbooks. An anonymous manual from 1278, dealing with enquiries of *credentes* in confession, echoed the terms of a consultation of 1242 about defining Waldensian *credentes*, who had been divided into one category of *discretus* and *litteratus* (prudent, literate), another of *simplex* and *ignorans* (simple, ignorant).[93] From a long time, back to St Dominic, converted or convicted *credentes* had carried letters stating this conviction and their penance. The formulae for these testimonial letters in Gui's *Practica*, a century later, lay down monthly presentation of these to a churchman who will translate for the bearer into the vernacular.[94] The action seems to include both discipline and the assumption that most of the bearers will not read Latin. The inquisitorial process can sometimes bear directly on the literacy of a suspect, for it involved writing and reading at every stage, the reading of formulae, and the translating and recording of answers, and occasionally a *credens* takes an active part in one of these stages. He receives a text with the charges, makes up a text for the inquisitors, even records his own deposition. Such cases are very rare, reaching their highest proportion in the (scanty figures) of d'Ablis's inquisition in 1308/9, when two out of seventeen wrote their own depositions.[95] The temptation to take such cases as (low) indices of proportions of literacy or

---

[91] See n. 60 above.   [92] Doat 24, fol. 115v.

[93] K.-V. Selge (ed.), *Texte zur Inquisition* (Gütersloh, 1967 = *Texte zur Kirchen- und Theologiegeschichte* 4), pp. 56–7; E. Martène and U. Durand (eds.), *Thesaurus novus anecdotorum ... multa* (Paris, 1717), vol. v, 1805.

[94] Gui, *Practica* 2.3, p. 38.

[95] D'Ablis, p. 42. See also Douais, vol. I, pp. 17, 74–5, vol. II, pp. 132, 139 (a woman wanting to see her accusations in writing), 155, 183; Toulouse BM 609, fol. 127v (two witnesses collaborated in writing testimony); Limborch, p. 283 (a Carcassonne professor of law writing his confession).

literacy in Latin needs to be resisted. A suspect needed familiarity and confidence with legal process, as well as literacy in Latin, to do such things.

The earliest substantial body of evidence, inquisitions in Quercy in 1241/2, show marked use of books by both Cathar and Waldensian *credentes*. The prohibition of vernacular books by the council of Toulouse suggests that we should project this picture back before the council's date, 1229. These are typical of the laconic data (extracts for the drawing up of sentences) which survive from the enquiries in Quercy: 'P. de Cassanholas . . . tenuit librum haereticorum . . . et legit in libro eorum' (P. de Cassanholas . . . kept a book of the heretics . . . and he read in their book); 'recepit de manibus haereticorum duos quaternos de erroribus eorum quos tenuit per octo dies et amplius et placuerint [*sic*] ei' (he received from the hands of the heretics two quires of their errors which he kept for eight days and more, and he liked them).[96] Some of the examples suggest deliberate policy by the *perfecti* – 'dederunt ei Pater Noster haereticorum scriptum' ([the heretics] gave him the text of their 'Our Father')[97] – and there is one dramatic example of a *credens* acting as a reading centre. R. Peregri, it is recorded, 'tenuit librum haereticorum ubi legebat quicunque volebat' (kept the book of the heretics where whoever wanted to would read it).[98]

After this early concentration in Quercy there are the inquisitions of the early 1240s and the enquiries of 1245/6, which preserve so much detail about rural and noble support of Catharism, stretching back via long memories easily into the 1190s and once into the 1180s. One finds a knight, who was bailli of Quié, with a mixed Latin and vernacular book:[99] but otherwise remarkably little. Then there are the inquisitions from the 1280s onwards which tell us so much about Catharism in the cities of Carcassonne and Albi, as well as smaller and more remote towns such as Ax and Tarascon. The

---

[96] Doat 21, fols. 202v, 228v.

[97] Doat 21, fol. 257v. Later examples of being given, or keeping probably for reading, or keeping and reading, books: Douais, vol. II, pp. 97, 106; Limborch, pp. 11, 50, 53, 54, 152, 160; D'Ablis, pp. 88, 372, 390; Fournier, vol. I, p. 285, vol. II, pp. 196–7, 204, 207, 419.

[98] Doat 21, fol. 211v. Other book examples, from this area, in Doat 21: fols. 187r, 201v, 'legit . . . evangelium in Romano' (read . . . the Gospel in romance); 210r: 'scienter legit in libro haereticorum' (knowingly read in a heretics' book); 221r: 'recepit librum haereticorum missum sibi a quodam' (received a heretics' book, sent to him by someone); 310v: 'Arnaldus . . . sacerdos venit ad haereticos et legit in libro haereticorum' (Arnold . . ., priest, went to the heretics and read in their book).

[99] Doat 24, fol. 248v.

milieu is socially distinguished and literate, and examples of *credentes* keeping and reading Cathar books easy to find. If earlier evidence of urban Catharism had survived less patchily, it is likely that we would find earlier parallels to the Toulouse citizen Peter Garcias, who was overheard talking in 1247 both about his Cathar beliefs and his possession and reading of a vernacular text of the passion.[100] The late examples, set among royal officials, law professors, consular families and notaries, are rich and full. Someone is riffling through a notary's books, and stumbles across a hidden Cathar/Catholic polemical treatise.[101] Social and intellectual distinction stand out. A judge had a heretic's book, and said he had read the heretics' books, knew their faith well and had discussed it with the count of Foix.[102] One Peter of Gaillac, notary of Tarascon, quoted the Gospel in Latin and discussed with another notary, who had read natural philosophy at Toulouse, the fact that many who read natural philosophy at Paris and Toulouse had doubts about the eucharist.[103] Nothing, perhaps, conveys more sharply the air of refinement within which books were set in this late urban Catharism than the civilised style of the *perfectus* Peter Autier when setting about the conversion of the cleric Peter of Luzenac, who had studied at the university of Toulouse. Peter Autier invited him to dinner. Good salmon and trout were provided, and then Autier went off, promising to lend Luzenac a book with texts on faith. Theological discussions are described in Peter's second confession, and drinking wine with Autier, who showed Luzenac the beautifully illuminated copy of a vernacular New Testament, written in best Bologna script, which has been mentioned earlier.[104]

4 IMAGES OF CATHARS AND BOOKS

An attempt has been made to reconstruct the lost reality of Cathar use of written materials. But how was this 'reality' seen by the *perfecti*, by their *credentes* and by Catholic writers?

According to one late Cathar sermon, the *perfecti* and the Roman Church possessed two texts, called *litterae*. The *perfecti*'s *littera* came from the true God, while the devil had forged the *littera* which the

---

[100] Douais, vol. II, pp. 97, 106.   [101] Fournier, vol. II, pp. 196–7.
[102] D'Ablis, p. 88, Fournier, vol. II, p. 419.
[103] D'Ablis, p. 358.   [104] D'Ablis, pp. 372, 380.

Roman Church possessed;[105] *carta diaboli* (devils' charter) springs to Cathar lips as a phrase of abuse.[106] The Roman Church had its *litterati* spreading this devil's *littera* – the *insensati litterati* (insensate men of learning) envisaged by one early southern French Cathar.[107] There is no hint of what one finds with the Waldensians, a proud counterposing of their own *illiterati* (unlettered), fishermen following the apostles. There is no direct expression of the *perfecti*'s view of themselves on this theme, but indirect reflection in one of their presentations of the *Vision of Isaiah*. Isaiah becomes a good man, a *perfectus*. This *perfectus* had read in books and began to have doubts about the Cathar faith. So he set himself to reading in books. And for three days and three nights he did not weary, nor did he sleep: he just read in books, on and on.[108]

To a *credens* the fact of someone reading was one of several grounds for suspecting he was a *perfectus*. 'Vidit ipsum legentem in quodam libro' (he saw him reading in a certain book), and from this and other things 'suspicatus tunc ipsum esse haereticum' (he then suspected he was a heretic).[109] The sharpness of the images of *perfecti* reading survive the filters of memory and translation into a Latin where they survive as word pictures, preserving frozen moments: a *credens* came across the *perfectus* Aimeri de Collet, standing in a forest holding a book open and reading,[110] while another *credens* in the early fourteenth century sees a *perfectus* near the top of a barn reading by sunlight. Inquisitors' curiosity, extended by that date to whether reading was by artificial light, and if so by what sort, helped elicit these glittering mental snapshots.[111]

In a late conversation a *credens* recommends giving money to a *perfectus* who is not *litteratus*, meaning that he cannot read Latin (we see him reading books, presumably vernacular).[112] The *credens* goes on to say that other *perfecti* were *litterati* and therefore more appreciated and got more money. Preaching and instruction were in the vernacular, but among *credentes* there could be higher prestige for Latin literacy.

Finally, what was the picture among Catholic writers? The *topos* of heretic as illiterate had played a great role in eleventh- and

---

[105] Fournier, vol. III, pp. 133, 236.   [106] Toulouse BM 609, fol. 247v.
[107] *Traité cathare* 14, p. 104.
[108] Fournier, vol. III, p. 200.   [109] Limborch, p. 23; another example, pp. 108–9.
[110] Doat 23, fol. 138r.
[111] Fournier, vol. I, p. 341; Limborch, p. 148.   [112] Fournier, vol. II, p. 416.

twelfth-century texts on heresy, as it continued to do in mid-thirteenth-century Germany. It briefly re-appears in Catholic reporting of the 1178 mission to Toulouse, where the appearance of *perfecti* with a written schedule containing Cathar articles of faith provided an 'opening to write about the poverty of their spoken Latin.[113] The slightness of the Church's knowledge of Catharism at this early stage may explain this mobilisation of the *topos*. Aside from one minor and precisely directed exception in the *Débat d'Izarn* (mentioned below), the *topos* now disappears in writing about Cathars – a silence underlined by some continuing mobilisation of it against Waldensians. In Alain de Lille (1190s), lack of literacy and knowledge is a polemical point against Waldensians, demonstrating their unfittedness to preach. But it plays no part in his polemic against Cathars, who by contrast are depicted using *rationes* (arguments) whose language smacks of the logic of the schools – beginning an argument, for example, saying 'si causa immutabilis, effectus immutabilis' (if the cause is immutable so is the effect).[114] Entwined with a perceived contrast in education was also the fact that a polemical attack against the Waldensians was appropriate in a way it could never be against Cathars. For Waldensians originated within the Church, and were seen as laymen preaching in it without licence, while *perfecti* were the clergy of an autonomous faith and Church. Perceived differences between Cathars and Waldensians in Latinity, literacy and use of books continued to play a part with Stephen of Bourbon. He laid emphasis on Valdes as 'not very literate', on Waldensian acquisition of texts in the vernacular, on their use of memory, and their avoiding *litterati* in their missions. However, when he turns to the Cathars, while Stephen has nothing systematic on the theme, he is silent on the use of memory or lack of literacy, and, more positively, he includes a scatter of allusions to Cathar schools and someone in their sect who was *litteratus*.[115] Finally, Gui describes Waldensian preachers as including *layci* and *ydiote* as well as *litterati* (*in this pairing*, illiterate and literate); but illiteracy is absent from his material on the *perfecti*.[116]

Books and sometimes high learning appear in most early- to mid-thirteenth-century Catholic writers. Peter of Vaux-de-Cernai

---

[113] See n. 50 above.   [114] Alain, 1.3, 309.

[115] Stephen of Bourbon, 289, on a *heretica* (female heretic) who had gone to *scolas Albigensium*; Stephen heard their *auctoritates* from a *litteratus* who was long in the sect, 303.

[116] Gui, *Practica* 3.35, p. 138.

set among the *perfecti* a former canon of Nevers who was highly esteemed among Cathars for his intelligence and because through him they had a defender from *Francia* (Ile-de-France), the *fons scientiae* (fountain of knowledge) – presumably, the university of Paris.[117] For Durand of Huesca the *perfecti* are *doctores*, they read to their followers in conventicles, they write and have books and treatises.[118] Luc de Tuy writes of *perfecti* carrying books when arrested, and a scribe who wrote for them. Since one Cathar treatise he describes contained extracts from philosophers, it may be significant of a link in Luc's mind that his treatise opposes both Catharism and philosophy.[119] Finally, at one point in his chronicle William of Puylaurens describes a theological dispute between the Catholic bishop of Albi and the Cathar bishop, Sicard Cellerier. At the end of it the Catholic bishop compares his opponent to a new doctor from Salerno, reading books in reverse:[120] this hostile *topos* against doctors, which goes back at least to John of Salisbury in 1159,[121] is significantly a *topos* of high learning. It is to be compared to the *perfecti*'s picture of themselves which has been glimpsed through one of their versions of the *Vision of Isaiah*.

This observation of high learning among Cathars was given a broad historical setting by Stephen of Bourbon. Earlier, he wrote, there had been fewer *litterati* in the Church, and few *docti*; the implied contrast of this earlier period was with the *litterati* and *docti* of the heretics then, who were therefore daring in disputations.[122] He is writing about the debates of *c.* 1200. The contrast is also with now (he is writing some time before 1261), when things are different. Similar is the historical view of the Anonymous of Passau, which has already been quoted, that there were *once* more schools of heretics than there were of theologians.

Two striking patterns in the depositions suggest two areas where this chapter should move, finally, from surveying to raising questions. The first question is about a contrast between the sexes. Female *credentes* hold and guard books in the same way as males. But otherwise there is silence about women and texts. Once there is a

[117] Peter of Vaux-de-Cernai, *Hystoria Albigensis* 1, vol. 1, pp. 24–6.
[118] Durand, *Liber contra Manicheos* 3, 6, 10, 14, pp. 113, 147, 188, 241, and the passages cited in n. 54 above.
[119] Luc de Tuy, *De altera vita* 3.2, *MBVP* 241B, and passages cited in nn. 1 and 52–3 above.
[120] Guillaume de Puylaurens, *Chronique* 4, ed. J. Duvernoy (Paris, 1976), pp. 34–6.
[121] John of Salisbury, *Metalogicon* 1.4, ed. C. C. J. Webb (Oxford, 1929), p. 13.
[122] Stephen of Bourbon, p. 312.

reference to some female *perfectae* using a scribe to draw up a testament or ordinance of their affairs.[123] Apart from this, and clearly women having contact with books where books were instruments in rites, there is no instance in the thousands of depositions which survive where a female *perfecta* or *credens* is described as reading a book. We also have a prejudicial statement in the *Débat d'Izarn*, which alludes to the analphabetism and lack of grammar of a group of Cathars, mainly women and headed by an aristocratic woman, who discuss theology in a Cathar weaving workshop:[124] a reminder of the immense role played by women, as seen in despositions, in *talking* about Catharism. A similar point could be made about Waldensians in southern France, where references are to men using books. Again, among the materialist atheists who appear occasionally in the depositions, men talking about their ideas tend to relate them more to texts than women do. Further enquiry is needed here. The role of women reading in Lollardy is well known, but rather less well known is an interesting group of female *credentes* who owned or read books among the Waldensians of Fribourg and Basle – where this is not specified of the men.[125] Further investigation could begin with one intelligible context, contrasts among orthodox lay women between northern and southern Europe.

The second question-mark comes after the word 'notaries'. It is well known that the last strong Cathar revival, that of the Autiers *c.* 1300, was headed by a notarial family and found a strong resonance among notaries and scribes. Going back to before 1250, we have seen the special role played by scribes and notaries in some formal Cathar assemblies. Go back even further, into the darkness of an (unknown) twelfth-century date: it was a notary from France (where 'France' probably means northern France) who brought Catharism into Lombardy. From the earliest to very near the last times, notaries are so prominent. They need more attention.

---

[123] Toulouse BM 609, fol. 94v; Wakefield, 'Heretics and inquisitors', p. 231.

[124] *Le Débat d'Izarn et de Sicart de Figueiras*, ed. P. Meyer, *Annuaire-Bulletin de la Société de l'Histoire de France* (1879), p. 247 lines 60–6. They expound and talk ('desponen ... fa sermo') of the Gospel and the devil being the author of all creation, but do not know grammar or how to write ('no saupro grammatica ni de letra ques fo').

[125] From the Waldensian trials of 1430 in Fribourg contained in Fribourg AE Geistliche Sachen 26, depositions bear on women and books: one called Perrotet had *aliquos bonos libros* (some good books) containing material against the notion that offerings, masses and almsgiving is of any use to the souls of the dead, *et multa alia* (and many other things), fol. 2v; a book containing 'expositiones evangeliorum et epistolarum beati Pauli' (exposition of the gospels and blessed Paul's epistles) had been sent to a sister in Basle (fol. 7r).

CHAPTER 5

Italian Catharism and written culture

Lorenzo Paolini

In recent decades Italian historians have tended to avoid the theme of Catharism and culture, partly because the historiographical trend has been more towards looking at heretics as people, living in a tangible, social setting, an approach which has favoured the use of inquisitors' trials with their 'daily life' material. A further explanation is the continuing appeal of Borst's pessimist view: for him Cathars could be stimuli or vehicles of thought at a popular level, but they were not a creative source, not able to assimilate and rework ideas or to exercise an influence on medieval culture.[1] Now, it must be remembered that if Cathar culture was marginal, it will have been so not just because of some internal weakness but also as a result of repression by the Church. But was it in fact so marginal? Cathars survived for nearly two centuries, and not in marginal areas, but in vigorously developing Lombard cities. And Cathars' initial expansion had rested in large measure upon their success in putting over a polemical criticism of the clergy and Church of Rome, and identifying a general malaise and need for religious participation.[2] In this missionary effort we can discern cultural force – though not 'learned' culture – and an area where Cathars often prevailed over a Catholic clergy which was ill-prepared for debate. There is less clarity about what Cathars were proposing positively, what human or religious values, thought or doctrine they were propounding, and in this second area we find the situation reversed: a 'Cathar scholasticism', or 'learned' culture', which was unsuccessful when competing with Catholic scholasticism.

---

[1] Borst, pp. 139–40, 225–6; see for an opposing view A. Brenon, *I catari. Storia e destino dei veri credenti* (Florence, 1990), pp. 143, 183, who underlines the 'intellectual and cultivated' character of Italian Catharism.

[2] Merlo, p. 214; G. Zanella, 'Hereticalia italica', in M. C. De Matteis (ed.), *A Ovidio Capitani. Scritti degli allievi bolognesi* (Bologna, 1990), pp. 248–50; Manselli, *Studi*, pp. 281, 309–15.

I THE VIEW OF CATHOLIC POLEMICISTS

Catholic polemicists had at their disposal two opposed equations: 'heretics = idiots, the simple, the illiterate', and 'heretic = *magister in superbia, sapiens in litteris* (master in pride, wise in letters), where pride in knowledge is not at the service of love of truth but is intended to deceive the simple.[3] These equations could be used simply as commonplaces, or deployed in propaganda in order to minimise or exaggerate. We must bear in mind that accepting the first equation (that heretics were unlearned and illiterate in the eyes of the Church because they were laymen) as a description of Cathars would not only oversimplify a complex reality, as Biller has suggested. It would also come up hard against the reality of Italian cities, where laymen wrote, studied, used books and knew Latin, and against the Cathar *perfecti*'s view of themselves, that they were not lay, and that they were *sapientes* (wise men).[4]

How, then, were these equations applied, and did they have any truth? Both of them can be found in the same treatise. Thus in the *Liber de duobus principiis* there are the accusations that the Cathars are *inperiti, indocti, ignorantes, adversarii veritatis, penes veritatem nullam habentes rationem* (unskilled, untaught, ignorant, enemies of the truth, having no reason as regards truth),[5] and at the same time that they resort to sophisms and *subtilitates*, artifices that are as cunning as they are futile.[6] Now, it is unlikely that the latter skills could have been acquired without intelligence and logical ability which had been further developed in schools and at university. Cathars aspired to be *the* authentic exegetes (*legis evangelii doctores esse cupientes* (wanting to be teachers of the law of the gospel)),[7] and their accompanying

---

[3] On this question see Grundmann, *Ausgewählte Aufsätze*, vol. I, pp. 313–27; Grundmann, 'Litteratus'; Stock, pp. 88–240 for heresy in the eleventh century; Biller 'Topos'.

[4] *Livre des deux principes*, pp. 210, 248, 278, 294, 306, 312, 318, 320, 340, 348, 360, etc.

[5] *Livre des deux principes*, *passim*.

[6] For example, 'Alii vero subtiliantes' (others indeed prevaricating), 'Sunt tamen aliqui inter istos qui distinguunt subtiliçantes inter angelos delinquentes' (there are some among them who distinguish minutely between the sinning angels), T. Kaeppeli, 'Une somme contre les hérétiques de s. Pierre martyr(?)', *AFP* 17 (1947), 323, 325; 'involvuntur ad subtilitates scripturarum explicandas inefficaces' (they tangle themselves in their useless attempt to explain the subtleties of scripture), Pseudo-James Capelli, *Summa contra hereticos*, Cesena, Biblioteca Malatestiana, Ms. S.I.VIII, fol. 12v; 'innituntur predicti haeretici, sed etiam rationibus quibusdam, quae eis naturales, vel logicae videntur, cum tamen sophisticae sint' (these heretics support themselves with certain reasons, which seem natural to them or logical, but in truth are sophistical), Moneta, p. 23B.

[7] Pseudo-James Capelli, fol. 23r.

presentation of themselves as *sapientes*[8] found some confirmation in the Catholic Church. The *Glossa ordinaria* on Honorius III's *Super specula* (November 1221, then *Decret.* x.iii.l) spelled out that it was encouraging theology in order to educate *bellatores* (warriors *qui possunt haereticis resistere authoritate divinae scripturae, qui contra nos surgunt* (who can oppose the heretics who rise up against us with the authority of divine scripture): an admission that Catholics lagged behind, and an indication that they would use the same tools as the Cathars.

If we accept some truth in the view of Cathars as *sapientes*, we must also see an element of authenticity in the horror and indignation expressed by Catholic polemicists when discussing the Cathars' approach to the great existential and theological problems of creation, evil and the origin and salvation of man. To describe the (ir-)rationality of Cathar thought they have a thesaurus of phrases such as *cogitationes evanescentes, neniae, vaniloquium, fabulationes, fabulae inefficaces, visiones, nugae, fantasticae rationes, inventiones, frivola, irrisoria, somnia, absurditates* (fleeting thoughts, nursery songs, idle chat, storytelling, worthless tales, visions, nonsense, imaginary arguments, devices, trifles, mockeries, dreams, absurdities), all the fruits of *dementia* or *deliramenta* (madness, raving).[9]

While the equation Cathar = illiterate clearly does not hold, there is a partial and complex truth to be found within the two contradictory equations, one which goes beyond the question of a hostile *topos* and the (in Catholic eyes) lay status of the *perfecti*. Catholic writers mount a substantial accusation against the content and method of Cathar thought: there is their continual debating, fondness for critical revision, which does not translate into something positive and constructive, but mere dogmatism. *Dogmatizant* ('they assert') is the constant term of reproach.[10] At the same time, while despising Cathar arguments,[11] Catholic polemicists do

---

[8] See n. 4; *De heresi catharorum*, p. 306; Pseudo-James Capelli, fol. 23v 'de sapientibus hereticorum' (concerning the wise men of the heretics); Borst, p. 127.

[9] This terminology, in varied form, is found especially in Pseudo-James Capelli and in Moneta, *passim*.

[10] For example, 'languentes circa questiones et pugnas verborum, semper discentes et numquam ad scientiam veritatis pervenientes' (tiring themselves about questions and verbal quibbles, always learning and never coming to the knowledge of the truth); 'ab invicem cum litigatione dissidentes' (falling out among themselves with quarrels), Pseudo-James Capelli, fols. 8v, 23r.

[11] 'silencio tamquam indigna responsione preterire decernimus' (we decide to pass over in silence as an unworthy reply), Pseudo-James Capelli, fol. 23v; and see further below n. 45.

confront their Cathar opponents at the level of learned theology, thereby implying a recognition of their scholastic training.

2 EVANGELISM AND PREACHING

Catharism took root and spread through Italy as a popular religious movement through itinerant missionary activity.[12] We are not admitting here either of two extreme and opposed views – one, that Catharism was *the* dominant element in the religious movement of the time, the other that Cathar radical-dualist theology never fused with the ideal of the apostolic life and popular piety.[13] Without playing a special creative role, Italian Catharism was fully a part of the lay piety which was emerging in western Europe in the second half of the twelfth century, and sometimes used some of its motifs in its propaganda.[14]

From the cultural point of view, there were several overlapping and complex stages.[15] During the first, the (probably) few written texts will have functioned to help an oral mission. The silence on both sides about theological and doctrinal issues and the exclusive attention paid to the appropriation of preaching by the laity (because it was against canon law) leads us to conclude that an absence of profound theological culture was a characteristic of the first Italian *perfecti*.[16] We must suppose that books were only resorted to out of necessity, and that only elementary training was given, what was necessary for a religious end – preaching – to which all uses of written texts were subordinated. Books may not have been absent, but written culture will have been accorded only marginal significance. Training and instruction in biblical exegesis (itself simple and unrefined at this period) must have existed, as a prelude

---

[12] E. Dupré-Theseider, *Mondo cittadino e movimenti ereticali nel medio evo* (Bologna, 1978), p. 248; Lambert, p. 117.

[13] Wakefield and Evans, p. 50.

[14] For example, the apostolic ideal and evangelical poverty, on which see L. Paolini, 'Esiti ereticali della conversione alle povertà', in *La conversione alla povertà nell'Italia dei secoli XII–XIV* (Spoleto, 1991 = Atti dei convegni dell'Academia Tudertina e del Centro di studi sulla spiritualità medievale n.s. 4), pp. 155–61.

[15] See the important comments of H. Grundmann, 'Hérésies savantes et hérésies populaires au moyen âge', in J. Le Goff (ed.), *Hérésies et sociétés dans l'Europe pré-industrielle, 11e–18e siècles* (Paris, 1968), pp. 212–13: 'Ces cathares chercheront à devenir savants, comme ils avaient cherché à devenir populaires' (These Cathars tried to become learned, as they had striven to become popular), p. 213.

[16] Grundmann, *Bewegungen*, pp. 68–9; Lambert, pp. 63, 65.

to missionary work. We must conjecture that they were given to novice *perfecti* during the year when they were *in abstinentia*, when they were taught the *secretum* (secret). But they are not documented.[17]

The introduction of radical dualism into Italy by Nicetas, and its subsequent adoption and spread, accelerated and perhaps even was the turning point in the shift of Italian Catharism from a predominantly ethical–practical to a theological cast. Dualism in both its moderate and radical forms emerged from the shadows where it had been, earlier, a reserved doctrine or 'secret'.[18] This dualism had philosophical and theological implications; and while its mythological guise could fascinate unlearned minds, it also needed learned inventiveness and elaboration, and a biblical exegesis which was often not literal but based in a 'different' allegory which demanded gymnastics from erudite minds. All this was not the fruit of popular culture of religion! Further, the 'secret' (dualist mythology) disorientated most people and scandalised the faithful. So the 'literary' element *par excellence*, doctrine and myth, came to be cultivated exclusively within the restricted group of the *perfecti*.

One can discern certain key points in a gradual development: from the culture of the grave-digger Mark, with his incisive and productive teaching, to the 'scholastic' theology of John of Lugio. Deeply influential on the Italian Cathars were doctrines imported orally by the missionaries Nicetas and Petracius, which disorientated and divided minds;[19] apocryphal writings such as the *Interrogatio Iohannis* and the *Visio Isaiae*; and voyages overseas to the churches of the various *ordines* (orders). However, these authoritative doctrines and texts were developed by Italian Cathars in their own ways, amalgamated with various Western cultural traditions (for example, Neoplatonism, and Averroism), and even shaped according to the traditions of Western catholicism.

3 DIVISION INTO CHURCHES; TECHNIQUES OF DEBATE

In the earlier period 'written culture' puts in a strong appearance at two points, the division of Cathars into six churches, and the birth of public debates as described by Joachim of Fiore. While many factors

[17] R. Manselli, 'Eglises et théologies cathares', *CaF* 3 (1968), 157; Lambert, p. 121.
[18] Manselli, *L'eresia*, pp. 181–2; Lambert, p. 132.
[19] Lambert, p. 121.

lay behind the Cathar fragmentation,[20] what is significant here is that diversity of *ordines* reflected in part doctrinal diversity, and that in Italy the birth of six separate churches gave birth to intellectual activity, which was intended to justify and perpetuate doctrines specific to each group, and resulted in the creation of new doctrines.

By the last quarter of the twelfth century a relationship with the book – not a uniform one – cannot be overlooked. The first *doctores* and *magistri* appear. At Orvieto between 1168 and 1170 'quidam florentinus ... nomine Diotesalvi ... doctrinam manicheorum pessimam ... seminavit' (a certain Florentine ... named Diotesalvus ... sowed the worst doctrine of the Manichees).[21] And again, between 1198 and 1199, 'quidam Petrus Lombardus, manicheorum doctor ... in Urbeveteri occulta cepit conciliabola cum quibusdam pravis doctoribus celebrare' (one Peter Lombard, a doctor of the Manichees ... began to hold secret assemblies with certain evil doctors).[22] These are leaders, and at the same the Cathar intellectual elite, men capable of putting into practice a planned and co-ordinated preaching campaign. Boncursus of Milan, a converted heretic and author or inspirer of the *manifestatio heresis* (1176–90),[23] is described as *magister* and *doctor*, expert in Cathar mythology and doctrine. A popular, mnemonic and oral culture no longer seems to be sufficient as the intelligible context into which to place such figures.

Turning to concentrate on the period of divisions, we should pause to look at the anonymous source *De heresi catharorum* (composed before 1214) for the light it throws on Cathar culture. The author's knowledge of arcana and his detailed historical information suggest the direct and personal involvement of a former *per-*

---

20 See Lambert, p. 131.
21 V. Natalini, *S. Pietro Parenzo* (Rome, 1936 = *Lateranum* n.s. 11/2), p. 153. His errors were collected together 'in libello contra hereticos hedito' (in a small book compiled against the heretics), p. 154.
22 Natalini, *S. Pietro Parenzo*, pp. 155–6; M. Maccarrone, *Studi su Innocenzo III* (Padua, 1972 = *Italia sacra* 17), pp. 30–48, with further comment by O. Capitani, 'Patari in Umbria: lo "status questionis" nella recente storiografia', *Bolletino dell'Istituto Artistico Orvietano* 39 (1983), 37–54.
23 Ilarino, pp. 155–203; R. Manselli, 'Alle origini della "Manifestatio haeresis catharorum quam fecit Bonaccursus"', *BISI* 67 (1955), 189–211; Rottenwöhrer 1.i. 48–50, 1.ii 71–8 presents a variety of interpretations of the relation to the *Confessio*. 'Bonacursus qui olim fuit magister eorum ... quendam ipsorum doctorem Bonacursum nomine' (Bonacursus who

fectus, now converted.[24] If this is the case, then the text's success as a synthesis of material and as a literary composition, as well as its fluency of expression and thought – all suggestive of a Cathar *doctor*, perhaps a notary or man of law – are indicative of Cathar intellectual and literary capacity at this time. The text tells of the existence among Cathars of a group of *sapientes* and of their role, sometimes mediating between different positions, sometimes taking sides;[25] a group of thinkers, enjoying authority, which could persuade the two branches of Catharism, moderate and radical, to come together in a council at Mosio, and not just to consider the issue of one bishop. This group was able to put exchanges onto a formal footing, in order to allow time for reflection on the bishop's power of orders and jurisdiction; it guided arduous negotiations; and once the break became final, it was at the spearhead in elaborating the diverging bodies of doctrine of what were, from then on, different *ordines*. Although the *De heresi* does not say this, rivalries of schools and doctrinal diversity may have been not only a consequence of the division: they perhaps played an active part in it. The *De heresi* does not refer to doctrine during this dramatic phase, although its wording, that Nicetas *cepit causari ordinem bulgarie* (began to declaim against the orders [consecration in the orders] of Bulgaria),[26] implies a doctrinal element in Nicetas' opposition. The author of the *De heresi*, who as a former moderate Cathar was a prejudiced witness, regards this only as a pretext for something else, and he confines his report to the themes of obedience and hierarchy, dealing with these in a juridic language which perhaps reveals his profession.[27] The text has much formulaic language which recalls written, even notarial, agreements. There is invocation *de iure* (by law),[28] and documents, in

---

was once his teacher ... a certain doctor of theirs called Bonacursus), Manselli, *Studi*, p. 207.

24 *De heresi catharorum*, p. 310; Wakefield and Evans, pp. 159–60, 690–4; Rottenwöhrer, i.i. 51–3, i.ii 83–90.

25 'Quidam vero de eius sapientibus, de hac divisione dolentes et ad unitatem eos reducere cupientes' (Some of their wise men, grieving over this division and desiring to bring them to unity), p. 306; 'Interea vero quidem sapientes adheserunt Johanni iudeo' (Meanwhile some of the wise men adhered to John the Jew), p. 307.

26 *De heresi catharorum*, p. 306.

27 This would confirm the general tendency in Catharism to be strong among the urban middle classes, headed by notaries and doctors – those imbued with a practical culture (Borst, p. 138 n. 13; Lambert, p. 118; E. Le Roy Ladurie, *Montaillou, village occitan de 1294 à 1324* (Paris, 1975), pp. 350–1); not by chance was the first missionary in Italy a notary from France.

28 *De heresi catharorum*, p. 307.

which aims are declared, which acquire thereby binding authority. The formal character of the promise of obedience suggests that a written formulary may have been followed. All this legal flavour indicates a phase in Catharism in which there was resort to legal solutions in the face of imminent division. Relationships were formalised, and the missionary effort institutionalised in churches and in a framework of dependencies and binding obediences. This process, explained in technical language, seems to be sustained by reflections on the power of the bishop.

The presence of notable personalities within Italian Catharism, from the last quarter of the twelfth century onwards, favoured something which became a constant characteristic: a penchant for controversy and doctrinal discussion, even acrimonious dispute. This disputatiousness made lines of division within Catharism even deeper,[29] and it was also displayed in public debate with Catholics.[30] Cathars became famed for their skill in argumentation, almost as if it were their exclusive prerogative. We can see how this feature alarmed over many years men such as Joachim of Fiore,[31] bishop Rainerius of Toscanella and Bernard Gui. Joachim was convinced that the new kind of heretics depended on a single unknown instigator,[32] who had used learned persuasion to make the movement adhere to the error that bodies were created by the devil. The Cathars *ostendunt se humanos et quasi simplices* (show themselves human and as though they are simple)[33] but the Calabrian monk clearly did not believe in their simplicity. Their technique and the way they seem to be *quasi rationabiliter concinantes* (joining [things] together as

---

[29] Salvo Burci, *Liber supra Stella*, mentions many fruitless meetings and councils between those of Albi and those of Concorezzi 'pluries convenerunt in unum et conscilia plurima fecerunt' (many came together and held many councils), Ilarino, p. 331; Wakefield and Evans, p. 31; Lambert, pp. 117, 132; G. Rottenwöhrer, 'Foi et théologie des cathares Bagnolistes', *Heresis* 7 (1986), 27–32, for the specific and developing identity of one group.

[30] R. Manselli, 'Una "Summa auctoritatum" antiereticale (ms 47 della Bibliothèque Municipale de Albi)', *Atti della Accademia Nazionale dei Lincei* 8th series, 28 (1985), fasc. 6, pp. 325, 329, 336. Two famous public disputations occurred in Vicenza between Bartolomeo da Breganze, bishop of the city, and Peter Gallus, the Cathar bishop, in the 1260s 'con alcuni membri di spicco della gerarchia catara locale, da lui imprigionati' (with other prominent members of the local Cathar hierarchy imprisoned by him), F. Lomastro Tognato, *L'eresia a Vicenza nel Duecento* (Vicenza, 1988), pp. x, 35–6.

[31] *Expositio in Apocalypsim* (Venice, 1527; repr. Frankfurt on Main, 1964), fols. 130v–133r, 167r, on which see R. Manselli, 'Testimonianze minori sulle eresie: Gioacchino da Fiore di fronte a catari e valdesi', *SM* 3rd series, 18/2 (1977), 8–17. The testimony of Raniero bishop of Toscanella is in P. Egidi, 'L'archivio della cattedrale di Viterbo', *BISI* 27 (1906), 140; Manselli, *L'eresia*, p. 291. See Gui, *Practica*, p. 236.

[32] *Expositio*, fol. 130vb.   [33] *Expositio*, fol. 132rb.

though according to reason)[34] produces a plausible discourse, which not only draws others into error but makes them prisoners of insoluble and dangerous problems.[35] Overridingly important was the search for public confrontation and challenge of heretics who were, in Joachim's eyes, conscious of the superiority of their dialectical abilities, of the validity of their arguments, of their support from biblical *auctoritates* – of their whole cultural arsenal.[36] Joachim is referring to this when remarking that 'videntur sagaciores esse, et quasi inter homines rationem habere' (they seem to be more wise, and as if they have [the better] reason among men),[37] and that they rely on *verba subtilia* (subtle words).[38] When looking at their interpretation of the Bible Joachim emphasises misuse and a complex of forced interpretations *per pravum littere intellectum* (through perverted understanding of the letter).[39] He implies that error is combined with exceptional intellectual talent. Later (*c.* 1222) bishop Rainerius of Toscanella complained to Honorius III, stating that he was powerless and that their dialectical superiority was overwhelming.[40] By contrast Bernard Gui – by whose time scholastic theology had developed far – positively hoped that public disputations would take place, to provide an arena for the opposition of Catholic *viri litterati* (learned men). He was also aware that the heretics' ability regularly put the learned into a difficult position and found them ill-prepared to counter-attack, and that this bewildered the faithful. However, the aim of preventing heretics from muddling both the simple unlearned and the inexperienced learned made this a risk worth running.[41]

---

[34] *Expositio*, fol. 131rb.   [35] *Expositio*, fols. 131vb, 132ra.

[36] *Expositio*: 'querentes cum quibus inhient commune vel singulare certamen, ut quasi vel prevaleant hoste prostrato, vel occisi (sicut asserunt) coronentur martyrio' (seeking with whom they can engage in general or individual battle, that they may either overcome the defeated enemy, or be killed and crowned (as they assert) as martyrs), fol. 131vb; 'ut quasi equi preparati ad prelium nihil vereantur adversi' (so that, like horses prepared for battle, they fear no enemy), fol. 132ra. Those of them who were kept back were the 'perfect of the perfect', 'quando veniunt ad conflictum ... stridentes et rugientes disseminant verba sua, ut videantur superare verbis quos non possunt vincere ratione' (when they come to battle ... shouting and roaring they send out their words, so that they may seem to overcome with words those whom they cannot convince by reason), fol. 132va.

[37] *Expositio*, fol. 135ra.   [38] *Expositio*, fol. 167ra.   [39] *Expositio*, fol. 132va.

[40] Egidi, 'L'archivio', p. 140: 'Nec, quocumque simplicitas me vertat, potest corriva paralogistice disolutionis eorum vitare. Nempe paralericus eorum superat meum clericum et malitia sapientiam vincit' (Nor, in whichever direction simplicity turns me, is it possible to escape from the stream of their fallacious refutation. Truly their para-cleric overcomes my clerk and their malice defeats wisdom). On unprepared clergy see Manselli, 'Una "Summa"', p. 327.

[41] Gui, *Practica*, pp. 236, 239.

All this implies that the Cathars were well prepared for discussion, equipped for public confrontation even with learned theologians and clerics, and that they had studied, above all, the bible. In deploring their polemical and instrumental use of the bible Joachim, Bonacursus[42] and all the controversialists indirectly conformed their profound knowledge of it. Did they possess, as Catholic preachers were soon to do, the *letteratura da battaglia* (literature for battle)[43] provided by *summae auctoritatum* (collections of authorities), collections of passages, often from the New Testament, subdivided by subject and intended for immediate use? Though no trace of one has yet been found, I am convinced (following an old, unrepeated suggestion of Morghen)[44] that such collections of authorities were in Cathar before they were in Catholic hands. In one passage of Bonacursus's *Manifestatio* it is possible to see his intention as this: to rise to the heretics' bait (their distorted use of scripture), and to follow them in their intellectual journeys (even if these are not worthy of answer), adapting himself to the choice of passages *they* have made.[45] A dim echo of Cathar possession of a collection of authorities? If Cathar possession did precede Catholic, there will have been on the Catholic side a precise mirroring of the literary forms of the Cathars, with Catholic polemicists using Cathar lists of *auctoritates* to construct their own works, giving each passage a different exegesis and combining them with others that disproved the interpretation given by heretics. Such mirroring certainly happened with treatises.

4 THE EMERGENCE OF MYTH

The first penetration of myth into Italian Catharism, oral or written, presumably gradual, is unrecorded. Bonacursus already registers a variety of myths, related to both moderate and radical

---

[42] *Manifestatio, PL*, 204.778: 'Prosternamus istos seductores, quos videmus quosdam errores suos Scripturarum testimonio perverso intellectu confirmare' (Let us throw down those seducers, whom we see confirm their errors by the witness of scripture wrongly understood).

[43] Manselli, 'Una, "Summa"', p. 330.

[44] R. Morghen, 'L'eresia nel Medioevo', in his *Medioevo cristiano* (Bologna, 1968, first edn, 1951), p. 229.

[45] *Manifestatio*, col. 778 'Quod ergo Scripturae testimonio asserere nituntur, ejusdem testimonio omnino destruamus. Quod autem velut deliramenta conjicere videntur, tanquam sint indigna responsione, pedibus conculcemus' (What they labour to argue through the

dualism. Sacconi, Anselm of Alessandria and the *explicit* of the version in the Carcassonne manuscript combine in attributing to Nazarius the initiative of having brought with him, on his return from a journey to Bulgaria where he had accompanied the bishop Garattus, the apocryphal *Interrogatio Iohannis*, a fundamental work of Bogomil literature (see plate 3).[46] This acquired the name of the *Secretum* (The Secret of the church of Concorezzo, to which Nazarius always remained faithful and which directly shaped the evolution of moderate dualism. Another apocryphon, but of the second century, perhaps written by a Jew influenced by Gnosticism, was the *Visio Isaiae*.[47] In the Latin version which was diffused in northern Italy and Provence, this decisively influenced parts of the radicals' doctrine, becoming part of the cultural and doctrinal heritage of the Cathars of Desenzano; at the time of Pseudo-James Capelli[48] and of Moneta[49] it still had devotees, deeply attached to its arcana.

The reception of these two texts in the *De heresi catharorum*, in the *Disputatio*, in the *Glossa* to the Pater, in the *Summae* of the Pseudo-James and Moneta, and in the *Brevis summula* (asserted by some critics and minimised by others)[50] raises the problem of the myths' role from a literary standpoint. For in these irrational fables, fantastic tales, biblical reminiscences, uncanonical or apocryphal christian legends, and fragments of Hebrew apocalypse and popular tradition, there was an extraordinary literary and psychological power. This stimulated the poetic and creative inventiveness of the *magistri*.[51] There was no rigid defence of the authenticity of myths, rather their modification and blending in difference schools in such varying

---

witness of scripture, let us destroy entirely with the same testimony. What they seem to interpret like fantasies, even if they are not worthy of an answer, let us grind under foot).

[46] See Hamilton, ch. 3 above, and his nn. 1 and 79–88.

[47] See Hamilton, ch. 3 above, and his n. 71–8.

[48] A. Acerbi, 'La "Visione di Isaia" nelle vicende dottrinali del catarismo lombardo e provenzale', *Cristianesimo nella storia* 1 (1980), 80–1; Rottenwöhrer, 1.i 42, 1.ii 57. Pseudo-James 'habent enim quendam libellum Ysaye ... Quem libellum, quia tales innectit fabulas, carius amplectuntur' (They have a book of Isaiah ... which book, because it encompasses such tales, they value more greatly), fol. 19r.

[49] See Hamilton, ch. 3 above, and his n. 77.

[50] Acerbi, 'La "Visione"', pp. 75–122. Less importance is attached to it by Borst, pp. 161–2; Manselli, 'Eglises', p. 135, and 'I commenti biblici', in *Fonti medioevali e problematica storiografica* (= Atti del congresso internazionale ... 22–7 ottobre 1973, Rome, 1976), vol. 1, p. 429, 'Evangelisme et mythe dans la foi cathare', *Heresis* 5 (1985), 11, 14, as not forming part of the Cathar faith. Bozóky (*Livre secret*, p. 198) suggests an essentially oral diffusion of the *Interrogatio Iohannis*.

[51] Lambert, pp. 122–6; Manselli, 'Evangelisme', p. 13, 'Una "Summa"', p. 340; *Livre Secret*, p. 217.

ways that an exact correlation between myths and Cathar groups cannot be traced. New myths were created, and the inventiveness of the *doctor* excited admiration: 'et qui maiora dicit de istis fabulis habetur multum sapiens' (and the man who says more concerning these stories is considered a very wise man).[52]

Myths seem to have helped to engender a theorising literature among Italian Cathars. For the majority of *perfecti* there remained preparation for preaching and debate and an elementary knowledge of the *secreta* (secrets), but at the same time an opening developed for those who had studied in more advanced schools and in universities, an opening for mythological, theological and exegetical reflection and elaboration. This was an area reserved for the few, professional users of the book: those who were soon to be fighting Catholic scholasticism through the literary form of the treatise. Reserved to these few, for example, was the myth of the abortion of pregnant women during the great battle in the sky: 'est illud unum de suis secretis archanis' (that is one of their arcane secrets). And the myth of the presence in domestic animals of spirits who will be saved: 'manifestabo tibi secretam secretissimam nostram quam pauci etiam ex nostris consolatis sciunt' (I will reveal to you the most secret of our secret things, which few even of our 'consoled' know).[53]

Yet there was no Cathar mythological literature which was fully independent of biblical exegesis and reflection, and the impulse to study and write came from various sources. Despite a perceptive analysis by Manselli,[54] we do not yet fully understand the complex relationship between scripture and myth. Here we can only note that this link survived even after there had come, both from within Catharism and from outside, a tendency towards rationalisation of the faith. In this process myths were not superseded, their hold was not broken. Rather attempts were made, on the one hand to give them a credible basis through appropriate exegesis, and on the other hand to adapt them to the bible, in particular to the New Testa-

---

[52] *Liber supra Stella*, in Ilarino, p. 336. Manselli, 'Evangelisme', p. 13, underlines the confusion produced by the many variations.

[53] Käppeli, 'Une somme', pp. 330, 331; *Liber supra Stella*, p. 360 'credere duo crucificamenta est unum de secretissimis eorum; ipsa duo crucificamenta palam populo predicare non attemptant, ne populus scandalizaretur' (belief in two torments is one of their most secret beliefs; they do not try to preach these two torments amongst the people, lest the people should be scandalized); Rottenwöhrer, I.ii 101, 114. Manselli, 'Evangelisme', p. 11, 'Una "Summa"', p. 340.

[54] *L'eresia*, p. 329; 'Eglises', p. 155, 'Evangelisme', pp. 11, 14, 16.

ment. But they persisted. One might suggest there was a preference for them, for the examples of lack of belief in myth seem exceptional. Desiderius provides one example: 'non tenet illud secretum sed reputat illum malum' (he does not believe that secret but accounts it evil); 'de istis nichil credit Desiderius' (Desiderius believes none of this).[55] Others are the anonymous author of the *Liber de duobus principiis* and John of Lugio. Thus there emerged contradictions and cultural tensions in Italian Catharism. The scholastic method, based on principles of reasoning in theology, defines as *stulta* (foolish) the *questio* (question) which cannot be demonstrated through scripture,[56] and with the same logic the author of the *Liber de duobus principiis* reproached his Concorezzo adversary for continuing to believe in the myth that the devil had corrupted the four elements of the true God: 'probare non potes per scripturam novi testamenti hanc fidem' (you cannot prove this belief through the writing of the New Testament).[57] This suggests that the Cathar myths, or at least some of them, were autonomous and pre-existing and resistant to biblical exegesis, and that Cathar scholasticism tended not simply to reject them *en bloc* but to use *auctoritates divine* and true argumentation to disprove them. This process eroded their previous autonomy, for now the gospel was the norm or *auctoritas* (authority) which authenticates doctrine and myth, both of which could be false if such verification were not forthcoming. The profound biblical knowledge of the Cathars and their faithfulness to orthodox *lectio* (reading),[58] allied to their methodical mode of study, had brought them to this: and they had also been forced to it by the rigours òf scholasticism.

5 SCHOOLS, BOOKS, *MAGISTRI*

For the thirteenth century we have quite a good indirect information about scholastic activity, centres of teaching, use of books and the compilation of treatises. We are not dealing with a sudden

---

[55] Anselm of Alessandria, pp. 311, 312.   [56] Salvo Burci, *Liber supra Stella*, pp. 356, 361.

[57] *Livre des deux principes*, pp. 61, 378.

[58] Most importantly the studies of C. Thouzellier, 'La bible des cathares languedociens et son usage dans la controverse au début du xiiie siècle', *CaF* 3 (1968), 42–58, esp. 43–4; 'L'emploi de la bible par les cathares (xiiie s.)', in W. Lourdaux and D. Verhelst (eds.), *The Bible and Medieval Culture* (Louvain, 1979 = *Mediaevalia Lovaniensia* i.vii), pp. 141–56; *Livre des deux principes*, pp. 83–157; and Manselli, 'I commenti', p. 407.

development, and our information throws light on the preceding period. There is an intensification towards the peak of Cathar literary production in the 1230s and 1240s.

This is not an appropriate place for a (necessarily incomplete) list of schools, works and masters. More to the point is providing evidence which may help towards assessing prevailing trends. Yvo of Narbonne, who fled from Italy about 1214, was informed by the Cathars of Como 'quod ex omnibus fere civitatibus Lombardiae et quibusdam Tusciae Parisius dociles transmississent scholares, quosdam logicis cavillationibus, alios etiam theologicis dissertationibus insudantes' (that from almost all the cities of Lombardy and some of Tuscany, they had sent apt scholars to Paris, some to study the sophistries of logic, others the discourses of theology).[59] This means that these young men already had a heretical scholastic training, acquired in their cities, which was an adequate preparation for university studies. When he asked them for permission to go to Milan, 'miserunt me Mediolanum, a suis comprofessoribus hospitandum' (they sent me to Milan, to live with their teacher colleagues). This reveals that there was a Cathar school in Como and one, or perhaps more, in Milan, where *Magister* Bonacursus had already taught, where probably, if not at Concorzzo, Nazarius taught, and where some time later Desiderius, an authoritative head of the school, also taught. In the 1220s, therefore, the Lombard and Tuscan Cathars had established school structures. John of Lugio was also head of a school in around 1230,[60] though we have no information about where he taught. The same is true of Rainier Sacconi, in whose description of himself as *olim heresiarcha* (once a leader of heretics) can be traced his position as school head. From Caesarius of Heisterbach we learn that in Rome in 1209 there were schools run by a Cathar *haeresiarcha*.[61] Caesarius also confirms the existence of heretical schools in many Lombard cities (he does not specify them as Cathar, and may be referring generally to all heresies). In these the *magistri* taught theology, *aperte legentes*[62] –

---

[59] Matthew Paris, *Chronica majora*, RS 57/4, 271.

[60] Anselm of Alessandria, p. 257; Lambert, p. 132; Käppeli, 'Une somme', p. 303.

[61] *Dialogus miraculorum*, ed. J. Strange (Cologne, Bonn, Brussels, 1851), vol. I, p. 309: 'simul ingressi sunt scholas cuiusdam haeresiarchae' (at the same time they entered the schools of a certain heresiarch). That this was Cathar is confirmed from one of his sermons (see Thouzellier, *Catharisme*, p. 166 n. 26).

[62] *Dialogus* p. 308: 'NOV.: Audivi quod multi haeretici sint in Lombardia. MON.: Hoc mirum non est, habent enim suos magistros in diversis civitatibus, aperte legentes, et

which must be understood technically, as 'publicly holding schools'. In Verona too, in the historic year of 1184, there had existed a school of heretics run by a *magister* which a certain young Everard had attended with profit. In this case Caesarius uses the ambiguous term *auditorium*; but since Everard studied there, and, as we are told, thus became qualified to teach others, it must have been a school.[63] The Cathar church of Florence had its schools in the thirteenth century at Poggibonsi, Pian di Cascia and Pontassieve.[64] Finally, the evidence of the Anonymous of Passau, somewhat generalised and perhaps second-hand, and referring to all heresies, can be considered as supplementary evidence of the existence of Cathar schools in Lombardy.[65] Thus every Cathar church had one or more schools, schools which were presumably at every educational level.

Because of the complex interweaving of mythology–theology and exegesis, Cathar teaching could not have managed without books. Reading and writing were part of the professional training and everyday activities of those middling social groups to which Catharism addressed itself with such assiduity. And the works composed by the *magistri*, mainly indirectly documented, required a certain range of books. What, then, was the Cathar library? The sparse surviving evidence does not permit a full reconstruction, but it is indicative of some of this library's elements. Undoubtedly the best known and most widely used book was the New Testament, and this in a Latin and orthodox text; there is no evidence of circulation in Italy of Latin texts of the New Testament which had been modified (for doctrinal reasons) or translations in the vernacular. It was the *Liber* above all others, read and commented upon on all occasions whether everyday or important, used in preaching, in disputations, in treatises, in the rite of the *consolamentum*. And it was accessible to all, not restricted as were the two apocrypha which were so jealously guarded in the various churches.

In their writings the Cathars cite the Fathers of the Church,

---

sacram paginam perverse exponentes' (Nov.: I heard that there are many heretics in Lombardy. Mon.: That is no surprise, for they have their teachers in many cities, reading openly and expounding the sacred page wrongly).

[63] *Dialogus*, p. 308.   [64] Brenon, *I catari*, p. 143.

[65] Patschovksy and Selge, p. 72: 'In omnibus eciam fere civitatibus Lombardie et in provincia Provincie et in aliis regnis et terris plures erant scole hereticorum quam theologorum. Et plures auditores habebant, publice disputabant' (In almost all the cities of Lombardy and in the region of Provence and in other kingdoms and lands there were more schools of heretics than of theologians. And they had many listeners, and argued publicly).

theologians, and ancient and medieval philosophers, sometimes verbatim, sometimes paraphrasing; it is not clear whether citation comes directly or second-hand through quotations from Catholic treatises or other heretical works. Thus, for example, the author of the *Liber de duobus principiis* quotes the *Physics* of Aristotle, the *Liber de causis* and the *Digest*, but also reflects the thought of various other authors such as Boethius, Tertullian, Irenaeus, Jerome, Augustine, Marius Victorinus and perhaps William of Auvergne, without reproducing the exact words of any of them.[66] The author of the Latin Ritual, on the final doxology of the *Pater Noster* (*Quoniam tuum est regnum* (for thine is the kingdom)), alludes indirectly to its presence *in libris Grecis vel Ebraicis* (in Greek and Hebrew books), and shows that he knew Bogomil and Catholic sources, theological and sacramentary treatises, and Chromatius of Aquileia's commentary on the Pater Noster.[67] Moneta tells us that the Cathars knew and used the *Glossa*, perhaps the *Glossa ordinaria* to Matthew (Matt. 3:5–17).[68] The anonymous Cathar author, against whom the layman George wrote in the *Disputatio*, knew the Fathers and cited John Chrysostom and Augustine.[69]

Amongst the Italian Cathars there also existed certain books which it is not always possible to distinguish from their more important treatises. In 1234 in Piacenza, 'the financial capital of heresy',[70] after the attack on Roland of Cremona it was discovered that there was a book of accounts belonging to the heretics, and that

---

[66] *Livre des deux principes*, pp. 47–56, 60. For the established citations, respectively pp. 398, 166, 226.

[67] See Hamilton, ch. 3 above, and his n. 70.   [68] Moneta, p. 279A.

[69] *Disputatio inter catholicum et paterinum haereticum*, ed. E. Martène and V. Durand, *Thesaurus novus anecdotorum*, vol. v (Paris, 1717), col. 1714: 'Audite Johannem Chrisostomum damnantem secundum matrimonium' (Hear John Chrysostom condemning a second marriage), col. 1744: 'coacta servitia Deo non placent, sicut dicit Augustinus' (forced service does not please God, as Augustine says).

[70] So defined by Y. Dossat, 'De singuliers pèlerins sur le chemin de Saint-Jacques en 1272', in his collected essays *Eglises et hérésie en France au XIIIe siècle* (London, 1982), no. xiv, p. 217, and P. Racine, 'Il movimento ereticale', in *Storia di Piacenza dal vescovo conte alle Signoria* (Piacenza, 1984), p. 379. The evidence is contained in a letter of Gregory IX (J. H. Sbaralea, *Bullarium franciscanum*, vol. i (Rome, 1759), p. 133): 'Quod Guglielmus de Fontana ... solverit denarios nuntio haereticorum, probatur per librum haereticorum. Quod Ansaldus de Allo ... scripserit, et vendiderit libros haereticis' (that William de Fontana gave money to the heretics' messenger is proved in the heretics' book. That Ansaldus de Allo wrote and sold books to the heretics). Guiraud, vol. ii, p. 462; Ilarino, p. 216 sees – perhaps straining the point – the existence and circulation of a heretical literature; Dupré-Theseider, *Mondo*, p. 245, 'una sorte di biblioteca di libri ereticali' (a kind of library of heretical books).

a certain Ansaldo de Allo (perhaps a copyist) had written and sold books to the heretics. The Florentine Saraceno Paganelli confessed to having read *in libro pactarenorum* (in a book of the Patarenes), and having recommended its excellence.[71] This was probably a Cathar doctrinal work, certainly not the New Testament, which he was none the less in the habit of hearing read and commented upon. In the archive of the Dominican inquisition in Pavia in 1307 were listed 'multos libros de erroribus hereticorum et alios ad refellendum errores' (many books of the errors of heretics and others to refute errors) – the distinction suggests that the first were of heretical origin. In 1317 there came confirmation that this same office possessed these books, together with specification of their nature and origin: 'quidam libelli qui fuerunt hereticorum ubi sunt scripti errores eorum' (some books which belonged to heretics, in which their errors were written).[72] In the second half of the fourteenth century the Cathars of Chieri possessed a *liber grossus* (big book) called *liber civitatis Dei* (book of the city of God), which also acted as a register for adherents to the group: was it a sacred text, a ritual or doctrinal work? Once more in the foothills of the Alps in Piedmont, Martino de Presbitero possessed a book whose contents, he explained, concerned the *fractio panis* (breaking of bread).[73]

The high point of Cathar literature was the theological treatises written by the Cathars themselves, and what we are told about these in Catholic polemical treatises amounts to much more than mere casual allusion. Just as Thouzellier was able to reconstruct the text of a Cathar treatise from its quotation and citation in Durand of Huesca's *Liber contra Manicheos* (see plate 4), so we can discern and even partly reconstruct the outline of heretical texts from Italian Catholic responses to them. For Catholic counter-polemic attended to specific points.[74] It also indirectly informs us about the form as well as the content of heretical treatises, for it developed as a parallel or mirror of the writing it was refuting.

[71] R. Manselli, 'Per la storia dell'eresia catara nella Firenze del tempo di Dante', *BISI* 72 (1950), 134–5.

[72] G. Biscaro, 'Inquisitori ed eretici lombardi (1292–1318), *Miscellanea di storia italiana* ser. 3.19 (1922), 527, 557; *Livre des deux principes*, p. 21 n. 17; Borst, p. 260.

[73] Both the references are in Merlo, pp. 59, 64, who notes how books, schools and epistolary contact were features common to all the groups of Piedmontese heretics.

[74] Thus Manselli, *L'eresia*, p. 245; Wakefield and Evans, pp. 60, 66–7.

Catholic polemicists' principal sources of information about heretical writings were the writings of the Cathars themselves, either directly or as reported by earlier Catholic polemicists. The scholastic method itself, in its dialectic of *questio, propositio, responsio, reprobatio*, etc. (question, proposition, response, counter-argument) required precise fidelity to the letter and thought of the adversary. Following scholastic practice, the polemicist adapted himself to his adversary, here the heretic, accepting his choice of *auctoritas* and reproducing his pronouncements, in order then to demonstrate a different exegesis (often combined with other scriptural authorities) and to produce different answers using philosophical and theological reasoning.

Here are some examples. When Rainier Sacconi explained the thought of John of Lugio, he had the work in front of him: 'quoddam volumen magnum x quaternorum, cuius exemplarium habeo et perlegi et ex illo errores supradictos extraxi' (a large volume of ten quires, a copy of which I have; and I have read through it and extracted from it the errors cited above).[75] George, the author of the *Disputatio*, followed the fiction of a dialogue, but he was clearly not reporting an oral debate. His precise references (including those to the Fathers already mentioned), frequent expressions based on the terms *expositio, argumentatio* (exposition, argument), and the reference to a heretical *glossa* which, if used in its correct technical sense, meant a written commentary – all these lead us to suppose he was using one or more heretical texts.[76] From these he was quoting passages, alternating them with his own refutation. Salvo Burci, a layman from Piacenza, states explicitly that he is confuting the work known as *Stella*, which came from the church of Desenzano, calling his own refutation of it the *Supra Stella*: 'Supra Stella autem dicitur ad differenciam cuiusdam libri hereticorum, qui Stelle nomine pretitulatur' (It is called 'The Higher Star' to distinguish it from a certain book of the heretics which is entitled 'The Star').[77] Since Peter Gallus, bishop of the church of Gallus, is cited four times in the

---

[75] Sacconi, p. 57.

[76] *Disputatio*, respectively cols. 1707, 1711, 1712, 1720, 1727, 1741, 1709, 1737; 'sed quod de glossa tua vis addere, non accipio' (but I cannot accept what you want to add from your gloss), col. 1734.

[77] Rottenwöhrer, I.2 101 n. 70; Ilarino, p. 305 argues for his direct and detailed knowledge; Manselli, *L'eresia*, p. 252 attributes it, without any particular evidence, to one Andreas, a doctor, who was said to be Burci's only informant (Ilarino, pp. 304, 357).

Summa attributed to Peter the Martyr from Verona, this *Summa* was perhaps written not just against Gallus but against a treatise by Gallus. For Gallus's notoriety is unlikely to have been entirely oral and confined to his ability in public debate, given that his high status as a Cathar thinker is implied by Albertus Magnus's taking the trouble of citing and confuting him on the theme of the battle which took place between the angels in heaven.[78] The Pseudo-James Capelli never cited either Cathar authors or texts, preferring, when using them, to break them down in order to fit in with his overall plan – which deprived them of their individuality. By contrast Moneta of Cremona was very explicit in declaring his sources right at the start of his treatise: 'ex ore eorum, vel ex scripturis illa habui' (I have had these things from their mouth[s] or from their writings).[79] His subsequent (and frequent) citations of named Cathar authors are only of two, the radical Tetricus and the moderate Desiderius, which is probably because the other Cathar books available to Moneta were anonymous.[80] For each of these two, Tetricus and Desiderius, he provides once a precise reference to their work: 'in quadam parte cujusdam libri sui, cap. II illius partis' (in a certain part of some book of his, chapter II, of that part): 'notavit in cap. suo de resurrectione' (he noted in his chapter on the resurrection). The more famous of the two was undoubtedly Desiderius, whom St Thomas also mentioned in his *Contra impugnantes*: 'sicut patet in quodam tractatu cuiusdam Desiderii haeresiarchae Lombardi nostri temporis' (as appears in a certain treatise of a certain Desiderius, a heresiarch of Lombardy in our time).[81] Moneta identifies some of the authors of anonymous tests as heads of schools, but how many such anonymous texts he had is unknown. The author of the *Liber de duobus principiis* also cited a *sententia* (pronouncement) – perhaps a written text? – of the Concorezzo *magister* Guglielmo, *sapiens in pluribus*.[82]

[78] See Käppeli, 'Une somme', pp. 306–7, who conjectures that a copy of the *Summa* was intended for Peter Gallus (p. 307), and that something written by Gallus will have been available to the author of the *Summa* (p. 310). The passages from Albertus Magnus and from the Bolognese jurist Odofredo are quoted from Rottenwöhrer, I.ii 110 n. 52. On this important figure see P. Marangon, *Il pensiero ereticale nella Marca Trevigiana e a Venezia dal 1200 al 1350* (Abano Terme, 1984), p. 15; Lomastro Tognato, *L'eresia a Vicenza*, p. 35.

[79] Moneta, p. 2B.

[80] Tetricus, 61A, 71A–74A, 79B; Desiderius 248A, 347A, 357B, 473B, 540A. For a complete outline, Rottenwöhrer, I.ii 138 nn. 2, 3.

[81] Rottenwöhrer, I.ii 88 n. 30.   [82] *Livre des deux principes*, pp. 58, 218.

To the *doctores*, *magistri* and *sapientes* mentioned so far should be added Giovanni de Cucullio, referred to by the *Brevis summula*;[83] Daniele de Giussano, *verbis et scientia prefulgidus* (pre-eminent in words and knowledge), bishop of the church of Concorezzo and later a Dominican and inquisitor;[84] Filippo, bishop of Desenzano, who maintained a particular doctrine; Lanfranchino de Vaure, *doctor Albanensium* (doctor of the Albanenses (a particular Cathar group));[85] among the Cathars of Concorezzo one *Alb*. . . (his name is incomplete in the manuscript) who is cited in the *Liber de duobus principiis*;[86] and perhaps even Peter Martyr himself, who was from a Veronese Cathar family and had been sent to study at Bologna (at the university?) *pro defensione perfidie* (for the defence of perfidy – possibly meaning 'defence of heresy').[87] And we should include a great number of *magistri erroris* and *litterati* (masters of error, learned men),[88] of all levels of culture from simple *perfecti* to great scholastic *sapientes coram simplicibus philosophiam dantes* (wise men, giving forth philosophy amongst simple people).[89] If this was their stance, and if the aim of proving and defending their faith had led them to the study of holy scripture, philosophy and theology, and to write theorising works, this was how a tradition of scholastic learning had come to be consolidated among the Cathars of Italy, a tradition which was recognised even beyond the Alps. As late as 1321 Arnaud Sicre recalled a phrase of Pierre Maury referring to Italy (Sicily and Lombardy) *ubi sunt magni magistri hereticorum* (where there are great masters of heretics)[90] exile in Italy. This tradition continued in the subalpine area throughout the fourteenth century.[91] Italian Catharism, both because of its ties with the churches of the Balkans, documented from the twelfth to the second half of the fourteenth

---

83 Ed. C. Douais, *La Somme des autorités à l'usage des prédicateurs méridionaux au XIIIe siècle* (Paris, 1896), p. 121.

84 Anselm of Alessandria, p. 293, from which Dondaine quotes the passage from Galvano Fiamma that concerns the ex-Cathar.

85 Anselm of Alessandria, pp. 310, 312.

86 *Livre des deux principes*, pp. 376–80.

87 Käppeli, 'Une somme', pp. 297, 315.

88 See Gregory IX, *Ille humani generis* 20.v.1237 (G. Bronzino, 'Documenti riguardenti gli eretici nella Biblioteca Comunale dell'Archiginnasio, 1235–1262', *L'archiginnasia* 75 (1980), 20); Innocent IV, *Truculentam unius hominis* 9.iv.1254 (*Bullarium privilegiorum ac diplomatum romanorum pontificium amplissima collectio*, ed. C. Cocquelines, 6 vols. in 13 (Rome, 1739–40), vol. I, p. 344); Caesarius of Heisterbach, *Dialogus miraculorum*, p. 303.

89 *Disputatio*, col. 1740.

90 Fournier, vol. II, p. 60.

91 Merlo, pp. 35, 47, 67, 94, where some Cathar *magistri* are mentioned.

century (when the example is Giacomo Bech)[92] and especially because of the scholastic training achieved in the early thirteenth century, exercised a kind of intellectual and religious leadership in western European Catharism.

[92] On the Balkans contacts of Bech, who was tried in 1388, see Merlo, pp. 20, 43, 94.

CHAPTER 6

Heresy and literacy: evidence of the thirteenth-century 'exempla'

Aaron Gurevich

It is hardly possible to doubt that heresy could be and often was, in fact, connected with literacy, and that the critical attitude towards the Church was usually fed by acquaintance with the bible or some of its literary commentaries. The interpretation of the scriptures was crucial, and some scholars have sought the main focus of contradiction between the official Church and the heretics in theological differences. I must confess that I feel unable to be completely convinced by this approach. He who approaches medieval heresy from a strictly theological point of view may run into the danger of becoming a victim of delusion created, consciously or subconsciously, by the opponents and persecutors of the heretics. However, the clergymen were interested not only in the maintenance and defence of the pure faith, but also power, ideological influence and control over the minds of the laity. Their interpretation of heresy depended on their biassed position.

Nevertheless, the point I should like to stress is not ideology. While discussing the problem of 'heresy and literacy', one should not forget that their interaction took place in a society which was basically alien to literacy and was not orientated towards the written word, but towards orality. Of course, what I have in mind is not the statement of the obvious, that is, that the bulk of the population remained completely unlettered. The most important fact is that the whole cultural context was determined by the predominance of the spoken word. The 'mental equipment' (*outillage mental*, to use Lucien Febvre's formula) of the people was not formed according to the structure of written texts, but in the total climate of the word-of-mouth culture, and it was primarily the oral culture that gave the frame of reference to the thought.

Even the most educated and learned people continued to live in an unlettered milieu, and the specific atmosphere of folk-lore could not but influence their minds very essentially. They functioned in the intellectual field formed by the opposition 'written text/oral word'. I believe that the historian of medieval scholarship and literacy cannot escape the problem of how this all-embracing mental atmosphere created by the dominance of the spoken word formed the very approach to the written texts and their comprehension.

May I, in this connection, recall certain facts? A lot of transactions were never fixed in documents and were executed in the form of ceremonies. Even when charters were used, people often saw in them the instruments of rite and ritual, which seemed to be an effective means, without any direct connection with the content of the written text. The preparation and delivery of the land deed was accompanied by the traditional custom of throwing or handing over a handful of earth, turf, twigs, etc. The deed (*carta*) was seen as an object, and before putting the text down it was customary to take the parchment and the writing equipment to the piece of land involved in the transaction, so that the 'power of the earth' would penetrate the material and make the inscription on the parchment effective and inviolable.[1] It was not the written text with its exact juridical content that was in the focus, but the magic ritual.

The combination of the *litterae* with ceremony, ritual and a system of gestures was widely practised. For the deed itself was accepted as a symbol. The ritual made the transaction substantive, irrespective of whether a document was provided or not. Even in those cases when the deed was made, the main point of transaction was the public ceremony in the presence of witnesses who could confirm the validity and legality of the bargain. As such, the document did not even have to have anything written on it, and *cartae sine litteris* were quite frequently used.[2]

Such practices testify to the specific attitude towards the written word. If the historian who studies the medieval frame of mind seen mainly through the eyes of the learned were, nevertheless, to take into serious consideration the basic mental disposition of the unlettered as well, he would admit that they saw in the written word something different. The text was considered not only as a sort of vehicle of factual information, but, and first of all, as part of a

---

[1] E. Goldmann, '*Cartam levare*', *Mitteilungen des Instituts für Österreichische Geschichtsforschung* 35 (1914), 1–59.
[2] M. Kos, '*Carta sine litteris*', *Mitteilungen des Instituts für Österreichische Geschichtsforschung* 62 (1954), 97–100.

certain ritual infused with magic. Magic, ritual, sorcery seem to be the essence of the comprehension of the text.

You may see that I am not completely happy with Professor Brian Stock's statement that the written word determined the form and content of the discourse in the West already in the eleventh and twelfth centuries.[3] This impression arises when the historian studies the learned texts. And yet, if he/she expands his/her field of research a little, the picture, I suspect, will be quite different. The texts addressed to a larger audience of unsophisticated people, inexperienced in reading and writing, reveal many connections with oral tradition, and the manners of thought which influenced such texts look quite different.[4]

I have already mentioned some documents which were used in legal transactions. However, the question arises of whether the same can be applied to theology as well. I am inclined to answer in the positive. The power of the sacral texts was first of all sought by the simple folk not in their content, but in other aspects. These texts were widely used in everyday practice as magic talismans. It is well known, for example, that the gospel could be laid onto a painful organ to heal it, and not only onto the sickly head, but onto the belly and even the genitals. The other sacral objects in their turn could function as amulets; the wafer was used as a disinfectant; the holy relics could help as medicine. It is difficult to describe the whole range of situations, outside the religious practice proper, in which the holy water was used.

The Church disapproved of this use of the holy objects as profane and, at the same time, was compelled to tolerate it, for the people needed magical help in everyday life. It would be enough just to look through Adolph Franz's publication[5] to be convinced of how deeply the propensity of the population for magic was rooted in their life and mentality. Such was the global setting in which, from my point of view, the problem of 'heresy and literacy' should be discussed. In any case, it seems to me that it would be incorrect to ignore this all-encompassing psychological context.

I should like to investigate some texts belonging to the genre of *exempla*, the short didactic stories which were in abundance from the

---

[3] Stock, *passim*.

[4] See D. Le Pan, *The Cognitive Revolution in Western Culture*, vol. I: *The Birth of Expectation* (London, 1989), p. 31.

[5] A. Franz, *Die kirchlichen Benediktionen im Mittelalter*, 2 vols. (Freiburg, 1909).

thirteenth century. Since then, the *exemplum* had become an invariable component of the sermon. There were several collections of *exempla* compiled, and each preacher could borrow from them the specimens he wanted to use to illustrate his sermon. The collections of Jacques de Vitry, Stephen of Bourbon and Cesarius von Heisterbach were the most popular ones.

The *exemplum* combined religious didactics with some entertaining story about human behaviour and miraculous events. The preacher who used *exempla* in his sermons addressed to a large audience wanted to be understood and, therefore, could not but try to use the system of images and notions which were not unfamiliar to his flock. There was of necessity a kind of feedback between the author of the *exemplum* and the preacher, on the one hand, and his audience, on the other. That is why I suppose that it is possible for the historian to penetrate into the popular mentality by means of studying such genres of medieval literature as *exempla*. There was expressed in them a popular world-view, though, of course, distilled by monastic interpretation.

As Jacques Le Goff and Jean-Claude Schmitt emphasized, the thirteenth century, when the genre of *exempla* flourished, was a 'period of the explosive expansion of the spoken word'. It was only during that century that the voices of the simple folk became audible. Neither before the thirteenth century nor later was the 'scholarly word' so closely connected with the 'popular word'.[6] The idiom of the town streets and public gatherings penetrated into certain categories of literary production, and first of all into the *exempla*. Some authors or compilers of *exempla* collections, especially Jacques de Vitry, felt it necessary to include vernacular words and expressions in the Latin texts of their stories. The voices of the crowd and of the individuals are clearly discernible in the sermons of the learned monk.

The rhetorical technique used by Berthold von Regensburg, the most famous preacher of the thirteenth century, included, in particular, the recurrent interruption of his speech by fictitious questions from his audience: 'O brother Berthold, tell me, please ... ', and so on. Such oratory devices were to attract the audience's attention and establish a dialogue between the preacher and his

[6] J. Le Goff, J.-C. Schmitt, 'Au XIIIe siècle: une parole nouvelle', in J. Delumeau (ed.), *Histoire vécue du peuple chrétien* (Toulouse, 1979), vol. I, pp. 257–79.

parishioners. Orality intrudes into the written text, and together with it the manner of thought characteristic of the ignorant, *simplices, idiotae*.

Let us now turn to the heretics in the thirteenth-century *exempla*. They tried to influence people not so much with the help of learned arguments as by means of miracles. Caesarius of Heisterbach describes the events which took place in Besançon. Two men came there, 'non mente ... sed habitu simplices, non oves, sed lupi rapaces' (simple in their dress, but not in their mind, ravening wolves and not sheep). Both were thin, barefoot and pallid. They constantly observed the fasts, went to church and attended all the holy services. They took charity, but nothing except food. These 'hypocrites', as Caesarius calls them, 'et novas atque inauditas haereses rudibus praedicare' (preached new and unheard-of heresy and deluded the whole population). However, Caesarius did not expound their teaching, and his attention was not concentrated on it. He said that they did not restrict themselves to preaching but also performed miracles: they covered the street with flour and stepped on it, leaving no footprints; they did not drown in water, and got out of burning huts unharmed. They said to the people 'Si non creditis verbis nostris, credite miraculis' (If you do not believe our words, believe our doings).

The clergy, headed by the bishop, feeling unable to persuade the heretics, were gravely worried by their actions. Meanwhile, the people's faith was shaken. What should be done? The bishop requested the cleric known to be quite expert in black magic to ask the devil for help and in this way to find out who these men were, where they came from and what was the source of their power to perform miracles. Sorcery and commerce with the devil were, of course, strictly forbidden; however, the bishop promised the cleric absolution of his sins, for he was gravely distressed by the extraordinary and dangerous situation.

Obeying the bishop's order, the cleric invoked the fiend, who disclosed to them that the strangers were his servants and preached his teaching. But why, the cleric asked him, had they remained unhurt in fire and in water. The devil's answer was: because they have sewn in their armpits the deeds (*cyrographa*) with the text of the oath which they gave to the devil, promising their obedience to him. These amulets protected them from any harm. If these talismans were forfeited, they would be defenceless.

Then the bishop hurried to call the town populace and announced that he wished to put these men to the test. 'Respondit populus: Nos plurima ab eis signa vidimus. Quibus Episcopus: Sed ego illa non vidi' ('We have seen a lot of signs from them', answered the crowd. 'But I have not', retorted the bishop). Both heretics were invited, and a fire was built. Before permitting them to undergo the ordeal, the bishop ordered the guard to search them, and the magic chartulae were found in their armpits and immediately cut out. The bishop demonstrated the talismans to the crowd, and the devil's servants were thrown into the fire and perished.

Thus, concludes Caesarius von Heisterbach, the heresy was eradicated, with God's help and the bishop's efforts, and the tempted townspeople cleansed by penitence.[7] It seems necessary to add: 'with the devil's assistance, as well'.

We can see that the main characteristic of the above-mentioned heretics (Caesarius meant Albigensians) was not their ideas based on the unorthodox reading of the bible and gospel (this teaching was only mentioned in parentheses, without any specification), but their magic abilities given them by the devil. The written texts which figured in the *exemplum* and played the main role in the episode were not the scriptures but demonic amulets hidden under their skin. The *exemplum* quoted above seems to be interesting, for not only are heretics identified by Caesarius as the devil's underlings involved in the manipulation with magic and sorcery, but also the bishop himself, who consulted with the same devil. The borderline between the God and his Church, on the one hand, and the devil and his slaves, on the other, is not very clearly defined in the cited story.

However, the authors of the *exempla* knew only too well that many heretics were quite experienced in theology. They often surpassed Catholic clerics and monks in their knowledge. It was difficult to dispute with them, and from time to time the Catholics could not find arguments convincing enough to suppress the heretics' objections. For there were, among heretics, persons who possessed deep knowledge of sacred texts, translated them from Latin into the vernacular and interpreted them not only before the educated but, what was especially dangerous, before the simple folk as well. Etienne de Bourbon knew a young shepherd who, during one year

---

[7] *Caesarii Heisterbacensis monachi ordinis Cisterciensis 'Dialogus miraculorum'*, ed. J. Strange (Cologne, Bonn, Brussels, 1851), vol. II, pp. 296–8.

spent by him in a Waldensian house, had been imbued with every kind of heresy and learned a lot of texts.[8]

Again, a certain heretic presented to the simple-minded orthodox theologian so many reasons that the *idiota* could not dispute with him. None the less, he was not perplexed at all. The triumphant heretic asked him: ' "Quare rides, cum contra concludatur?" Respondit "Rideo quod tibi resistere nescio; scio tamen quod fidem rectam teneo et quia ab heretico me tractari ita viliter conspicio" ' ('Why do you laugh, if you proved unable to draw the true logical conclusions in our altercation?' The *simplex* answered, 'I am laughing because, though I cannot contradict you, I nevertheless know that it is my faith that is true, and I will be rewarded, for I am disputing with the heretic who treats me so meanly').[9] Thus, even though it was admitted that a heretic could be better educated and more lettered than a true Catholic, at the same time it was shown that the *sancta simplicitas* should win. The deciding factor is faith, not knowledge.

Catholics could not change the Albigensians' way of thinking during their public dispute, when they quoted many authorities. However, they managed to demonstrate publicly their opponents' errors, for when an orthodox proposed that a heretic should cross himself, the latter was only able to begin making a sign of the cross, but could not perform it.[10]

In conclusion, I should like to recall an episode in the war against the Albigensians. When the crusaders approached Béziers, from the wall of the besieged town the heretics threw on their heads the gospel, on which they had urinated. 'Clamaverunt: "Ecce lex vestra, miseri" ' ('There is your law, wretches!', they cried). The result of that unheard-of action, Caesarius of Heisterbach added, was that when the Catholic army rushed into town, they massacred all its inhabitants, making no distinction between the heretics and the faithful, in obedience to the bishop's words: 'Caedite eos. Novit enim Dominus qui sunt eius' ('Kill all of them, the Lord will separate His own').[11] Is not the heretics' contempt and aversion mixed with

---

[8] *Anecdotes historiques, légendes et apologues tirés du recueil inédit d'Étienne de Bourbon*, ed. A. Lecoy de la Marche (Paris, 1877), no. 349.

[9] *La Tabula Exemplorum secundum ordinem alphabeti. Recueil d'exempla compilé en France à la fin du XIIIe siècle*, ed. J. T. Welter (Paris, Toulouse, 1926), no. 279.

[10] *The Exempla or illustrative stories from the 'Sermones vulgares' of Jacques de Vitry*, ed. T. F. Crane (London, 1890), no. 26.

[11] *Dialogus miraculorum*, vol. II, pp. 300–3.

sarcasm and intended infamy demonstrated in this incident (if we may believe Caesarius of Heisterbach) an evident expression of their attitude towards literacy?

I am not inclinèd to generalise from this evidence. Nevertheless, it seems to me that the interaction between orality and literacy cannot be dismissed when one studies heresy. Medieval orality was not only the absence of learning, but something much more significant. It was an expression of a distinctive state of mind and a specific world-view.

CHAPTER 7

The literacy of Waldensianism from Valdes to c. 1400

Alexander Patschovsky

A visitor to Torre Pellice, the geographical and spiritual centre of contemporary Waldensianism, cannot overlook the references to the prime symbol of literary education at a focal point in the town: in the middle of a monumental fresco painted by Paolo Paschetti at the front end of the Aula Sinodale in the eastern wing of the so-called Casa Valdese he will notice an open book.[1]

The book, of course, is the bible, and the emphasis placed upon it reveals both the educational foundations and limitations of Waldensian piety. Its sole point of orientation is the bible, 'the Book of Books'; consequently, a literary document, and hence literacy, is the foundation stone of Waldensianism. At the same time, however, the pronounced biblicism of the Waldensians, together with the implicit reserve, if not explicit rejection, which they show towards exegetical tradition, doctrinal interpretation and rational disputation, may lead us to doubt whether the Book is anything more than a mere fetish for Waldensian believers, as the characteristic quality of literacy is lacking: namely, the intellectual penetration of a subject by means of the written word. Brian Stock has elucidated the idea that orientation towards the written word without the accompanying communicative articulation in the medium is a characteristic of the heretical groups of the eleventh century in the phase of transition from oral to written culture.[2] Although I doubt the general validity of his observations for the eleventh century, they can be applied

---

[1] Paolo Paschetti created the fresco in 1939 at the 250th anniversary of the so-called 'Glorioso Impatrio' of 1689, when the inhabitants of the Valli Valdesi in the duchy of Piedmont who had survived persecution and exile managed to return to their homelands. The fresco depicts an oak tree, in the middle of whose crown the open book is to be seen, bearing the inscription (Apoc. 2:10): *Sii fedele fino alla morte.* See *I Valdesi e le loro valli. Testi di Augusto Comba. Immagini di Mario Benna ed Ernesto Bertone* (Turin, 1989), pp. 85, 111, 112, 128.

[2] Stock, pp. 90f. On the point of their relationship to the written word Stock does not distinguish sufficiently between the different heretical groups.

without hesitation to the Waldensian movement which began a century and a half later.

The questions I wish to deal with in this chapter are derived from this tension between orientation towards a book and, at the same time, lack of intellectual interest. What is the significance of literary education, 'literacy', in Waldensianism in the first two centuries of its existence? This means asking, on the one hand: 'In what way was literacy a constitutive factor in Waldensian spirituality?' And, conversely: 'What was the contribution of Waldensianism to the literacy of European culture?'

I

I would like to begin with a *tour d'horizon* through the documents which testify to the relationship between Waldensianism and literacy.[3] First we have the famous report by Stephen of Bourbon on the translation into the vernacular of the bible and certain statements of the Fathers of the Church which was commissioned by the founder of Waldensianism, the Lyonese merchant Valdes (see plate 5).[4] The task was carried out by two clerics of his home town for a fee. One of them, Stephen of Anse, described as *grammaticus*, did the translation (see plate 6); the other, Bernard of Ydros, wrote the translation down from dictation. According to Stephen's own words, the language was *Romanum*. Whether this refers to the Franco-Provençal spoken in the region of Lyons or to the Dauphinois spoken in and around Grenoble is debated; but the text itself has been lost, and the problem is anyway irrelevant to the main issue.[5] The main issue is that the translation commissioned by Valdes provides us with the oldest certain testimony for the existence of a bible, or at least of really significant parts of the bible,[6] in the French vernacular.[7]

---

[3] See Gonnet and Molnar, pp. 319f.; Gabriel Audisio, *Les 'Vaudois': naissance, vie et mort d'une dissidence (XIIme–XVIme siècles)* (Turin, 1989), pp. 153ff. The following statements are in part very close to G. G. Merlo, *Identità valdesi nella storia e nella storiografia (Valdesi e valdismi medievali* 2, Turin, 1991) pp. 71–92. Helpful for the problem in general is Peter Biller, 'Oral and written', pp. 19–28.

[4] Patschovsky and Selge, pp. 15ff.

[5] See the references in Thouzellier, *Catharisme*, p. 453, n. 1 referring to p. 429.

[6] To be more precise, Stephen of Bourbon testifies to the translation of the Gospels and 'many books of the bible', that is, the Old Testament, and not of the entire text. The selection was probably made on practical grounds and is not connected with the later formation of a typically Waldensian canon, which entirely or partially excluded the Book of Machabees. On the versions of the bible regarded as Waldensian see the survey in Gonnet and Molnar, pp. 323f. and 394 and n. 121.

[7] On this point see Grundmann, *Bewegungen*, pp. 445f.

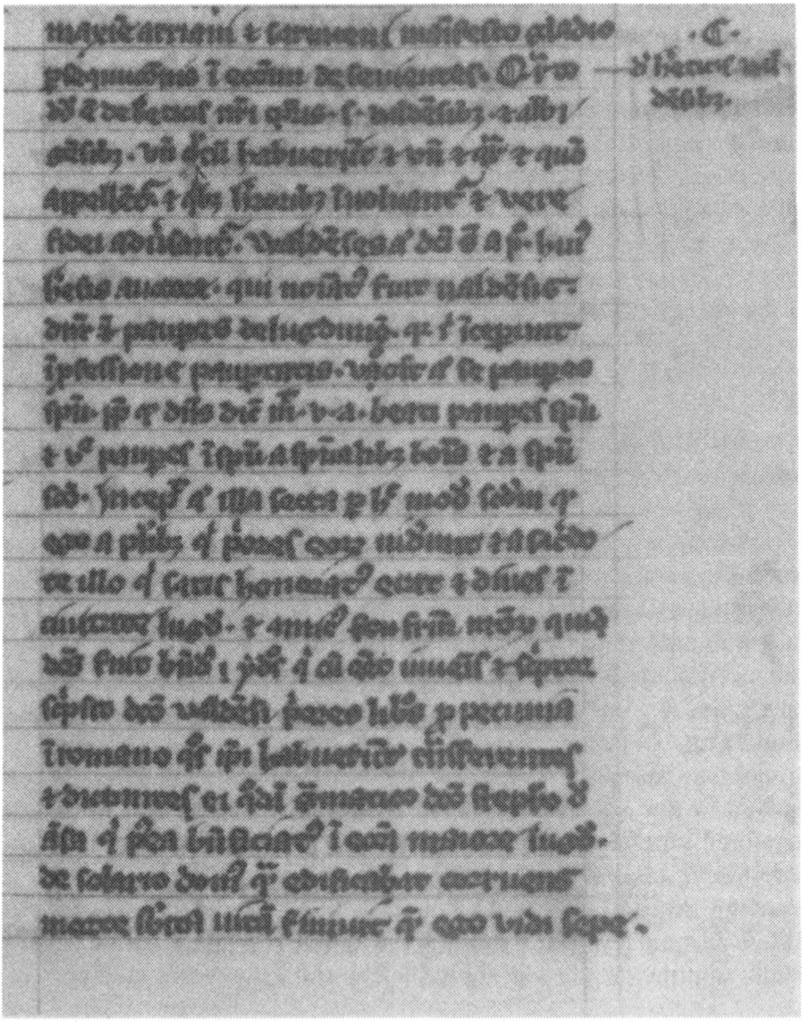

Plate 5 The Dominican Stephen of Bourbon describing the founder of the Waldensians, Valdes, commissioning translations of parts of the bible and patristic authorities into the vernacular, with the priest Bernard of Ydros acting as a scribe and Stephen of Anse dictating to him. Paris, Bibliothèque Nationale Ms. Lat. 15970, fol. 404r. (With permission of the Bibliothèque Nationale.)

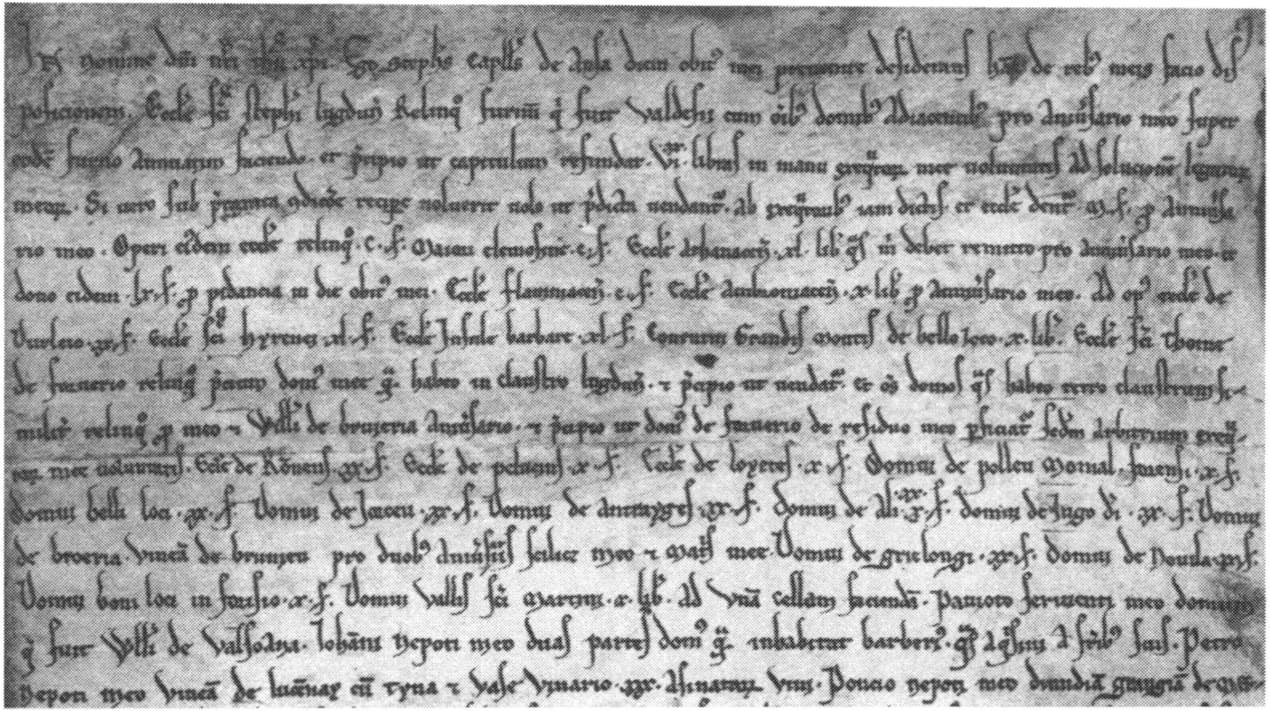

Plate 6 The will of Stephen of Anse, in the second line of which he specifies the *furnum qui fuit Valdesii* (bake-house which belonged to Valdes), which presumably had been his payment for the translating for Valdes described by Stephen of Bourbon (see plate 5). (Archives du Rhône, 10 G 1002, pièce no. 9. cliché P. Ageneau, Conseil Général du Rhône, with permission of the Archives Départementales du Rhône.)

Valdes therefore, and through him Waldensianism, was a prime cause for the use of the Romance vernacular in imparting know-ledge of the basic text of all christian religious writing. That is an epoch-making achievement, although it should not be seen in iso-lation.[8] Valdes's action soon found followers elsewhere. Around 1200 bible translations appear in the dioceses of Metz and Liège,[9] at first in the Romance language and quite soon afterwards in German. The Synods of Toulouse (1229), Rheims (1230/1), Trier (1231), Tarragona (1233) and Béziers (1246) provide similar testi-mony. Heretics are regularly associated with these bible translations both by the ecclesiastical authorities of the time and by modern scholars, on occasion with explicit reference to the Waldensians.[10] Arguably, Waldensianism and the work of translating the bible into the vernacular were virtually synonymous around the year 1200.[11] Admittedly, it was only in the first phase of the emergence of religious writing in the vernacular, the phase restricted to translation, that Waldensianism played an important, if not leading, role. Herbert Grundmann has rightly pointed out that the Waldensians no longer participated in the productive application of the biblical knowledge gained from such translations by an intellectually active readership (the true meaning of reception according to Hans Robert Jauss),[12]

---

[8] On the French versions specifically the fundamental treatment is still S. Berger, *La Bible française au moyen âge* (Paris 1884), pp. 35-50, who on pp. 49ff. correctly points to the existence of translations made at the same time as that of Valdes at Liège in the Flemish circle of Lambert le Bègue and associated with the beginnings of the Beguine movement. Berger, 'Les bibles provençales et vaudoises', *Romania* 18 (1889), 353-422; additions from Paul Meyer, in the same issue of *Romania*, pp. 423-9 and 430-8. That the reception of the bible was the crux of all religious movements in the middle ages which were termed heretical, and hence is not specifically Waldensian, is rightly emphasised by Robert Lerner, 'Les communautés hérétiques (1100-1150)', in Pierre Riché and Guy Lobrichon (eds.), *Le Moyen Age et la Bible* (*Bible de tous les temps* 4, Paris, 1984) pp. 597-614, 629f.

[9] See L. E. Boyle, 'Innocent III and vernacular versions of scripture', in *SCH, Subsidia* 4 (1985), 97-107. See also the earlier study by H. Rost, *Die Bibel im Mittelalter* (Augsburg, 1939), pp. 72ff.

[10] References in Grundmann, *Bewegungen*, pp. 447ff.; see also Selge, vol. I, pp. 22ff., 290ff.

[11] See also K. Schreiner, 'Laienbildung als Herausforderung für Kirche und Gesellschaft, Religiöse Vorbehalte und soziale Widerstände gegen die Verbreitung von Wissen im späten Mittelalter und in der Reformation', *Zeitschrift für Historische Forschung* 11 (1984), 257-354, especially 287-9.

[12] See, for example, H. R. Jauss, *Die Theorie der Rezeption – Rückschau auf ihre unerkannte Vorgeschichte* (Konstanzer Universitätsreden 166, Konstanz, 1987), pp. 15, 17. On our case see Jauss, *Ästhetische Erfahrung und literarische Hermeneutik* (Frankfurt on Main, 1982), pp. 673ff.

or in the development of religious writings of their own based on such reception of religious writings of the bible.[13]

II

The translation arranged by Valdes was commissioned work, done by clerics who had no spiritual connections with Valdes and the movement he initiated. The production of the translation is not, therefore, evidence of the educational horizons of Valdes and his followers. On the contrary: translations are needed by those who have difficulties with the original text. In the words of Stephen of Bourbon, Valdes was *non multum litteratus*. What does this mean? It is a known fact that the meaning of *litteratus* and its opposite *illiteratus* is by no means unequivocal. Herbert Grundmann, who devoted one of his most brilliant articles to this topic, interpreted *illiteratus* in this place as ability to read, but not to understand Latin.[14]

Valdes must in fact have been able to read, as the making of a translation would otherwise have been meaningless. But did he have no knowledge of Latin? Apparently, not enough to understand the Vulgate effortlessly. But since Michael Clanchy's investigation of the English material we know that the acquisition of reading skills in Valdes's time was inseparably linked with a knowledge of Latin and that the process of achieving literacy in the vernacular by no means presupposed a lack of Latin.[15] Emphasis must therefore be placed on the *non multum* in regard to Valdes's literacy. As a *litteratus*, Valdes knew some Latin; as a merchant of the dominant social class in an area whose cultural contacts with the traditions of antiquity were unbroken, he certainly knew no less than what we know others of the same estate and profession from Flanders, England and much later the German Hansa towns to have possessed.[16] But, admittedly, it cannot have been 'much'.

---

[13] Grundmann, *Bewegungen*, pp. 449ff; H. Grundmann, 'Die Frauen und die Literatur im Mittelalter. Ein Beitrag zur Frage nach der Entstehung des Schrifttums in der Volkssprache' in *Ausgewählte Aufsätze* 3 (1935), 67–95, particularly 86ff.

[14] Grundmann, 'Litteratus', p. 58.   [15] Clanchy, particularly pp. 158ff., 184.

[16] This is termed 'pragmatic literacy' by M. B. Parkes, *The Literacy of the Laity* (1973; repr. *Scribes, Scripts and Readers* (London, 1991), pp. 275–97, particularly pp. 278ff.). See also Clanchy, pp. 188, 189ff., 197f.; Henri Pirenne, 'L'instruction des marchands au moyen âge', *Annales d'histoire économique et sociale* 1 (1929), 13–28, particularly 20ff.; F. Rörig, 'Mittelalter und Schriftlichkeit', *Die Welt als Geschichte* 13 (1953), 29–41, particularly 37ff.; Edith Ennen, 'Stadt und Schule in ihrem wechselseitigen Verhältnis vornehmlich im Mittelalter', *Rheinische Vierteljahrsblätter* 22 (1957), 56–72, expanded in C. Haase (ed.), *Die*

But how much was it in fact, or could it perhaps have been? The question is not aiming at the Ciceronian quality of his Latin, but at his command of the cultural contents expressed in what he read. The translations Valdes commissioned, the New Testament, parts of the Old Testament and *sententiae* of the Fathers of the Church, are all texts of an authoritative kind, works of reference, texts intended to instruct and pronounce judgement, not to initiate discourse. Preoccupation with them presumes the existence of religious sentiment, but not necessarily of theology.

Naive unquestioning belief in authoritative sacred texts without profound theological education is also the intellectual profile of the earliest Waldensian, as depicted by Walter Map in his much quoted report on the appearance of a group of Waldensians before pope Alexander III at the Third Lateran Council of 1179. There they requested permission both to preach the gospel in general, and, specifically, to propagate the writings from which they wished to preach. This led to an examination by a theological commission of the Council, in which the questions were put by Walter Map himself, an Englishman who knew all the tricks of the clerical–curial trade. They were catch questions, and the answers required no particular profundity of thought. But they did require knowledge of theological distinctions of the kind which were crammed in the schools. 'Do you believe in God the Father?' Answer: 'Yes!' 'And in the Son?' Again the answer: 'Yes!' 'And in the Holy Ghost?' Yet again: 'Yes!' And now the trap: 'And in the mother of God?' Here too the answer was 'Yes', to the great amusement of the academically schooled audience.[17]

It has been pointed out that this anecdote should not be over-rated historically.[18] Alexander III reacted differently from what might have been expected after the Waldensians had failed the test. He approved of the vow of poverty which Valdes had intended as a guideline for the way of life of his community and granted the

Stadt des Mittelalters, vol. III (Darmstadt, 1984), pp. 455–79, particularly pp. 463ff.; K. Wriedt, 'Schulen und bürgerliches Bildungswesen in Norddeutschland im Spätmittelalter', in B. Moeller, H. Patze and K. Stackmann (eds.), *Studien zum städtischen Bildungswesen des späten Mittelalters und der frühen Neuzeit*, (Abhandlungen der Akademie der Wissenschaften in Göttingen, philosophische-historische Klasse, 3, Folge 137, Göttingen, 1983), pp. 152–72.

17 Walter Map, *De nugis curialium* D.1 c. 31, ed. and trans. M. R. James, revd. C. N. L. Brooke and R. A. B. Mynors (Oxford, 1983), pp. 124–7.

18 See Selge, vol. I, p. 24.

permission to preach, which they had requested, provided the approval of the local clergy was sought and given from case to case.[19] The lack of theological training was not so important for the fate of the Waldensian movement as Walter Map's account suggests.

Nevertheless, the fact that methodical theological training was lacking cannot be denied. In the eyes of Walter Map this lack branded the Waldensians as *idiotae illiterati*. But this is by no means true of all Waldensians. The most famous example demonstrating the opposite is Durand of Osca, a cleric whose knowledge was sufficient for him to be able to engage in a literary campaign against the Cathars.[20] Literacy in the sense of a clerical education was a matter of course for him and his companions, as it was presumably for Bernard Prim and his followers. Both of these groups were persuaded by Innocent III to return to the fold of the Church, where they formed small communities of their own, which, however, did not prosper.[21] Durand's Latin is cultivated, occasionally even recherché;[22] he not only has a command of the bible, but also possesses knowledge of the Fathers of the Church, although the source of this knowledge is by no means clear. Most of the references in his *Liber Antiheresis* can be traced back to Gratian, which suggests an acquaintance with florilegia in the style of the Waldensian anthologies of ecclesiastical authorities rather than direct recourse to the *originalia patrum*. The critical apparatus of quotations, approximate references and allusions to the *Liber Manicheos* (see plate 4), however, betrays a breadth of education which passes far beyond the general knowledge of the clergy and permits us to include Durand in the first rank of the theologians of his time.[23]

Literacy in the full sense of the word and of the highest quality for that time was thus by no means unknown to the early Waldensians. Apart from the work of Durand of Osca, their missionary operations

---

[19] Anonymous of Laon, *Chronicon universale*, ed. A. Cartellieri and W. Stechele (Leipzig and Paris, 1909), p. 29 (written around 1219); Moneta, p. 402[b]. On this point see Selge, vol. 1, pp. 21ff. On the legal and practical problems involved in the exercise of the preaching office by laymen see in general R. Zerfass, *Der Streit um die Laienpredigt* (Freiburg, 1974), particularly pp. 59ff. on the activities of the Waldensians.

[20] He did this in two works: in the *Liber Antiheresis*, composed when he was still a Waldensian, and in the *Liber contra Manicheos*, written after he had returned to the bosom of the Church. See editions by Selge and Thouzellier respectively.

[21] See Selge, vol. 1, pp. 188ff., 193ff.

[22] Above all in the *Liber contra Manicheos* he reveals a love of rare, and especially Greek, words.

[23] Unfortunately, neither Selge nor Thouzellier have investigated Durand's educational horizons closely.

against the Cathars, involving open disputations,[24] provide ample proof of this, as the polemical treatment of Cathar dogmas and myths required knowledge which could only be acquired from books. It is also confirmed by the production of further literary works. These include compilations of ecclesiastical authorities on certain issues, of which two examples have been handed down to us: the one has recently been identified by Mary and Richard Rouse as the work of Durand of Osca,[25] the other is a compilation on the worthiness of priests handed down by the so-called Anonymous of Passau.[26]

One could question whether compilations of this kind are literary productions at all, in the sense that literary activity requires creative and argumentative treatment of a topic and not merely the collection of a set of reference texts in accordance with certain principles of selection. In the case of the new work by Durand of Osca this question can certainly be answered positively. It is a compilation of biblical *distinctiones* based on the *Alphabetum in artem sermocinandi* of the Parisian professor of theology Peter of Capua (died 1214). Such *distinctiones* provide assistance in the preparation of sermons by giving the user references for the exegesis of the words of the bible with corresponding examples; this is a type of text to which Louis-Jacques Bataillon has attributed the function of mediating between the theology of the universities and lay culture.[27] This work can, however, only be described as Waldensian in as far as Durand of Osca was once a Waldensian; it must be dated in the period after his reconciliation with the Roman Church. Consequently, it is equally possible to regard it as a product of a newly won scholarship or as a demonstratively presented proof that Waldensianism and literacy are not mutually exclusive.

The situation is different with the compilation of *sententiae* in the Anonymous of Passau, a collection that is almost certainly Waldensian. The test is a short tract in the simplest of forms. At first a series

---

[24] See Selge, vol. I, pp. 271f. and n. 123.

[25] M. A. Rouse and R. H. Rouse, 'The schools and the Waldensians: a new work of Durand of Osca', in S. L. Waugh and P. D. Diehl (eds.), *Christendom and its Discontents: Exclusion, Persecution and Rebellion, 1000–1450* (1996) pp. 86–103.

[26] Preliminary edition by Patschovsky, in Patschovsky and Selge, pp. 44–6.

[27] L.-J. Bataillon, 'Intermédiaires entre les traités de morale pratique et les sermons: les *distinctiones* bibliques alphabétiques', in *Les Genres littéraires dans les sources théologiques et philosophiques médiévales. Définition critique et exploitation (Université Catholique de Louvain,*

of sentences of the Fathers are listed, with the intention of proving that the dignity of the priestly office is tied up with the personal worthiness of the bearer of the office; the source is quaestio 3 of causa 11 in Gratian's *Decretum*, a work which time and again could be detected as Waldensian authority.[28] But then the compilatory form is abandoned, conclusions are drawn, and a large number of further quotations from the bible and the Fathers are presented, which can no longer be found in any of the known compilations of canons. These are used, furthermore, to suggest a clear ecclesiastical attitude, the quintessence of which can be found in a quotation allegedly stemming from Ambrose 'Qui in spiritualibus presunt, si publice criminosi sunt, etsi bona precipiunt, non sunt audiendi' (Those who are high in religious office, if they are publicly known as sinful, even if they teach good things are not to be heard).

A text of considerable literary quality which is indubitably Waldensian is the letter of information sent by the Poor Lombards to their brethren in Germany, which only survived within the manuscript tradition of the Anonymous of Passau.[29] In this letter twelve brethren of the Lombard wing of the Waldensian movement, whose names are stated, inform their transalpine, that is German, companions about their position on certain controversial issues, on which the differences between them and the ultramontane primitive community of Valdes were irreconcilable. The main issues were the structure of authority in the community and the labouring congregations, which were important to the Lombards. There were also deep differences on the question of the standing of Valdes, the founder of the community.[30] What does the letter tell us about the level of literacy in the Waldensian movement in 1218, the year in which it was written? The first point to be made concerns the language. It is written in Latin, a respectable functional Latin of average standard, not in any of the vernacular tongues. Moreover, the insertion of excerpts from a letter of the ultramontane primitive

---

Publications de l'Institut d'Etudes Médiévales, 2ᵉ série: Textes, Etudes, Congrès 5, Louvain-la-Neuve, 1982), pp. 213–26, particularly p. 222.

[28] See P. Biller, 'Medieval Waldensian abhorrence of killing pre-c1400', *SCH* 20 (1983), 129–46, here p. 131 with n. 14, could show that the arguments referred by Alain de Lille, *PL* 210.394–5 as proofs against killing are mostly taken over from Gratian, *Decr.* II c. 23 q. 5, and with high probability of Waldensian origin.

[29] Preliminary edition of the *Rescriptum heresiarcharum Lombardie ad Leonistas in Alemania* in Patschovsky and Selge, pp. 20–43.

[30] For a detailed account see Selge, vol. I, pp. 172ff.

community reveals that the correspondence between the 'ultramon-
tanists' and the Lombards was also in Latin. There could be purely
practical reasons for this: the transalpine German brethren would
probably have had more difficulties with the Lombardian *volgare*
than with Latin, the *lingua franca* of the educated Western world. But
the situation is different with the correspondence between the Ultramontanes and the Lombards. Strikingly, the names of the brethren
of the two communities do not follow geographical demarcation
lines – they cannot be neatly separated into names of French and
Italian origin. One of the Lombards, for example, was called Johannes Francigena, and one of the Ultramontanes Oprandus de Bonate,
which suggests that he came from Bergamo.[31] 'Ultramontane' and
'Lombard' turn out not to be the designation of Waldensians from
different geographical areas, but to denote different observances –
on the one side the followers of the primitive community of Valdes,
on the other the followers of John de Ronco. In view of the inter-
mingling of nations among the parties to the dispute, communication in the *volgare* would definitely have been possible. This seems
all the more likely in view of the well-known fact that Provençal or
French, in which even the Umbrian Francis of Assisi is reported to
have composed poems, were something like a vernacular koiné, at
least for the better-educated classes, in Italy at the time.[32] There
were probably other reasons, therefore, for the choice of Latin in the
letter and in the correspondence between the two estranged Waldensian communities. It can safely be assumed that the reasons lie in
the status of the subject matter. For theological disputations there
was a preference for *clergie*. In the Lombard, Provençal and German
cultural zones of the early thirteenth century the vernacular was
obviously not yet respectable enough.[33]

---

[31] *Rescriptum*, ed. Patschovsky and Selge, pp. 26 and 28 with n. 103.

[32] Basic for the use of French in Upper Italy is P. Meyer, 'De l'expansion de la langue
française en Italie pendant le Moyen Age', in *Atti del Congresso Internazionale di Scienze
Storiche (1903)*, 4 (Rome, 1904), pp. 61–104, here pp. 68f. concerning the often quoted
report of Thomas of Celano that Francis produced his poems *lingua Francigena*. See also,
with special reference to the Provençal, M. Lenzen, 'Wann beginnt die italienische
Literatur?', *Archiv für das Studium der neueren Sprachen und Literatur* 208 (1972), 1–22,
particularly 16ff. Summing up the discussion, B. Guthmüller, 'Die volgarizzamenti', in
A. Buck (ed.), *Grundriss der romanischen Literaturen des Mittelalters*, vol. x: *Die italienische
Literatur im Zeitalter Dantes und am Übergang vom Mittelalter zur Renaissance*, part 2: *Die Literatur
bis zur Renaissance* (Heidelberg, 1989), pp. 228ff.

[33] On the status of languages in relation to certain subject matters see the highly instructive
observations in Clanchy, particularly pp. 155ff.

This is testimony to a literacy which in quality and usage differs in no way from that of the educated clerical world in the Church at large. This is true even of the form of argument; opposing opinions are exchanged, positions are justified by means of reference to authorities. As is only to be expected from the Waldensians, arguments are based on the testimony of the bible,[34] but the *doctores* of the Church are also quoted from Gratian's *Decretum*.[35] Such procedures were gradually becoming antiquated in the beginnings of the high age of scholasticism, and are not abreast of the theological discussions of the time. But they do correspond entirely with the methods of theological argument and disputation which then existed and continued to be practised long after the discovery of the scholastic method.

The letter of information also contains other peculiarities. Its apostolic pathos is particularly noteworthy. This is evident, above all, in the exordium of the letter, which repeats virtually word for word the exordium of the Epistle to the Philippians[36] and generally reveals a striking preference for the Epistles of St Paul, which the author uses to express his own views with particular grandiloquence.[37] For a religious community which, more than any other, has committed itself to following the example of the apostles in its missionary activities, demonstrative quotations of this kind cannot be dismissed as incidental. They serve the purpose of legitimation, emphasizing the tradition to which the authors of the letter believe they belong.

III

The letter of the Poor Lombards to their German brethren is the last manifestation of Waldensian writing for more than a century. We encounter the next witnesses to the existence of genuine Waldensian literacy only towards the middle of the fourteenth century in Piedmont in the form of the *Liber electorum* (see plate 7) and the related correspondence between the Austrian Waldensian renegades,

---

[34] See, for example, the *Rescriptum*, in Patschovsky and Selge, pp. 31ff. on the question of the ability of unworthy priests to perform the act of transubstantiation.

[35] c. 1 q. 1; See Patschovsky and Selge, pp. 40ff. The order of the quotations makes it highly unlikely that any source other than Gratian was used.

[36] *Rescriptum*, in Patschovsky and Selge, pp. 21f.

[37] See *Rescriptum*, in Patschovsky and Selge, p. 36.

Johannes Leser and Siegfried, and their former companions in Italy and Austria. These date from the 1360s and 1370s, as Peter Biller has pointed out.[38] The *Liber electorum* is a kind of historically based proof of the legitimate apostolic succession of the Waldensian preachers. Church history serves as an apologia, the historical experience in time as an argument for eternal truths. The contents of the work are briefly as follows: the primitive Church was the true Church as founded by Christ. In the time of Constantine came the turning point and the parting of the ways. Under pope Sylvester the main body of the Church, corrupted by power and property, took the wrong path. But one of the pope's companions broke with him and maintained the true apostolic succession in a poor, spiritually pure Church, which survived in secret, never completely disappearing. With Valdes, who is here given the christian name Petrus in analogy to the Prince of the Apostles,[39] the true Church appears on the scene again and can at first develop relatively undisturbed, until recent times, when it again suffers persecution. In the polemical correspondence which follows from this apologetic work of history the central question is the legitimate *ordo* of the Waldensian preachers.

Here again the language was still Latin, or at least predominantly Latin. There was a version of the *Liber electorum* in *volgare* in circulation in Piedmont at the time (see plate 8), but its relationship with the Latin version is not yet clear. Latin could again serve as the medium of communication between the German and the Italian brethren; for reference texts with canonical content (as Peter Biller rightly classifies the work),[40] Latin remained the language most appropriate to the subject matter. The use of Latin indicates that at the end of the period we are investigating there was no difference between the educational horizon of an ordinary priest in the established Church and that of a Waldensian preacher.

This is also true of the standard of education. The letters of the

[38] Only fragments of the material are at present available in an edited form. A critical edition is being prepared by Peter Biller (I have used his 'Aspects'). See, for the time being, C. Schmidt, 'Actenstücke besonders zur Geschichte der Waldenser', *Zeitschrift für die historische Theologie* 22 (1852), 238–62, particularly 239–42; Emilio Comba, *Storia della reforma in Italia*, vol. I (Florence, 1881), pp. 539–41; Döllinger, vol. II, pp. 351–62.

[39] Giovanni Gonnet, 'Waldensia', *Revue d'histoire et de philosophie religieuses* 33 (1953), 202–54, particularly 239ff.; Gonnet, 'Pierre Valdo ou Vaudès de Lyon?', *Bulletin de la Société de l'Histoire de Protestantisme français* 126 (1980), 247–50; Selge, vol. I, p. 2 and n. 3.

[40] Biller, 'Aspects', p. 253.

two German Waldensians Siegfried and Johannes Leser are written in a simple, clear and functional Latin, which is grammatically correct by the standards of the time, whereas the formal style of the Italian brethren even suggests training in the *ars dictaminis*.[41] The quotations they intersperse are revealing: there are references to Horace and Seneca made by the Italians, which nevertheless are probably ornamental remnants of elementary Latin instruction, and do not necessarily betray an acquaintance with the classics. There are also numerous quotations from the Fathers of the Church included by both the Italians and their German opponents. This source is not one of the specifically Waldensian florilegia which we have already encountered in Valdes's time. The two renegades quote the Fathers from Gratian, which could be both a consequence of their conversion and evidence for the continuing vitality of the tradition documented in the letter of 1218. The letter of the Italian brethren, however, leads to more definite conclusions. They quote entire series of 'Allegations' from the *Sentences* of Peter Lombard.[42] This is a work with which anyone taking an introductory course in theology would be acquainted, and leads us almost inevitably to the conclusion that the Italian Waldensian *Magistri* at least had received their training in a *studium generale* in a theological faculty of a university or in the *studium particulare* of one of the religious orders.

This may come as a surprise to anyone who examines the documents on the inquisition in Brandenburg and Austria dealing with the activities in the 1390s of the Celestinian provincial Peter Zwicker, and discovers that the Waldensians interrogated by Peter Zwicker expressed themselves in a very derogatory fashion on the value of university education.[43] This could indicate a general hostility towards education in the milieu of the German Waldensians, especially as they are also said to have a low opinion of the tradition of the Church Fathers.[44] Both points may be polemical: contempt

---

[41] Biller, 'Aspects', p. 229.   [42] Biller, 'Aspects', editorial section pp. 292, 293ff.

[43] See the list of Waldensian articles circulated in connection with the inquisition of Peter Zwicker, ed. G. E. Friess, 'Patarener, Begharden und Waldenser in Österreich während des Mittelalters', *Österreichische Vierteljahrschrift für katholische Theologie* 11 (1872), 260 (= Döllinger, vol. II p. 340) 'Item universitates scholarum Parisiensium, Pragensium, Wyennensium et aliorum locorum reputant inutiles et temporis perditionem' (They considered the universities of the schools of Paris, Prague, Vienna and of other places to be of no use and a waste of time). Peter Zwicker deals with this article in connection with the passage quoted below, n. 53.

[44] Waldensian Article, ed. Friess 'Patarener, Begharden und Waldenser', p. 261 (= Döllinger, vol. II p. 340) 'Item dicta sanctorum doctorum nihil curant, nisi quantum [*quam*

for university education seems to have been the result of an awareness of the dangers involved when theology was studied by men like Johannes Leser and Siegfried or by the Waldensian *magistri* whose conversion had led to the wave of persecution in the 1390s.

The fact that such studies were undertaken is, however, beyond doubt. This is shown by the example of the Waldensian deacon Raymund de Costa, who was interrogated by Jacques Fournier in his own diocese of Pamiers in 1319. Raymund himself informs us not only that he had acquired the basics of philology by studying the grammar part of the Trivium in Orange and Montpellier but that he had also attended the *studium* of the Franciscans at Montpellier to study theology.[45] That this was not an isolated instance, even if we include the eastern areas of Germany in our considerations, is demonstrated by a list drawn up in 1391 of Waldensian *magistri* who had returned to the fold of the Church, one of whom is described as a 'scholar' who had attended the (elementary) school in Wittenberg for two years.[46]

IV

Literacy in the sense of the characteristic ability of the clergy to express themselves in Latin, the command of a degree of school knowledge in theology and the arts, the use of letters as a form of communication and treatises as a form of intellectual articulation, the mediation of and orientation towards canonical texts – this kind of literacy was peculiar to the Waldensians throughout Europe at the beginning and end of the period under consideration. But is it also a permanent aspect of Waldensian intellectuality? And is the literacy of the educated man the most distinctive feature of Waldensianism?

These questions can hardly be answered with an unqualified 'yes'.

Friess] pro secta confortanda retinent, sed tantum [*sic, totum* Friess] novum testamentum ad literas observant' (They took no heed to the sayings of the holy doctors except to back the sect's beliefs, but observed the whole of the New Testament to the letter).

[45] Fournier, p. 102. For the studium of the Franciscans at Montpellier, which at least after 1346 ranked as *studium generale*, see J. Moorman, *A History of the Franciscan Order, from its Origins to the Year 1517* (Oxford, 1968) pp. 138, 366. See also G. G. Merlo, 'Sul Valdismo "colto" tra il xiii e il xiv secolo', in *I Valdesi e l'Europa* (*Collana della Società di Studi Valdesi* 9, Torre Pellice, 1982), pp. 67–98, here p. 75 with n. 20.

[46] See Kurze, p. 67, n. 2. In Wittenberg before the foundation of the university in 1502 a school existed run by Franciscans; see *Deutsches Städtebuch. Handbuch städtischer Geschichte*, ed. E. Keyser, vol. II (Stuttgart and Berlin, 1941), p. 738.

It has already been pointed out that evidence for the existence of genuine Waldensian writing between the letter of 1218 and the *Liber electorum* composed roughly a century later has not survived. Since older documents generally have a poorer chance of survival than later ones, one can only conclude from the relative abundance of Waldensian documents of the early years in comparison with the period immediately following, and from the concentration on the *Volgare* of Piedmont in the later Waldensian writings, that the continuity of literary productivity in the Waldensian movement was not particularly strong.

On the other hand, there is an abundance of sources which testify that from its very beginnings Waldensianism was at the educational level of an illiterate oral culture. Of course, the sources stem without exception from the opponents of the movement and do not merely transmit the facts, but serve the purpose of justifying the verdict of heresy. They are accordingly characterised by a tendency towards the formation and perpetuation of clichés.[47] The characterisation of Waldensians – *all* of them, without distinction – as illiterate idiots begins with Walter Map, and there is scarcely a single 'catholic' author who does not join the chorus when he has occasion to speak of the Waldensians. Most statements of this kind were stereotyped, following fixed patterns of thought and expectation, and using reality at best as a cue for predetermined responses, in as far as reality was taken into account at all. The restricted mental horizon of their opponents produces the same stereotype for *all* Waldensians: because they are lay they are illiterate; because they are illiterate they are incapable of interpreting texts correctly; and consequently, because they stubbornly insist on their own interpretation of the texts they are rebels against the Church and, therefore, heretics.

Alain de Lille is a perfect example of schematic thinking of this kind: 'They take the name Waldensians from the founder of the sect, Valdes, who, guided by his own spirit and not sent by God, founded a new sect, in order to presume the right to preach without due authorisation, without divine inspiration, without knowledge, without literary education. [He is] a philosopher without reason, a prophet without vision, an apostle without a mission, a teacher without training. His followers, or rather ratcatchers, lead simple

---

[47] See further Biller, 'Topos'. On the problem of lay education in the middle ages see the detailed treatment by Schreiner, 'Laienbildung'.

spirits astray everywhere and bring them from the true path instead of leading them to it.'[48]

In view of this kind of polemic, replete with clichés and serving only to justify apologetically the condemnation of the Waldensians as heretics, the accusation of a lack of literacy can be seen for what it is: a sweeping judgement which unmasks its authors. This applies not only to Alain de Lille, but also to Geoffrey of Auxerre,[49] Pseudo-David of Augsburg[50] and all those who, like Bernard Gui[51] and Nicolaus Eymericus,[52] took over the picture drawn by the polemicists of the twelfth and thirteenth centuries and ensured its persistence in the future. The accusations of Waldensian lack of literacy were taken to such extremes that those acquainted with the catholic clerical semi-literacy of the time must gasp in amazement, when, for example, Peter Zwicker in all seriousness accuses the Waldensian 'donkeys' not only of knowing no Latin, but also no Greek or Hebrew.[53] The catholic-polemical literature of the period generates a caricature, designed to present its object as the incarnation of all possible negative clichés. In the words of Stephen of Bourbon, after an account of Valdes's translation of the bible, he describes the beginnings and the impact of his missionary activity with these words: 'He sent his followers, men and women of the lowest occupations, to preach in the surrounding villages. They then prompted others to do the same: men and women, *idiote et illiterati*, who went into the villages, insinuated themselves into families (*domos*) and preached in the open and in the churches.'[54] Every

---

[48] Alain, 2.1, 377f. (*EFV*, p. 103): 'Hi Waldenses dicuntur a suo haeresiarcha, qui vocabatur Waldus, qui suo spiritu ductus, non a Deo missus, novam sectam invenit, scilicet ut sine praelati auctoritate, sine divina inspiratione, sine scientia, sine litteratura praedicare praesumeret. Sine ratione philosophus, sine visione propheta, sine missione apostolus, sine instructione didascalus, cuius discipuli, imo muscipuli, per diversas mundi partes simplices seducunt, a vero avertunt, non ad verum convertunt.' See also *PL* 210.379; *EFV*, p. 104.

[49] Geoffrey of Auxerre, *Super Apocalypsim*, sermo XIV, ed. F. Gastaldelli and J. Leclercq (*Temi e testi* 17, Rome, 1970), p. 179; *EFV*, p. 46.

[50] *De inquisitione hereticorum* c. 4, ed. W. Preger, *Der Tractat des David von Augsburg über die Waldesier*, ABAW 14, 2 (1878), 205f.

[51] See Gui, *Practica*, 34ff. His account is based largely on Stephen of Bourbon and Pseudo-David.

[52] Nicolaus Eymericus, *Directorium inquisitorum*, pars 2 qu. 14, ed. Franciscus Pegña (Rome, 1587), pp. 278f. The account is based largely on Bernard Gui.

[53] Petrus Zwicker (Pseudo-Petrus of Pillichdorf), 'Tractatus "Cum dormirent homines"', c. 35, ed. J. Gretser, *Lucae Tudensis episcopi scriptores aliquot succedanei contra sectam Waldensium* (Ingolstadt, 1613), pp. 271ff.

[54] Stephen of Bourbon (as above, n. 4), p. 16 'Quos eciam per villas circumiacentes mittebat [*sc.* Valdes] ad predicandum, vilissimorum quorumcumque officiorum. Qui eciam, tam

single element of this description indicates the violation of a social taboo and thus unmasks itself as a social cliché: the contempt for the lower estate, the coming and goings in the villages, the insidious intrusion into families and, last but not least, the preaching by women (which Alain de Lille also flays as an abomination)[55] – this is the world out of joint, described in part with literal allusions to the well-known warnings of St Paul.

Illiteracy is also a sign of a world gone wrong. It was far less easy, however, to dismiss it lightly for, after all, the apostles had also been uneducated people.[56] For their part, the Waldensians seem to have been influenced by this side of the apostolic model in their preferences. It is striking that the statements of Raymund de Costa, the materials stemming from Peter Zwicker, and the protocols of the Bohemian interrogations all regard virtues such as a decent family background, good behaviour and, above all, chastity as criteria of the suitability for acceptance in the circle of the brethren and advancement in the hierarchy, but never make reference to any special education requirements.[57]

This fits in with the report of Raymund de Costa, which suggests that the educational standard reached by the Waldensian brethren, and even by the *majorales*, was rather modest. Asked why they based their preaching and exegesis on the bible in the vernacular rather than in Latin, Raymund answers: 'quia non omnes sunt clerici vel laici, sed commixti' (because they are not all either clerical/learned nor lay, but are mixed).[58] This statement requires interpretation. I follow Clanchy's view that a distinction of that kind does not mean a distinction between the estates of the clergy and the laity in the strict sense of the words, but between literary education with a knowledge of Latin and oral culture without knowledge of Latin. The vernacular would then be something like a third way, fitting for both groups,

---

homines quam mulieres, idiote et illiterati, per villas discurrentes et demos penetrantes [2 Tim. 3:6] et in plateis predicantes [cf. Luke 12:3] et eciam in ecclesiis, ad idem alios provocabant.'

55 See above, n. 48.

56 See Acts 4:13. See also Schreiner, 'Laienbildung', pp. 264ff. and n. 21 on the apostolic state of being *idiota et illiteratus* as something praiseworthy, for example in Francis of Assisi's description of himself.

57 For Raymund de Costa: cf. the interrogatory register of Fournier, pp. 59, 71, Merlo, 'Sul Valdismo "Colto"', pp. 77ff. For materials from Peter Zwicker's circle: see Friess, 'Patarener, Begharden und Waldenser', pp. 257ff.; for Bohemia, see Patschovsky, *Quellen*, p. 250.

58 Interrogatory register of Fournier, p. 81.

lay and clerics alike, corresponding to the educational standard of someone like Valdes.

Sometimes the level of literary training seems lower still, even for the *majorales*. At any rate, Raymund de Costa describes the *minister maior* Christian as *ydiota et sine litteris* (an idiot and without letters).[59] Although these are exactly the words used in the Acts of the Apostles to describe Christ's disciples Peter and John,[60] it was by no means Raymund's intention to express his esteem. He wanted rather to illustrate the contrast with Christian's much admired predecessor, who had given him instruction in the bible or, as it is expressed elsewhere, 'in theology', and had made him a deacon.[61]

If then we can take it as a fact that academic education was obviously not particularly popular with the core of the Waldensian community,[62] we can be sure that it scarcely existed at all among the simple believers. Their opponents never tire of emphasising this point, but it can also be found in fact in various protocols of inquisitorial proceedings against the Waldensians. In view of their social composition one could hardly expect anything else. For although far more members of the leading strata of the urban and agrarian population were part of the Waldensian movement than was assumed in the past, the great bulk of their followers neverthe-less came after all from the middle and lower classes in town and country. And as we can safely assume that the literacy of the leading strata of lay society, at least north of the Alps and east of the Rhine, was at best modest until well into the fifteenth century,[63] the lack of such skills, and hence the dominance of oral culture in spiritual education, must have been characteristic of the simple Waldensian believer.

The lack of scholarly academic training did not, however, exclude either an orientation towards textual monuments or the command and transmission of textual knowledge. Quite the contrary: more than one opponent of Waldensianism felt there was something uncanny about the power of the Waldensian mission; and their

---

[59] Fournier, p. 100.   [60] See above, n. 52.   [61] Fournier, pp. 99, 121.

[62] Further references are Ermengaud, Abbot of St-Gilles, *EFV* 155f. and material of the inquisition of Peter Zwicker, ed. Friess, 'Paterener, Begharden und Waldenser', pp. 578ff. The attitude of hostility towards education was, moreover, not specifically Waldensian; see Schreiner, 'Laienbildung', pp. 264ff.

[63] See Peter Moraw, *Von offener Verfassung zu gestalteter Verdichtung. Das Reich im späten Mittelalter, 1250–1490* (*Propyläen Geschichte Deutschlands* 3, Berlin, 1985), pp. 323ff.

zealous advocacy of an evil cause awakened apocalyptic fear. The best example is the so-called Anonymous of Passau, a cleric and almost certainly a Dominican, who provides an illuminating account of the Waldensians in his diocese based on his own experience. He names six causes for the spread of heresies, by which he means, in particular, Waldensianism. One reason is

because all of them, men and women, big and small, learn and teach incessantly, day and night. An artisan who works during the day learns and teaches at night. Such is their eagerness to learn that they scarcely have time to pray. They also teach and learn without books. They also teach in the leper houses. Even a disciple who has been with them for only seven days searches for someone he can teach, like one fold of the curtain pulling the next. If one of them makes excuses, saying he cannot learn, they say to him 'Learn just one word each day and after a year you will know three hundred; in this way you will make progress.' I have personally heard a believer tell of a certain heretic, whom I also knew, who swam to him on a winter's night across a river called the Ybbs, in order to estrange him from our faith and convert him to his. The lukewarmness of our doctors should make them blush with shame for not spreading the truth of the catholic faith with the same zeal as the faithless Waldensians show in spreading their errors and unbelief![64]

The picture painted here of a community of believers who make certain written testimonies of canonical validity the exclusive content of their missionary message, who have them disseminated by their preachers and try to commit them to memory themselves can be encountered frequently throughout the entire period we are investigating.[65] The descriptions incidentally inform us of typical details of oral reception and transmission. Stephen of Bourbon, for example, mentions a tendency to present a series of quotations rather than making a systematic presentation under a controlling

---

[64] Anonymous of Passau, *De causis heresum*, ed. Patschovsky and Selge, pp. 7of. 'Heresis sex cause sunt ... Secunda est, quia omnes: viri et femine, parvi et magni, nocte et die non cessant discere et docere. Operarius in die laborans, nocte discit vel docet. Ideo parum orant propter studium. Docent eciam et discunt sine libris. Docent eciam in domibus leprosorum ... Item discipulus septem dierum alium querit quem doceat, "ut cortina cortinam trahat". Qui excusat se, quod non possit discere, dicunt ei: "Disce cottidie unum verbum, et post annum scies trecenta, et sic proficies!" Audivi ex ore credentis cuiusdam, quod quidam hereticus – quem eciam novi – ad hoc tantum, ut eum a fide nostra averteret et ad suam perverteret, nocte hyemali tempore per aquam, que dicitur Ibis, natavit ad ipsum. Erubescat negligencia fidelium doctorum, qui non sic zelant catholice fidei veritatem, sicut perfidi Leoniste zelant infidelitatis errorem!' Stephen of Bourbon tells us a similar story. See below, p. 132.

[65] Stephen of Bourbon (1230s), ed. Patschovsky and Selge, pp. 47–8.

idea.[66] The view that the scriptures are a treasury of precious gems rather than a functionally defined object of critical interpretation points in the same direction.[67]

Above all, the number of examples is legion which tell of rote learning of the bible and its transmission. Much of this can be dismissed as a rhetorical *topos*, like the effective technique of contrasting the simplicity of a person with the wealth of his biblical knowledge. But the accounts obviously also reveal authentic details of Waldensian piety. Stephen of Bourbon, for example, tells of a cowherd who had acquired an astounding knowledge of the bible in a year, achieved, among other things, by committing to memory all the forty evangelical pericopes which he heard at the Sunday services in a Waldensian household. The cowherd may well be a *topos*, but the supposed source of his wisdom does not arouse suspicion. It permits us to conclude that regular services took place in private households, which must have been held by the heads of households who belonged to the class of *credentes*, as the wandering preachers cannot have remained in one place over a longer period of time.[68]

Whoever exceeds his competence will inevitably be called to book for meddling in other people's business if he makes a slip. Consequently there is no lack of examples of mistranslations of passages in the bible. To quote the Anonymous of Passau:

And because laymen are uneducated they interpret the Scriptures falsely and corruptly: for example they translate John 1:11 'Sui eum non receperunt' as 'The pigs/sows did not accept him', confusing *sui*, 'his own', with *sues*, 'the pigs/sows'. Again, Psalm 67:30 'Increpa feras arundinis', 'Rebuke the Beast of the Reeds', is translated as 'Refele diu tier der swalwem' (which presumably means 'Rebuke the Beast of the swallows'), confusing *arundo* with *hirundo* ('reed' with 'swallow').[69]

On the other hand, their confident command of the bible, which was said to be superior to the biblical knowledge available to some scholars, and which they used for propaganda purposes, was recog-

---

[66] Stephen of Bourbon, ed. Patschovsky and Selge, p. 48.

[67] Anonymous of Passau, ed. Patschovsky and Selge, p. 75. See also Pseudo-David of Augsburg, ed. Preger, *Der Tractat*, pp. 213ff.

[68] Stephen of Bourbon, *De septem donis spiritus sancti*, ed. Patschovsky and Selge, p. 48.

[69] Anonymous of Passau, *De causis heresum*, ed. Patschovsky and Selge, p. 71: 'Et quia sunt layci ydiote, false et corrupte scripturam exponunt, ut Io. 1°: "Sui" – id est porci – "eum non receperunt", *sui* dicentes pro *sues*. Et in psalmo: "Increpa feras arundinis", dicunt: *Refele diu tier der swalwem, yrundinis* pro *arundinis*.'

nised as enviously as its significance was played down.[70] A good example is provided by Pseudo-David of Augsburg, who sees their knowledge of the bible as evidence of arrogance:

All of their pride resides in the uniqueness they see in the superiority of their knowledge, because they are capable of reciting a few words from the Gospels and the canonical letters off by heart in the vernacular. In this they feel themselves to be superior not only to our laymen but also to our scholars, idiots who are incapable of recognising that a twelve-year-old schoolboy knows a hundred times more than a sixty-year old teacher of heresy, because the one only knows what has been inculcated by permanent repetition, whereas the other has a philological training which enables him to read a thousand books in Latin and to understand their meaning in all possible ways.[71]

Such reports do not necessarily have to be taken literally. Allowances must also be made for rhetorical effects and literary function. Stephen of Bourbon wants to present instructive examples; Pseudo-David and the Anonymous of Passau do not merely wish to provide documentation but to rouse their contemporaries from their apathy. In view of this function of the reports of our non-Waldensian informants, therefore, a good dose of scepticism towards them is called for. Consequently, in assessing the reports on the supposedly inferior quality of the translations circulating among the Waldensians, we must remind ourselves that the bible was translated for Valdes by 'catholic' clerics of orthodox faith, so that it is unlikely that the Waldensian vernacular versions were significantly different in quality from those used in the established church. The view that the Waldensians were well versed in the bible, however, seems plausible. This is evident enough from the fearful respect this knowledge engendered. Furthermore, the Anonymous of Passau reports in various passages of his work: 'They feign the behaviour of the faithful, attend church, offer sacrifice, confess, go to communion and listen to sermons, but only to discredit the preacher'; and again 'For

---

[70] Anonymous of Passau. Chapter on 'Recruitment methods of the Waldensians', ed. Patschovsky and Selge p. 76.

[71] Pseudo-David c. 13, ed. Preger, *Der Tractat*, p. 212 'Omnis gloriacio eorum est de singularitate, quod videntur sibi pre ceteris scioli, quod aliqua ewangelii verba vel epistolarum sciunt corde vulgariter recitare. In hoc preferunt se nostris non solum laycis sed eciam literatis, stulti, non intelligentes, quod sepe puer XII annorum scolaris cencies plus scit quam magister hereticorum LX annorum, dum iste sola illa scit, que usu corde affirmavit, ille vero per artem grammaticam mille libros scit legere Latine et ad literam intelligere quoquo modo.'

if the preacher says anything that he cannot prove from the Old or
New Testament, they call such preaching a lie.'[72]

v

A careful investigation of the evidence from the pens of the opponents of Waldensianism, together with the insights gained from
genuinely Waldensian sources, leads us to the following overall
picture of Waldensian literacy. The relationship of the Waldensian
religious community as a whole to literacy turns out to be surpris-
ingly complex, varying considerably in different times and places.
Its fundamental inspiration is, of course, the bible, and particularly
the gospels and the epistles. But the principle of *sola scriptura* seems to
form the basis of Waldensian piety only in as far as it corresponds, in
an oral culture, to an orientation on sacrosanct canonical texts
which are mechanically recited but not reflected upon. However,
this kind of strict biblicism was only characteristic of the simple
members of the community, but not of the preaching brethren.
Although they flirted with the apostolic attribute of illiteracy, the
spiritual and organisational elite of the community was literate, and
sometimes even highly literate. The educational level of the Waldensian preacher can scarcely have been inferior to that of the
founder of the community. And although it did not compare with
the level of intellectual ability and knowledge to be found among
trained theologians, it can by no means be equated with the intellectual horizons evidenced by the oral culture of lay society.

However, the dichotomy between the intellectual horizons of the
leaders of the movement and the simple adherents is not the actual
cause of the complexity of Waldensian attitudes towards literacy.
This lies rather in the obviously ambivalent approach of the leading
stratum towards education based on books. At the beginning of the
movement the difference from the 'catholic' side is not recognisable,
especially when the Franciscans and even the Dominicans in the
early phase of their development are taken as a point of comparison.
What mattered was the emulation of the apostles, and this required

---

[72] Anonymous of Passau, ed. Patschovsky and Selge, p. 74, 'Item ad ecclesiam ficte vadunt et
offerunt et confitentur et communicant et predicacioni intersunt – sed ut predicantem
capiant in sermone'; p. 72, 'Quinta causa est insufficiencia doctrine quorundam, qui
predicant quandoque frivola vel falsa. Unde quidquid ecclesie doctor docet, quod per
textum novi testamenti non probat, hoc totum pro fabulis habent.'

poverty as a postulate for the way of living and mission for the way of acting. However, mission in the form of the conversion of heretics did, of course, require theological training, just as it involved disputation as the intellectual form of articulation. But there seems to be very little trace of such assumptions in later Waldensianism, even in the top ranks. The polemical and apologetic writings associated with the *Liber electorum* do not provide a refutation of this conclusion. Quite the contrary. We are obviously dealing here with an *ad hoc* event, which was by no means part of an ongoing debate rooted in some tradition or other of literary controversy. It is probably not just a case of stereotyped and abstract polemics divorced from reality, when Peter Zwicker, criticising the Waldensian contempt for university education as the characteristic feature of academic intellectuality in his anti-Waldensian tract, points out that the apostle Paul had not merely preached but also participated in disputations, 'But you, Waldensian heretic, seldom or never enter into a dispute!'[73] This would probably have been a rather risky thing to do anyway, but the way in which works in the style of a Durand of Osca or the letter of the Lombard brethren peter out suggests that the entire genre of polemical writing involving literary argument and justification was no longer cultivated in the later period of Waldensianism.

This points to a consolidation of the movement, but also to stagnation. The Waldensianism of the later period is as sympathetically simple in its pious way of life as it is intellectually unassuming in its spiritual manifestations. A child of the reforming and social dynamics of the twelfth century in its early phase, Waldensianism became a sect in which even the leading circles were intellectually anaemic. The light of literacy, which, in the early period, had illuminated Waldensianism no less than its ultimately triumphant 'catholic' rival, flickered and failed among the leaders of the movement; it never went out completely, but it never enjoyed any particular prestige and consequently failed to stimulate a productive activity which might have moulded the movement in some way. It cannot be denied that literacy, at least of a rudimentary kind, was always present, but its primary purpose was to serve as an instrument for the mediation of canonised texts to adherents whose socio-

---

[73] Peter Zwicker, 'Cum dormirent homines', pp. 271f.: 'Sed tu, Waldensis heretice, raro vel nunquam venis ad disputandum!'

cultural environment was oral. When the process of emancipation from the established church and the internal developmental struggles were over, the written word was repeated parrot fashion, but no longer applied in discourse. This led to a high degree of unanimity, both within the movement and against its external enemies, which was probably necessary if Waldensianism were to survive at all. Admittedly, it survived at a rather low level, which could lead to disaster, if the Waldensian leaders who acquired their academic training in the educational establishments of their religious enemies were affected by their point of view, intellectual methods and breadth of knowledge to such an extent that the plain and simple literacy of the Waldensians also appeared to them not as an apostolic virtue but as pure asinity.[74]

[74] Peter Zwicker, see above, n. 53.

CHAPTER 8

The Waldensian books

Anne Brenon

This chapter will consider the Occitan language manuscripts traditionally known as the 'Waldensian collections' of Cambridge,
Dublin, Geneva and elsewhere. 'The Waldensian books' will refer
here only to the Romance texts, which will be examined from an
inclusive point of view, without any regard to the effects of chance
on documentary survival. The approach is based on a study of two
dozen manuscripts which make up these collections, a study which I
began many years ago and have continued since.[1] Recent research
and publications on the subject have confirmed the conclusions of
this work.[2]

In the desire to avoid the impasse of the idea of individual

For Jacques Monfrin

[1] A. Jolliot-Brenon (later A. Brenon), 'Les livres des Vaudois' (unpublished thesis, Ecole des
Chartes, Paris, 1970), vol. I: 'Les manuscrits vaudois', vol. II: 'La literature vaudoise' – copies
deposited at the Bibliothèque de l'Ecole des Chartes (Paris) and the Centre National des
Etudes Cathares (Villegly); 'Les manuscrits littéraires vaudois, présentation d'ensemble',
Cultura Neolatina 38 (1978), 105–28; 'Localisation des manuscrits vaudois', in G. P. Clivio and
G. G. Queirazza (eds.), *Lingue e dialetti nell'arco alpino occidentale* (Turin, 1978 = *Atti del
Convegno Internazionale di Torino, 12–14 Aprile 1976, Centro studi piemontesi*), pp. 193–203.

[2] The approach followed in this chapter is not as opposed as it might appear to the approach
adopted by a team of Italian scholars and philologists under the direction of E. Balmas and
M. Dal Corso, when studying and editing the 'Waldensian collection' of Geneva in the
series *ATV*, for publication by Claudiana in Turin. In fact, the editors of the Geneva
collection themselves reject the idea of 'collection'; see L. Borghi Cedrini (ed.), *Vertuz e altri
scritti (manoscritto GE 206)* (Turin, 1984 = *ATV* 2), pp. xlvi ff. So far two manuscripts have
been published in the *ATV* series: Ge 9 by A. Degan Checchini, *Il Vergier de Cunsollacion e
altri scritti (manoscritto GE 209)* (Turin, 1979 = *ATV* 1), and Ge 206 by Borghi Cedrini,
Vertuz. Among modern editions one should note that of Carpentras MS. 9 by H.-R. Nüesch,
Altwaldensische Bibelübersetzung. Manuskript Nr.8 der Bibliothèque municipale Carpentras (Bern,
1979 = *Romanica Helvetica* 92A–B), and that of the Bestiary by A. M. Raugei, *Bestiario
Valdese* (Florence, 1984 = *Biblioteca dell'Archivum Romanicum'* series 1, *Storia–Letteratura–
Paleografia* 175). I have published the six texts of the treatise *Las Tribulacions*, from all the
manuscripts, as follows: text A in *Heresis* 1 (1983), 25–31; text B in *Heresis*, 2 (1984), 21–33;
texts C–E in *Heresis* 3 (1984), 35–43; text F in *Heresis* 4 (1985), 25–36. I have also published
the three sermons *Judici*, again from all the manuscripts, in *Heresis* 9 (1987), 11–32.

'Waldensian collections', I will approach the texts as a single group. This will do no violence to the facts, as the texts all derive from the same pivotal period in which the Waldensian communities opened themselves to the new and radical thought of the Hussites and Taborites of Bohemia, and to the first Reformers.

This was something that could hardly have happened without recourse to some degree of theological reflection, to a certain book-ishness in the Waldensian culture. From its very beginnings, in fact, from the last third of the twelfth century, and before even having been rejected by the Roman church, the Waldensian movement had, to some extent, the character of a literate culture.

I THE WALDENSIAN BOOKS

There is a corpus of Waldensian literature which is recognisable by its common origin, language, form and content. It is dispersed among several European libraries, in small collections or isolated manuscripts. For present purposes we will consider only those volumes in Occitan coming from the Waldensian valleys of Pied-mont. These amount to twenty-four collections of scriptural, literary and moral texts. Excluded are two volumes kept at Dublin which are in fact Latin collections of various judicial pieces concerning the Italian Waldensians,[3] and a manuscript in Zürich which is nothing more than a late copy of the *Nobla Leyçon*.[4]

Of these twenty-four books, for which I have added an appendix of references and sigla, six are held in the University Library at Cambridge, and are traditionally known under the sigla Ca A–F. Nine are to be found in the library of Trinity College Dublin, and they are designated Du 258–64, Du 267, Du 269. Five are held in the Bibliothèque Publique et Universitaire of Geneva: Ge 6–9 and Ge 9a. There is one at the Bibliothèque Municipale at Dijon: Di; one at the Bibliothèque Municipale of Carpentras: Car; one in the Biblio-thèque Municipale of Grenoble: Gre; and one in the Zentralbiblio-thek of Zürich: Zü.

Although the collection of correspondence and theological debates which the Waldensians exchanged with Bucer and Oeco-lampadius at the time of the Reformation (Du 259) is only slightly

---

[3] These are the Dublin TCL manuscripts formerly with the sigla C.1.6. and C.4.18, now 265–6.
[4] Zürich, Zentralbibliothek, Simmler Collection Ms. 590.

removed from this coherent library, discussion of it is confined to Paravy's chapter below (ch. 9). Paralleling this set of documents is the near contemporary collection of exchanges between the same Waldensians and the Bohemian Brethren (Du 262). At the other end of the chronological scale is the Du 269 collection, which has an archaic and Catharist character.

It is striking, however, that there is no other evidence in the rest of Europe of a religious Waldensian literature with the exception of a few Occitan New Testaments preserved in the Bibliothèque Nationale in Paris, which could be of Waldensian origin;[5] the Latin text of a *Liber electorum*, emanating from the Piedmontese Waldensians, which has survived in an Occitan version (see plates 7 and 8);[6] and finally the correspondence which took place in the second half of the fourteenth century between the Waldensian brethren of the valleys and the Austrian Waldensians, grouped around John Leser, who had recently converted to catholicism.[7] The theological propositions in these exchanges can be useful in throwing light on the meaning of several of the texts we are going to consider.

Origins

The Piedmontese and Waldensian origins of the literature that concerns us here is confirmed by the detailed accounts of two of the earliest historians of Waldensianism. These men had these manuscripts in their hands, used them, described them and collaborated with one another to preserve them. Jean Léger, pastor of Saint Jean

---

[5] See the studies of these by S. Berger, 'Les bibles provençales et vaudoises', *Romania* 18 (1889), 353–422, and P. Wunderli, *Die okzitanischen Bibelübersetzungen des Mittelalters. Gelösten und ungelösten Fragen* (Frankfurt, 1969 = *Analecta Romanica* 24). Several categories of texts are not at issue here: (i) the early Waldensian translations and texts discussed by Patschovsky, chapter 7 above; (ii) texts, attested by references in inquisitors' treatises, which have not survived (see, for example, Gui's reference to a lost or no longer identifiable compendium, Gui, *Manuel*, vol. 1, p. 54); (iii) texts which have not survived or are no longer identifiable whose existence is implied by reference in trials – for example, probably German vernacular books used in preaching (see examples cited in P. P. A. Biller, '*Multum ieiunantes et se castigantes*: medieval Waldensian asceticism', *SCH* 22 (1985), 220, n. 25); (iv) the German *Codex Teplensis*, the alleged Waldensian nature of whose contents produced indecisive controversy in the late nineteenth century, references to which are given in A. A. Hugon and G. Gonnet, *Bibliografia Valdese*, *BSSV* 93 (1953), 110–11, nos. 1312, 1318–21, 1323.

[6] The *Liber Electorum*, which was edited by Biller, 'Aspects', pp. 264–70, is predated by a letter of 1368 which cites it. Biller suggests a probable date of composition between *c.* 1335 and *c.* 1350. The Occitan version is in Ca A, fols. 236r–40r.

[7] See the study and edition of this correspondence by Biller, 'Aspects', pp. 223–63, 271–353.

in the Val Luserna and moderator of the Valley Churches, published at Leiden in 1669 his *Histoire générale des églises évangéliques des vallées de Piémont ou vaudoises.* On pages 21–3 he describes in detail the books of the Cambridge collection and adds that it was he who, with his brother Antoine, also a pastor, 'handed over [the books] to Mr. Morland, special representative of my Lord Oliver Cromwell, protector of Great Britain'. It was this same Morland who donated the books to the University of Cambridge in August 1658.

Jean Paul Perrin, another pastor of the valleys, published at Geneva in 1618 two volumes under the titles *Histoire des Vaudois* and *Histoire des Chrestiens albigeois.* In the first he used as a source several books which had been sent to him by the Synod of the Valleys, and which had been collected by Dominique Vignaux, another pastor. On pages 55–8 of the first book of his *Histoire des Vaudois,* he described these books in great detail and they can easily be identified with the Dublin manuscripts.[8] One can also recognise with near certainty at least three of the Geneva manuscripts (Ge 6, Ge 8 and Ge 9) among the manuscript books used and described by Perrin.

If we add the fact that one of the other Genevan books carries the words 'Ce livre appartient aux Eglises du Piemont qui prient les Genevois de le leur conserver' (this book belongs to the Churches of Piedmont, who ask the Genevans to keep it safe),[9] and that several other volumes retained various inscriptions, dedications and signatures from their Waldensian owners in the valleys,[10] the geographical origins of these books cannot be questioned any more than the Waldensian character of their contents. It is important to underline the deliberate and concerted action of sixteenth- and seventeenth-century protestantism in collecting and preserving these 'witnesses' to the evangelism of the Waldensians of the valleys. It should also be noted that some books, such as the Dijon manuscript or the bibles at Carpentras and Grenoble, are closely linked to the Waldensian library though their external characteristics and their contents, even though their provenance and tradition are not known.

General characteristics

Immediately striking points about these bibles, sermons and moral treatises are the homogeneity of their external appearance and their

---

[8] Du 258, 267, 260, 262, 261, 263, 259. See Brenon, 'Localisation', pp. 196–7.
[9] Ge 7. See Brenon, 'Localisation', p. 198.   [10] Brenon, 'Localisation', pp. 199–200.

'pocket' format. It is true that the largest of the manuscripts, some of the bibles, can reach 20 by 15 cm, or thereabouts (Du 258 is 20.4 by 15.3 cm but the Grenoble bible only 17.8 by 11.8 cm). However, for the most part they hardly exceed 10 by 7 or 8 cm; Ca A is 10 by 7.3 cm (see plate 8), while Ca C is no more than 9 by 6 cm, and Ca D only 8.8 by 6.5 cm. All volumes are small and written in almost every case in long lines with rubrics. Only the bibles were written in two columns.

The manuscripts are varied in their physical characteristics. Ten are parchment, fourteen paper, both groups showing the same sobriety in their decoration. Of the parchment books four bibles or New Testament collections stand out: Mss. Ca F, Du 258, Car and Gre are of particularly fine workmanship with even writing, large gilt and brightly coloured illuminated initials at the beginning of every text, alternating red and blue initials at chapter headings, the text framed with stylised floral motifs and the folios numbered with red Roman numerals. The Dublin bible, dating from 1522, is somewhat simpler. Nevertheless, there can be no doubt that the Waldensian bibles, with the exception of the example in Zürich, display a very traditional appearance at the heart of the Waldensian library.

The paper manuscripts, like the six or seven collections of treatises on parchment, have a distinctly duller appearance and more restrained decoration. They are much more clearly set apart from the standard format of medieval books. Their writing in long lines is often rudimentary and careless, sometimes even clumsy. Only the titles, initials and running titles, where they exist, are rubricated. Mss. Ca A (see plate 8) Ca C and Di do, however have a finer hand than the rest of the group, while Di and Du 260 even have some decorated initials. However, these are minor qualifications to the generally homogeneous appearance of these Waldensian books.

Language, script, abbreviations

The fundamental unity of these manuscripts becomes even clearer when we consider their language and script. The cement of Waldensian literature was, above all, the language in which it was written. Despite the variety of ways in which it was written down, this was a completely unified language and closely identifiable with the north Occitan dialects of the Alpine region. The remarkable linguistic

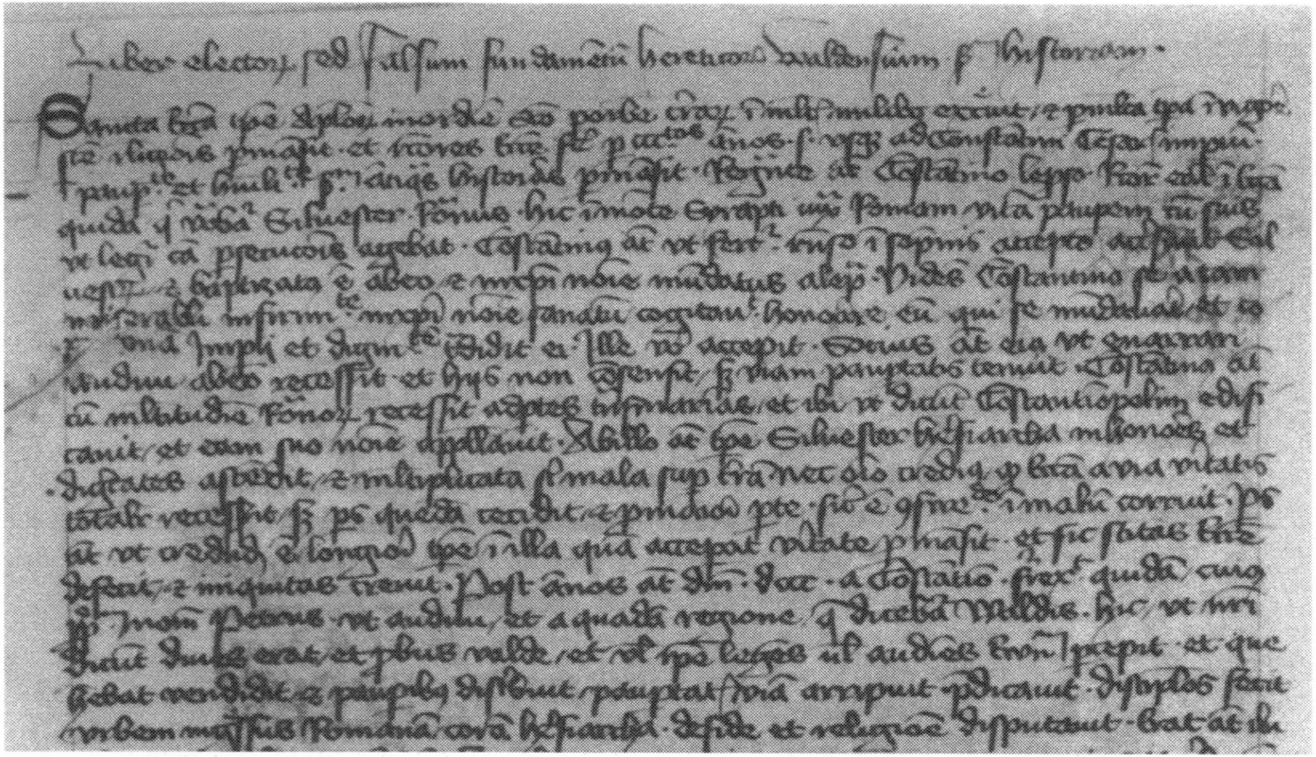

Plate 7 The beginning of a Waldensian historical text which was written before 1368. It circulated in a Latin version among Waldensians of German-speaking areas, and this is the only manuscript which has its title, *Liber Electorum* (Book of the Elect). Linz, Bundesstaatliche Studienbibliothek Ms. 292 (63), fol. 7v. (With permission of the Bundesstaatliche Studienbibliothek, Linz.)

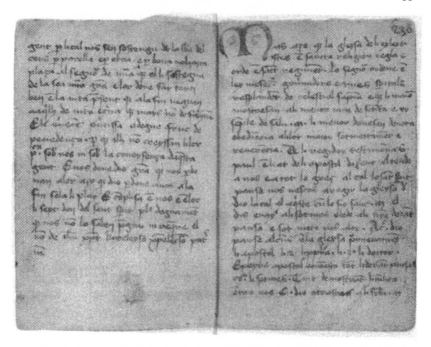

Plate 8   On the recto leaf, the beginning of the *Liber Electorum* (see plate 7) in the dialect, and in a manuscript, of the Waldensians who lived in the Alps between Piedmont and the Dauphiné. Note the tininess of the manuscript, which is reproduced here size for size. Cambridge, University Library, Ms. Dd.15.29, fols. 235v–236r. (By permission of the Syndics of Cambridge University Library.)

homogeneity which unifies the different Waldensian collections led Morosi, in 1890, to suggest that they were written in a koiné, a literary and somewhat artificial language distinct from the fluid and evolving dialects of the populations of the valleys, in effect 'the official language of the congregation'.[11]

I have already published a study of the main types of variants found in the twenty-four Waldensian books, together with a table of the main types of abbreviations used by their copyists.[12] I need only repeat here that the Waldensian system of abbreviation appears to be as uniform and flexible as the language they used.

Standard abbreviations and their signs were inherited from abbreviations of academic works, for example sbia = substantia,

[11] 'La lingua "officiale" della congregazione'; cited by Borghi Cedrini, *Vertuz*, p. xlvii.
[12] Brenon, 'Livres des Vaudois', vol. II, pp. 110, 115–20.

mia = misericordia, snia = sententia (the signs of abbreviations are
not reproduced here, but see plate 8, for examples of them). One
finds these mixed with home-made abbreviations and their signs,
such as endegna = endegnacion, or mesc°secza = mesconeisencza,
where the Latin system is adapted to the needs of the Occitan text.

This uniformity of these manuscripts, both internal and external,
prompted Balmas, who was concerned only with the Geneva collection, to raise the problem of the workshop or workshops which
produced them.[13] I am not so sure that one can see the hand of
professional or specialist copyists, but there is still a problem. Of a
small format, plain decoration, often hastily produced, all in the
same language and showing, for the most part, the technical characteristics typical of the scriptorial culture of the later middle ages:
what milieu produced such manuscripts? Clearly, a grasp of the
conditions in which these volumes were manufactured would
greatly help our understanding of the medieval Waldensians.

The problems of dating

There has been hypothesis upon hypothesis on the dating of these
manuscripts. Borghi Cedrini, in an excellent philological and
linguistic analysis of Mss. Ge 6 and Ge 9 in the introduction to her
edition of *Vertucz e altri scritti*,[14] gives a perfect synopsis of the
numerous interpretations. I am entirely in agreement with her in
seeing these manuscripts as witnesses to a single chronological
period in which the deposit of Waldensian literary traditions was
organised and clarified.

The dates traditionally ascribed, based either on formal indications of the date or the contents of the texts, range from the
fourteenth century for the parchment bibles until well into the
sixteenth century in the case of the latest collections on paper.
The uniformity of the manuscripts suggests a close chronology for
the production of the library. The exact dating of several of the books
– four volumes in Dublin are from the years 1520, 1522, 1523 and
1524, one at Cambridge from 1530 and another successively bears
the dates 1519, 1520 and 1522 – gives us a very precise chronological
reference point.[15]

[13] Balmas and Dal Corso, pp. 8–9.   [14] Borghi Cedrini, *Vertuz*, pp. xli–xlix.
[15] Brenon, 'Livres des Vaudois', vol. II, p. 109.

There is no doubt, then, that this corpus of texts represents the state of Waldensian literature at the very end of the middle ages, at the moment when Waldensian communities were opening themselves to the Reformation and to the modern world. Some of the books are more or less archaic. The parchment bibles, for example, have a truly classical medieval appearance and could have been copied several decades earlier than the collections of treatises and sermons on paper, or perhaps produced by another more 'professional' scriptorium. Some others clearly belong to a slightly later period: the middle of the sixteenth century in the case of Du 259, Du 262, Ge 8 and Ge 9, the second half of the sixteenth century for Ge 9a, and the beginning of the seventeenth for Du 264.

In all probability, the nuances of theological interpretation noted by Montet in different manuscripts of the same treatise do not indicate, as he thought, the order in which the manuscripts were produced, but merely the diversity of the Waldensian traditions which these manuscripts contained. In fact, Montet himself had already noted that none of the manuscripts is an original, and that what we have are copies of lost originals.

The only manuscript in the Waldensian collection which carries a date clearly divergent from the 1520–30 range, or from the sixteenth century in general, is Du 269. Dated by an Easter table for the year 1376, it is written in a language distinctly different from the Occitan of the Waldensian library. Thirty years ago Venckeleer identified a fragment of a Cathar ritual in it, establishing that it was not a Waldensian book.[16]

2 THE RELIGIOUS LITERATURE OF THE WALDENSIANS

The homogeneity of the Waldensian library, already clear to the external observer, reveals itself fully to the attentive reader of the texts it contains. The small number of Latin texts will not be discussed here. They are generically similar to the Occitan corpus – an interesting indication of the co-existence of Latin with the Romance vernacular in the dissemination of Waldensian culture.

The twenty-four volumes of this collection are made up of five

---

[16] T. Venckeleer, 'Un Recueil cathare, le manuscrit A.6.10 de la collection vaudoise de Dublin', *RBPH* 38 (1960), 815–34, and 39 (1961), 759–92. See also A. Brenon, 'Syncrétisme hérétique dans les refuges alpins? Un livre cathare parmi les recueils vaudois de la fin du Moyen Age: le manuscrit 269 de Dublin', *Heresis* 7 (1986), 5–23.

bibles (Car, Ca F, Du 258, Gre and Zü), fifteen collections of
sermons and moral treatises (Ca A, B, C and D, Di, Du 267, 264,
261, 260, 263, Ge 6, 7, 8, 9 and 9a), a fragment of Cathar ritual (Du
269), one scholarly collection (Ca E), and two collections of theological exchanges with the Hussites (Du 262), and the early
reformers (Du 259).

Waldensian religious literature itself is divided into scriptural
texts (predominantly New Testament), moral and dogmatic
sermons and treatises in prose and verse, and finally sermons of a
liturgical character.

Characteristics and difficulties

When, at the end of my work on the Waldensian manuscripts, I
drew up a general table of all the texts which made up this literature, I was able to list almost ninety treatises and more than 200
different sermons. All these texts had been copied and recopied,
usually with variants in different manuscripts and of course in
different collections of manuscripts – something which detracts from
the value of studying a single Waldensian manuscript, isolated from
its family. The majority of these texts are still unpublished.[17]

The first point to be made is that the religious literature of the
Waldensians is, in itself, a genre. All the texts have a common spirit
and style, It is a simple literature, essentially evangelical and moral,
even moralising, and of a markedly oral character. The texts are
permeated with a latent anxiety about the Last Judgement, and the
morality of the sermons and treatises, which concentrate on the
necessity of good works, virtuous behaviour and the avoidance of
capital sin, is entirely directed towards the goal of personal salvation.

It is often difficult to distinguish between the sermons and
treatises. In essence, the sermons are commentaries on passages of
scripture intended for use in preaching. They usually open with a
liturgical reference and a quotation, abbreviated or *in extenso*, of the
chosen piece of scripture, which is then developed at varying length.
Numerous sermons, however, contain no liturgical references, and
there are some treatises based on biblical texts. The treatises usually
have a title, but quite often they do not, and the sermons can also

---

[17] See n. 2.

have titles. The style and the themes are the same. It is often the case
that a treatise does not restrict itself to the opening theme but strays
off, following associated ideas, while it is equally possible for a
sermon to restrict itself to comment on a single word or idea from the
selected text. The subject matter and the methods of its development
are the same. For example, we are dealing with seven different
treatises or sermons on the subject of marriage.

The entanglement of these texts with one another is total. Each
anthology volume gives the impression of having been copied for
pastoral or preaching purposes. All are relatively late copies of a
single, or several, lost originals. There are discrepancies in the texts
from one volume to another, and even contradictions. The contrary
also occurs: by a process of collage, the superimposition of one text
on another, sudden relationships are thrown up between ideas
which would have no connection in another context. Analysis of the
contents confirms what linguistic analysis has already suggested. For
the most part these pieces represent different versions of the same
text; chronologically, they fall within the 1520–30 margin, and they
differ from one another only in their particular traditions. As we
shall see, their common roots can go back to the fourteenth or even
thirteenth century.

It is therefore a delicate business, and perhaps imprudent to
attempt, as Montet did in 1885, to write a literary history of the
Waldensians on the basis of these books, and to establish the chronology of the texts on a reconstituted intellectual chronology of
Waldensian doctrinal development. It is safer to restrict ourselves,
for the time being, to an empirical observation of the literature and
to ask what we can learn about the Waldensians from their books,
rather that what we can learn about the books from what we think
we know about the Waldensians.[18]

Translations of Biblical texts

The five Waldensian bibles are New Testaments, usually with a few
fragments of the Old Testament attached.

The Cambridge bible contains chapter 6 of Proverbs, chapters 5
and 6 of the Wisdom of Solomon, and an incomplete New Testa-

---

[18] What follows is based on vol. II of my unpublished thesis, 'Livres des Vaudois'. Contrast the
approach in E. Montet, *Histoire littéraire des Vaudois du Piémont* (Paris, 1885).

ment. The Carpentras bible contains Proverbs, the Song of Solomon, the Wisdom of Solomon, Ecclesiasticus and a complete New Testament. The Dublin bible contains, apart from the New Testament, Proverbs, Ecclesiastes, Song of Solomon, Wisdom of Solomon and the first twenty-three chapters of Ecclesiasticus. The Zürich bible contains only the New Testament.

Several isolated Old Testament fragments can be found in various other Waldensian manuscripts: in Ca A (Gen. 1:1–9, 29), in Ca B (the seven pentitential Psalms), in Ca C (2Mac. 7:5–41; chapters 1, 2, 3 and 42 of Job; the entirety of Tobit), in Di (Eccli. 30:22–31:11 and Eccli. 33:19–24), in Du 267 (Wis. 5:1–6). Mss. Ca B and Ca E also contain a few scriptural extracts in Latin.

There is clearly a strong preference for the New Testament over the Old, and, from the Old Testament, for the sapiential books. It is also notable that the vocabulary of the Occitan versions suggests a sort of harking after Latinity – this feature becomes very obvious when one compares these texts with the Cathar New Testament at Lyons (Ms. Pa 36). There are several readings which are exclusive to the Waldensian versions: *Filh de la Vergena* for *Filius hominis, pena* for *gehenna*, or *lo Filh* for *Verbum*.[19]

These facts might give too strong an impression that the Old Testament was neglected by the Waldensians. There were, however, several works preserved in other parts of the collection which made use of it. There is a biblical reckoner for calculating the variable feast days, a table of references to the parables, the use of prophetic and apostolic texts to illustrate the articles of the faith and, finally, in Ms. Ge 7, an *Expositio Canticorum Salomonis*, which explains the symbols of the Song in a very orthodox way, and even takes issue with heresy.

Amongst this collection of scriptural Authorities we can also find numerous compilations of the Fathers and Doctors with titles such as *Crisostimo di, Doctor, De li parlar d'alcuns doctors, Li parlar del philosophe, Philosophus, Versus morales* and the Homilies of John Chrysostom on Matthew. Chrysostom appears to have been particularly prized by the Waldensians. Two collections are devoted to his work and one can find many references to him in the majority of Waldensian treatises and sermons. He appears randomly throughout the five other compilation volumes in the company of the Fathers and

---

[19] See A. Brenon, Survivances "cathares" dans les manuscrits vaudois du XVe siècle', *CaF* 20 (1985), 142–3.

Doctors as well as Greek philosophers and Latin thinkers led by Aristotle and Seneca.

Lectionaries and liturgy

The Waldensian library includes three books which conform strictly to the idea of a lectionary, that is, tables of epistles and gospels for the Sundays of the liturgical year. Two of the books have only this schematic arrangement, but the third includes models of 'Sunday' sermons on a considerable number of texts.

Ca B contains, under the title *Trecenas*, the incipits of the epistle and gospel texts for the Sundays of the liturgical year divided into four *trecenas*, or groups of thirteen, running from the first Sunday of Advent. The biblical citations were taken from the Cambridge bible (Ca F).

The Grenoble bible ends with a similar liturgical collection, entitled *Registre de li Evangeli e de las Epistolas*, followed by incipits of the epistle and gospel texts for the whole of the liturgical year, again starting with the first Sunday of Advent, and finally another table of incipits for the feast days of the saints. This lectionary does not refer to the text of the bible which precedes it. It is, in fact, a copy on paper of a Hussite lectionary from Prague and has no connection with the parchment bible with which it is bound.

Ms. Du 267 is almost entirely taken up with the *Epistolas e Avangelis de tot l'an*, which covers fols. 56a–351a. Unlike the other lectionaries, which only give incipits, here the scriptural citations are given in full. The manuscript also contains sermons based on these texts for most of the Sundays and feast days of the liturgical year from the first Sunday of Advent to the fifth Sunday after Pentecost. A significant number of these liturgical sermons can be found out of context in most of the other Waldensian manuscripts.

The interest of these lectionaries and liturgical sermons rests on the questions they force us to ask about how they were used in the communities of the valleys. In this context we should keep in mind Biller's suggestion of a shift in the radicalism of Waldensian opposition to the sacraments in the mid-fourteenth century.[20] Also of importance is the Hussite origin of one of the lectionaries.

In his introduction to the edition of Ge 206, Dal Corso insists on

---

[20] Biller, 'Aspects', p. 226.

the importance of the Waldensian sermons.[21] Whether they are liturgical or informal, they speak eloquently of Waldensian evangelism at the end of the middle ages.

Sermons on scripture

Either as part of the liturgical collection of *Epistolas e Avangelis* or dispersed among the other volumes of the Waldensian library, the model sermons are very largely based on New Testament texts. I have only been able to find nine sermons based on the Old Testament, and these share only seven different texts between them (from Job, Psalms, Ecclesiasticus, Isaiah, Jeremiah, Ezekiel and Zachariah).

By far the most popular of the gospels for Waldensian preachers was Matthew, from which 40 texts are cited in 52 different sermons. Luke follows with 26 texts cited in 42 sermons, then John with 17 texts cited in 20 sermons and Mark with only two texts cited in three different sermons. Of the Epistles, Paul to the Romans was the most frequently chosen with seven texts cited in eight different sermons. The other Pauline Epistles, however, were on an equal footing with James, Peter and John (five texts from 1 Peter, but otherwise one or two texts cited in anything between one to five sermons). If we add the single citations in single sermons of Acts and Apocalypse we have a total of 122 New Testament texts cited in 146 sermons, a frequency out of all proportion with the modest usage of the Old Testament. Waldensian literature, on the point of death as it entered the modern world, still had the evangelical impulse as its most profound characteristic.

We have already noted that many of these scriptural sermons also carried a title and could be found in isolation in other Waldensian volumes. Their tone is for the most part moralising and their themes developed from an eschatological perspective. This is very clear in such sermons as the *Judici*, based on Mt. 24:30 (two versions can be found in Du 263 and Ge 206), the *Vergenas* sermons based on Mt. 24 and 25 (two versions again in Di and Du 267), and the *Ensegnas seren al sollelh e en la luna* based on Luke 21:25–33 (a series of four texts in Du 267). All these weave together the sombre themes of the Last Judgement, the *Filh de la Vergena* (Son of the Virgin) who will come

---

[21] Borghi Cedrini, *Vertuz*, p. xviii.

from the clouds amidst holy signs, and the parable of the wise and foolish virgins.

In a similar way, others series of sermons such as the *Noczas* and the *Del matrimoni*, based on Mt. 22:4 (one example in Ge 6), Luke 14:8 (two versions in Du 263 and Ge 6), Luke 14:16 (two versions in Du 267 and Ge 9), Jo. 2:1–2 (two groups of texts and five different sermons in Du 267, Du 260 and Di) and Heb. 13:4 (a single sermon in Du 267) somewhat laboriously combine biblical commentary with moral instruction and doctrinal argument in favour of the sacrament of marriage. Except for some formal details, these sermons are hardly distinguishable from the *Del matrimoni* series of treatises in Mss. Di, Du 260 and Du 263.

Altogether, the Waldensian sermons provided the models for a preaching which effectively instilled an evangelical confidence into the everyday life of the communities. Their numerical importance and their near ubiquity throughout the Waldensian collection must play a major part in any analysis of the realities of medieval and post-medieval Waldensianism.

Moral and doctrinal texts

The example of the texts on marriage shows that, as sermons and treatises often make use of identical religious themes, they can be used only as very formal categories in Waldensian literature. Under the heading of moral and doctrinal texts, then, I will include all Waldensian literature which develops a religious theme but makes no express reference to preaching. This large category of 'theoretical' texts will include a fair number of sermons, large treatises in the form of theological *summae*, and some small independent texts, sometimes drawn from these *summae*, sometimes without any known derivation.

It would be impossible to treat such a large body of material in detail here. What follows is confined to a discussion of the two principal sources of literary influence on Waldensian texts.

The Waldensian books, copied in the first half of the sixteenth century, have preserved for us several theological *summae*. These treatises, 'univeralist' in character and typically medieval in style, deal with the vices and virtues, the twelve articles of the faith, the ten commandments, the seven sacraments, the twelve punishments of hell and the twelve delights of paradise, the four future things and the six things to honour in this world and so on, all in the manner of the great classical treatises of medieval religious literature.

The *summa* of the *Vergier de Consolacion* is organised in just this way, covering in order the capital sins, other sins, theological and cardinal virtues, other virtues, heaven and hell. The incomplete version of this text which appears in Ms. Ge 9 has been edited in the *ATV*.[22] Other copies exist in Mss. Di (fols. 29a–71a) and Du 264. Similarly with the treatise on *Vertucz* or *Liber virtutum*, which has been edited in *ATV* in its Ge 6 version,[23] but which also appears in Ms. Du 260 (fols. 1a–70b). Ge 6 lists twenty-eight virtues while Du 260 adds the two supplements of *fortalecza* and *perseverancza* (courage and perseverance). The treatment of the first five virtues is cut off in Ge 6. The sequence of the virtues is identical in both texts with the exception of the twenty-first grace, which appears as *satisfacion d'obralh* (the satisfaction of having done good works) in Du 260, and as *penedenza* (penitence) in Ge 6.

Even more 'universalist' are the two *summae* to which I am now turning. The first is the large anonymous and untitled treatise contained in Ms. Ca B, which Montet recognised as an abbreviated Waldensian version of the *Somme le Roi* of Laurent d'Orleans (1279). The second is a long doctrinal treatise, also anonymous and untitled, but christened *Exposé de doctrine chrétienne* by Montet, which appears in Mss. Di, Ca D, Du 260 and Ge 8 and which gives evidence of a much more complex array of influences, particularly from Hussite writings.

The Waldensian *Somme le Roi* is arranged in eight parts: *Li Comandament; Li Article de la sainta fe catholica; Pecca; De li set Dons del Sant Sperit; De las tres Vertucz tehologials e de las quatre Vertucz cardenal; De li Ben de fortuna, de natura et de gracia; De seys Cosas que son honorivol en aquest mont.* We have already seen that the whole of this treatise is contained in Ca B (fols. 125r–237v).

Separate copies of certain chapters can be found elsewhere. The small 'treatises' on *Bal* and *la Taverna*, for example, which make up part of the chapters on sin, seem to have been enormously successful with Waldensian moralisers. Copies can be found in five other manuscripts.[24] The commentary on the gifts of fortune, nature and grace can also be found on its own in two other manuscripts.[25]

---

[22] Degan Checchini, *Vergier*, pp. 151–83.   [23] Borghi Cedrini, *Vertuz*, pp. 3–54.

[24] Leaving aside Ca B, these are Ca A, Di, Du 267, 260 and 263.

[25] Du 260, 263.

Indirect borrowings from the *Somme* are also numerous. The chapter on *Pecca* (sin), for example, which is divided into three sections (the seven deadly sins; taverns and dancing; the sins of the tongue or speech), has had an evident influence on most accounts of sin in the whole of the Waldensian archive. Some versions add *Remedi* (remedies) for the sins in question, almost all include a section on sins of speech, and all include occasionally incoherent re-arrangements and overlaps which show that several originals have been recopied according to different schemes.

On the dogmatic rather than moral level, we find that the chapter on the seven gifts of the Holy Spirit, the fourth part of the Waldensian version of the *Somme le Roi*, is a faithful abridgement of the original Latin text. It lists the seven traditional gifts: *Temor del Segnor, Pieta, Sciencia, Forcza, Conselh, Entendament* and *Sapiencia*. The appearance in Ms. Ca C of an independent treatise on *Temor del Segnor* (based on Prov. 1:7), and the fact that this gift can be found among the virtues described in *Vertucz* and *Vergier de Consolacion*, indicates clearly the importance the Waldensians attached to the fear of God. The chapter on the gifts of fortune, nature and grace is also a fairly accurate translation of the original text (book 2, chapter 4), and can be found independently under the title *Tot Don noble* in two other Waldensian books (Du 260 and Du 263). A small tract based on Ja. 1:17 in Ms. Du 267 (fols. 300v–303v) under the same title appears to be closely related to it. The argument is that the only valuable gifts are the gifts of God, that those of fortune are worthless, and those of nature hardly less so.

Retaining the theme of 'classical' medieval religious literature, we should note finally that the chapters on the twelve articles of the faith and on the ten commandments are also an accurate translation of Laurent's texts; that analogous chapters appear in the *Exposé de doctrine chrétienne*, that one of the versions of the twelve articles in the *Exposé* hardly diverges from the version in the *Somme le Roi*, and that its chapter on the ten commandments, particular in Du 260 and Ge 8, is curiously close to Laurent d'Orléans.

The *Exposé de doctrine chrétienne* is a moral and doctrinal *summa* which bears a particularly heavy imprint from influences outside the 'classical' medieval christian tradition. Thanks to the works of Gonnet and Molnar, the connections between the Alpine Waldensians and the Hussites, particularly the Bohemian Brethren, are well known.[26] One book in the Waldensian library, Ms. Du 262, is a collection of correspondence between the Waldensians and the Taborites.[27] The *Exposé* is organised in eight sections which deal successively with (i) the Athanasian creed, (ii) the Catholic faith, (iii) penitence, (iv) purgatory, (v) the invocation of saints, (vi) pontifical authority, (vii) the power of the keys, (viii) indulgences.

The only complete copy of the *summa* is in Ms. Di (1r–28r), but here it is in schematic form, with only chapter 10 on the commandments, written out in full. Mss. Ca D, Du 260 and Ge 8 contain more developed but fragmentary versions.[28] The second part, made up of three sections on the articles of the faith, the seven sacraments and the ten commandments, appears in four manuscripts. The third part, divided into two sections on true and false penitence, is copied on its own in Ge 7 and Ge 9; the appendices to this section on prayer, fasting and alms-giving are widely diffused throughout the library (Du 260, Ge 8, Ge 9). Extracts from the whole treatise were published by Perrin as evidence of the character of pre-Reformation Waldensian literature.[29]

While the parts of the *Exposé* devoted to the articles of the faith or to the ten commandments are entirely orthodox, the accounts of the seven sacraments contain the occasional variation and the chapters on purgatory, invocation of the saints and pontifical authority are nothing less than a polemical attack on the Catholic position. This is hardly surprising, as they are direct borrowings from a Taborite *Confession of Faith* of 1431,[30] and even include extracts from the writings of John Hus and Nicholas of Dresden.

The *Exposé* lists the seven sacraments and then contrasts those based on scripture with those based on Church custom. Confirmation is simply replaced by the laying on of hands, in the words of the Taborite *Confession*, 'de sacramento, manus impositionis, in fide Scripturae habente fundamentum' (concerning the sacrament of the laying on of hands, with its foundation in the faith of scripture). We

---

26 Notably in Gonnet and Molnar, chapter 5, 'L'Internationale Valdo-Hussite'.
27 See Gonnet and Molnar, p. 348, for a detailed list of Hussite and Taborite texts and compilations translated or used in the Waldensian library.
28 Ca D, fols. 81r–100v contains the prologue, parts 1 and 2, and half of part 3; Du 260, fols. 176v–242v, contains parts 1–3, and, in fols. 373r–383r, parts 4–5; Ge 8 in its entirety (145 fols.) contains parts 2–6.
29 J. P. Perrin, *Histoire des Vaudois* (Geneva, 1619), notably on purgatory (pp. 295ff.) and invocation of the saints (pp. 310ff.).
30 Ed. A. Molnar and R. Cegna (Rome, 1983 = ISIME, *Fonti per la Storia d'italia* 105).

should be careful not to confuse this with the Cathar baptism. The Waldensian text, translating the Taborite original, indicates only that the laying on of hands 'es segnal de robor spirital per laqual gracia es fayta de Dio' (is a sign of spiritual power through which grace comes from God).[31] Both Taborite *Confession* and Waldensian *Exposé* recognise the value of baptism with water. In the case of the eucharist, however, things are less clear. The denial of transubstantiation in the Waldensian version is a great deal less categorical than in the Taborite *Confession*. Christ is said to be 'Lo nuriment spiritua, de l'om en Dio' (the spiritual food of man in God'), the bread is truly the body of Christ, but 'non entendent ydempticament, d'una numeral idemptita, mas sacramentalment, realment et verament' (one should not understand it to be identical, with a numerical identity but it is [the body of Christ] sacramentally, really and truly).[32] The Waldensian text seems to imply a *spiritual* presence of Christ under the species of the bread. We are at the very heart of the preoccupations which gave birth to the Reformation. For the remainder, *Exposé* and *Confession* both reject the sacraments of Orders and Extreme Unction.

Penitence occupies an entire chapter of the *Exposé*. The issue appears to have been a crucial one for the Waldensians as it forms the subject matter of four other separate tracts. We have six copies of the chapter on *Penitencia* from the *Exposé*, each one different, more or less abridged[33] and reworked from different copies of the same original text. Some have additions, prologues and appendices which do not appear in the others and some internal contradictions have arisen, particularly on the power of the priest to bind and loose. They all, however, distinguish between true confession, which is internal, necessary and sufficient for salvation and directed towards God, and auricular confession, which has value only as advice and only if the minister is worthy. The point is made in the same language with which the Taborite confession asserts that absolution is given by God, without a priest's absolution.[34]

Chapter 4 is a refutation of Purgatory with very direct Hussite sources. It is, in effect, a translation of two fragments from the Taborite *Confession* linked by a passage citing various scriptural and patristic authorities right up to *Mestre Johan de sancta recordancza*

---

[31] Du 260, fol. 192r.   [32] Du 260, fols. 188r–v.   [33] In Ca D, Di, Du 260, Ge 7–9.
[34] See Molnar and Cegna (eds.), *Confessio Taboritarum*, p. 81.

(Master John of holy memory),[35] that is, John Hus himself, who blithely maintained that the invention of purgatory was due entirely to the greed of priests who wanted gifts and offerings in exchange for arranging an easy passage to heaven.

The non-existence of purgatory made prayers for the dead quite pointless and undermined the whole idea of indulgences. In this, the Waldensian *Exposé* faithfully followed its Hussite model once again and offered Hus as its authority. In this area the 'Waldensian–Hussite International', to use Gonnet and Molnar's phrase, fully deserves to be known as the first Reformation.

We should add, as final details, that sections 6 and 7 on the powers given to the vicar of Christ and the powers of the apostolic keys, take issue with the temporal power of the pope and follow, almost to the letter, John Hus's *Tractatus de Ecclesia*. By contrast, the language of part 5 of the *Exposé*, which rejects the invocation of the saints, is much milder than the Taborite original, which denounces such practices as idolatry.

Eschatological characteristics

One cannot draw up an adequate picture of this literature without saying something about its sombre and dramatic tone. The most persistent themes which sound throughout this material are anticipation of the Last Judgement, the prophecies and a certain anguish. One separate tract, *de las 4 cosas que son a venir*, has survived in six copies,[36] and it systematically develops the themes of Waldensian eschatology. For the most part, however, this eschatology is to be found in a series of small treatises on the antichrist, the perils, the tribulations, or in particular sermons on related gospel texts. On an even larger scale, it would be fair to say that the entire corpus of Waldensian literature is rooted in eschatology.

This could be the result of direct Hussite influence. The treatise *Qual cosa sia Antichrist*[37] is translated from three works of Luke of Prague; the *Barka* (1483/1512), the *Causes of Separation from the Roman Church* (1496) and the *Foundations of the Faith* (1525). However, one can find in all the texts the idea that the reign of the antichrist has

---

[35] Du 260, fol. 377r.
[36] Text A in Di, fols. 87r–143v, Du 264, fols. 19v–48v, Du 260, fols. 301r–334r, Ge 9, fols. 91r–130r; Text B in Ca B, fols. 48v–64r, Ge 6, fols. 102r–113r.
[37] Du 267, fols. 377v–390r.

arrived and that this explains the persecutions perpetually suffered by the Waldensian communities. All these evils presage Judgement Day. They are also the tests by which God can recognise his own people. This is why God allows the devil to tempt christians; it reveals who the true faithful are and helps to lead them to salvation.

The *Li Perilh* tract analyses the three dangers to christians which will arise in the world in the time of the antichrist. The collection of treatises and sermons under the title *Las Tribulacions*[38] has a similar purpose. In these works one finds, with the support of scriptural and patristic references, divine justification for the persecutions and temptations of this world. All these tracts are crowned with the ascetic morality of the Waldensians, an entirely practical morality in anticipation of the Last Judgement.

It is important to point out that the series of treatises on the tribulations, which at first sight appeared to Gonnet and Molnar to be perfectly orthodox and probably inspired by Catholic analogues, are in fact texts of resistance and struggle produced by a persecuted Church, and intended to denounce the Church of Rome which had become the Church of the Antichrist and of the Wolves.[39] The Waldensians had more than enough experience of persecution to be able to write about it without any borrowings from the Bohemian Brethren. They knew that 'li herege [persegan] li christian, non li christian li herege: donca de li fruc de lor, vos conoissere lor' (Mt. 7:16) (heretics [persecute] Christians, Christians do not persecute heretics: for by their fruits you shall know them).[40]

The Waldensians and their books: conclusions

First and foremost, these books are late. They appear to us, in their portable format, as adapted practically for the needs of the preachers who carried them. Their contents, often contradictory in substance, are the final expression of a tangling and mixing of medieval and post-medieval texts.

---

[38] See the editions of *Las Tribulacions* detailed in n. 2 above.
[39] See A. Brenon, 'Christianisme et tolérance dans les textes cathares et vaudois du Bas Moyen Age', in P. Blumental and J. Kramer (eds.), *Ketzerei und Ketzerbekämpfung im Wort und Text. Studien zur sprachlichen Verarbeitung religiöser Konflikte in der westlichen Romania* (Stuttgart, 1989 = *Zeitschrift für französische Sprache und Literatur*, 14), pp. 65–77.
[40] *Las Tribulacions*, Text A, p. 14, discussed and cited more fully in Brenon, 'Christianisme et tolérance', pp. 73–4.

At the very moment when Waldensian communities were aligning themselves with the Reformation (Chanforan, 1532), the copying of weighty and very medieval and Catholic treatises was still going on. These treatises contained dogmatic assertions of the transubstantiation which they had just rejected officially, and which the Bohemian Brethren had renounced decades before.

Certainly, the minor revolution in theological attitudes which led the medieval Waldensians to join with the Reformation movement may have taken place in the heart of the communities less quickly and less systematically than a rapid historical sketch such as this might suggest. Be that as it may, the Waldensian books blended several things together, in the archaic form of hand-written manuscripts and medieval *summae*: the clichés of an older popular christianity, which were based on a good patristic culture, with the new ideas inspired by the first Reformers of Bohemia or by the newer modern evangelism.

The fundamental originality of this literature is its profound commitment to scripture. It is above all a resource of handbooks for the preaching of the gospel. There is also in it the imprint of the intense trauma of these christian communities, which had been driven by repeated and bloody persecutions into isolation and the rejection of all compromise. It is a literature heavy with the melancholy of a moribund middle ages, at a time when the dawn of the Reformation was beginning to offer the possibilities of a new culture and a new hope.

APPENDIX

Sigla of the Waldensian manuscripts

Cambridge UL: Ca A = Cambridge UL Dd xv 29; Ca B = Dd xv 30; Ca C = Dd xv 31; Ca D = Dd xv 32; Ca E = Dd xv 33; Ca F = Dd xv 34.

Carpentras BM: Car = Carpentras BM 8.

Dublin TCL – equivalents of current and former sigla: Du 267 = Dublin TCL A.6.2.; Du 269 = A.6.10; Du 258 = A.4.13; Du 264 = C.4.17; Du 259 = C.5.18; Du 260 = C.5.22; Du 261 = C.5.21; Du 262 = C.5.25; Du 263 = C.5.26.

Dijon BM: Di = Dijon BM 234.

Geneva BPUL: Ge 6 = Geneva BPUL 206; Ge 7 = 207; Ge 8 = 208; Ge 9 = 209; Ge 9a = 209a.

Grenoble BM: Gre = Grenoble BM 43.

Zürich Zentralbibliothek: Zü = Zürich Zentralbibliothek c.169.

CHAPTER 9

Waldensians in the Dauphiné (1400–1530): from dissidence in texts to dissidence in practice

Pierette Paravy

What shaped the minds of Alpine Waldensians during the decisive generations between the crusade of 1488 and acceptance of the Reformation? First to be considered is that Waldensian library which was well known to Samuel Cassini at the time of the 1488 crusade and to Claude de Seysell in the 1520s, the library which is analysed in Brenon's chapter (ch. 8). Second is the concern about the inadequacy of their learning which the Waldensians expressed when confronting the masters of the new reform – witness here the *barbe* from Freissinières, Georges Morel:

> omnes nostri recipiendi emanant fere a bestiarum custodia aut ab agricultura aetatisque viginti quinque et plerunque triginta annorum et prorsus literarum expertes. Et inter nos trium aut ad summum quatuor annorum tantum duobus aut tribus mensibus hybernis probantur, si congruis praesent moribus. Et etiam his mensibus docentur literas coniungere et legere et memoriae mandare omnia Matthaei et Joannis omniumque epistolarum, quae dicuntur canonicae, capitula et bonam partem Pauli.

> (Our people come almost always from herding animals or agriculture, aged twenty or, in most cases, thirty, and utterly unlettered. During just two or three winter months they are put to the test amongst us over three or at most four years, to see if they show suitable character. During these months they are also taught to read and write, and to commit to memory all of Matthew and John, chapters from all the epistles which are called canonical, and a good part of Paul.)[1]

Several levels are discernible here. One is theoretical, the level of learned teachers who were interested in the contents of the library. That they were also concerned to bring it up to date is also clear from the speed with which stimulating Hussite literature entered it. Another was the practical level of the missionary pupil, well trained

---

[1] Vinay, p. 36.

in the fervent repetition and proclamation of scripture, but broadly unaware of contemporary debate, the question-mark now hanging over the traditional clandestine pastorate of the Waldensians, and the fact that the Protestant experiment was making another choice unavoidable. The third was the level of the Waldensian 'faithful', whose minds and attitudes, steeped in Catholicism, were going to need transformation.

The problems evident at these three levels provide the intelligible framework for an examination of the evidence from Dauphiné.[2] The dossier, richly suitable for an enquiry into the relation between Waldensian literature and the society in which it was produced, consists of the following. (i) Trials, abundant from the period round the 1488 crusade, and from the following years, when banished and condemned banded together in a legal battle which led to their obtaining rehabilitation by royal sentence in 1509. (ii) Fifteenth-century fiscal enquiries which illuminate socio-economic themes and structures of power and authority in Waldensian communities. (iii) Waldensian manuscripts, showing the contents of the Waldensian library during this period of exceptional tension (see the description of these manuscripts in chapter 8, by Brenon). (iv) The observations of Catholic controversialists, from Samuel Cassini to Claude de Seyssel, archbishop of Turin, in the 1520s. (v) The views of the *barbes* of the generation of the great debates in 1530, which led to the fusion of Waldensianism with the Reform movement in 1532.

These sources are used in the three parts of the following account, to describe the Waldensian Dauphiné (section 1), and to compare the contents of the Waldensian library with what took place on the ground (section 2). In section 3 the library is looked at as a source for the tension between conservatism and change. Far from being static, the library renewed itself through massive importation of Hussite material. What effect did this have on the Waldensians?

---

[2] I gave an analysis of the whole in 'Un autre modèle ee vie chrétienne, les Vaudois du Haut-Dauphiné', which is the fourth section of my Doctorat d'Etat thesis 'Recherches sur la vie religieuse en Dauphiné du milieu du XIVe siècle à la Réforme' (3 vols., Paris, 1988); the thesis is currently in press under the title *De la Chrétienté à la Réforme en Dauphiné: église, fidèles et déviants (XIVe–XVIe siècle)*. Recent comments on research concerning the Waldensian world appear in *Vaudois des origines à leur fin (XIIe–XVIe siècles)*, ed. G. Audisio (Colloque international d'Aix-en-Provence 1988, Turin, 1990), and Audisio, *Vaudois: Naissance, vie et mort d'une dissidence (XIIe–XVIe siècles)* (Turin, 1989).

I THE WALDENSIAN DAUPHINÉ

(a) Implantation, persecution and the rehabilitation of 1501–9

Waldensians were present in the more coastal areas of the Rhone region and the Valentinois, and in the high valleys of the dioceses of Embrun and Turin. Evidence for the two zones is uneven. As a result of precocious mendicant presence the first prosecutions in the coastal area had taken place in the thirteenth century. In the 1320s Jacques Fournier's interrogations of four Dauphinois, including the Waldensian deacon Raymond de la Côte, make the frequent links which they maintained with their home region remarkably clear. In the fifteenth century trials at Chabeuil and then Valence-Romans move the spotlight towards the Valentinois. One thing is certain: these Waldensians belonged to a group unified by the travelling missions of the *barbes*, and they were in no way ignorant of the fortunes of their brothers in the Haute-Dauphiné.[3]

The latter lived in three valleys of the diocese of Embrun, carved by tributaries of the upper Durance, Vallouise, L'Argentière and Freissinières, and also in the Italian Valcluson (an area belonging to the diocese of Turin but an integral part of the Dauphiné until the treaty of Utrecht in 1713). These Dauphinois lands constituted but one element of the large heterodox grouping studied by Merlo. Finally, inhabitants of these areas supplied the Waldensian emigrés to the Luberon who have been studied by Audisio.[4]

Evidence from the 1330s show already well-established communities. Although opponents were still to be found (1501–9) holding to the idea of 'refuges' for fugitives from Lyons in high mountain caves,[5] in fact, as de Seysell knew, Waldensians had been missionaries before persecution condemned them to clandestinity. This

---

[3] For the proceedings at Pamiers see Fournier, vol. 1, pp. 40–127, 508–32; French translation by Duvernoy (Paris, The Hague and New York, 1978), vol. 1, pp. 55–150. See G. G. Merlo, 'Nel mezzogiorno di Francia tra XIII e XIV seculo', *Valdesi e valdismo medievali* (Turin, 1984), pp. 43–92. The Waldensians of Chabeuil, AD Isère B 2752, fols. 128v–132; see the texts edited by J. Colombi, *Opuscula varia* (Lyon, 1668), pp. 330–1, P. Allix, *Some Remarks upon the Ecclesiastical History of the Ancient Churches of Piedmont* (London, 1690), pp. 318–31, Chevalier, p. 139–45.

[4] Merlo; Audisio; E. Cameron, *The Reformation of the Heretics: the Waldenses of the Alps (1480–1580)* (Oxford, 1984); P. Paravy, 'Reflexions sur les Vaudois en Dauphiné aux XIVe et XVe siècles', *Echanges religieux entre la France et l'Italie au Moyen Age et à l'époque moderne (Chambèry, 1984)* (Geneva, 1987), pp. 147–62.

[5] BN lat. 3375(2), fol. 434v. Seyssel, fol. 6.

initial momentum had led to numerous and unified communities. However, after the trial of Raymond de la Côte in Pamiers in 1320, Jacques Fournier made the eradication of the movement a top priority, and from the 1330s persecution was uninterrupted. Merlo's work shows the dense chronology of persecution on the Piedmontese side of the Alps. This is matched on the Dauphinois side, beginning with valleys of the Embrunais and Valcluson in the 1380s, and accompanied in the Embrun area by an unprecedented pastoral effort in the shape of a preaching mission by St Vincent Ferrer, the effects of which can be followed throughout the fifteenth century.[6]

The endpoint was an anachronistic attempt at complete eradication, the crusade of 1488. Undertaken from the diocese of Embrun, this followed on earlier episcopal reforming action. It was a local man, the archbishop Jean Baile, strongly supported by the Parlement of the Dauphiné (long presided over by his father and namesake, Jean Baile), who wanted to put an end to the matter. He managed to obtain from pope Innocent VIII a crusading bull which empowered Albert Cattaneo to intervene in the Piedmontese area and in Valcluson as well as within the diocese of Embrun. Autumn and winter 1487 witnessed inquisitorial summonses, spring 1488 the violent events of crusade,[7] whose effects were threefold: loss of life; confiscations and exile; a new diaspora.[8]

Since the communities' tally, drawn up in 1507, coincides with Cattaneo's own estimate, the figure of 160 dead can be accepted. This shared experience was now the most powerful cement binding these communities: irreconcilable, now, in the memory of their martyrs. Confiscations of goods were crushing; they led to proceedings brought by the communities against their persecutors at the beginning of the sixteenth century.

Of greater importance was the new diaspora, composed by flight and judicial banishment. Its directions included Lombardy (in the medieval sense of the term), already denounced by Benedict XII in 1336, where one could find refugees from Vallouise and L'Argentière in 1488. Calabria had been mentioned by Innocent VI in 1358,

---

[6] Merlo, and for the mission of St. Vincent Ferrier, P. Paravy, 'Remarques sur les passages de saint Vincent Ferrier dans les vallées vaudoises (1399–1403)', in *Croyances religieuses et sociétés alpines* (= Colloque de Freissinières, October 1981, 1987), pp. 143–55.

[7] Amongst the numerous accounts of the crusade see Marx, pp. 158–67.

[8] See the collection of depositions put together during their enquiries of 1501–7, BN lat. 3375(2), *passim*.

at a time when repression was extending to all Alpine communities and compelling them to look for more distant refuges, and it remained a Waldensian destination. A more recent refuge was Provence. Its refuge locations were cited by Innocent VIII in 1489, in the bull which commissioned a new inquisitor, François Plouvier, to pursue Waldensians – whose community is now known perfectly through Audisio's work.[9]

An incurable haemorrhage, which reduced Dauphinois Waldensianism to a residual phenomenon? This initial impression is incorrect. The exiles remained united by their sense of belonging to the high valleys and their solidarity with those who remained in them, and what is evidenced by the actions they took is the vitality of this Alpine group, dispersion notwithstanding. The trials connected with the 1488 crusade were to be sources revealing to the later historian the lived experience of the Waldensians of this period; they also provided the occasion for testing the solidarity of these communities – as the 'trial of the trials' showed.

Behind eventual rehabilitation lay support which the communities received during Louis XI's reign, support itself rooted not in religious preference but in politics. The desire was to obstruct an archbishop, Jean Baile, who was son of the president of the Parlement which had taken Charles VII's side in the dispute between him and the Dauphin Louis during his stay in the Dauphiné. In the appeals which preceded the unleashing of the crusade, the inhabitants of the valleys had continually cited the favourable judgements obtained from the king in 1478–9, reserving everything concerning the Waldensians to royal jurisdiction. The memory of this remained.

More immediate roots were those methodical and effective contacts which give us such a vivid impression of the solidarity of the dispersed Romance Waldensians. From inhabitants, formerly, of Vallouise and L'Argentière who had taken refuge in Piedmont (in Angrogna and Val Luserna) there came a list of appellants in 1489 and 1490. One finds former inhabitants of Freissinières at Gap,

[9] Lombardy: bull of Benedict XII (1335) in J. M. Vidal, *Bullaire de l'Inquisition française au XIVe siècle et jusqu'à la fin du Grand Schisme* (Paris, 1911), doct. 147, p. 224; refuge at the end of the fourteenth century G. G. Merlo, 'Circulation d'hérétiques entre la France et le Piémont au XIVe siècle', *Provence historique* 27 (1977), 325–34; refuge at the end of the fifteenth century, see BN lat. 3375(1), fols. 53v, 60–62v. For southern Italy, bull of Innocent VI in 1353, in Vidal doct. 213, p. 329. F. Reynaud, 'Quelques documents sur l'émigration vaudoise au XVe siècle', *Provincia* 263 (1964), 155–6, and AD Isère B 3757, fol. 394. Provence: Audisio, pp. 45ff.

Chorges and even in the Dauphiné, where they are numerous from 1490; ten years later a witness spoke of 400 at Gap. They were also at Cabrières-d'Aigue, where, in 1504, sixty-eight of them banded together to defend their rights against neighbours from Vallouise and L'Argentière.

Rehabilitation was established first in 1501, and then definitively in a judgement of 1509, after the failure of an appeal by the Parlement of the Dauphiné.[10]

(b) Structure and organisation

The enquiries generated by these legal procedings constitute evidence which can be put beside the fiscal archives of the Dauphiné (for the fifteenth century, up to 1475), which add families other than those accused.

The sentence of rehabilitation of 1509 only holds the *barbes*, among the Waldensians, as responsible. According to the sentence, at the time of trial it had been held that there were grounds for inquisitorial enquiry and action; evidence had then appeared which had been taken to show that the Waldensian faithful were not heretics or obstinate deviants from the faith. There follows in the sentence an exhortation to the Catholic clergy to carry out its pastoral task; a threat of repression is reserved for Waldensian missionaries, who are seen as pseudo-apostles who deceive the simple with their clandestine preaching.[11]

Why did the sentence thus dissociate Waldensian masters and faithful? It could have reflected the reality of powerlessness in the face of Waldensian communities, but more probably it rests upon a Catholic view in which pastor is distinguished from flock: the former responsible and active, the other a passive recipient of teaching. Such clericalisation reaches back to the Gregorian reform and beyond, to Gregory the Great's *Regula pastoralis*, and it helps to explain the Church's inability to grasp a very different reality. For Waldensianism's pillars were its communities just as much as its missionaries, and they are described here first.

The juxtaposition of the names of Waldensians known through

---

[10] BN lat. 3375(1) and (2). Comments of Marx, pp. 178–98.

[11] The sentence of rehabilitation is ed. by P. Guillaume, in M. Fornier, *Histoire générale des Alpes maritimes et cottiènes et particulière de leur métropolitaine Ambrun* (Paris and Gap, 1892), vol. III, pp. 409–23.

legal proceedings and the lists of names of those liable to pay tax allows one to reconstruct communities among about 500 hearths. Although two of the communities in the Embrunais, Vallouise and L'Argentière, had been declining numerically since the fourteenth century, this did not entail loss of identity. Rather, the experience of trying to live as a minority produced forceful leaders. Despite long erosion, the community of Freissinières was also to remain important until the crusade, as did that of Valcluson south of the mountains.[12]

Immediately striking, socially, in these communities, are the dominance of some lineages and the importance of families, households, the *domus*. Take the confessions of Thomas Guiot (1495). Speaking of a neighbour, Pierre Pastre, he said he did not know if he was a Waldensian, but he said that all the others *de ejus domo* (of his household) were Waldensian. Again, always Waldensian were those *de progenie Vilhotorum* (of the Vilhot lineage). Pierre Griot accepted that his father, like Thomas Guiot's, were Waldensians, and in this they followed their ancestors.[13]

If families were the basis of cohesion, it was a few determined men belonging to the most powerful lineages who took the initiative in defending communities, preparing the texts of petitions, addressing the authorities and putting their names at the heads of lists of appellants. And during periods of crisis their mandate came from regular assemblies.

Examples of the importance of the local level in Waldensian practice are easy to find. In 1451 the confessions of Philippe Regis show missionaries coming annually into his valley, the Piedmontese Val S. Martino, staying in his house. Before leaving, they would appoint him and one other, as deputies, to hear confessions. Three generations later Georges Morel wrote of leading men elected in each community to ensure peace and concord: men of trust.[14]

In the trials of 1487–8 three defendants from the community of

---

[12] P. Paravy, 'Recherches sur la mobilité de la population des vallées vaudoises du Dauphiné à la fin du Moyen Age: l'évolution de la communauté de Vallouise aux xive et xve siècles', in *Migrazioni attraverso le Alpi Occidentali* (= Colloque International de Coni, 1–3 Juni 1984, Turin, 1988), pp. 471–85, and 'Les Vaudois du Haut-Dauphiné de la croisade de 1488 à la Réforme', *Heresis* 13/14 (1989), 268–73.

[13] BN lat 3375(1), 1237, 246, 258r–v; the same witness of Antoine Marie in 1507, BN lat. 3375(2), fol. 502.

[14] Ed. G. Weitzecker, 'Processo di un Valdese nell'anno 1451', *Rivista cristiana* 9 (1988), 363–7. G. Morel, ed. Vinay, p. 42.

Freissinières, Turin, Jean and Brunet Bertrand, were named by neighbours as *barbes*. Now, nothing else supports their having been true *barbes*, but they had played an active role in defence during the crusade: probably, therefore, they were similar men of trust.[15] Meetings took place in their houses, in Valcluson as well as the valleys of the Embrunais. Other reception houses are known: those of the Maret at Pragelas, of the David at Usseaux, of the Challier at Fenestrelle, of François Ripert at Freissinières, of the Bérard at L'Argentière. Family was also the first milieu and source of Waldensian doctorine for children: it was from his relative Aude that Antoine Blazy was first taught rejection of the Roman Church and the necessity to confess to one of the *barbes*.[16]

To these we should now turn: men who were central to the conception and practice of Waldensianism. A description of their origin and elementary education has already been quoted from Georges Morel, writing in 1530. Morel's account also includes the asceticism of their form of life, an allusion to a period of noviciate in an unspecified place (the need for secrecy lies behind this silence), annual general councils, the itinerancy of missions, and the centrality in these of hearing confessions. Twenty-one individual, named, *barbes* recur in our documents, at least eleven of whom certainly had regional links. Whether born locally, or, like the *barbe* Fernand, from the Valentinois but a Piedmontese speaker, they were moulded by the region.[17] They were also present, whether on regular missionary travels or in emergencies, during the crisis year of 1487–8.

2 WALDENSIAN ATTITUDES AND THEIR FOUNDATIONS

Integration between these two key elements in Waldensianism – on the one hand families and communities, on the other hand the *barbes* – stands out when we turn to the evidence of the trials of 1487–8 and 1501–9. Those of 1487–8 give the responses of the accused to their judges, and in these what is salient first is a stereotyped and large corpus of Waldensian rejection. Here the most frequent formula was a contrast between the lives of abundance of churchmen and of justice and goodness of the *barbes*, a lietmotif for the insistence on authority depending upon sanctity. Condemnation of taking oaths,

---

[15] AD Isère B 4351, fol. 26v.   [16] Marx, p. 238.
[17] Paravy, 'Les Vaudois', pp. 273–7.

of lying, rejection of belief in purgatory or prayers for the dead, disdain for the cult of the Virgin and the saints and allied practices, indifference to Roman sacralisation of the space of material churches or cemeteries:[18] these rejections form a coherent structure but, as we shall see, they are incompatible with the actual attitudes revealed by confessions. The second feature we see, a positive one, is the operation of the Waldensian mission. The *barbes* appear in pairs, usually at night, carrying a book; the comment of one of the accused, that it was in the vernacular, shows that he could read it himself.[19] Family and neighbours would gather round the hearth in one of the meeting-houses to hear the sermon, before or after which there was confession. This could also be in a secret or isolated place – there are examples in a field under an apple tree, or in a barn.[20] The penitent would kneel before the *barbe*, who would place his hands on his head during confession, like the parish priest; penance would be recitation of the *Pater Noster*. In the lowlands Péronette Fournier, tried in Valence in 1494, described in similar terms two men coming into her house and, after a meal, one of them beginning his sermon by reading from a little book.[21]

The rehabilitation trials of 1501–9 provide us with the evidence of witnesses who had seen Waldensians in exile and earlier. Very important were enquiries held in July 1591 at Gap and Chorges, where there were altogether thirty-two witnesses, ranging from nobles to merchants, notaries, priests and innkeepers. These men of substance, maturity and experience testified about the numerous Waldensians who had lived among them, and also about what they had seen on journeys to the valleys going back to the 1480s.[22]

First to stand out is that all, without exception, underline conformism in religious practice, both now and in the past: going to church, taking the sacraments, and (in priests' depositions) discussion prior to receiving extreme unction. Occasionally what is revealed is extremely catholic. Journeying on the business of the *prévoté* had enabled François Farel to witness the participation of a good 2,000 people from the valleys of Freissinières and L'Argentière in a pilgrimage on the feast of St John, hearing mass, receiving holy

---

[18] AD Isère B 4350, B 4351, *passim*; numerous references in the whole of the regional bibliography.
[19] AD Isère B 4350, fol. 154.   [20] AD Isère B 4351, fols. 200, 239v; Marx, p. 238.
[21] Ed Allix, *Some Remarks*, p. 322.
[22] BN lat. 3375(1), fols. 431–464v, Lat. 3375(2), fols. 1–46.

water, genuflecting, in particular at the elevation of the Host, and going into a chapel one by one to offer candles.[23] Secondly, witnesses insisted on Waldensian knowledge. One judge who had lived for a few months in Freissinières, taking refuge there from the plague, knew there a local man who knew the Old and New Testaments perfectly. At mass, he said, Waldensians learnt the *Pater Noster* and the *Credo* both in Latin and in the vernacular, with the priest saying, 'I believe in God almighty', and parishioners repeating it after him. Witnesses admired the *optime* (very good) quality of their knowledge, described as superior to that of other christians.[24]

Finally, everyone testified to the good character of the Waldensians. Accusations of licentiousness at nocturnal meetings were given horrified rejection.[25] Priests spoke strongly, one even expressing his admiration of the heroism of those condemned to death. A servant accused by a master of being a Waldensian says that he is just as good a Christian as his master. A merchant of Gap describes the good death of one of his servants from Freissinières, receiving the last rites, declaring that he always lived and wished to die in the Catholic faith, and crossing himself.[26]

While the two sets of trials are both biassed, in opposing directions, they agree in pointing us to two themes: the existence of a double loyalty, and the precise character of the Waldensian mission. Firstly, throughout a Waldensian's life as a Christian, from baptism through marriage to burial, there was not a single step which was not taken in the local (Roman) parish church. Although two confessions of 1487–8 speak of the possibility of *barbes* consecrating if they wanted, there is no confirmation of this.[27] De Seysell, who knew the Waldensianism of *c.* 1518–20 very well, never located rivalry between *barbes* and parish priests in this or any area other than preaching and confession.[28]

In 1530 Morel was to express a feeling of destructive anxiety and guilt about this situation, but to previous generations it was not only a reality but perhaps also not yet seen as tragic. One confession of 1487 shows a *barbe* positively recommending going to church because of the celebration there of Jesus Christ.[29] As we have seen,

---

23 BN lat. 3375(1), fols. 450r–v.   24 BN lat. 3375(2), fols. 9v, 33v, 42.
25 BN lat. 3375(1), fol. 447.
26 BN lat. 3375(1), fols. 455v, 458v–459.   27 AD Isère B 4350 and 4351, *passim*.
28 Seyssel, fols. 52, 55.
29 AD Isère B 4351, fols. 115v, 294.

Waldensians learnt prayers from their parish priests. In discussions with a neighbour Péronette Fournier draws on both reference to the *barbes* and a sermon of her parish priest for an interiorised under-standing of the saving value of the lives of the just.[30]

On what was of decisive importance for the Waldensian mission, confession and exhortation, there is unanimity in the evidence, from the earlier Dauphinois trials to de Seyssell's treatise *Adversus errores Valdensium* (as we have just seen) and Morel's letter to Oecolampa-dius in the following generation. Morel wrote thus:

Plebeculam nostram semel singulis annis, quia per diversos vicos habitat, adimus ipsamque personam in confessione clandestine audimus. Admone-mus coniugatus, ut invicem debito proprio honeste et tantum ad medici-nam et non ad voluptatis societatem utantur ... in dicta confessione admonemus omnes secundum suam qualitatem et capacitatem, ut pro viribus se abstineant a peccatis.

(Once a year we visit our people, who live in various villages, and hear them individually in secret confession. We urge the married to render the (marital) debt worthily and only as a remedy and not in order to unite in sensuality ... in the said confession we urge everyone, according to their nature and capacity, to avoid sin with all their strength.)[31]

Trial testimonies from the Haut-Dauphiné insisted on the need for keeping Sundays holy, fasting on Fridays, confessing sins to every last detail before Easter communion, praying frequently, the valid-ity of prayer anywhere (i.e. outside church as well), avoiding evil-doing, doing to others as you would wish done to yourself, marital fidelity, not denouncing one's neighbour, not lying. Among similar exhortations received by Péronette Fournier in the Valentinois there was also the instruction that although not all feast-days needed to be observed, the most important should be, in particular feasts of the apostles, and again insistence on the holiness of Sunday and Friday fasting.

The emphasis on prayer and the teaching of the faith explains the perfect knowledge which struck observers, while the centrality of repentance and confession of sin lies at the root of an interiorisation which was fundamental. A call to conversion, implicit in penitence, took precedence over all other religious practice.

We must now turn to the 'little books' which were the source of

---

[30] Ed. Allix, *Some Remarks*, p. 325.   [31] Vinay, p. 42.

the missionaries' teaching. The possession of texts and the commission of some to memory (Morel's description is quoted above) rested on a long and living tradition. There was recourse in these Waldensian books to the writings of the Fathers, and to those pastoral moral works of the thirteenth-century authors Guillaume Peyraut and Lorens d'Orléans which generalised the twelfth-century shaping of moral theology by a Hugh of St Victor or an Alain de Lille.[32] The famous eight poems constitute a good example of the way their library nourished the *barbes'* mission, in particular *La Nobla Leyçon* (The Noble Lesson).[33] This last, as a manifesto against a repressive church, was an assertion of Waldensian identity, but also much more. Preaching on the destiny of man since the fall, it located the faith of a small flock in the long history of a dialogue between God and his creation, man, called to salvation but left with freedom of choice. Conversion of life is the central theme. Conversion and penitence are at the heart of the other poems. The first part of *La Barca* (The Bark) is an adaptation of pope Innocent III's *De contemptu mundi*; *Lo Despreczi del mont* (Contempt of the World) shares title and perhaps an atmosphere. Both invite man to tear himself away from his abjection and examine his conscience. As it was at the beginnings of Waldensianism, 'Awake' is the key word.[34] The impassioned contrition of *La Oracion* (The Prayer), and the deepening of the theme of penitence and the projection of a model of the Christian life in *Lo Novel Sermon* (The New Sermon), *Lo Novel Confort* (The New Comfort), and *L'Evangeli de li quatre semencz* (The Gospel of the Four Seeds) all share fidelity to scripture and extensive use of patristic writings. Their use, further, of vernacular works which further diffused the generalising moral works of the thirteenth century (Peyraut and Lorens) shows how they were broadly rooted in the pastoral project which the twelfth- and thirteenth-century Church had developed. Arguments and categories beloved of the Doctors of the Church make this clear: flesh versus spirit; the distinction between thought, word and deed; the concept of mortal sin.

---

[32] See the account of the manuscripts by Brenon above, chapter 8.

[33] Edited from the manuscripts of Cambridge, Dublin and Geneva in F. Apfelstedt, *Zeitschrift für romanische Philologie von G. Groeber* (Halle, 1880), pp. 330–46, 521–41; G. Balme, 'I Poemi valdesi', *BSSV* 21 (1904), 39–61; 23 (1906), 4–55; H.J. Chaytor, *Six Vaudois Poems from the Waldensian Manuscripts in the University Libraries of Cambridge, Dublin and Geneva* (Cambridge, 1930); A. de Stefano, *La 'Noble leçon' des Vaudois du Piémont* (Paris, 1909).

[34] Selge, vol. I, pp. 95ff.

Similar analysis of sermons produces categories: works based on Catholic sources; works adapting them to Waldensian purposes; original Waldensian compositions. Commentary on a scriptural passage, the first among many, shows attachment to texts. Scholasticism leaves its mark in the use of examples, modes of exposition and an interest in symbolic connections which is shown particularly in *De la Propriotas de la animanczas* (On the Properties of Animals, sometimes known as The Waldensian Bestiary). Arguments use traditional schemas, particularly triadic groups such as the three accusers at the Last Judgement and the three great enemies of the World, the Flesh and the Devil.

The educational intention throughout is to show that the world passes away, and, most sharply in the sermon *La Temor del Segnor* (Fear of the Lord; Prov. 1:7), that one must repent while there is time.[35] The treatises and sermons help in the exploration of all varieties of man's sin and emphasise his will and responsibility in turning to the right path.

Waldensian epistles, leaning heavily in content and form on canonical epistles, show a desire to return to the primitive church. Examined here is an epistle which is linked with the Dauphinois trials, the letter which the *barbe* Barthélémy Tertian addressed to the Dauphinois community of Pragelas. A 1488 trial indicates that there was a *barbe* of the Tertian family at that time.[36]

The letter is based on three texts, 'What will it profit a man if he gain the whole world but lose his soul' (Mt. 16:26), 'If you will enter into the life, keep the commandments' (Mt. 19:17), and 'To whom they have committed much, of him they shall demand the more' (Lk. 12:48). The principal themes are the pastor's responsibility, defined as 'lo meo debit, de mi a vos, de la part de Dio, maximament sobra la cura de la salù de las vostras armas, segond lo lume de verità' (the duty I have towards you, on God's behalf, mostly concerning care for the salvation of your souls according to the light of truth), and an exhortation to shun the ways of the world and assume responsibility towards God. As in *The New Comfort*,[37] love of God and of one's neighbour are the two fundamentals of christian

---

[35] CUL Dd.15.31 fols. 14–24v.

[36] AD Isère B 4350, fol. 296v; numerous editions of the epistles, see notably S. Morland, *The History of the Evangical Churches of the Valleys of Piemont* (London, 1658), pp. 180–2.

[37] Editions of *The New Comfort* appear in Balme, 'I Poemi', *BSSV* 23 (1906), 10–17 and Chaytor, *Six Vaudois Poems*, pp. 34–48 (translation on pp. 102–9).

life. The collective consequences of sin are emphasised more than
their individual aspect: 'Fazé que entre vos non se musse juoc ni
gourmandarias ... ni l'engan, ni barat, ni usura, ni malvolencas, ni
discordias ... ma carità et fidelità regne entre vos' (Make sure that
amongst you there is no gaming, gluttony ... no deception, fraud,
usury, malice, discord ... but rather let charity and trust reign
amongst you). This exhortation is directed more pressingly at *regi-
dors et gouvernadors* (rulers and leaders), whether of families or communities, 'car quand li cap son enferm, tuit li membres ensemp se
dolon' (for when the head is sick all members suffer). Thus Tertian
sketches the ideal for a peaceful and structured society.

This Waldensian library – an examination of which deepens our
understanding of the valleys during the period of the trials – was still
the staple of basic training a generation later, when Morel was sadly
contemplating the new reform movement and the inevitable decline
it would cause.

3 BETWEEN CONSERVATISM AND DISLOCATION

What we have seen here, the use of scripture and penitential–moral
literature developed in the twelfth and thirteenth centuries, links the
situation in the Dauphiné *c.* 1500 with a remote past. We cannot
debate here whether geographical dispersion and the long passage of
time may have led to the emergence of distinct 'Waldensianisms',[38]
we need simply to note similar traits among Waldensians in Languedoc *c.* 1320, as well as those in Peter Zwicker's Germany in the
1390s.[39]

Alongside such uniformity and conservatism we should also see
openness. Take as an example the multiplication of glosses on the
Pater Noster and the *Credo* in the Waldensian library. This did not
arise from collectors' mania. Rather we should see in it a search for
expressions which could nourish the life of the faith, speculative
research rooted in the desire to be absolutely faithful to the message,
and finally, underlying what could appear as conservatism, an
openness to new formulations.

This is the context within which we need to set our last theme, an

---

[38] See on this point the crucial research of Merlo, *Valdesi*, and *Identità Valdese nella Storia e nella
Storiografia* (Turin, 1991).

[39] P. Biller, 'Les vaudois dans les territoires de langue allemande vers la fin du XIVe siècle',
Heresis 13/14 (1989), 199–234.

importation of Hussite material which paved the way for the dislocations of the Reformation. There had been links with Hussites. In the 1430s the searches in the Dauphiné for Hussites fighting against German crusaders imply connections of sympathy.[40] Whereas there has been no appeals after the persecutions of the 1380s, the appeals we have seen after 1488 showed a will to resist which, plausibly, borrowed much from the example of those who had negotiated every inch of the way at the Council of Basel to get their differences and right to exist recognised. Finally there is the evidence of the valley of Paesana, where in 1510 there was expressed hope of support from the king of Bohemia.[41]

Hussite texts and treatises entered progressively and then massively into the Waldensian library – according to Cassini and de Seysell, proliferating after the journey of Luke of Prague. The entry of the *Tresor e lume de fe* (Treasure and Light of Faith) was decisive, marking a dogmatic break from Catholic faith on the question of transubstantiation.[42] Though not unaware of this work, de Seysell does not mention it, and in his chapter on the eucharist in his anti-Waldensian treatise he simply refers back to his more abstract treatise *De Divina Providentia* where, after designating more symbolic interpretations, he simply provides a formal restatement of the Catholic definition.[43] However, he did use Nicholas of Dresden's ardent missionary manifesto, which had been translated as *Alcuns volon ligar la Parolla de Dio* (Some wish to tie the Word of God).[44] From de Seysell's choice of emphasis it seems that he still saw as the central problem the fact that Waldensians preached and thus disturbed the Roman monopoly of preaching – not dogma.

What should we see as the general significance of the importation of Hussite texts? There was an obvious gulf between the radicalism of Hussite manifestos – full of talk of a complete break with Rome – and the restraint of the Waldensian mission and conformism of Waldensian religious practice, and this led Molnar to see the importation as an infusion of new life into an exhausted movement.[45] Clearly time was needed for assimilation, and Morel's

[40] Mansi, *Sacrorum conciliorum nova et amplissima collectio* (Florence and Venice, 1759–98), xxix.402D.

[41] A. Pascal, 'Margherita di Foix e i Valdesi di Paerana', *Athenaeum* 4 (1916), 85–8.

[42] R. Cegna, *Fede ed etica valdese nel quatrocento. Il 'Libro Espositivo' e il 'Tesoro e Luce della Fede'* (Turin, 1982).

[43] Seyssel, fols, 55v–56. *De Divina Providentia* (Paris, 1520), fol. 45.   [44] Seyssel, fol. 52.

[45] A. Molnar, in Gonnet and Molnar, ch. 5.

continuing attachment to the old ways in 1530 shows that there had not been enough time. However, what is implied here is not weakness or inertia but the tensions which existed between a living tradition, new ideas and a still limited audience. Waldensian appetite for Bohemian literture shows openness. The copy of Nicholas of Dresden shows quick realisation of its interest in providing a view of the practice of Waldensian missionaries which was entirely unacceptable to Rome. The quest for texts relating to the debates between Calixtines and Taborites shows the same keen desire for information.

The Waldensian world was by no means exhausted when, despite the opposition of such figures as John of Molines and Daniel of Valence,[46] it joined with the new Reformation movement which was being set up in Switzerland and the region round the Rhône. In the new dispensation the compromise with Rome – cemented by acceptance of its sacraments – had become pointless. To borrow an image from a text in the Waldensian library, *Herman* (Pastor of Hermas), that of the vine and the elm, one could say that the Waldensian vine had grown up the trunk of the Roman elm, but now that this elm was shattered it would have to find its support elsewhere.[47]

Into a new world Waldensianism was bringing several things of its own. One was a powerful, historically conditioned identity, which was going to have a large role to play in historiography. Brought forward also were the synodal organisation of the *barbes*, the exercise of responsibility in the heart of the community, and the tradition of heads of families taking the initiative in times of trouble. Thirdly, there was the precedence of scripture over tradition. At the beginning of this chapter the paradox was stated: a contradiction between the fine Waldensian library, which ranged from the earliest texts to Hussite disputes, and Waldensian confession of inadequacy and ignorance when faced with the vigour of the reformers. Waldensian structure, built on families, communities and the *barbes*, was strong. It was within this structure that Waldensians lived their lives and developed in that spiritual laboratory of the sixteenth century, when the present meant breaking with the past and the future was long.

---

[46] G. Gonnet, 'Les relations des Vaudois des Alpes avec les Réformateurs franco-suisses avant Calvin (1526–1533)', in *Croyances religieuses et sociétés alpines* (= *Colloque de Freissinières*, October 1981, 1987), pp. 165–78; Audisio, pp. 178ff.

[47] CUL Dd.15.29, fols. 172–7. E. Balmas, 'L'adattamendo Valdese del "Pastore d'Erma"', *BSSV* 148 (1980), 3–17.

CHAPTER 10

Were the Waldensians more literate than their contemporaries (1460–1560)?

Gabriel Audisio

Historians usually establish two enduring links: one between 'heresy' and holy scripture, and another between rural people and illiteracy. In these terms, the Waldensians constitute a particularly interesting case. On the one hand the Waldensians were religious dissenters; on the other hand most of them were peasants – apart from a few urban exceptions, this is true of the Waldensians of Provence, the Dauphiné, Piedmont, Calabria, Apulia, Pomerania and Brandenburg.[1] These was a direct opposition between these two features. As a religious movement which was founded on a literal reading of the bible and a refusal of any interpretation of it, Waldensianism invited its members to read holy scripture. These members needed, therefore, to be able to read. However, these same members nearly always came from a rural population which was unlikely to produce readers and writers.

The theme here, then, is the existential and structural tension created by these opposing elements, and the question is this: in terms of literacy, was it 'heresy' or 'peasantry' which ultimately prevailed? Were the Waldensians illiterate, as other peasants were, or were they more literate than other peasants, as was the case with the French Protestants of the later sixteenth century?

The extraordinary European extension of the Waldensian diaspora of the fifteenth and sixteenth centuries makes an overall answer difficult to achieve. One needs, first, local investigations. The case examined here is that of the Waldensians who were settled

[1] Waldensians were also in some cities, such as Strasburg, Basle, Fribourg, Marseilles. However, when the preacher Georges Morel in 1530 described in his official account of the Waldensian people, he wrote about *cuiusdam plebis indigae et pusillae* (a certain poor and insignificant little flock) and about their preachers: 'Omnes nostri recipiendi emanant fere a bestiarum custodia aut ab agricultura' (Those of us who are to be received [as *barbes*] nearly always come from tending animals or agriculture), Vinay, p. 36.

in the Luberon area in Provence. The sources for their study are not only judicial and inquisitorial records but also notarial deeds. The range and variety of this evidence allows the historian, for once, to get close to popular Waldensian culture in a particular time and area.[2]

I WRITTEN CULTURE IN PROVENCE

The first element in what was specific to the culture of Provence was its language: most people spoke nothing but Provençal. There was considerable understanding of French, of course, especially among those who lived in towns, and this became more widespread during the sixteenth century. However, many could not speak French. Provençal was what they spoke: and Provençal was only a spoken language. So, in the southern provinces of the kingdom of France, there were two obstacles in the path of the text: language, as well as illiteracy. This may explain why for several centuries the area was more illiterate than the northern provinces. One area of backwardness was printing. While the 'new art' had arrived in Lyons and Avignon by the end of the fifteenth century, it took another century for it to reach the two most important cities of the province, Aix and Marseilles.

Although it was not a centre of production, Provence did not lack printed books, and there were manuscripts. But who possessed these written materials? And who could read them? When looking at the culture of the Luberon area where the Waldensians lived, the first question, then, is where books and written materials were to be found. Three groups possessed written documents. First is the clergy, and in this group the regulars stand out. Here are two examples. An inventory of the library of the collegiate church of L'Isle-sur-la-Sorgue was drawn up in 1477. At that date it numbered twenty-one books – manuscript books, since it was specified that they were parchment. The books were mainly of canon law, alongside theology.[3] The choir of the church of the Franciscan convent in Apt had twenty-eight books in 1485: all concerning services and liturgy.[4] Though not large, these libraries were not

---

[2] See Audisio, based, among other sources, on more than 2,000 notarial registers of the period 1460–1560; see the notarial sources indicated, pp. 449, 452.

[3] Vaucluse AD, 3 E 33/402, 1 April 1477.   [4] Vaucluse AD, 3 E 2/10, fol. 182v.

negligible, and they constitute something of a contrast with the case of the secular clergy.

Precise knowledge of the parish clergy's books is difficult to obtain. For example, the chapter of Apt ordered the printing of a new breviary in Lyons in 1532.[5] However, it is not known how many of the clergy bought it. The only evidence in which one can find books is the inventories drawn up for probate after the deaths of property-holders, and documents relating to the disposal of their goods and chattels. Such evidence throws up very little – and this is in itself significant. Only one parish priest is found in possession of some books. Pierre Mazel was the parson of Ansouis and he lived in Cucuron. On 20 October 1514, after his death, his personal goods were shared between his brother, Elzéar, and another priest, Audet Bossie. His brother received three books, all religious: 'Ung libre appellat *Rationale divinorum officiorum*; item *la Bible* en papier en molle; item ung autre libre petit appellat *Anima fidelis*' (A small book called *Rationale of Sunday Offices*; item, the *Bible* printed on paper; item, another book called *Faithful Soul*).[6] One slender example and otherwise silence: the resulting cultural image of the clergy is not exactly a glowing one.

Turning from the clergy to the literate laity, one finds university men constituting the second group of those who possessed written materials. Thus in 1483 one sees Jean Redortier, bachelor of law and an inhabitant of L'Isle-sur-la-Sorgue, buying five printed books.[7] Dominique du Gay, a professor of law who lived in Carpentras, is another example. An inventory of his property which was drawn up after his death, in 1555, includes a large number of books, mainly law books: a real library.[8] The point needs no further insistence: the university was literate, but university men were few in number.

Landlords and the nobility constitute the third literate category. Two contrasting examples are given here. In one there was a correlation between wealth and the possession of books. The landlord of La Tour-d'Aigues, Raymond d'Agout, came from a powerful family in Provence. After Raymond's death a long inventory of his

---

[5] A copy of this breviary is kept in Bibliothèque Méjanes (Aix-en-Provence): *Breviarium in usum maioris et cathedralis ecclesiae Apten. Noviter impressum et emendatum* (Lyons, 1532).

[6] Vaucluse AD, 3 E 36/94, fol. 145r. The first title *Rationale divinorum officiorum* is Guillaume Durand's book, which was written in the thirteenth century and printed in Mainz in 1459. It was a very common handbook. I am grateful to P. Biller for its identification.

[7] Vaucluse AD, 3 E 38/500, fol. 195r.   [8] Vaucluse AD, 3 B 3410, fol. 13r.

goods was drawn up, by his usual notary, in 1503. Thirty-six books were itemised; two were manuscript. The titles reveal romances, texts of classical antiquity, law books, works of piety. If Latin predominates, French, Italian and German are also present.[9] Very different is the case of the landlord of Cabrières-d'Avignon, Jean d'Ancézune. In the 1490s, he owned many manuscript charters and papers and also printed books. Yet, through a deed written in Latin, it is known that he was not able to read them: 'Cum ipse sit ignarus literarum et latina verba non intelligit ... ' (As he is illiterate and does not understand Latin words ...).[10] While landowning and nobility tended to encourage literacy, they were insufficient to ensure it.

Some books can be found outside these three categories. These cases are exceptions, and sometimes it is not clear that the 'books' in question are 'books' in the modern sense of the term. In the sources used here only two examples crop up, both, it should be noted, from the very end of the period. In 1544, Master Damas Debert, an inhabitant of Cucuron, possessed 'ung libre dict *Virgille vieulh*' (a book called *Antique Virgil*), and another one without cover or title.[11] In 1558, an inhabitant of Mallemort, Antoine Boutier, had among other papers – especially notarial deeds – 'ung livre appelé *le Guidon* en français' (a book called *The Guide* in French) and another one in paper with only ten sheets written and the rest blank. While the first was clearly an actual book, a kind of guidebook, the second was just a manuscript copybook or register, and not exactly what is now called a 'book', even though that is the word used by the notary.[12]

To sum up: in Provence, few members of what was a rural society had books in their homes. These people were heirs to Roman Law, and in their society it was not rare for some documents, particularly notarial deeds, to be kept in these homes, in case of lawsuits. As far as books were concerned, most people only had the opportunity to see them, in church, in a castle, or in a notary's office. To these people a book was unfamiliar, strange in two senses of the word – foreign and bizarre. At the same time there was among these people a deeply felt veneration for the written text. This, in short, was the cultural milieu within which the Waldensians lived.

[9] Vaucluse AD, 3 E 55/35, fols. 409v–421r.   [10] Vaucluse AD, E Familles 331.
[11] Vaucluse AD, 3 E 36/134, fol. 26r.
[12] Bouches-du-Rhône AD, 418 E 226, fol. 103r.

2 THE *BARBES*: MEN OF THE BOOK

Although different forms of organisation can be found in the first centuries of Waldensianism, by the end of this religious movement, in the later middle ages, one simple form prevailed.[13] On the one hand there was the flock of the believers, and on the other the body of preachers who were called 'barbes', a Piedmontese word meaning 'uncles'. These *barbes* were always recruited from the broader Waldensian community, that is to say, from a rural populace. They were given three or four years of education, and then they were allowed into the body of the *barbes*, taking the three traditional vows of poverty, chastity and obedience, and receiving new names. They could then begin to preach to their people, going round in twos and in secret. They were undertaking a clandestine and itinerant mission, risky and sometimes dangerous. They would at the same time carry on some innocuous official trade, in order to avoid the attention of the authorities. The mission to their faithful flock had two parts, preaching to them and hearing their confessions.

Important to the present theme is the training which was given to the future *barbes*, of which we have two early sixteenth-century descriptions. During three or four winters of instruction they learnt to read and write. Here there was a contrast with the lack of education of the Roman clergy. They learnt in a *barbe*'s house, and probably directly from holy scripture. In addition they learnt by heart several books of the bible, in particular Matthew and John and some Epistles. They learnt in the vernacular, that is Romance or Provençal, in order to be understood by their people, and, of course, they preached in the same language.

Small manuscript books, almost always written in Romance, were

---

[13] On the *barbes* see Audisio, pp. 225–58, and G. Audisio, *Le Barbe et l'inquisiteur. Le procès du barbe vaudois Pierre Griot par l'inquisiteur Jean de Roma, Apt 1532* (Aix-en-Provence, 1979). On the books used during the training of the *barbes* see the latter pp. 105–6, where Pierre Griot says 'Evangile sainct Mathieu et sainct Jehan, et les apostres Thimoteum et Titum et les épitres de sainct Pierre, sainct Jehan, sainct Jacques et sainct Jude. Et mesmement ledict qui parle dict qu'il scavoit desjà sainct Mathieu et les épitres canonicalles en sa langue maternelle briansonnoys et deux chapitres de sainct Luc' (the gospel of St Matthew and [the gospel] of St John, and the apostles [to] Timothy and Titus [*correctly*: and the Apostle's [St Paul's] epistles to Timothy and Titus] and the epistles of St Peter, St John, St James and St Jude. And in particular the said person who is speaking said that he already knew St Matthew and the canonical epistles in his mother tongue of Briançon [in the Briançonnais dialect] and two chapters of St Luke); and also the passage from Morel quoted above, p. 160.

used by the *barbes* to help them in their mission. Even if many of them were lost or burnt, along with their 'heretic' owners, some of these have survived and can still be seen in several European libraries (see plate 8). Examples are the splendid parchment bible in Carpentras and, probably more representatively, the five small parchment or paper books which are now in Geneva. These treatises of piety written in Romance provide an important access to the piety and outlook of the *barbes* themselves. They are described more fully in the chapter by Brenon (ch. 8).

Now, how literate were the *barbes*? And how learned? Different and contradictory evidence bears on these questions. The Waldensian faithful were positive about their spiritual guides. The *barbes* seemed literate to Waldensians who were being brought to trial both in the Stettin area at the end of the fourteenth century[14] and in the Alps a hundred years later.[15] During his trial in 1532, the young Pierre Griot, who had not yet been received as a *barbe*, talked about 'hommes doctes' (learned men) among the *barbes*.[16] On the other hand on several occasions they were described as illiterate and ignorant. In 1530 Morel's formal account of the Waldensians given in a document which itself played a part in early contacts between *barbes* and the Reformers – described the training of illiterate novices who were recruited among peasants.[17] There is, further, the testimony of the Dominican inquisitor Jean de Roma, who prosecuted heretics, principally Waldensians, in Provence in the 1530s. In a treatise against the Waldensians, which was sent to the Parlement of Aix, he wrote about the *barbes*: 'Dicti predicatores sunt multum ignorantes et nullas habent litteras nisi aliquis eorum humanitatum et valde barbaras' (The said preachers are very ignorant and apart from some of their humanists they are totally ignorant and barbarian).[18]

Pierre Griot may have come near the truth when discriminating two groups among the *barbes*: on the one hand the majority who

---

[14] For instance, Kurze, p. 164, *aliqui litterati*.
[15] Isère AD, B 4350–1: Procédures contre les vaudois du Dauphiné, 1487–8. The *barbes* hold books: B 4350, fols. 87r, 119r, 286r, 300v. For example Peyret Griot, from Pragelas, questioned by the inquisitor on 10 October 1488 said: 'The *barbes* hold a book written in French in which their sect is written and when they come to Waldensians' homes they read this book [which is] written in the vernacular' (B 4350, fol. 153v).
[16] Audisio, *Le Barbe et l'inquisiteur*, p. 102, especially speaking about the *barbe* Georges.
[17] Vinay, p. 37.
[18] Paris, Archives Nationales J 851, no. 2, fol. 14r.

were less learned, though able to read and write, and on the other hand a few who were more learned, like Morel or the *barbe* Georges. Talking about the latter, Pierre Griot declared 'que c'est ung des hommes doctes de la compaignie' (that he is one of the learned men of the company). In Provence itself the duality is exemplified by Pierre Griot, who was just a novice and still being trained, and his master Jean Serre, who owned several books in Latin, Italian and French.[19] These can be set against both the general educational level of the Roman clergy, and also the Reformers and a Dominican like Jean de Roma. The academic minds of the latter filtered literacy: anyone who claimed to preach and teach the people while not knowing Latin was an illiterate, and a literate man was someone who spoke Latin. The general picture seems, then, to have been this. The *barbes* were more literate than most of the Roman clergy, but less learned than contemporary intellectuals; learned in the eyes of their rural flock, but they were lacking in learning when seen through the eyes of the learned of the time and compared to them.

One needs to underline, alongside the pastoral and spiritual roles of the *barbes*, their cultural role; for at a time when books were rarely visible, ordinary Waldensians could see them in their own houses. *Barbes* visited them, and took books out of their bags: everyone present could see these books, hear the words read in them, touch them. Thus the *barbes'* organisation and pastoral work was a vehicle which brought the written word closer to the Waldensians than to their contemporaries.

3 THE WALDENSIANS: LITERATE PEASANTS?

How far did the *barbes'* teaching raise the educational level of their flock? Put another way: were ordinary Waldensians, and not just the *barbes*, more literate than Roman Catholics?

In Provence, as in other areas of Europe, when reformed ideas spread they were linked with 'heretical' books.[20] Between 1530 and 1559 about thirty people were prosecuted by the Parlement of Provence simply for possessing some book which was supposed to be heretical. They all lived outside the Waldensian area. Thus in 1540

---

[19] About this declaration concerning the *barbe* Georges, see Audisio, *Le Barbe et l'inquisiteur*, p. 102. About Jean Serre see Audisio, pp. 250–3.

[20] On this general topic see J.-F. Gilmont (ed.), *La Réforme et le livre. L'Europe et l'imprimé, 1517–v. 1570* (Paris, 1990).

Noë Tabueys and his son Vincent, both from St Vincent in the diocese of Embrun, were condemned for heresy because a book entitled *Les grands pardons et indulgences* (The Great Pardons and Indulgences) was found in their house. The father was burnt alive in a public square in Aix and the son was branded on the forehead with a red-hot iron, which left the mark of a cross, and banished forever from Provence.[21] Most of these people who possessed books were not peasants but, rather, craftsmen, teachers, students, lawyers and doctors.

The ordinary Waldensians, were, by contrast, peasants. Did they own books? Some evidence suggests they did. In 1532 an inhabitant of the little Waldensian village of Gignac, Tomas Dauphin, was denounced to the inquisitor of Apt on the ground that he or his brother had books: an almanac, and a book of sermons.[22] Philippe Sambuc was denounced because while walking in the road he had showed the person travelling with him some *Matines* (Matins) in which there were many prayers of the Old Testament.[23] A tailor from Roussillon, a certain Pierre Fadier, could read; he attracted attention through his imprudent showing of a red book which, according to him, had been written by Luther.[24] In 1540 the property of the Pellenc family was confiscated because of heresy. Several papers and books were found, among them a copy of the bible which was printed in Neuchâtel in 1535 and paid for by the Waldensian community after the decision of the synod of Chanforan in 1532.[25] There is no doubt that the book was present in Provence among ordinary Waldensians. Nor is there doubt about the implication of this: that they – or some of them – could read it. The question is how they learned to read, since schools were few in number and principally to be found in towns.

Judicial records from the 1530s point to an answer. In 1532 Barthélemy Dauphin was denounced as a Waldensian by a cleric of the cathedral of Apt. The latter declared to an inquisitor that, when visiting a friend, he had found Barthélemy in the house, standing at a table, like a preacher. Antoine Pellison declared that he saw 'ung maître qu'on appeloit Barthomio Daulphin qui enseignoit les

[21] Bouches-du-Rhône AD, B 5443, 16 October 1540.
[22] Aix-en-Provence, Musée Arbaud Ms. MQ 755, 25 May 1532.
[23] Aix-en-Provence, Musée Arbaud Ms. MQ 755, 25 May 1532.
[24] Aix-en-Provence, Musée Arbaud Ms. MQ 755, 26 May 1532.
[25] On the Waldensian bible see Audisio, pp. 183–7.

enfants et les pères desdicts enfans, lesquels estoient de la terre de Saignon' (a master who was called Bartholomew Dauphin who taught children and their fathers, who were from the land of Saignon).[26] During his trial Pierre Griot declared to Jean de Roma that 'la coustume des barbes est de tenir les jeunes enfans en escoliers tout l'yver' (barbes are wont to keep young children as pupils throughout winter).[27]

This evidence opens the way for the suggestion that, although ordinary Waldensians were peasants, they were distinct from others in their greater concern with reading and writing. In 1534 Hugon Bertin, of Lourmarin, a totally Waldensian village in the Luberon region, was condemned for heresy by the archbishop of Aix because he 'tenoit les escolles de la dicte secte luthérienne en sa maison, a esté remys par le dict official et inquisiteur au bras séculier, et que la dicte maison seroit rasée et démolie, au milieu de laquelle seroit mise et plantée une grande croix: ce que fut faict' (held the schools of the said Lutheran sect in his home; he was to be handed over to the secular arm, and his house was to be razed and demolished, [and] in the middle of its [ground] a large cross was to be placed and implanted: which was done).[28] A few years later another totally Waldensian village of the Luberon, Mérindol, became a small centre for schools and printed books: a literary and cultural meeting-place.[29]

4 CONCLUSION

Waldensians held a special place in the general picture of the culture of Provence of that period. As in other French provinces, what was most widespread was an oral culture. Clearly, the preaching of the barbes was something which worked very effectively within this oral

---

[26] Aix-en-Provence, Musée Arbaud Ms. MQ 755, 23 and 21 May 1532. Saignon is a village near Apt.

[27] Audisio, Le Barbe et l'inquisiteur, p. 126. [28] Bouches-du-Rhône AD, G 205.

[29] Several discussions of the particular cultural situation of Mérindol exist: see, for example, for 1539–40 J. Aubery, Histoire de l'exécution de Cabrières et de Mérindol (Paris, 1645), re-edited by G. Audisio (Mérindol, 1982), p. 30: 'there was a bookseller in Mérindol'. Paris BN Ms. fr. 16545, fol. 58v: 'Helion Barbaroux, after dinner, at home in Mérindol read L'Antithèse, that is, the difference between Christ and the pope.' See also the condemnation act issued by the Parlement on 18 November 1540 against the inhabitants of Mérindol: 'in the said place there is a school of errors and wrong doctrines of the said sects, people who teach the said errors and wrong doctrines and booksellers who printed and sell books full of such wrong doctrines' (Audisio, p. 531).

culture. At the same time there was a divide between the generality of the Roman Catholic population and ordinary Waldensians, in that the latter, unlike the former, did not have to look far for books. Books came to them, came into their homes. They could touch the book brought in by the *barbe*, and, perhaps, even read it. Given the nature of the sources it is impossible to measure precisely how literate country people were at this time. However, one can confidently put forward the following relative statements on this theme. Waldensians were closer than their contemporaries to written culture. Books, earlier in manuscript and later in printed form, held a greater attraction for them. Both propositions need to be borne in mind when one examines the decision of the synod of Chanforan in 1532 to have the bible printed, and in French. Provençal Waldensian peasants were more literate than contemporary Provençal Catholic peasants. Waldensian peasants saw their *barbes* as learned, relative to themselves, while the same *barbes*, ignorant of Latin, seemed illiterate to both learned Catholics and the Reformed clergy.

An apparent paradox is the fact that Waldensians were nearer to books than other rural people but felt less awe for the written word: quite reasonably, perhaps, because it had less mystery for them? It was not difficult for the Waldensians of the first half of the sixteenth century to be more literate than their contemporaries – a pattern which was to be repeated with Provençal Protestants. The link between literacy and 'heresy' is once again evident, and it should not surprise one. The Waldensians, like other 'heretics', had a real worship for the Word of God, the holy bible. This was the best way to meet God through his Word: reading the Book. Consequently one had to learn to read. Clearly not all Waldensians were literate, but it is highly probable that some of them were. At this social level, even a small number of the literate is unexpected and remarkable. What now needs further investigation is the relative status that oral, written and image had among the 'heretics' compared to contemporary Catholics. But that is another story, and probably another history.

CHAPTER II

Writing and resistance among Beguins of Languedoc and Catalonia

Robert E. Lerner

Vernacular propaganda. Modern revolutionary and resistance movements would be inconceivable without it: 'these are the times that try mens' souls'; 'qu'est-ce que le tiers état?'; 'Arbeiter aller Länder vereinigt euch.' Did any remotely comparable propaganda exist in the medieval period? The chapters by Professors Hudson and Šmahel in this volume (chs. 13 and 14), treating respectively Lollardy and Hussitism, demonstrate that the answer must be 'yes'. Here I propose that the earliest incidence in western Europe of the use of vernacular propaganda to support religious dissent and resistance occurred in the first quarter of the fourteenth century among Beguins of Languedoc and Catalonia. Before then western European Cathars had produced some original religious writing, but not in the vernacular,[1] and Waldensians circulated vernacular texts, but not original ones.[2] Thus the Beguins opened a new chapter in the history of the relationship between writing and resistance.

Definitions both of *propaganda* and of *Beguin* are immediately necessary. Propaganda grows out of pedagogy; the word itself derives from the Latin for *propagating* – earnestly disseminating – the faith, as in *Congregatio de propaganda fide*. No sharp line of demarcation can be drawn between propaganda and instructional manuals

---

[1] Cathar writing was primarily disputational (i.e. learned works meant to convince learned readers) or liturgical (i.e. handbooks of prayers and rites). Passages in the inquisitorial records of southern France indicate that Cathar believers (*credentes*) possessed books acquired from their religious leaders (*perfecti*), but most of the references in question are opaque or ambiguous regarding the language and/or the contents of the books. So far as I can judge, there is no indisputable evidence that Cathar *perfecti* wrote discursive works of their own in the vernacular meant for the instruction of their flocks. See further the chapter in this volume by Peter Biller (ch. 4), who may be inclined to give more benefit of the doubt to the disputable evidence than I am.

[2] Until the middle of the fourteenth century the only known writings of Waldensians were translations, with rare exceptions translations of scripture. See the chapter in this volume by Alexander Patschovsky (ch. 7).

meant to clarify tenets and codify precepts of behaviour for groups of believers. Nevertheless, egregious propaganda *reveals, denounces* and *arouses*; that is, it communicates truths long hidden or hitherto unknown, identifies enemies and instills emotions of partisanship. Although propaganda can serve to recruit non-believers, it need not be designed primarily for that goal; instead it may aim to sustain the morale of those already converted. Similarly, although it aims to influence conduct, it need not intend to incite violent action.[3]

Following arbitrary but standard scholarly usage, I distinguish *Beguin* from *beguine*. The latter term usually designates semi-regular women of northern Europe, mostly cloistered, whereas I use Beguin to denote male and female Franciscan tertiaries, solely of Languedoc and Catalonia, who gained religious guidance from Spiritual Franciscans. The practice of calling these people Beguins descends from inquisitors (the term was pejorative); their own self-designation was 'Poor Brethren of Penitence'. Some lived communally; others lived at home in family units. In either case all sought to follow Franciscan ideals of poverty and humility while living to a greater or lesser extent in the world and without taking monastic vows. All attended communal devotional meetings, and all were partisans of Franciscan rigourism.[4]

Let a succinct passage from the inquisitor's manual of Bernard Gui, written around 1324, serve to establish the central point I wish to pursue:

By lawful inquisition ... the source of the Beguins' errors and pernicious opinions has been discovered. They have culled these, at least in part, from the books and pamphlets of Brother Peter of John Olivi ... that is, from his commentary on the Apocalypse, which they have both in Latin and vernacular translation, and also from some treatises which they say

---

[3] My thinking about propaganda has been clarified by discussion with R. W. Scribner and by Scribner's article, 'Reformatorische Bildpropaganda', in B. Tolkemitt and R. Wohlfeil (eds.), *Historische Bildkunde: Probleme – Wege – Beispiele* (Berlin, 1991), pp. 83–106.

[4] The standard work remains R. Manselli, *Spirituali e beghini in Provenza* (Rome, 1959). For Catalonia see J. Perarnau, *L'"Alia informatio" beguinorum d'Arnau de Vilanova* (Barcelona, 1978), and A. Rubio Vela and M. Rodrigo Lizondo, 'Els beguins de València en el segle xiv', in *Estudis en memòria del professor Manuel Sanchis Guarner*, vol. i (Valencia, 1984), pp. 327–41. An attempt at drawing a sociological profile of Occitan Beguins is J.-L. Biget, 'Autour de Bernard Délicieux: franciscanisme et société en Languedoc entre 1295 et 1330', *Revue d'histoire de l'église de France* 70 (1984), 75–93; the result remains very impressionistic, especially Biget's assertion (83) that the Beguins came predominantly from the 'upper middle class'.

and believe that he wrote, ... all of which they have in vernacular translations. These they read, believe in, and treat as veritable Scriptures.[5]

How did groups of people come to revere the works of a near contemporary as 'veritable Scriptures' in defiance of ecclesiastical prohibition? A full treatment of this question would have to consider the political and social history of the regions concerned, the internal history of the Franciscan Order, and the politics of the papacy between 1290 and 1320.[6] Needless to say, this cannot be done in a short article. Instead I will concentrate here on examining the emergence of a propaganda literature among the Beguins, as well as on the modes of transmission of teachings inscribed in vernacular texts.

To begin with 'Brother Peter of John' himself, by the last decade of his life – that is, from 1289 until 1298 – Peter Olivi had become a notoriously controversial theologian and the unquestioned leader of the 'Spiritual' party within the Franciscan Order.[7] In this period Olivi had returned from a two-year stay in Florence to his native territory of Lower Languedoc (he had been born near Béziers and he died in the Franciscan convent of Narbonne), and was engaged in a variety of literary as well as pastoral activities. Olivi's crowning written achievement was his *Lectura super Apocalypsim*, completed very shortly before his death, a work in which he formulated more clearly and explicitly than ever before a theology of history indebted greatly to Joachim of Fiore but containing numerous original aspects.

A sketch of the story Olivi told in his *Lectura* is necessary before proceeding.[8] In his view poverty and prophecy confirmed each

---

[5] I use the translation from Gui, *Manuel*, vol. I, p. 110 by Wakefield and Evans, p. 412. An edition of the original Latin of Gui's classic description of the Beguins, with variant readings from a manuscript ignored by Mollat is by Perarnau, *L'"Alia informatio"*, pp. 15–16.

[6] Guidance on some of these matters may be found in K. Balthasar, *Geschichte des Armutsstreites im Franziskanerorden bis zum Konzil von Vienne* (Münster, 1911); M. D. Lambert, *Franciscan Poverty* (London, 1961); and *Franciscains d'Oc: Les Spirituels ca. 1280–1324 (CaF* 10, 1975).

[7] The best survey of Olivi's career and doctrines is D. Burr, *The Persecution of Peter Olivi* (Philadelphia, 1976). Olivi's name appears in the sources as 'Petrus Iohannis', hence the English translation (unwieldy as it may be), 'Peter of John'. Here and throughout I use English equivalents for first names in order to avoid having to choose between French, Occitan and Catalan equivalents – as between 'Pierre', 'Peire' or 'Pere'.

[8] The *Lectura* remains unpublished; an edition by P. Vian is expected shortly. See provisionally the translation of some of the *Lectura* in P. Vian (ed.), *Pietro di Giovanni Olivi: scritti scelti* (Rome, 1989), pp. 115–44, and D. Burr, 'Olivi's apocalyptic timetable', *Journal of Medieval and Renaissance Studies* 11 (1981), 237–60.

other. The prophetic meaning of the bible could be penetrated most deeply if the reader abstained from the flesh by practising poverty. Conversely, biblical prophecy showed infallibly that God's plan entailed a march from 'carnality' to 'spirituality' characterised by ever greater collective abstinence from all worldly goods. Progress towards 'spirituality' continued within the framework of Church history, reaching a penultimate stage with the coming of St Francis. Yet the forces of Antichrist continually sought to check this progress and were succeeding best at the present time. In Olivi's day 'practically the whole Church [was] infected from head to toe and almost turned into a new Babylon'.[9] Worse, the 'great Antichrist' himself would appear soon; Olivi knew this would happen some time during the fourteenth century, and most likely before 1340.[10] The true followers of St Francis, the 'spirituals', would be persecuted brutally, but by their patient endurance they would help accomplish spirituality's final victory, a wondrous earthly Sabbath of universal illumination to come before the Judgement.[11]

Although this story surely was designed for evoking a partisan sense of calling, Olivi himself apparently had no intention of telling it in detail to his lay followers, the Beguins. A form less appropriate for the dissemination of propaganda among laity than Scholastic exegesis can hardly be imagined, and Olivi's exegesis in particular was very dense. (Current teachers of undergraduates today are always at a disadvantage when they wish to present selections from medieval exegesis as primary source readings for their students.) Yet probably before the end of Olivi's life and surely right after his death, aspects of his story were reaching the Beguins of Lower Languedoc by another route, the dissemination of some exhortative tracts penned by the master.

One was by means of works Olivi wrote himself. Although Olivi dedicated his literary efforts primarily to technical exegesis and theological *quodlibeta*, he also wrote several simple and affective pastoral works meant for lay readers, among which are four short

---

[9] Burr, 'Timetable', p. 238.   [10] Burr, 'Timetable', p. 260.
[11] It may be noted for purposes of comparison that late-medieval Waldensians also drew on a legend of history that helped buttress their faith; see, most recently, Biller, 'Construction'. Yet Olivi's narrative differed from that of the Waldensians in two crucial respects: it depended entirely on interrelated close readings from the bible, thus claiming infallibility, and it extended into the future.

treatises meant almost certainly for communities of Beguins.[12] In these Olivi by no means set forth his historical schemata systematically, but he did urge affective devotions and readiness to endure suffering in the face of the imminent eschatological crisis. According to him the devout lay christian should resist those who 'prepare the throne of Antichrist', meditate on 'the revilings, vituperations, privations, dolours, torments, and passions sustained by the Son of God', and don the defensive armour of faith and contempt of self.[13]

Such expressions were surely designed to encourage militant 'spiritual' faith, and it would be appropriate to categorise them immediately as 'vernacular propaganda' if only they had been written in the vernacular. In fact they were not. Given Olivi's ease in employing the exhortatory mode, one might have expected him to have written in the vernacular, yet it seems as if he never did so. Apparently he assumed that his Latin exhortatory works would be communicated to lay audiences by means of vernacular translations made by others.

In fact all four of Olivi's short treatises for Beguins survive in Provençal translations; two indeed survive in two different Provençal translations.[14] Were Beguins meant to read these translations themselves? Before I began the present enquiry I assumed that Olivi's teachings came to be revered by numerous laypeople because of the growth of vernacular literacy: laity attached themselves to certain doctrines because most of them could read these doctrines. On examination, however, I have found this assumption to be anachronistic, for the transmission among Beguins of vernacular teachings was accomplished mostly by means of ears rather than by eyes.[15]

[12] See R. Manselli, 'Les opuscules spirituels de Pierre Jean-Olivi et la piété des béguins de Langue d'Oc', in *La Religion populaire en Languedoc du XIIIe siècle à la moitié du XIVe siècle (CaF* 11, 1976), pp. 187–216. The treatises are edited in Manselli, *Spirituali e beghini*, pp. 267–90, and are discussed and translated into Italian by Vian, *Scritti scelti*, pp. 145–69. Another of Olivi's works that may have been meant for a lay audience was his commentary on the *Pater noster*. In this he sketched out his view of the history of the Church and declared that because of the struggle against Antichrist the words 'lead us not into temptation' must be said 'with strong crying': see Vian, *Scritti scelti*, pp. 179–80.

[13] Ed. Manselli, *Spirituali e beghini*, pp. 282, 279, 288.

[14] For bibliography, Vian, *Scritti scelti*, p. 150; on the two treatises that survived in two different versions, Manselli, *Spirituali e beghini*, pp. 269–70.

[15] Ideally a study of this sort should be accompanied by statistics about literacy rates, but I am aware of no studies of lay literacy in Languedoc or Catalonia during the period in question. J. M. Madurell i Marimon, *Manuscrits en Català anteriors a la impremta (1321–1474)* (Barcelona, 1974), is scarcely relevant because it lists only six documentary references to

The earliest hints about the transmission of Olivi's works in the vernacular concern the case of the Franciscan Matthew of Bouzigues, one of Olivi's adherents from the convent of Béziers.[16] In 1300 Matthew fled to Italy because of measures taken against the Provençal Spirituals by the majority in the order, and he was joined in his flight by five male and thirteen female Beguins. According to a hostile source, Matthew's company elected him 'pope' when they were in Rome. Of interest here is the fact that the group fled with some of Olivi's books, including at least two of Olivi's pastoral works in Provençal translations. Although we know no more, it seems likely that the works would have been read aloud to the circle of Beguins by Matthew in his capacity as their pastoral guide.

Unfortunately virtually nothing reliable is known about the use made of Olivi's writings by Beguins between 1300 and 1318, but considerable evidence exists regarding the composition and propagation of vernacular writings for Beguins during that span of time on the southern side of the Pyrenees. The author of the writings in question was Olivi's most prominent Catalan disciple, Arnold of Villanova (*c.* 1240–1311).[17] Arnold had achieved great fame and fortune as a medical doctor, serving as physician to James II of Aragon and professor of medicine at Montpellier; then, in the last decade of his life, he began a second career as an evangelical–eschatological prophet and became the most prominent living champion of the Spiritual Franciscans. Although Arnold did not

manuscripts in Catalan before 1350. The earliest statistics for lay literacy offered in a recent survey pertain to Nuremberg in 1487: see A. Wendehorst, 'Wer konnte im Mittelalter lesen und schreiben?', in J. Fried (ed.), *Schulen und Studium im sozialen Wandel des Hohen und Späten Mittelalters* (Sigmaringen, 1986), p. 32, n. 176. It may be added that those who commissioned and bought Latin and vernacular manuscripts and printed books in the fifteenth and early sixteenth centuries were predominantly higher clergy, lawyers, physicians, merchants and higher nobility: see T. Brandis, 'Handschriften- und Buchproduktion im 15. und frühen 16. Jahrhundert', in L. Grenzmann and K. Stackmann (eds.), *Literatur und Laienbildung im Spätmittelalter und in der Reformationszeit* (Stuttgart, 1984), p. 179.

[16] F. Delorme, 'La Confessio Fidei du Frère Matthieu de Bouzigues', *Études Franciscaines* 49 (1937), 224–39; D. Zorzi, 'Testi inediti Francescani in lingua Provenzale', *Miscellanea del Centro di Studi Medievali*, ser. 1 (Milan, 1956), 249–68; Manselli, *Spirituali e beghini*, pp. 42–6. Matthew's flight to Italy definitely transpired between 1298 and 1304; I infer that it happened in 1300 on the grounds that legislation against Franciscan owners of Olivi's books as well as against Beguins was passed in 1299 and that Matthew must have gone to Rome during the jubilee year.

[17] On Arnold's career, with emphasis on the religious aspects, P. Diepgen, *Arnald von Villanova als Politiker und Laientheologe* (Basel, 1909); F. Santi, *Arnau de Vilanova: l'obra espiritual* (Valencia, [1987]); and H. Lee, M. Reeves and G. Silano, *Western Mediterranean Prophecy:*

take the Franciscan habit (he continued to act as professor and practitioner of medicine), he courageously espoused the cause of the Spirituals in the courts of kings and popes until his death in 1311 and was considered by some in the Spiritual party to be a messianic 'anointed one'.[18]

Here I wish solely to discuss Arnold of Villanova's role as religious author and 'publisher'. Arnold wrote many exhortatory and pastoral works meant explicitly for laypeople. Sometimes he wrote for lay recipients in Latin, choosing the more formal language when he knew a layperson could understand Latin or could be expected to have a Latin translator immediately nearby.[19] Clearly the prestige of writing about religion in the 'proper' language was overwhelming. Yet Arnold chose often to write in the vernacular as well. Some of his vernacular works are Catalan reworkings of his own Latin treatises. In this category are Catalan versions Arnold made of earlier Latin declarations of faith – searing works of propaganda that urged recipients to awaken to his truths and join his side.[20] In addition, Arnold wrote original vernacular compositions for laity, including two Catalan manuals of pastoral guidance designed expressly for Beguin communities. The first, dating from between 1302 and 1311, was directed to Beguins of Narbonne (apparently

---

the School of Joachim of Fiore and the Fourteenth-Century Breviloquium (Toronto, 1989), pp. 27–46. Santi and Lee et al., cite additional literature.

[18] He is hailed as unctus in the commentary to the Liber de Flore written by a Spiritual Franciscan, probably shortly after the election of pope Clement V in June 1305; see Grundmann, 'Liber de Flore', Ausgewählte Aufsätze 2, 101–65, esp. 128–32, 159–63. Although the paths of Olivi and Arnold may possibly have crossed in Languedoc in the 1290s (this is not certain), Arnold did not turn to eschatological prophecy under the influence of Olivi, but became a champion of the Spirituals after Olivi's death. Grundmann, 'Liber de Flore', pp. 129–31, establishes this point convincingly, but was unaware of evidence that Arnold drew on Olivi in 1302 now adduced by J. Perarnau, 'L'Ars catholicae philosophiae (primera redacció de la Philosophia catholica et divina) d'Arnau de Vilanova', Arxiu de textos Catalans antics 10 (1991), 20–1.

[19] Arnold's letter of spiritual guidance addressed to a Catalan female sympathiser, Bartholomea Muntaner, was written in Latin, in answer to a request by Bartholomea apparently sent to him in Latin: see the text in Diepgen, Arnold von Villanova, pp. 100–2. Arnold usually wrote for royalty in Latin, apparently because this was still the 'correct' procedure. An inventory of Arnold's religious writings (not without imprecisions) is F. Santi, 'Gli "Scripta Spiritualia" di Arnau de Vilanova', SM ser. 3, 26 (1985), 982–1005, repr. in Santi, Arnau, pp. 250–77.

[20] Arnold's Confessió de Barcelona of 1305, printed in Arnau de Villanova, Obres catalanes, vol. 1: Escrits religiosos, ed. M. Batllori (Barcelona, 1947), pp. 101–39, was a version of Arnold's Confessio Ilerdensis of 1303. His Raonament d'Avinyó of c. 1310, in Arnau, Obres catalanes, vol. 1, pp. 167–221, was a version of a manifesto that Arnold had read before a papal consistory in 1309. Note that Arnold (or an associate) made a Catalan translation (now lost) of his major Latin treatise, De tempore adventus Antichristi: see Santi's inventory, no. 79.

Arnold's Catalan was sufficiently comprehensible to a Provençal audience); the second, probably written between 1305 and 1311, seems to have been written for a Beguin community of Barcelona.[21]

Arnold's teachings in his Catalan works (both the reworkings of Latin texts and the original ones) were akin to Olivi's. God's chosen were those who renounced property, both individually and in common. Rampant ecclesiastical 'carnality' was a manifestation of Antichrist's imminent reign. A crescendo of evil would soon be reached in the 'great Antichrist's' open reign, but then would come a marvellous earthly Sabbath for the Church. Meanwhile devout laypeople should pursue lives of humility, charity, poverty, mortification and endurance: 'in renouncing all earthly goods we fear neither hunger nor thirst, neither heat nor cold, neither nakedness nor any other kind of affliction'. Just as Christ was 'scorned, and blasphemed, and mocked, and persecuted' so should his disciples be ready to be scorned, blasphemed, mocked and persecuted.[22]

An intriguing glimpse into the activities of a scriptorium Arnold set up in Barcelona, probably in 1305, gives some idea of how he intended his works to be propagated.[23] The scriptorium was located in the house of one of his associates in Barcelona, and seems to have been financed from income that Arnold himself provided. As we learn from an inventory made in 1311, when news of Arnold's death at sea reached Barcelona, the owner of the house in question, together with a disciple of Arnold's from Valencia, acting in their joint capacity as executors of Arnold's will, went to the scriptorium and there took possession of seventeen manuscript volumes containing Arnold's religious works. According to the inventory, these volumes were then in different stages of completion, some bound, some unbound. Most could not have been cheap, for most (perhaps all) were made of parchment. Six were illuminated and bound in

---

[21] Respectively, *Informatio beguinorum seu lectio narbone*, in Arnau, *Obres catalanes*, vol. I, pp. 141–66, and *Alia informatio beguinorum*, ed. Perarnau, *L'"Alia informatio"*, pp. 19–85.

[22] *Confessió de Barcelona*, pp. 114–15, 136–7; *Raonament d'Avinyó*, pp. 169–70; *L'"Alia informatio"*, pp. 37, 45. In the *Raonament* Arnold followed Olivi in specifying that the 'great Antichrist' would reign and meet his demise within the first forty years of the fourteenth century.

[23] For the following see R. Chabás, 'Inventario de los libros, ropas y demás efectos de Arnaldo de Villaneuva', *Revista de archivos* II Epoca 9 (1903), 189–203, meticulously analysed by Perarnau, *L'"Alia informatio"*, pp. 111–26. For a more extensive summary of Perarnau's findings than space allows here, see Lee *et al.*, *Western Mediterranean Prophecy*, pp. 55–8.

red.[24] Given that fourteen of the seventeen volumes contained works by Arnold in both Catalan and Latin and only three contained works solely in Catalan, it is clear that most of the intended recipients were supposed to be reasonably learned.

Who were the intended recipients? The inventory answers that question when it states that Arnold's two executors assigned all seventeen volumes to 'various people of penitence', that is, Beguins. Ambiguity exists only as to whether 'various people of penitence' meant various individual Beguins or various communities of Beguins. Nevertheless, independent evidence shows that the scriptorium in Barcelona must have been manufacturing books meant for the main communal house of Beguins in Barcelona, for a notarial instrument of 1312 shows that the 'minister' of the Barcelona community was able to cite for the record the entire text of Arnold's second vernacular manual for Beguins.[25] Other pieces of relevant evidence are that the minister was literate and that a ruling of the province of Tarragona against Catalan Beguins of 1312 prohibited them from coming together in 'congregations or conventicles'.[26] Since Arnold himself referred in his second manual for Beguins to public readings and to the need for Beguins to assemble to listen to 'holy words',[27] it seems warranted to infer that many or all of the books manufactured in the Barcelona scriptorium were meant for several Beguin houses in Catalonia, and that the mode of communication of Arnold's teachings in such cases would have been public readings in Beguin 'conventicles' by learned intermediaries such as the Barcelona minister.[28]

Evidence concerning the presence of Arnold's vernacular works in Valencia is complementary. I have mentioned that one of the two persons who drew up the inventory of 1311 and distributed the

---

[24] Chabás, 'Inventario', p. 190: 'invenimus ... vi preparata illuminata et ligata cum coopertis rubeus'. In addition to six volumes specified as made from parchment, the six 'illuminated and bound in red' must have been of parchment as well. None of the seventeen volumes are said to be of paper even though paper manuscripts are mentioned frequently elsewhere in the inventory.

[25] Ed. Perarnau, L'"Alia informatio", pp. 90–101.

[26] Ed. Perarnau, L'"Alia informatio", p. 104.

[27] Perarnau, L'"Alia informatio", p. 52, and Perarnau's commentary, pp. 52–3.

[28] The document of 1312 shows that the Barcelona minister, William Martí, was capable of reading and writing in the vernacular: see Perarnau, L'"Alia informatio", p. 96: 'la confessió per mi feta en scrit'. His Latinity is uncertain. Perarnau, pp. 91–2, hypothesises that William was the same person who appears elsewhere in the Barcelona records as the brother of a wealthy priest.

volumes then in Barcelona scriptorium to 'people of penitence' was a disciple of Arnold's from Valencia. Specifically, Raymond Conesa was a cleric who served as the bishop of Valencia's 'provost of alms' and was one of four men designated by Arnold in 1305 to be executors of his will.[29] (The others were all Barcelonans.) Raymond was so devoted a servant of Arnold's that after his master's death he attended to his testamentary affairs for two years in southern France – in Avignon, Marseilles, Montpellier and elsewhere – distributing books as part of this office.[30] Raymond was also linked to the Beguin community of Valencia by family ties. In 1315 his widowed mother entered a novitiate among the Beguins of Valencia and in 1316 she made her profession, her son being present as a witness.[31]

In the same year, 1316, Raymond Conesa's role as Arnold of Villanova's surrogate was fully put to the test when the vicar of the archbishop of Tarragona condemned thirteen of Arnold's works – nine of which were in the vernacular – as heretical and because 'many simple men and women' who 'used such books' were prone to be led by them into error.[32] In response, Raymond engaged in a courageous but hopeless legal campaign to defend Arnold's books and reputation.[33] The surviving documentation shows that in January of 1318 he and several others in Valencia, including the 'minister' of the local Beguin community, volunteered to exhibit some of Arnold's books in order to demonstrate their orthodoxy. But after a council of Tarragona meeting in February of 1318 not only again inveighed against Beguin 'conventicles', but broadened the ruling of 1316 by specifying that all Beguins in the province be prohibited from owning any theological books in the vernacular whatsoever, Raymond Conesa was required to surrender in Valencia a chest full of Arnold's books and also a volume containing

---

[29] Ed. R. Chabás, *Boletin de la Real Academia de la Historia* 28 (1896), 87–92.

[30] See the instrument of 22 October 1318, edited by R. d'Alós, 'De la marmessoria d'Arnau de Vilanova', *Miscel. lània Prat de la Riba* (Barcelona, 1923), pp. 289–306, at 301. I am indebted to John Bollweg for calling my attention to the importance of this publication.

[31] See the document published in Rubio Vela and Rodrigo Lizondo, 'Els beguins de València', p. 337.

[32] An edition of the condemnation appears in Santi, *Arnau*, pp. 283–9, as well as in Santi, 'Gli "Scripta Spiritualia"', pp. 1006–10.

[33] The complete documentation is assembled in M. Rodrigo Lizondo, 'La protesta de Valencia de 1318 y otros documentos inéditos referentes a Arnau de Vilanova', *Dynamis* 1 (1981), 241–73 (John Bollweg acquired a copy of this article for me). See p. 260 for Raymond Conesa's report of November 1316 that a Dominican had accused merchants of Valencia of being supporters of Arnold. It is unclear from the context, however, whether these

Arnold's complete vernacular oeuvre, now not for examination but for destruction.[34] Thus it appears certain that Arnold of Villanova's books were being made available to the Beguin community of Valencia for reading in communal gatherings by the learned cleric, Raymond Conesa.[35]

To return now to Languedoc, while nothing certain is known about links between Beguins and books there until 1318, it is clear that an Olivi cult was gaining enormous momentum between 1300 and 1318 among laity in the areas in and around Narbonne, Béziers and Carcassonne. Although legislation against the 'secta fratris Petri Iohannis' issued in 1299 by the Franciscan Order and parallel legislation against Beguins issued by a provincial council of Narbonne meeting at Béziers in the same year resulted in some persecution of Olivi's followers (especially within the Franciscan Order) until about 1305,[36] from then until 1317 the persecution fell into abeyance, apparently owing to the temporising policies of pope Clement V (a patient of Arnold of Villanova's) and the interregnum following Clement's death. The result seems to have borne out the wry observation of E. R. Dodds that 'the blood of the martyrs really is the seed of the Church, always provided that the seed falls on suitable ground and is not sown too thickly'.[37] Olivi gained a reputation for having been divinely illuminated: word spread that he had said on his death-bed 'he had received all his knowledge from God through infusion'; some of his disciples began to insist that his

---

merchants were supposed to have been owners of Arnold's books or adherents of Arnold's teachings.

[34] The condemnation of February 1318 (sometimes mistakenly dated to 1317) is edited by J. M. Pons i Guri in *Analecta sacra Tarraconensia* 48 (1975), 129. For the surrender of the books, Rodrigo Lizando, p. 250, n. 40: 'quandam caxietam plenam libris et operibus dicti magistri Arnaldi et unum volumen, extra ipsam caxietam, de omnibus operibus dicti magistri Arnaldi in romancio compilatis, tam per ipsum inquisitorem damnatis quam non damnatis'.

[35] The resident minister, Bernard Costa, could have done the reading, since he was definitely literate; on him see Rodgrigo Lizondo, 'La protesta de Valencia', pp. 251–2, 267, and Rubio Vela and Rodgrigo Lizondo, 'Els beguins de València', pp. 319, 337–9; Bernard's appearance in several Latin documents proves his Latinity.

[36] Manselli, *Spirituali e beghini*, pp. 40–1, 53–4, 81–90; Burr, *Persecution of Olivi*, p. 74. Overlooked supplementary evidence regarding persecutions in Languedoc appears in a complaint by Arnold of Villanova to pope Benedict XI of 2 June 1304: see Perarnau, *L'Ars catholicae*', p. 210. Although two or perhaps three Franciscans died from barbarous prison treatment in this period, almost certainly there were no burnings at the stake and no mass round-ups of either Franciscans or Beguins. In fact it is uncertain whether any Beguins were arrested at all.

[37] *Pagan and Christian in an Age of Anxiety* (Cambridge, 1965; repr. New York, 1970), p. 133.

teachings were 'just as true as the Gospels'.[38] In 1313 more crowds were said to be flocking to Olivi's tomb in Narbonne than were visiting the relics of St Francis at the Portiuncula; and around 1315 the Spirituals and Beguins in Béziers were said to have gained such respect among the clergy and 'the entire city' that they were considered 'saints of God and fundaments of the Church of God, called by God as if they were apostles'.[39]

Soon after ascending the papal chair in nearby Avignon, John XXII moved ruthlessly to make clear where the fundaments of the Church really lay.[40] In *Sancta Romana* (30 December 1317) the pope in effect ordered the destruction of Beguin communities in the provinces of Narbonne and Toulouse. Simultaneously he initiated formal investigations into the orthodoxy of Olivi's works. One result was the condemnation in 1318 of a vernacular compendium of Olivi's Revelation commentary.[41] Although a definitive condemnation of the full Latin commentary was delayed until 1326 because of unforeseen theological complications concerning the entire Franciscan Order, a general chapter of the Franciscans meeting at Marseilles in 1319 proscribed Olivi's Revelation commentary and other of his writings for use within the Order.[42]

---

[38] On Olivi's alleged death-bed statement, Burr, *Persecution of Olivi*, p. 5, n. 1 and p. 73. For assertions about his infallibility, the charges against the Spirituals lodged by the Franciscan community in March 1311, in *ALKG* 2 (1886), 371: 'dixerunt quod doctrina Fratris Petri predicti erat ita vera sicut evangelica' (they said that the doctrine of the aforesaid brother Peter was as true as the gospel); 'quod doctrina ... erat defendenda sicut articulus fidei' (that the teaching ... was to be defended as an article of faith). The allegations of the community seem trustworthy since they are confirmed by later Beguin trial records.

[39] On the crowds, a letter by Angelo Clareno in *ALKG* 1 (1885), 544; on the situation in Béziers, the statement of the Dominican Raymond Barrau, ed. P. Botineau, 'Les tribulations de Raymond Barrau, O.P. (1295–1338)', *MEFR* 76 (1965), 475–528 at 505: 'dominus episcopus predictus et officiales sui ... sustinebant beguinos et fratres predictos spirituales ... quos dicebant sanctos Dei et fundamentum ecclesie Dei, missus a Deo in mundum tamquam apostolos Dei, sic quod tota civitas Bitterrensis sequebatur eos'.

[40] The highlights of John's activities against the Spiritual Franciscans are recounted by Lambert, pp. 200–2. See also T. Turley, 'John XXII and the Franciscans: a reappraisal', in J. R. Sweeney and S. Chodorow (eds.), *Popes, Teachers, and Canon Law in the Middle Ages*, (Ithaca, 1989), pp. 74–88.

[41] The articles drawn up in 1318 by the Carmelite Gui Terrena and the Dominican Pierre de la Palu, from a Catalan treatise, *De statibus ecclesie secundum expositionem Apocalypsis*, are edited by J. Pou y Martí, *Visionarios, beguinos y fraticelos catalanes (siglos XIII–XV)* (Vich, 1930), pp. 489–512. The missing treatise was identified as a compendium of Olivi's Revelation commentary by J. Koch, 'Der Prozess gegen die Postille Olivis zur Apokalypse', *RTAM* 5 (1933), 305, a judgement upheld by subsequent scholarship.

[42] E. Pásztor, 'Le polemiche sulla "Lectura super Apocalypsim" di Pietro di Giovanni Olivi fino alla sua condanna', *BISI* 70 (1958), 365–424; see pp. 377–80 for the Franciscan condemnation. Inquisitors also knew of the *Littera magistrorum*, a judgement of eight

The records of trials conducted in Languedoc from 1318 until 1328 show that Olivi's reputation for infallibility had become deeply entrenched among the Beguins.[43] One examinee conceived of Olivi as a new Saint Peter: Peter Olivi and Saint Paul were the only infallible christian doctors whose teachings the Church should observe and guard 'without removing a single letter'.[44] According to others Olivi was Revelation's 'angel with a face like the sun, who held in his hand an open book' (Rev. 10:1-2); for them the 'open book' signified 'clear knowledge of the truth', or 'knowledge of what would happen in the future'.[45] Awe for Olivi's Revelation commentary was so great among the inculpated Beguins that one said: 'if all the heads of all the men in the world were in one head they would not be able to make such a book, unless through the work of the Holy Spirit'.[46]

The same records show how Olivi's 'clear knowledge of the truth' was spread in Beguin communities. Two points are central. First, the most influential of Olivi's writings by far was a vernacular version of his Revelation commentary. It is impossible to tell when this version was made. Already in 1299 the conciliar legislation of Béziers inveighed against *litterati* from approved orders who were preaching to Beguins that the end of the world was approaching and that the present was already the time of Antichrist, 'or almost'.[47] Doubtless the doctrine was Olivi's but whether the preachers were

theologians against Olivi's Revelation commentary delivered in Avignon to John XXII but not formally promulgated: see Koch, 'Der Prozess', pp. 305-6, and Gui in Wakefield and Evans, p. 413.

[43] The two repositories of evidence are: (1) the sentences handed down by Bernard Gui as inquisitor in the diocese of Toulouse from *c.* 1318 until *c.* 1324 and printed in Limborch (from what is now BL Add. 4697); (2) the records of Beguin hearings in Languedoc from *c.* 1323 to *c.* 1329 gathered in 1668 and 1669 by Colbert's agent Jean de Doat and preserved in volumes 27, 28, 34 and 35 of the Collection Doat of the Bibliothèque Nationale, Paris. See Manselli, *Spirituali e beghini*, pp. 297-345, for analysis of the entire contents as well as a large selection of edited texts. I am exceedingly grateful to Walter Wakefield for making available to me microfilm copies of volumes 27 and 28 of the Collection Doat, now on deposit at Northwestern University.

[44] Limborch, p. 306; passage cited by Leff, p. 220 n. 3.

[45] Limborch, p. 316; passage cited by Leff, p. 219 n. 1. Same view in the confession of Na Prous Boneta: Doat 27, fol. 79r; passage cited in W. H. May, 'The confession of Prous Boneta', in J. H. Mundy, R. W. Emery and B. N. Nelson (eds.), *Essays in Medieval Life and Thought Presented in Honor of Austin P. Evans* (New York, 1955), pp. 3-30, at 29-30.

[46] Doat 28, fol. 230r; passage cited in Leff, p. 222 n. 3.

[47] *Concilium provinciale anno MCCXCIX Biterris celebratum*, ed. E. Martène and U. Durand, *Thesaurus novus anecdotorum* (Paris, 1717), vol. IV, p. 226: 'plurimi litterati ... non immerito inter religiones ceteras approbata ... predicantium multis finem mundi instare et iam adesse, vel quasi, tempora antichristi'.

making use of a vernacular version of the Revelation commentary just a year or two after the Latin work had been completed is anyone's guess. All that is certain is that by 1318 a vernacular version was widely available.[48] Unfortunately, no copy of the vernacular Revelation commentary survives, but there is strong reason to believe that it was a compendium rather than a complete literal translation.[49] On this assumption it must have been a more effective work of propaganda than the original, not only in language but in form.[50]

Other writings by Olivi – and apparently also some by other Franciscan Spirituals – were available in the vernacular too. These are difficult to identify confidently from the trial evidence, but it seems as if some of Olivi's questions on poverty were circulating in vernacular translations or adaptations, as well as an assortment of pastoral and exhortatory tracts.[51] Nevertheless, the references to

---

[48] M. Bartoli, 'Jean xxii et les Joachimites du Midi', in *La papauté d'Avignon et le Languedoc* (*CaF* 26, 1991), pp. 237–56, takes it as certain (following Manselli) that the Provençal version of Olivi's Revelation commentary was made no earlier than 1318. To my mind, however, this point is open to doubt; see further note 49. It is generally assumed that the Catalan work examined in 1318 (as n. 41 above) was substantially the same as the Provençal version of the Revelation commentary mentioned frequently in the Provençal trial records.

[49] The work examined in 1318 was certainly a compendium: note that the Latin title given to it was *De statibus ecclesie secundum expositionem Apocalypsis*. Koch, 'Der Prozess', p. 305 n. 16, points out that Bernard Gui uses the words 'transposita in vulgari' (the same expression appears in the trial records), which Koch believes implies an adaptation rather than a translation. David Burr has kindly called my attention to the fact that the Catalan work identifies *Olivi* as the angel of Revelation 10:1 and hence cannot have been taken verbatim from Olivi. See Pou y Martí, *Visionarios*, p. 501. Since the representatives of the Franciscan majority at the Council of Vienne charged that Olivi's followers conceived of him as the angel of the Apocalypse who came after the one 'who has the sign of the living God' (see *ALKG* 2 (1886) 371) they may have been alluding to a teaching in the compendium; if so, this would constitute proof that the compendium was composed before 1318.

[50] Further study would be necessary to determine whether all the positions imputed to Olivi in his 'postilla' in the trial records can actually be found in the Latin original. Provisionally it seems that the vernacular version was more extreme, or else that those who communicated its contents exaggerated them.

[51] Gui's manual, as Wakefield and Evans, pp. 412–13, refers to three treatises the Beguins 'say and believe [Olivi] wrote' – respectively on 'poverty', 'mendicancy' and 'dispensations' – and also to 'other writings they attribute to him, all of which they have in vernacular translations'. In addition a passage from Doat, ed. Manselli, *Spirituali e beghini*, p. 335, refers to 'libellos et scripturas editas per dictum fratrem Petrum Johannis, videlicet in spetiali quendam libellum in vulgari scriptum facientem mentionem de oratione et ieiunio, et alium libellum facientem mentionem de paupertate Christi' (books and texts written by the aforesaid brother Peter of John, namely and in particular a book written in the common language mentioning prayer and fasting, and another book dealing with the poverty of Christ). Other passages refer to specific books but do not indicate whether they were in the vernacular: see Manselli, *Spirituali e beghini*, p. 308/11–16, and p. 336/1–4; also a reference in Doat 27,

Plate 9   Bernard Gui's inquisitor's manual: beginning in the second column, line 6, Gui describes the dissemination among Peter of John Olivi's followers of vernacular versions of Olivi's works. Toulouse, Bibliothèque Municipale Ms. 387, fol. 146v. (With permission of the Bibliothèque Municipale de Toulouse.)

these works in the records are much less frequent than those to the vernacular version of the Revelation commentary.

The second central point about the spread of vernacular propaganda among the Beguins of Languedoc is that it was customarily communicated orally.[52] Almost always the Beguins in the trial records did not *read* books; they *heard* them read. William Ruffi 'heard' vernacular works by Olivi 'read to him and to others in different places'; Blaise Boyer 'heard' a work of Olivi's read at a meeting of Beguins; Peter Hospitalis 'heard' Olivi's Revelation commentary read aloud in the vernacular 'more than thirty times'.[53]

Whereas in the case of Catalonia it can only be inferred that propaganda was recited in regular devotional gatherings, in the case of Languedoc it is certain. Bernard Gui once more comes to our aid:

> Both the occupants [of the houses of poverty] and those who dwell in their own homes frequently gather together in these houses with associates and friends of the Beguins on feasts-days and Sundays. There they read or listen to the reading in the vernacular from the aforementioned pamphlets or tracts ... although certain other things are read there such as the commandments, the articles of faith, the legends of the saints and the *Summa of vices and virtues*. Thus the school of the devil ... seems to imitate the school of Christ in ape-like fashion. [See also plate 9.][54]

Gui's remark about the devil's school imitating the school of Christ could be translated into the modern sociological vocabulary of a Weber or Troeltsch as meaning that the Beguins had a 'church-like' rather than 'sect-like' organisation and mentality.[55] Of greater

---

fol. 86v to an Apocalypse commentary by one 'Bertrandus Joannes' (to the best of my knowledge this has been overlooked; nor am I able to identify the author).

[52] It is salutary to bear in mind how long oral transmission of ideas expressed in books was prevalent. The point is made in reference to nineteenth-century rural England by B. Reay, 'The context and meaning of popular literacy', *Past and Present* 131 (May 1991), 116–18.

[53] Ruffi: Limborch, p. 316; passage cited by Leff, p. 219 n. 2: 'ipse frequenter audivit legi sibi et aliis in diversis locis in scriptis fratris P. Johannis in vulgari transpositis' (he frequently heard read to himself and others in various places from the writings of brother P. of John translated into the vernacular). Boyer: Doat 27, fol. 84r: 'audivit quandoque legi scripturam fratris Petri Johannis' (he once heard read the writing of brother Peter of John). Hospitalis: Limborch, p. 338, passage cited by Leff, p. 218 n. 2: 'de qua postilla audivit ipse pluries legi etiam plus quam xxx vicibus in vulgari' (from this commentary he heard read many times, indeed more than thirty times in the vernacular) (Leff, p. 218, mistranslates this as 'at more than thirty different places').

[54] Wakefield and Evans, p. 414 (I follow that translation with slight alterations). For the Latin see Perarnau, *L'"Alia informatio"*, p. 16.

[55] In this regard they resemble the Waldensians. See my 'Waldenser, Lollarden und Taboriten: zum Sektenbegriff bei Weber und Troeltsch', in W. Schluchter (ed.), *Max Webers Sicht des okzidentalen Christentums* (Frankfurt, 1988), pp. 326–54.

relevance here is the fact that Gui's remark is borne out in so far as those who read aloud to the Beguins were a handful of dedicated organisers who not only acted very much like priests, but in most cases actually were priests.[56] Some of these literate men may have served as resident ministers for given communal houses in Languedoc before the persecutions began. All were forced to pursue their activities clandestinely, often on the run, once inquisitors started searching for them.

The organiser whose activities appear most prominently in the records, Peter Trancavel of Béziers, is the only one whose original profession is never designated.[57] Certainly he was neither a Franciscan nor a priest, but he may have been in minor orders because he was a close associate of priests and seems to have known Latin. Before the persecutions began, Trancavel was an active propagandiser for the teachings of Olivi among laypeople in the region of Béziers and Narbonne. Arrested around 1319, he managed to escape from imprisonment in Carcassonne and elude recapture for several years by moving from town to town and gaining refuge with sympathizers. In 1327 he was finally apprehended and doubtless burned. As a fugitive Trancavel continued missionising, and he always travelled with books. On one occasion he brought writings, including glosses by Olivi on the Psalter, to a priest in the diocese of Béziers; once he brought a collection of works by Olivi to another priest of the neighbourhood.[58] Seeking shelter across the Rhône in Apt, Manosque, Aix and Marseilles, Trancavel carried with him several books by Olivi, which he said he was carrying so that they and Olivi's teachings might never be destroyed.[59]

All the other organisers known from the records who transmitted Olivi's teachings from books were priests. John Rogerii, a priest

---

[56] In what follows I take a position that varies considerably in emphasis from that of Biget, 'Autour de Bernard Délicieux', p. 88: 'les plus instruits lisent aux autres'. When Gui refers to 'Beguins' reading to others he is evidently referring to the learned organisers and not the rank and file.

[57] On Trancavel, Manselli, *Spirituali e beghini*, pp. 188, 190, 234–7. (Unfortunately Manselli does not piece together Trancavel's career from the scattered records as methodically as one might prefer.) When Trancavel is labelled 'beguinus de tercio ordine' (Manselli, *Spirituali e beghini*, p. 188 n. 2) this tells us nothing more than that he was not a Franciscan or a priest.

[58] Records from Doat, ed. Manselli, *Spirituali e beghini*, pp. 307, 308.

[59] Manselli, *Spirituali e beghini*, p. 335: 'dictus Petri Trencavelli constituerat se in fugam ... cum multis libris doctrine fratris Petri Johannis ad hoc ut dicti libri et doctrina non destruentur nec dampnarentur'.

from the diocese of Béziers, travelled with Trancavel and received books from him containing writings by Olivi.[60] Both Rogerii and Trancavel stayed in the home of another priest, John Adzoriti, where they all read together various Spiritual Franciscan writings, including works by Olivi.[61] Bernard Maurini, a priest of Narbonne, took flight across the Rhône after an initial recantation. When he was recaptured Maurini confessed to having 'commended, approved, and praised' Olivi's teachings 'frequently and in many places'.[62] Raymond Johannis, a Spiritual Franciscan driven from the order, travelled with Trancavel, carried books by Olivi to Provence, and often read aloud from Olivi's Revelation commentary to others.[63]

Two exceptions to the rule of verbal dissemination of vernacular written works by learned intermediaries may be mentioned in conclusion as signs of things to come. Berengaria Donas, the wife of a cloth preparer of Narbonne, apparently could not read vernacular works of theology herself. But Berengaria owned a version of Olivi's Revelation commentary that had been given to her by another Beguin woman, and someone read to her from this book 'frequently'.[64] Clearly the mere ownership of a work of learned exegesis by Berengaria Donas represents a new departure in the dissemination of doctrine. Not only does it display the awe held for learned teachings by a simple laywoman, but it apparently facilitated 'frequent' reading in the home whenever someone could be found to do the reading aloud.

In one other case we actually have a layperson who could read on his own and hence form his own opinions. This was Peter Tort of Montréal near Carcassonne, whose occupation is unknown, but who attended Beguin meetings without being a leader. In his trial Tort said that he came to his views by listening to sermons of Franciscans in Narbonne and to what was said by Franciscan fugitives and fellow Beguins. In addition he developed his own ideas on the grounds of what 'he himself had read in the books of [Olivi], translated into the vernacular' and especially in 'the postilla on the

---

[60] Manselli, *Spirituali e beghini*, pp. 306–7.   [61] Manselli, *Spirituali e beghini*, p. 308.
[62] Manselli, *Spirituali e beghini*, pp. 335–6.   [63] Manselli, *Spirituali e beghini*, p. 302.
[64] Doat 28, fol. 221r: 'item a quadam Begguina unum librum de doctrina fratris Petri Johannis habuit quem frequenter legi audivit'. The contents of the book that emerge from fol. 221v make clear that it was a version of Olivi's Revelation commentary. Leff, p. 225, mistakenly refers to Berengaria Donas 'having read in Olivi'.

Apocalypse of the said brother, which he himself read often'.[65] Tort
maintained that 'the whole world would be in darkness if it were not
for brother Peter of John and his writing'. Although Tort was
exceptional, his ability to engage in private vernacular reading
despite ecclesiastical prohibition makes him at least as memorable a
figure as brother Peter of John himself. There would be many more
like him in the future.

---

[65] Limborch, pp. 329–30; passage cited by Manselli, *Spirituali e beghini*, p. 202 n. 3: 'tam per
ea que audivit ... quam per ea que ipsemet legit in libris dicti fratris P. Johannis positis in
vulgari'; 'que omnia dictus P. Tort dixit se credidisse informatus per dictos apostatas et
beguinos et ex postilla dicti fratris P. Johannis super Apocalypsim in qua ipsemet frequenter legit, ut dixit'.

CHAPTER 12

Religious reading amongst the laity in France in the fifteenth century

Geneviève Hasenohr

Any consideration of the relation between heresy and literacy, especially if the suggestion is made that heresy in some way fosters literacy, must raise the questions of orthodoxy and literacy. *Were* heretics more susceptible to acquiring the skills of reading than the orthodox? Did their preachers advocate literacy, overtly or implicitly, to advance their cause more than the regular parish clergy? Were heterodox books better suited to their potential audience than comparable traditional works? Being more at home with literary sources than with sources strictly historical, it seemed to me that it could be enlightening to look at the production and spread of orthodox vernacular books in the last two centuries of the middle ages, and particularly in the period 1380–1480, in an area relatively untouched by heresy in that period, northern France.[1] Two categories of material provide the most useful information on this subject: lists of books that the clergy recommended for reading by the laity, and wills and inventories of private libraries, however incomplete their evidence. A survey of the texts most widely distributed in French manuscripts at the end of the medieval period serves to complete, even to correct, the picture which these witnesses provide of the religious culture of the privileged. For, it is important to remember, though learning to read was increasingly encouraged

---

[1] My chief source of information has been the documentation, much of it still unprinted, which has already provided the basis of the following studies: 'La littérature religieuse', *Grundriss der romanischen Literaturen des Mittelalters* 8/1 (1988), 266–305; 'Aperçu sur la diffusion et la réception de la littérature de spiritualité en langue française au dernier siècle du Moyen Age', in N. R. Wolf (ed.), *Wissensorganisierende und wissensvermittelnde Literatur im Mittelalter* (Wiesbaden, 1987), pp. 57–90; 'L'essor des bibliothèques privées aux xiv et xve siècles', in A. Vernet (ed.) *Histoire des bibliothèques françaises*, vol. 1: *Les Bibliothèques médiévales* (Paris, 1989), pp. 215–63. Further bibliographical references, and clarification of the questions discussed here, can be found in these papers.

in all circles and especially amongst women,[2] and though in the fifteenth century the development of primary schools ensured that literacy was no longer the prerogative of a few,[3] to acquire a book remained a major capital outlay.[4] In France few outside the higher ranks, whether ecclesiastical or lay, or those professionally involved in writing, seem to have been sufficiently motivated to take this step: the evidence of inventories of goods after death demonstrate this. The situation did not change before the turn of the century, when printed books in French spread more and more widely amongst different levels of society.[5] It is equally crucial to grasp that the important matter is not so much what was written as what was read – these are two very different issues, and they require distinctly different modes of enquiry.

Often it is treatises directed towards women which reveal indications about the place of reading in the devotional life of the end of the middle ages. This arises partly because a high proportion of the moral writing of the fourteenth and fifteenth centuries was addressed to women;[6] but partly, and more importantly, because the frequent habit amongst spiritual directors of providing for women, even wives and mothers, a model of life based on the contemplative model produced simultaneously denigration of bodily labour and exaltation of meditation and of reading to forestall idleness and wandering thoughts.[7] Apart from the recitation of

[2] See, for example, the Knight of the Tour Landry, *Enseignements a ses filles*, ed. A. de Montaiglon (Paris, 1854), cap. 90, and the chancellor Gerson, speaking to his sisters, *Discours sur l'excellence de la virginité*, ed. Glorieux, no. 337.

[3] The enquiry undertaken by A. Derville concerning northern France concludes that elementary instruction was widespread amongst countryfolk, normal in the towns at the level of artisans, and occasional amongst workers anxious to better themselves ('L'alphabétisation du peuple à la fin du Moyen Age', *Revue du Nord* 66 (1984), 761–72). Less detailed, but equally optimistic, figures appear for Champagne and Burgundy in S. Guilbert, 'Les écoles rurales en Champagne au xve siècle', *Annales de l'Est* (1982), 127–47; D. Viaux, 'L'école élementaire dans les pays bourguignons à la fin du Moyen Age', *Annales de Bourgogne* 59 (1987), 5–19. See also D. Alexandre-Bidon, 'La Lettre volée: apprendre à lire à l'enfant à la fin du Moyen Age', *Annales Economie, Société, Civilisation* 44 (1989), 953–88.

[4] On this matter, as on other financial aspects of the making and selling of manuscripts, see C. Bozzolo and E. Ornato, *Pour une Histoire du livre manuscrit au Moyen Age. Trois essais de codicologie quantitative* (Paris, 1980), and *Supplément* (Paris, 1983), and E. Ornato, 'Les conditions de production et de diffusion du livre médiéval (XIIIe–XVe s.)', in J. P. Genet (ed.), *Culture et idéologie dans la genèse de l'Etat moderne* (Rome, 1985), pp. 57–84.

[5] According to the basic article of D. Coq, 'Les débuts de l'édition en langue vulgaire en France: publics et politiques éditoriales', *Gutemberg-Jahrbuch* (1987), 59–72.

[6] Still valuable is A. Hentsch, *De la Littérature didactique du Moyen Age s'addressant aux femmes* (Cahors, 1903; repr. Geneva, 1979).

[7] See my paper 'La vie quotidienne de la femme vue par l'Eglise: l'enseignement des journées chrétienes du Moyen Age', in *Frau und mittelalterlicher Alltag (Veröffentlichungen des Instituts für mittelalterliche Realienkunde Österreiche* 9 (1986)), 19–101.

hours and of regular prayers, all recommended pious and devout reading for the daily life of the christian woman, following the monastic model. Reading took on greater importance the higher up the social scale one looks, and manual tasks equivalently are devalued. Christine de Pisan, at the beginning of the fifteenth century, was hardly specific in her recommendations,[8] whilst a middle-class Parisian, around 1390 who undertook the education of his young wife, defined her reading as 'the bible (the *Bible historiale*), the *Golden Legend*, the Apocalypse, the *Vie des Pères*, and many other good books in French which I own'.[9]

The advice was more explicit when, in accordance with Gerson in the *Canticordum du pèlerin*, they were directed to 'simple pious hearts'.[10] In order to advance 'on se doit exercer ou appliquer a la dottrine morale des vices et des vertus, et plus especialment a aucuns livres qui sont fais a venir a devocion, puis a speculacion, puis a contemplacion' (one must exercise or apply the moral teaching concerning vices and virtues, and especially turn to some books which direct one to come to devotion, then to speculation, then to contemplation). Gerson continued to describe works that could be found, in French and in Latin, in the houses of the Celestines and Carthusians:

books describing temptations and the distinction between mortal and venial sins, the *Mont de contemplacion* and the *Medecine espirituele*,[11] the *Theologia mistica*,[12] *Horologium Sapiencie*,[13] the *Meditationes sanctorum Augustini, Anselmi, Bernardi*,[14] *Collaciones Patrum*,[15] *Vite et narraciones eorum*,[16] works of Gregory, Augustine, Bernard, Hugh, Richard,[17] Bonaventura, William of Paris and many others 'qui singulierement ont eu la foy et la loy de Dieu

[8] See M. Laigle, *Le 'Livre des Trois Vertus' de Christine de Pisan* (Paris, 1912), pp. 166, 174.
[9] *Le Menagier de Paris*, ed. G. E. Breton and J. M. Ferrier (Oxford, 1981), pp. 45–6.
[10] Ed. Glorieux, no. 305.
[11] All French works by Gerson himself, ed. Glorieux, respectively nos. 324, 328, 297 and 317.
[12] Ed. Glorieux, no. 100, and A. Combes (Padua, 1958); no vernacular version known.
[13] Henry Suso; widely disseminated in French.
[14] This refers to short apocryphal works attributed to Augustine and to Bernard translated, often more than once, in the course of the fourteenth and fifteenth centuries: by the former the *Soliloquies* and the *Manual* (PL 40), by the latter *Meditationes piissime de miseria humane conditionis* (PL 184).
[15] John Cassian; no French translation known.
[16] *Vite patrum, Historia monachorum* and *Verba seniorum*; many partial adaptations, in verse or in prose, were widely popular.
[17] Hugh and Richard of St Victor. By the first only the *De arrha anime* exists in French. None of the work of Richard, Bernard or William of Auvergne was accessible in northern French, and only some of Gregory (*Homilies, Dialogues*), Augustine (*City of God*), Bonaventura (*Stimulus amoris*).

comme le signacle de la croix emprainte dedens leur cuer' (who especially
had imprinted the faith and law of God like the sign of the cross in their
hearts).[18]

This programme of books, not all of which were available in French,
could only have been useful to those already well advanced in the
spiritual life and also with the advantage of an assured written and
theological education. Elsewhere Gerson specifically discouraged
the reading of the Victorines, of Bernard (*Sermones in Cantica*) and of
Henry Suso (save for his *Meditations on the Passion and on the Last
Things*) for 'simple people without learning' and especially for
women.[19] It was for the same reason that, a quarter of a century
earlier, thinking of his sisters, he had devised the scheme of the
Montagne de contemplation, and had transposed the teaching of the
great contemplatives for the use of 'simple people', whose ignorance
should not prevent them from climbing the ladder of spiritual life in
their own fashion, different though that might be from that of great
clerks. In guidance he had recommended some books as likely to
excite compunction and then devotion: Bonaventura's *Aiguillon
d'amour divine (Stimulus amoris)*, lives of saints, to which he returned
many times, the prayers and meditations of St Anselm, William of
Auvergne's *Rhetorica divina*. In the *Mendicité spirituelle*, written also for
a 'simple woman', and inspired by Bernard and the Victorines, the
only recommended reading was the *Somme le roi* – a work certainly
more accessible, from all points of view.[20]

If Gerson never stopped repeating that the reform of the Church
had to begin with the children, he was also convinced that the
renewal of christian society would remain an empty phrase unless
the initiative came from the top. He thus paid attention to the
education of the French Dauphins whenever the opportunity arose.
Three texts are relevant.[21] The most consistent is the *Opusculum de*

---

[18] Ed. Glorieux, vii. 133.   [19] *Montagne de contemplation*, ed. Glorieux, no. 297.
[20] Ed. Glorieux, no. 317.
[21] Limiting discussion to the last identifications, since the identity of the recipients is debated:
the letter to Jean Cadart, doctor and teacher to Charles the Dauphin, later Charles VII,
(ed. Glorieux, no. 52); the letter to the newly appointed teacher to the later Louis XI, and
not Charles VII (ed. Glorieux, no. 86); *Opusculum de considerationibus*, composed either for
the teacher of the Dauphin Louis, duke of Guyenne, in 1407, or for the teacher of the
Dauphin Charles, duke of Touraine, in 1417 (ed. Glorieux, no. 42). The rather disappoin-
ting investigation by M. L. Picascia, 'Messaggi al precettore del delfino: *Tractatus* e
Instructiones di Jean Gerson', *Mélanges Ecole française de Rome. Moyen Age–Temps modernes* 93
(1987), 235–60, takes no account of the suggestions of M. Lieberman, 'Chronologie
gersonienne', *Romania* 73 (1952), 480–96 and 74 (1953), 289–337.

meditationibus seu considerationibus quas princeps debet habere, very different in its conception from the traditional *Miroirs des princes*. It is in the fourth and fifth reflections, in which he praises reading, *doctrix discipline Dei tamquam ancilla sapientie* (the governess of divine discipline and the handmaid of a wisdom), that the author sets out the ideal library from which the prince should never allow himself to be separated. Religious writers are represented there by the bible, but *presertim quoad historias et documenta moralia* (especially histories and moral texts), a description which refers better to the *Bible historiale* or the *Historia scolastica* than to the Vulgate; the *Postille* of Nicholas of Lyra, because they remain closest to the literal sense (as before there is a desire to move away from an allegorising reading of scripture); William Peraldus's *Summa de vitiis et virtutibus*, the *Somme le roi*, a martyrology, legends of saints, *Vies des Pères* and the *Speculum historiale* by Vincent of Beauvais, *meditationes et orationes devote* by men such as Augustine, Anselm and Bernard, and a whole series of short French works by himself (*Triparti*, the *Miroir de l'âme*, *Examen de conscience, Science de bien mourir*),[22] *Montagne de contemplation, Mendicité spirituelle, Ecole de la raison*[23] and many sermons (on the Passion, for the dead, for the restoration of the kingdom, for peace, for justice[24]); the *De regimine principum* of Giles of Rome; the *De quattuor virtutibus* of Martin de Braga; the *City of God* translated with commentary (by Raoul de Presles for Charles V). Even for a prince, what remains the concern of Gerson is conversion and piety much more than doctrinal education: in his eyes the temporal and spiritual health of the kingdom depends on this. In this he was in complete agreement with the line taken rather earlier by Philippe de Mézières in regard to the young Charles VI.[25]

The most basic characteristic of the models set out for religious literature is their ascetic and spiritual tendency: stress is placed on the conscience, improvement of the moral life, progress in the spiritual life; their ideal is contemplation. Any doctrinal or ecclesiological dimension is entirely lacking. In this they were fundamentally identical to the models provided for recluses, novices or even for seasoned religious.[26] In this area, a special place is reserved

---

[22] Ed. Glorieux, nos. 312, 330, 332.   [23] Ed. Glorieux, no. 304.

[24] Ed. Glorieux, nos. 341, 390, 398, 396 and 348.

[25] *Songe du vieil pelerin*, ed. G. W. Coopland (Cambridge, 1969), ii.c.229.

[26] For comparison: Gerson, letter to the recluse of Mont Valérien (ed. Glorieux, no. 21); *De libris legendis a monacho* (ed. Glorieux, no. 464); letter to the master provincial of the

for hagiography, and not only in the rules of life for women. A good example amongst many is the *Epistre du miroir de chrétienté* by Jean de Varennes.[27] Elsewhere the chancellor Gerson, speaking to the students of theology in the college of Navarre, warned them against scorning these saints' legends.[28] Also worth noticing is the preference for translations rather than short works directly composed in the vernacular, and the preference for treatises by medieval writers rather than the Fathers. This conservatism, which contrasts with the openness shown at the same date by Italian religious, is the natural result of the great ignorance which the French clergy, even the best informed, had of a proliferating but anarchic literacy output in the vernacular, which was often for private use; it reflects also the cultural gap between France that was still 'scholastic' and Italy, already humanist and aware of the value of its vernacular literature.

Did the make-up of libraries match these models?[29] Even though the picture provided by catalogues, inventories and wills is very incomplete, some trends can be discerned.[30] In the small collections made by women, of noble or middle class, the kinds best represented, with the exception of books of hours and Psalters, are saints' lives on the one hand, and moral and ascetic spirituality on the other. Two titles stand out: the *Pèlerinages* of Guillaume de Deguilleville and the *Soliloquies* attributed to Augustine. Also found in the possession of the middle class in Tournai are the *Somme le roi*, the *Aiguillon d'amour divine* (a translation of the *Stimulus amoris*), the *Ad*

Celestines, Jean Bassandi (Glorieux, no. 83). The list set out by Denis the Carthusian in article 9 of his *Exhortatorium novitiorum* (*Opera omnia*, vol. xxxviii, pp. 542–3) is exactly matched by that in *Canticordum du pèlerin* (ed. Glorieux, no. 305). The headings are the same in Gerard Groote and the followers of the *devotio moderna* (see *DSP* 3 (1955), cols. 741–2).

27 Brussels Bibliothèque Royale 10384–10414, fol. 45.

28 Ed. Glorieux, no. 5. The *Vies des Pères* and the legends of saints were obligatory parts of the equipment of parish clergy; see the letter to a newly named bishop, ed. Glorieux, no. 29.

29 Copies of bibles and of biblical books are omitted here, since I plan to devote a separate paper to the questions associated with the reading of the bible in French at the end of the middle ages.

30 Wills often mentioned only articles to which their testators were particularly attached, or which fell outside the normal disposition of goods. With notable exceptions, for example the libraries of the Louvre and of Burgundy, inventories and catalogues only mention the preliminary material of the books or the text whose title appears on the binding. Consequently we are ignorant concerning the majority of works too short to form a volume of their own, but which circulated within more or less homogeneous collections. Only the evidence for works sufficiently bulky to have had an autonomous circulation of their own is at all reliable. For this reason it is necessary to correct the impression against a systematic list of the surviving works.

Deum vadit and the *Mendicité spirituelle*.[31] In princely collections, the richest of which exceeded 150 books (though the average was between thirty and forty), saints' lives, books of instruction and spirituality formed the basis, though with variations in which personal preference may be discerned. A half-dozen titles recur constantly: in the areas of hagiography the *Légende dorée*, the *Vies des Pères*, the *Miracles de Notre-Dame*; in the area of the creed and christian ethics the *Somme le roi*; more directed towards ascetic spirituality the *Miroir des dames* (a translation of the *Speculum dominarum* by Durand de Champagne OFM), a feminine counterpart to the thirteenth-century mirrors for princes; finally, directed towards the improvement of christian life but set in an exuberant allegorical form, the trilogy of *Pèlerinages* by the Cistercian Guillaume de Deguillevile (*de vie humaine, de l'âme, de Jesus-Christ*). If one adds to this the *Ci nous dit* and Jean de Meung's *Testament*, occasionally found, this is a remarkably conservative set. It would be tempting to think that this was the result of tradition, were it not that the majority of these books continued to enjoy some success into the fifteenth century. Collections that were receptive of contemporary compositions, such as that of Charlotte de Savoie (died 1483),[32] were the exception. Even the writings of Gerson do not appear frequently. Only the *Vies* and the *Passions* of Christ were widely distributed in the second half of the century.

The *Somme le roi* and the *Légende dorée* form the basis of book collections of middle-class men and of artisans, amongst which appear also one of the *Pèlerinages* or, at the end of the period, a *Vie de Jesus-Christ*.[33] These are the same titles as appear in the castles.

---

[31] So in 1438 a widow left to different recluses the *Vies des Pères*, the *Somme le roi*, the *Pèlerinage de Jesus Christ*, the *Aiguillon d'amour*; to the Beguines the *Soliloquies*; to a female cousin in the *Abbaye du Saint Esprit*, a thirteenth-century allegorical guide to the devout life (A. de La Grange, *Choix de testaments tournaisiens antérieurs au XVIe siècle* (Tournai, 1897), no. 801).

[32] Religious works make up more than a half of the hundred volumes in the library. In addition to the books traditionally owned by women, authors such as Gerson, the pseudo-Peter of Luxembourg Jean Saulnier, Jean Henry, Robert Ciboule, Pierre de Caillemesnil, Etienne des Arpentis, translations (*City of God, Horloge de Sapience, Livre des anges, Vita Christi* of Ludolph of Saxony), mirrors for princes and, amongst numerous anonymous works, the prose redaction of the *Pèlarinage de l'âme*.

[33] For example, the bequests by a townsman of Chauny in 1419 of a copy of the *Légende dorée* in French and a *Catholicon* to the church of Notre-Dame, along with a *Miroir du monde* to the town's Hôtel Dieu (Archives Hospitalières de l'Aisne, Hospice de Chauny B.1), and by Jacques Piaudeveil, townsman of Tournai (1400, 1405), who left a translation of the *Consolatio Philosophiae*, the *Roman de la Rose*, the *Livre du pelerin*, the *Somme le roi* (A. de La Grange, *Choix de testaments*, no. 447).

Certainly, the contents of aristocratic collections, very variable in size (about forty volumes being the average?), were more diverse, and religious books did not form the whole of the library; but the selection of titles, apart from a few variations, remains the same:[34] the emphasis on hagiography, predilection for works of education (from Giles de Rome to the Knight of La Tour Landry), some translations of the Fathers or of medieval doctors (*City of God, Livre des anges*). Only those aristocratic libraries set up after 1380 (thus excluding the Louvre collection to which the contribution of Charles VI was tiny), and which show their owners to have a predominant taste for vernacular writing (thus excluding the collections of the princes of Orléans, Angoulême and Anjou, as also of parliamentarians and members of the legal profession) are relevant here. It is enough to recall the duke of Berry (died 1416), whose instincts, even if dominated by a passion for art, remained traditional: amongst forty-six religious books in French, ten were hagiographic, seven of the mirror of princes kind, about ten translations of the Fathers (primarily *City of God*); amongst the remainder may be noted *Pèlerinages*, the *Trésor* of Jean Chapuis, the *Ci nous dit*, the *Miroir des dames*, the *Trésor de Sapience* (an extract from Henry Suso) and *Passions*.

More illuminating, because it allows one to perceive permanence and change, is a comparison between the various inventories of the library of Burgundy made after the deaths of the three dukes Philippe le Hardi, Jean sans Peur and Philippe le Bon.[35] Continuing to leave out books of prayers, liturgical books and books of scripture, in 1404 out of ten religious books three were of saints' lives (*Vies des Pères, Légende dorée, Vie de saint Bernard*), two translations of Augustine (*City of God*), and the others, under a literary guise, give direction in the christian life: Jean de Meung's *Testament*, the *Trésor* of Jean Chapuis, *Ci nous dit, Pèlerinage de vie humaine, Echelle du ciel*. By 1420 the number of religious books had risen to thirty, excluding the *Miroirs des princes*. Added to the preceding titles, some of which were

---

34 The religious basis of the library (eighty-two volumes altogether) of Guichard de Jaligny, master of the Hôtel du roi and governor of the Dauphiné, killed at Agincourt in 1415, is formed by the *Somme le roi*, the *Légende dorée*, the *Testament* of Jean de Meung, a commentary on the Pater Noster and the translation of the *Homiliae* of Gregory the Great, together with books of hours, Psalters and books of prayers (see *Bulletin du bibliophile* (1843–4), pp. 518–27).

35 Bibliographical references are in G. Hasenohr, 'L'essor des bibliothèques privées', cited in no. 1.

by then available in several copies, had been added the *Miroir du monde* (a survey of vices and virtues), the *Somme le roi*, a work by the Reclus de Moliens, a *Vie de saint François*, but no identifiable work of contemporary composition. In 1467 the hagiographical content had been quadrupled: many *Légendes dorées*, numerous lives of saints (Louis, Colette, etc.), the *Dialogues* of Gregory the Great, a half-dozen *Miracles de Notre-Dame* and about the same number of *Vies des Pères*. The *City of God* remains the only patristic, non-hagiographical translation (eighteen copies). The remaining twenty-four other religious books, to which may be added about twenty books of advice to princes, demonstrate the major themes of fifteenth-century spirituality: living well to die well (*Sommes des vices et des vertus*, the pseudo-Augustinian *Miroir des pécheurs*, the *Miroir de l'âme pécheresse* of Jacques de Guythrode, *Voies d'enfer et de paradis*, *Horloge de Sapience*, in addition to the traditional literary works); laments for the human condition (the pseudo-Bernard *Méditations*) and for the last things (a translation of the *De quattuor novissimis* of Gérard de Vliederhoven, the *Vigiles des morts* of Pierre de Nesson); preparation for death (Gerson's *Médicine de l'âme*); compassionate devotion to the suffering Christ (various lives and passions of Christ, the *Lamentations* ascribed to Saint Bernard); devotion to the cross, to the blood and the wounds (translations of the Franciscan *Lignum Vite* and the *Stimulus amoris*); encouragement to affective union and to mysticism (various meditations, *Mendicité spirituelle*, *Montagne de contemplation*, a translation of Hugh St Victor's *De arrha anime*, like its Latin model the pseudo-Augustinian *Soliloquies*, more informed by the desire to praise). Some writings set out a schematic form of doctrinal direction (such as the short works of Gerson), summary (*Doctrinal aux simples gens*), or more elaborate (*Chemin de paradis* by the bishop of Châlons, Jean Germain), though two enterprises seem unusually to extend the range: the translation of Anselm's *Cur Deus homo* because of its speculative nature, and the translation of the *Lectura de oratione Domini* by Godefroy d'Erlach (1342–6) because of its gestures in the direction of eucharistic theology.[36]

A survey of surviving manuscripts confirms the extent of devotion to saints (to actual saints' lives must be added the prayers appended to books of hours); the dissemination of Jean de Meung's *Testament*

---

[36] See *Romania* 107 (1986), 407–16; the text became the source for the *Glosa Pater* of Waldensian origin.

(116 copies), often added to the *Roman de la Rose*, whose popularity doubtless contributed to it; the success of the *Pèlerinages* of Guillaume de Deguillevile (eighty copies), and especially of the *Pèlerinage de Vie humaine*, and to a lesser extent the *Somme le roi* (more than a hundred copies, but only fifty complete copies from the fourteenth and fifteenth centuries). A significant number of the copies of these last two works, however, belonged to clergy or monks. On the other hand, it seems that the attention given to other texts must have been greater than the surviving mentions in inventories suggests: the *Trésor* of Jean Chapuis (about sixty copies, but in a style so contorted that it must have restricted its impact), the *Horloge* and *Trésor de Sapience* (seventy-five copies of all), passions and lives of Christ where narrative and meditation were mixed in the style of the *Meditationes Vite Christi*, of the *Ad Deum vadit* or of Ludolphus of Saxony (a body of about twenty texts surviving in more than a hundred copies and carried on into the books of hours through a multitude of meditations and prayers to the cross, to the five wounds, to the seven sorrows, and so on).[37] Some points should be stressed. The perception by readers of the *Horloge de Sapience* was of a passion of Christ together with an *ars moriendi*, as Gerson had wished. It is significant that from the start extracts had been made from the original text making up a complete *Trésor de Sapience*, which was at one and the same time a mirror of the good life and a mirror of the good death – the first in French literature. The translation of *De civitate Dei* only circulated in princely and courtly circles; it was strictly for collectors, and if it was ever consulted it was regarded, as Raoul de Presles wanted it to be, as a summary of history and of classical mythology.[38] Finally it is worth asking whether the project so patiently and passionately set in train by Gerson for the benefit of the 'simple folk' received its due welcome: amongst spiritual works there are about thirty copies of the *Montagne de contemplation*, a few more of the *Mendicité spirituelle*, some fewer of the *Traité des diverses tentations de l'ennemi*, but only six of the *Canticordum du pèlerin*; amongst pastoral works, the *Examen de conscience* and its expansion *Le Profit de savoir quel est pechié mortel et pechié veniel* (addressed to a more advanced

---

[37] It should be remembered that it was the printing press that ensured the success of translations of the *Ars moriendi* and of the *Imitatio Christi*. Circulation of these two classics of western devotion was non-existent in French before the sixteenth century.

[38] See G. Hasenohr, 'Place et rôle des traductions dans la pastorale française du XVe siècle', in G. Contamine (ed.), *Traduction et traducteurs au Moyen Age* (Paris, 1989), pp. 265–75.

audience, and pushing its analysis further) survives in a total of about seventy copies (39 + 28); the *Miroir de l'âme*, a commentary on the commandments, survives in about forty copies, but the *A.B.C. aux simples gens*, a guide to the essential elements of belief and behaviour for the avoidance of hell, only achieved about twenty copies. It must be remembered that these texts, the first directed to 'contemplative souls', the others to the direction of 'simple folk' – the *Triparti* especially was very often prescribed for parish clergy in synodal statutes of the fifteenth and sixteenth centuries – were used as much, if not more, by the clergy as by the laity.[39] It is essential to ponder these numbers to come to any view, even relatively, of their use for reading by the laity.

What can be concluded from this long review? As the clergy hoped, the two poles around which the laity's reading matter was organised were morality, more or less internalised, and devotion. A first group of writings, often with titles such as *Voie*, *Pèlerinage*, *Miroir*, provides directives towards the christian life under various literary forms, from the *somme* of the thirteenth century to the short pastoral work of the fifteenth, through the long allegorical poem of the fourteenth. The most down-to-earth were content to exhort obedience to the commandments; others, which fostered a more spiritual outlook on morality, set out to bring about through an alteration of habits a change in the heart, and repeated insistently themes of the contempt of the world and the vileness of the flesh, fitting in with lessons drawn from the lives of saints. A second group sought to enliven devotion, setting out meditative themes which, alongside the more or less mechanical recitation of the hours (which usually were in Latin), were to encourage the soul to eager prayer of repentance, the action of grace, of love or of compassion. The pivot of this, even more than fear of death, was compassion for the sufferings of the Saviour.

This was a timeless literature, whose limitations are readily apparent: even if there was nothing in the material which gave any encouragement towards the least heresy, there was equally nothing in it which, if a seed of heresy were planted, could hinder its growth. Whilst there was plenty concerning the moral and spiritual component of the christian faith, at the same time there was a blatant lack of dogma. Admittedly, the *Somme le roi* in a systematic fashion,

---

[39] See 'Aperçu sur la diffusion', cited n. 1.

the *Trésor* in a more discursive fashion, and Gerson's *Miroir de l'âme* in a very schematic way went over the articles of the creed. But always, and even more with Gerson than with Friar Laurent, they proceeded by specifying the truths of the faith and not by reflecting upon them or explaining them, as the *Elucidarium* had done in the twelfth century.

As the guides to reading indicate, the imbalance between morality and doctrine was deliberately sought: in the fifteenth century even more than in the thirteenth, the clergy thought it useless and indeed dangerous for the laity to endeavour to gain enlightenment concerning the theological foundation of their faith. The creed need not be known verbatim by laymen:

Est assavoir que chascun bon chrestien est tenu de savoir et croire lesdits articles explicitement, c'est a dire du tout es singulierement – et a ce sont tenuz les prestres et clercs –, ou implicitement, c'est a dire ainsi que l'Eglise les croit et entent – et a ce sont tenuz les labouriers et simples gens, sans en faire grandes inquisicions. Et s'ilz en ont scrupules ou temptations, ilz les doivent laisser et mespriser, et avoir voulenté et desir de croire ce qui est a croire et a desirer.

(It is to be known that every good christian is bound to know and to believe these articles either explicitly, that is to say as a whole (and to this are obliged priests and clerks), or implicitly, that is to say according as the Church believes and understands them (and to this are bound the labourers and simple people, without looking further). And if they have queries or doubts, they should check and despise them, maintaining the will to believe that which is to be believed and to be desired.)

So one reads in a fifteenth-century treatise *De conscience* which calls on the authority of Aquinas.[40] The argument is the same in the long *Livre de la maison de conscience*, which the theologian Jean Saulnier (died 1430) dedicated to Catherine d'Alençon, sister-in-law to queen Isabeau, which could have taken over from the *Somme le roi* but actually never gained popularity (only six copies survive). Another Franciscan, speaking to a lay correspondant of high rank, contented himself with commenting very shortly on the Apostles' Creed 'sans nulle subtillité, car ton amy pour qui cesti labeur as empris n'est pas clerc mais homme lay, auquel doit souffire de croire simplement sans reins doubter la fay Sainte Eglise. Et par curiosité on ne doit riens en ceste matiere anquerir ou demander' (without

40 Paris BN fr 1881, fol. 228.

any subtlety, for your friend ... is not a clerk but only a layman, for whom it should be enough to believe very simply the faith of Holy Church without doubting anything. And in this matter it is not right to question anything out of curiosity.)[41] This was a faithful echo, three quarters of a century later, of the view of Gerson.[42] Amongst ordinary people *devotio* and implicit trust in the faith of the Church should always have taken the place of *cognitio*.[43] They must take great care to keep themselves from that idle and dangerous curiosity which Gerson never gave up denouncing – when arguing against the direct reading of the bible by the laity. Even commentaries on the truths of the faith were intended to increase *devotio*, not *cognitio*; as the *Ordinaire des chrétiens* (1468) explained.[44] For a long time the Creed had stopped being considered by or for the ordinary christians as a profession of faith; it had become, like the *Pater Noster* and *Ave Maria*, a prayer characteristic of the daily life of simple people.

But this restricted view of the faith was not limited to directions intended only for the simple people. Writings intended to instruct the clergy charged with the cure of souls, manuals of pastoral care devised to furnish the curates with the means of carrying through their task of educating the laity,[45] both gave an absolute pre-eminence to morality over theology. Looking only at two guides which were available before being largely replaced by the printed *Ordinaire des chrétiens*, the *Doctrinal aux simples gens*[46] and Gerson's *Miroir de l'âme*, neither trouble with theological reflection. This was not the case, it should be said, with the fourteenth-century *Second Lucidaire*, the last version of the work of Honorius of Autun.[47] But

---

[41] *Vision de la Rose*, Cambrai BM 178, fol. 84v, of the third quarter of the fifteenth century.

[42] *Miroir de l'âme*, ed. Glorieux, no. 312.

[43] The same conclusion, relating to a period two centuries earlier, is reached by J.-C. Schmitt, 'Du bon usage du Credo', in A. Vauchez (ed.), *Faire croire: modalités de la diffusion et de la réception des messages religieux du XIIIe au XVe siècles* (Rome and Paris), 1981), pp. 337–61.

[44] Incunable edition *c.* 1498 (Paris, BN Rés.D 2203), fol. 32.

[45] Synodal statutes from the thirteenth century onwards continually revert to this need; for example, those of the archbishop of Bourges, Jean Coeur, in 1451 (ed. G. Godineau, *Revue d'histoire de l'Eglise de France* 72 (1984), 64–6). On this type of text see A. Gurevich, 'Popular culture and medieval Latin literature from Caesarius of Arles to Cesarius of Heisterbach', in *Medieval Popular Culture: Problems of Belief and Perception* (Cambridge, 1988), pp. 1–38.

[46] Known in two versions: the first earlier than 1370, commissioned by Gui de Roye, archbishop of Sens, and wrongly included amongst the works of Gerson (ed. Glorieux, no. 532); the other, considerably amplified by a monk of Cluny, and dated 1389 (see C. Amalvi, '"Le Doctrinal aux simples gens" ou "Doctrinal de Sapience"', *Positions des thèses de l'Ecole des Chartes* 1978, 9–14).

[47] See most recently D. Ruhe, 'Savoir des doctes et pratique pastorale à la fin du Moyen Age', *Cristianesimo nella storia* 11 (1990), 29–60.

this was the exception, and its reception (a half-dozen copies, as against about thirty of the *Doctrinal*) shows well enough that it went against the trend of anti-intellectualism and moralisation.

To set up the faith of the coalminer as a model at the moment when an increasing number of the faithful had access to reading; to deny to the laity the right to try to understand the why and the wherefore of the truths of the faith concerning whose importance writing, reinforcing the spoken word, never ceased to insist; to refuse, as a result, to assist their reflection and to guide their reading – this was to leave the field wide open to all interpretations, to all deviant ideas. Gerson's *Examen de conscience* outlined, amongst the sins of pride, the risk of this situation; but he did nothing himself to avoid it.[48] And most of the manuals of confession, always quick to spot lukewarm practice, made no attempt to deal with doubts, questions or arrogant interpretations, as if none of them ever existed.[49] It is necessary to look to Jean Germain (died 1460) to find confirmation of the danger, so strongly felt in regard to the bible. Germain complained:

Plus tost courent hommes et femmes a ung ygnorant qui se mesle de medicine que ne font aux licenciez et docteurs en ycelle. Dont ainsi pluseurs noz subgetz plus tost se applicquent a lire romans, faubles et falses doctrines non approuvees, mais que elles leur soyent recitees par vielles, bigotz et ypocritez en chambres, maisons et lieulx secretz, qu'ilz ne font a la saincte doctrine qui leur est tous les jours en l'esglise preschee en publicque et devant tout le monde et par gens approuvés, clers et seurs en leurs doctrine et sciences; et querent meileur pain que de froment et ayment mieulx boyre de l'eaul trouble que de l'eau clere et necte, comme tous degectez et malades et enfumés de la maladie de mauvaise foy.

(Men and women run with more enthusiasm to an ignoramus who dabbles in potions than to the qualified doctors of medicine. It is the same habit with our subjects: they give much more attention to romances, to fables and to false doctrines, as long as they are recited by old women, bigots or hypocrites within walls, in houses or secret places, than they give to the holy doctrine which is preached to them every day in public, and before all, in the church by authorised people, certain and assured in their doctrine and their knowledge. They look for bread better than bread made from wheat, and prefer muddy water rather than clear and limpid, like fervent men out of their senses whose spirit is darkened and obscured by evil faith.)[50]

[48] Ed. Glorieux, no. 330.
[49] Thus The Hague Koninklijke Bibliotheek 76.G.3, fol. 293r–v.
[50] *Deux pans de la tapisserie chrétienne*, Lyon BM 1209, fols. 73v–74.

Just as the spiritual writings ignored the ecclesiological dimension of christianity and developed a strictly individualistic piety,[51] so the guides that have been reviewed gave no room, even in a limited way or in metaphors, to a theology of the church, the mass or the sacraments, even of the eucharist. Just as the *Somme le roi*, preoccupied by the desire to interiorise the truths of the faith in the conscience, was content to exhort the reader 'mengier hastivement et gloutement [l'hostie], ... c'est a dire, croire en gros que c'est li verais cors Jhesucrist, et l'ame et la deité tout ensemble, senz encerchier comment ce puet estre, car Diex puet plus fere que homme ne puet entendre' (to eat the host quickly and eagerly, ... that is to say, to believe entirely that it is the true body of Jesus Christ, his soul together with his divinity, without seeking to know how that can be, for God can do more than man can understand).[52] The most widely disseminated of the commentaries on the mass amongst the books of hours and collections of prayers, that which the author of the *Ménagier de Paris* offered as a model to his wife, consists of enumerating the subjects of prayer for each moment of the sacrifice without obvious reference to the liturgy, and passes in complete silence over the consecration and the communion. No more is said about the creed than: 'Quant on commence le *Credo*, adont vous devez penser en disant en vostre cuer: "Beau Sire Dieu, je crois que vous convient donner a vos amis ce que vous leur avez promis, et que vous vengerez de vos ennemis, car vous le pouez bien faire"' (When the creed begins, you should think and say in your heart: 'Good Lord God, I believe that it is right that you should give to your friends that which you have promised them, and that you should avenge yourself on your enemies, for you are well able to do so').[53]

So far as I am aware, only one composition in French was devoted during this period to the church: the pastoral text, unfinished at his death, which Jean Germain put together at the end of his life for the

---

[51] See similarly F. Rapp, 'La réforme religieuse et la méditation de la mort à la fin du Moyen Age', *La Mort au Moyen Age: Congrès de la Société des historiens médiévistes* (Strasbourg, 1977), pp. 53–66.

[52] Quoted from the duplicated thesis of the Ecole des Chartes by E. Brayer (Paris, 1940).

[53] Wrongly edited amongst the works of Gerson (it goes back to the thirteenth century) by Glorieux, no. 532b. No mention is made of the Creed in the commentary, either more substantial or closer to the liturgy, than has been transmitted in, amongst other collections, the *Ci nous dit* (see the edition by G. Blangez, *Société des anciens textes français* (1979–86), ii.c.604).

clergy of his diocese. *Les deux pans de las tapisserie chrétienne*, such is its
title, contains pages, produced by experience as much as by knowledge, concerning the church triumphant, the church militant, the
ecclesiastical church, preaching, scripture and tradition. If, like all
prelates, he was more concerned to alert parish priests and their
flocks against superstitious practices than to enter into the details of
possible heresies, the bishop of Châlons nonetheless considered it
useful in passing to refute Hussite tenets (which had an echo in
Burgundy in the years 1450–60?). In part 5, chapter 4, expounding
the Creed according to the commentary of Aquinas on *Sentences* III,
Jean Germain explained that the Church militant is united to God
through faith and charity, united or incorporated in Jesus Christ
through the sacrament of the altar. He continued:

Par cet article est condampnee la fole oppinion d'aucuns heretiques comme
Jean Husse et Augustin de Rome, qui ont dit que le lyen et moyen par
lequel l'Eglise est joincte et unie a son chiefz Jhesu Crist et dicte saincte et
unie, estoit la grace de predication. Et aussi l'Eglise selon eux estoit seule-
ment de ceux qui estoyent predestinez et qui seront saulvez en paradis.

(In this article is condemned the foolish opinion of some heretics like John
Hus and Augustine of Rome, who said that the link and mean through
which the Church is joined and united to its head Jesus Christ, and called
holy and one, was the grace of preaching. And also the Church, according
to these men, consisted only of those who were predestinate and would be
saved in paradise.)[54]

But this is an isolated case, and his work never gained the success it
deserved (six manuscripts survive). Without doubt, it was considered too learned.

So the very foundations of the ecclesiastical edifice were exposed
to the danger of the most discordant interpretations. It should,
however, not be forgotten that these impressions derive from the
analysis of written texts, and, to add a further limitation, from
writings in the vernacular which could be read in the fifteenth
century. Their evidence should be set over against that of iconography, liturgy and preaching – matter more important than the
mass for the faithful – whose influence on the common people was
crucial in many ways.[55] None the less there remained a persistent

[54] Lyon BM 1209, fol. 132v.
[55] Even if it is highly likely that, from the thirteenth century to the Reformation, they had
universally worked in the same direction. See, for the daily pastoral life, J. Longère and

refusal in the northern French language to allow theoretical reflection, and this left the faithful defenceless before the Reformers: the church was caught off its guard, at a time when reading acquired a decisive weight in the formation of belief. Literacy, even where it did not foster heresy, might offer little with which to combat heterodoxy.

N. Lemaître in *L'Encadrement religieux des fidèles au Moyen Age et jusqu'au concile de Trente: Actes du 109e Congrès de Société Savantes* (Paris, 1985), pp. 391–418 and 429–40; and, for images, P. Boespflug, 'Autour de la traduction picturale du *Credo* au Moyen Age (xiie–xve siècle)', in P. de Clerck and E. Palazzo (eds.), *Rituels, Mélanges offerts au Père Gy, O. P.*, (Paris, 1990), pp. 55–84.

CHAPTER 13

'Laicus litteratus': the paradox of Lollardy

Anne Hudson

From October 1390 to October 1393 bishop Trefnant of Hereford found himself dealing with a Lollard from his diocese, one Walter Brut.[1] Brut's domicile is not specified in the long details of the investigation in Trefnant's register, though from other sources we know that he held property at Lyde, a few miles north of Hereford.[2] He describes himself as 'peccator, laycus, agricola, cristianus, a Britonibus ex utraque parente originem habens' (sinner, layman, farmer, christian, having my origin from among the Britons from each parent; p. 284); he was plainly proud of the Welsh extraction his name reflects, and thought his race specially chosen by God.[3] But *laycus, agricola* though he may have been, he was also *litteratus* (p. 285), *laycus literatus nostre diocesis* (p. 278); more remarkably, he was able to defend himself at length in writing; most worthy of note is the fact that he was able to compose this defence in Latin. He states that he had been accused on a number of counts by Trefnant 'a quo sum requisitus *quod scriberem responsionem in latinis* ad omnes illas materias' (by whom I am required to write my reply to all these matters in Latin; p. 285). Brut's tracts were not penned in prison but, as the notary attests (p. 285), sent 'diversas papiri cedulas manu propria ... partim per seipsum ... partim vero per nuncios

---

[1] The trial and associated papers are to be found in *Registrum Johannis Trefnant*, ed. W. W. Capes (*CYS*, 1916), pp. 278–394; John Foxe, *The Acts and Monuments*, ed. S. R. Cattley and J. Pratt, 8 vols. in 16 (London, 1853–70), vol. III, pp. 131–86 gives an accurate translation of pp. 278–358, though he abruptly summarises (p. 179) pp. 345/9–347/14, where Brut deals with the question of a woman's power to administer the sacraments.

[2] *Calendar of Patent Rolls 1401–5* (London, 1905), p. 412, mentioned by C. Knightly, 'The early Lollards: a survey of popular Lollard activity in England, 1382–1428' (D.Phil. thesis, York, 1975), p. 173.

[3] Trefnant reg., pp. 285, 293–4 especially 'sic videtur michi Britones inter omnes alias gentes quasi ex Dei eleccione specialiter fuisse ad fidem vocatos et conversos' (so it seemed to me that the Britons amongst all other races had been specially called and converted as by the choice of God).

suos ad hoc specialiter deputatos, nobis presentavit presentarique fecit' (in various paper documents in his own hand ... some brought by himself ... some hę caused to be brought to us by messengers specially organised for the purpose). The fluency of his extensive writing, recorded *seriatim de verbo ad verbum*[4] makes it plain that *sum requisitus* cannot imply that Brut was set to a task for which he was linguistically incompetent; it is more likely, though admittedly unstated in the surviving record, that, like most of his fellow heretics, he would have preferred to use the vernacular as a matter of principle.

The seriousness with which Trefnant took Brut is evident from the assemblage of advisors that the bishop called when Brut appeared before him on 3 October 1393: fifteen officials, two masters and three bachelors of theology, two doctors of civil and canon law, drawn from his own and the Worcester dioceses but also from Exeter, Oxford and Cambridge (pp. 359–60). Within the episcopal register are brief summaries of the answers which two of these worthies prepared at Trefnant's request against Brut; the two were John Neuton, currently chancellor of Cambridge University, and William Colvyll, a recent predecessor in the post.[5] Trefnant, however, evidently took opinions beyond the range of those present at the trial: William Woodford, one of Wyclif's own earliest adversaries, was consulted on the matter. Part of his refutation of Brut, *iste aduersarius* who 'capitose et presumtuose loquitur contra determinacionem ecclesie et sanctorum doctorum' (this enemy in quarrelsome and presumptuous fashion speaks against the determination of the church and of holy doctors; f. 123v), survives in a manuscript now in Paris; it covers at length only a short section of Brut's tract.[6] At least

---

[4] As will appear later, the record in Trefnant's register is incomplete. From an examination of the register itself it appears that this incompleteness must go back to an earlier stage; it is not due to excision of material from the surviving book.

[5] Their answers are divided into two sections, pp. 368–76 and 376–94; it is not clear whether each scholar was responsible for one of these sections, and if so for which. There is a good deal of overlap between the two sections, and neither follows straight through the sequence of condemned articles (pp. 361–5) which they purport to answer. They are also complicated by the combination of Brut's case with that of Swinderby, for which see below. For the two men see Emden, *Cambridge*, pp. 421–2 and 151.

[6] Paris BN lat. 3381, fols. 115–124v, answering Brut's material in Trefnant reg., pp. 328–35. In the Paris manuscript the text is unattributed, but Woodford refers to his own efforts in his *De causis condemnatis articulorum 18 damnatorum* (see Bodley 703 fols. 16rb, 17va); Woodford there mentions both a letter *missa domino Herford contra librum Walteri Breet* (*sic*) (sent to the bishop of Hereford against the book of Walter Brut), and arguments *magis diffuse in quadam determinacione* (more diffusely in a certain determination) – from the length of the Paris text it

one other anonymous reply to one of Brut's more radical notions
survives, entitled *Utrum mulieres sint ministri ydonei ad conficiendum
eukaristie* (Whether women may be suitable ministers to consecrate
the eucharist); this mentions Brut by name and quotes from his
writing.[7] It is probable that three other texts found in the same
manuscript, though they do not mention Brut by name, arose from
his case.[8] The trial of Brut was then something of a *cause célèbre* – not,
it should immediately be said, because of the incompetence of the
bishop, for Trefnant himself was a noted legalist, a DCL, involved in
a number of legal disputes, and leaving at his death a library of over
seventy books, many of them reflecting his legal interests.[9] More
significantly, it is plain that the interest in the trial spread far
beyond the bounds of Hereford or its diocese: Woodford was at the
time based at the London Franciscan convent, and from his own
words wrote to Trefnant rather than physically visiting him. The
anonymous material is couched in the form of university determinations; even if not written in Oxford or, more probably given the
summaries of the views of Neuton and Colvylle, Cambridge, apparently designed for an academic audience for whom the views out-
weighed in interest the suspect who had originally expressed them.

The views of Brut are not here my primary concern. They were
outspoken and in many ways extreme: the eucharist was primarily a
memorial, papal pretensions to powers of absolution, along with the
pontiff's claims to temporalities, demonstrated his identity with
antichrist, war and legal execution were against the christian insistence on charity, oaths were illegal, the children of baptised parents
themselves needed no baptism and true baptism consisted not in

seems that this is part of the latter. The style of the Paris text is certainly that of Woodford,
and it is accepted as such by J. I. Catto, 'William Woodford' (D.Phil. thesis, Oxford, 1975),
pp. 29–30. The text is certainly incomplete at the end, breaking off seven lines down fol.
124v; whether it is incomplete at the beginning is less clear, since, although it starts in the
middle of Brut's tract with no obvious introduction, it follows straight on from Woodford's
De causis condempnacionis and is not obviously defective. The manuscript is English in origin,
and was sold from the Cecil collection in 1687.

[7] The determination in London BL Harley 31, fols. 196v–205; fol. 201v quotes Trefnant reg.,
p. 345, fol. 202 p. 347, fol. 204v p. 344; this item is not known elsewhere.

[8] BL Harley 31, fols. 194v–6, 216–18, 218–23. The first, *Utrum liceat mulieribus docere viros publice
congregatos*, appears to be unique. That on fols. 216–18, *Utrum quilibet laicus iustus sit sacerdos
noue legis*, and the last, *Utrum mulieres conficiunt vel conficere possunt*, are also found in London BL
Royal 7 B.iii, fols. 1–4v. Margaret Aston, 'Lollard women priests?', *JEH* 31 (1980), 441–61,
pointed out (pp. 450–1 and n. 34) the apparent summary of some of Brut's arguments in the
last.

[9] See the summary in Emden, *Oxford*, vol. iii, pp. 1900–2.

material water but in faith and hope, the just layman and, more
outrageously to his readers, the just laywoman was a priest and had
a duty to preach publicly, and, most flagrantly of all, since the
church allowed that a layperson of either sex might *in extremis*
baptise, there was no outright bar to the possibility that a woman
might consecrate the host. With such views it is hardly surprising
that Brut attracted orthodox condemnation from the clerical hierarchy. More interesting from our present viewpoint is the evidence
of Brut's *Latin* learning. Woodford described his material as a *liber*
(book; fol. 117v). Brut apologises that his tract is written *plano stilo
etsi rudi* (in plain and rude style), but that it was composed *iuxta
exilitatem literature mee* (according to the limitations of my literary
knowledge; p. 289); he invokes Christ to help him 'quia pauper sum
et notarios non habeo nec habere possum in testimonium hic scripto-
rum' (because I am a poor man, and I cannot emply a notary to set
down my testimony here; p. 289). He knows the biblical tropes of
humility, and of inadequacy with words, and so allies himself with
Isaiah and with Daniel, when God wishes to reveal himself *peccatori-
bus et laycis ydiotis* (to sinners and ignorant laymen; p. 291). But his
claim that *non cognovi litteraturam* (I know no letters; p. 286) is
controverted by his practice: his style is not unpractised, as the
balance of clauses in his creed shows (p. 286). His knowledge of the
bible is extensive, with nearly 200 passages, some of them lengthy,
quoted with verbatim accuracy.[10] He refers to canon law eleven
times, in eight cases according to the normal medieval academic
method, in a fashion that is readily identifiable; he alludes to the
chronicle of Martinus Polonus and once to Jerome.[11] Canon law he
knew as a whole, not just in extract: he refers widely and jumps from
the beginning of a chapter, correctly acknowledging 'et *in fine*
eiusdem capituli sic scribitur' (and *at the end* of the same chapter it is
written; p. 340). More interesting is his evident acquaintance with
traditional modes of argumentation in canon law: he wonders why
canon law and the fathers quoted there so often base themselves on
the Old Testament shadow of the law and not on the light of Christ's
gospel (p. 334); he is not prepared to accept the testimony of
Augustine cited there that infants dying before baptism are destined

---

[10] Though the marginal notes in the edition of Trefnant's register are almost all editorial, in
many cases the reference is also given within the text.
[11] Canon law references pp. 309, 317, 325, 332, 340 twice, 341, with more general references
pp. 328, 331, 344, 350; the others pp. 357, 350.

for eternal fire; he mocks at the diversity of patristic opinion cited in the sections dealing with the eucharist.[12] His own avoidance of patristic citation is evidently not the result of ignorance but of conviction: he comments that sacerdotal claims to absolution are 'determinata tam in decretis quam in decretalibus' (set out in the decrees as in the decretals) but not 'expresse fundentur in plana et manifesta Cristi doctrina' (clearly based in the open and declared teaching of Christ; p. 325). Repeatedly he avers that the only matters that can be accepted are those 'ex auctoritate scripture sacre aut racione probabili in scriptura sacra fundata' (from the authority of holy scripture or by probable reasoning grounded in holy scripture).[13]

Here then is a *laicus litteratus*, heretic. But how typical was Brut? Earlier historians have been understandably unwilling to take his testimony at face value: some sought to see Brut as a cleric *manqué*, and to identify him as a fellow of Merton in 1379;[14] others have exaggerated the undoubted eccentricities of his views (especially those on apocalyptic subjects), whilst playing down his learning.[15] For the first the evidence is poor. The second does little justice to the perceptions of his bishop and of those consulted by him: Brut to them might be an extreme case, but he was clearly seen as a significant straw in the wind.

Brut was accused as the adherent of views previously alleged against William Swinderby, and the two cases are not easy to disentangle in parts of the record.[16] Swinderby was, to judge by the surviving evidence, a more long-standing heretic: first encountered

[12] Trefnant reg., pp. 303–4, 317, 330–1, 340–1.

[13] Trefnant reg., p. 358; cf. pp. 286, 333, 335–6, 344.

[14] See the summary of the evidence in Emden, *Oxford*, vol. I, pp. 270–1. Brut had, according to his accusers (p. 279), been cited for heresy previously by the archbishop (Courtenay) and by Trefnant's predecessor (John Gilbert, 1375–89), but had not responded; the latter puts Brut's troubles with the ecclesiastical authorities in the Hereford diocese back before May 1389.

[15] For instance, see the comments of K. B. McFarlane, *John Wycliffe and the Beginnings of English Nonconformity* (London, 1952), pp. 135–8; McFarlane's description of Brut's 'strings of not very intelligible quotations from scripture' (p. 136) is hardly a fair reflection of their accuracy.

[16] The process against Swinderby fills fols. 97–106v of Trefnant's register, pp. 231–78 of the printed edition. But the opening of the accusations against Brut (fols. 107r–v, slightly abbreviated without notice in the edition on pp. 279–83, note the reference back to Swinderby's statement at the end) makes clear the close association of the two. Aston, 'Lollard women priests?', p. 446, n. 21, rightly observed that the editorial heading on p. 368 wrongly refers to Swinderby rather than Brut; but that on p. 365 is confirmed by the text's own specification of Swinderby even though the material interrupts Brut's case.

in Leicester in 1382, though apparently not a native of the town, he had abjured before bishop Buckingham of Lincoln that year before leaving for Coventry and later for the Hereford diocese, where Trefnant obtained a copy of the earlier abjuration in 1390.[17] Swinderby described himself as *bot sympully lettered* (p. 262) but, though his preference in his surviving texts was for English rather than Latin, his arguments were scarcely less erudite than Brut's.[18] Repeatedly he sent to Trefnant defences of his position against his accusers, twice these were stated to be *in quodam papireo quaterno* (in a certain paper booklet; pp. 237, 262), once described as *quandam cedulam papiream in modum indenture dentatam* (a certain paper document indented in the form of a legal document; p. 252), but to judge by the record of their contents in the bishop's register, neither was a negligible production. Even if he preferred English for preaching, it seems plain that Swinderby was not ignorant of Latin: he quotes his sources in Latin, even when this is the bible.[19] Since the case against Swinderby depended in large measure on these statements that he submitted, in default of the suspect's actual appearance for interrogation, it seems reasonable to deduce that the early attestation that the case is presented *de verbo ad verbum* (p. 237) should be credited in regard to the whole process. This is confirmed by the fact that the letter that Swinderby sent to the knights of parliament after Trefnant's condemnation of him *in absentia*, whilst it is a tissue of biblical allusions and quotations, contains only four Latin phrases and all of them are immediately translated (pp. 275–8).[20] Swinderby's acquaintance with canon law seems to have been even more impressive than Brut's: almost every article of his first defence (pp. 240–7) concludes with an identifiable reference to parts of the *Decretum*. Yet there is no suggestion anywhere that Swinderby had an academic background. It is, of course, possible that, since Swinderby produced his answers, as Brut was to do, not in prison but at

---

[17] His early history is given in *Chronicon Henrici Knighton*, ed. J. R. Lumby (*RS* 1889–95), vol. II, pp. 189–98, and Lincoln reg. Buckingham, fols. 236–44.

[18] The *allegaciones* of Swinderby and his supporters are given in Latin on pp. 257–61, but it is not absolutely clear that this was their original language (cf. p. 255, where mention is made of the divergence between Swinderby's preaching *in Anglicis verbis* whilst the article is in Latin).

[19] Note, for example, the material on pp. 266–7, where Latin figures as largely as English, or pp. 269–70, where all biblical citations are presented in Latin without translation or paraphrase.

[20] The side-notes in the edition, whilst they are all editorial and are not in the register itself, far from exhaust the allusions.

liberty, both may have had an academic disciple in the background
to pen these erudite documents. But of this there is absolutely no
suggestion in the record: Brut and Swinderby, though themselves
allied, are the only suspects actually named in the long process of
Trefnant's register.

The Lollard heresy was in origin learned, indeed academic.
However much it took up ideas and attitudes that had a long
medieval history, its immediate source was the thought of John
Wyclif: despite the attempts of some critics this century to divorce
Lollardy and Wycliffism, contemporaries saw the two as synonymous terms – *Wycliffisti* and *Lollardi* are merely stylistic variants in
the proclamations and writings of the orthodox both in England and
in Bohemia.[21] Netter, in his *Doctrinale* that attempted to restore
English theological respectability in the eyes of pope Martin V and
of the Council of Basel, saw the refutation of Wyclif as the answer to
his followers; the master of William White, William Taylor and
John Purvey, whose arguments all occupy Netter's attention at
various points in his long polemic, was without doubt John Wyclif.[22]
So much is by now usually accepted. Equally, the importance of
books throughout the history of the Lollard movement, from the
1380s to the 1530s, has been amply established and needs no repetition here: Thomas Maryet of Southwark who in 1496 admitted to
having kept and read in his house 'bookis, libellis, volumes, tretes
and other werkis wretyn in Englissh compiled by John Wykcliff, a
dampned heretik' neatly brings together the origin of his errors, the
mode by which he maintained his beliefs (if not the source of his
books), and the vernacular language in which those notions were
expressed.[23] But it also resumes the paradox of Lollardy: in origin
literacy begot heresy – so much is clear since Wyclif's own beliefs
evolved during his academic career; but Maryet was a layman, who
admitted to keeping English heretical books, and had to promise not
to resort or consent to read or hear such books, 'nor to pryvate and

---

[21] See Hudson, pp. 2–4.
[22] See Hudson, pp. 50–5, and on the manuscripts M. Harvey, 'The diffusion of the *Doctrinale*
of Thomas Netter in the fifteenth and sixteenth centuries', in L. Smith and B. Ward (eds.),
Intellectual Life in the Middle Ages: Essays Presented to Margaret Gibson (London, 1992),
pp. 281–94.
[23] For recent discussion of Lollard books see M. Aston, 'Lollardy and literacy', *History* 62
(1977), 347–71; Hudson, especially pp. 200–8, 231–77 and also 'Lollard book production;
in J. Griffiths and D. Pearsall (eds.), *Book Production and Publishing in Britain 1375–1475*
(Cambridge, 1989), pp. 125–42; Maryet's admission is Winchester reg. Langton, fol. 66.

dampned lecturus', it seems clear that heresy in turn fostered, even if in this case it cannot be shown to have originated, literacy. One modification between the academic world and the popular, in origin illiterate, audience of later Lollardy, the transition between Latin and English, has come to be regarded as crucial and indeed inevitable. The Brut and Swinderby cases, however, raise some interesting doubts about various aspects of the story.

In the first place, it is clear from that investigation that Brut in particular challenged many of the assumptions of his accusers: *laicus* by definition should be *illiteratus*, but Brut was far from that, and could even be brought to defend himself in fluent Latin; a lay heretic should be incapable of defending his case before the bishop's officials, let alone of quoting the bible at length, of citing canon law and the fathers. The taunts of Trefnant's helpers, whether present at the trial or not, show how they tried to push Brut back into the stereotype of the lay heretic: Brut's name was used by his opponents for predictable jokes 'Walterus est brutus idest obrutus' (Walter is stupid, overwhelmed).[24] Yet at the same time Trefnant's use of a formidable team of experts, and his resort to the expert opposition of the absent William Woodford, reveals his unwilling realisation that Brut could not be assimilated to that comforting convention.

I have spent perhaps too much time on Trefnant's dilemma: the cases might be seen as exceptional, far from paradigmatic for Lollardy. The enquiries into Brut and Swinderby occurred within ten years of Wyclif's death, a time when, as I have argued elsewhere, the causes for which he was condemned were still alive in academic circles and the outcome of the battle was not absolutely clear. But it is worth observing that laymen, even if laymen of education, were apparently setting the intellectual agenda: Trefnant saw Swinderby as expounding scripture in a new way, 'more moderno ... ubi vocabula a propriis significacionibus peregrinantur et novas divinari videntur, ubi non sunt iudicanda verba ex sensu quem faciunt sed ex sensu ex quo fiunt, ubi construccio non subjacet legibus Donati, ubi fides remota a racionis argumento sed suis principiis, doctrinis, et dogmatibus publicis et occultis' (in the modern fashion ... where words are moved from their correct meaning and appear to bring in new meanings, where the words are not to be judged by the sense they make but from the sense from which they are made,

[24] Paris BN lat. 3381, fol. 117v.

where the construction is not bound by the laws of Donatus, where
faith is taken far from the force of reason according to their principles, doctrines and teachings in public and in secret; p. 232).
Arguments in favour of the preaching of women, let alone for their
powers to consecrate, are not to be found in the heresiarch's manifold writings – these are new issues, and ones that, to judge by
surviving evidence, were raised by Brut. However, can these two
cases be paralleled elsewhere, and later, in the course of the Lollard
heresy? Predominantly, of course, Lollardy is associated with the
vernacular: the heretics, as I have suggested Brut hinted, held that
the use of the common language that all could understand was the
only proper instrument of christian instruction. But preference for
English did not universally mean rejection of Latin. The early
compilations, the *Floretum* and its abbreviation the *Rosarium*, probably originated in Oxford and were, despite the proclamations of the
prologue to the longer work, designed for an academically trained
audience. The Latin sermons that in one manuscript travelled
alongside the *Rosarium* are less evidently directed towards learned
men, though the author himself was plainly erudite. The *Floretum*
must have been compiled before 1396; the date of the sermons is
harder to ascertain but was probably before 1401. William Taylor's
notorious sermon at St Paul's Cross in 1406 was disseminated,
according to the evidence of William Thorpe, both in English and in
Latin.[25] More puzzling than these is the *Lanterne of Liʒt*. Its date of
origin is uncertain, but our first certain information about it comes
from the trial in 1415 of the London skinner John Claydon, whose
ownership of the work and agreement with its content were the chief
evidence cited in favour of his condemnation and burning for
heresy. The work quotes from the bible and at considerable length
from a number of patristic works; what is remarkable is that each of
these quotations in the two surviving medieval copies is given first in
Latin and only secondly in English. Claydon's own copy was burnt
with its owner, but there seems no reason to think that it differed in
this respect from those we have.[26] Claydon was by his own admission

[25] The sermon survives in Bodleian Ms. Douce 53, fols. 1–30; its context is described in my
edition of it and of Thorpe's work (Early English Text Society 301, 1993); see also Hudson,
pp. 13–14.

[26] It should be noted, however, that when the work was put into print by Robert Redman
about 1535 (*STC* 15225) the Latin material was throughout omitted. The case is discussed
in Hudson, pp. 211–13 and also 'Lollard book production', pp. 125–7.

illiterate; he paid to have the copy made and bound for him, and listened to the scribe and later to servants who read the book aloud to him. Unfortunately the details given in the case against him do not reveal whether this reading included the Latin sections. But the story of Claydon merely emphasises the puzzling nature of the *Lanterne*: was Latin regarded, despite its unintelligibility – or perhaps because of that – as more authoritative? At the very least the text brings to the fore the paradox in traditional medieval terms of a heresy, derived from academic circles but increasingly located amongst the laity, which never conformed to the stereotype.

Grosseteste's definition of heresy, a definition repeated by Wyclif, 'an opinion chosen by human perception contrary to holy scripture, publicly avowed and obstinately defended', makes no overt mention of literacy or of language.[27] But applied to the Lollard heresy this mnemonic involves both. The public avowal of Wyclif's ideas was from a very early stage, discernibly before Wyclif's own withdrawal from Oxford, taken out of the academic world and into the wider arena of secular debate; the increasing use of the vernacular was an inevitable concomitant of that process.[28] Equally, however, the advantages of book learning were plain to the early university-trained dissidents from the start, and these advantages were evidently transmitted: greatest of all, the written word could stay when the persecuted preacher could not; a book is more easily hidden than a man; the text is constant if not permanent, where the spoken word is fleeting. To the Lollards access to the written word was crucial: a recurrent objection to the friars was that they locked up their books from common access in their private houses.[29] Lollard beliefs were not only publicly preached, they were also publicly displayed in written form: in 1382 John Aston disseminated his heterodox views on the eucharist around London in English and Latin on flysheets, whilst Philip Repingdon and Nicholas Hereford the same year nailed a list of their beliefs to the doors of St Mary's and St Paul's

---

[27] *De civili domino*, ed. R. L. Poole and J. Loserth (Wyclif Society, 1885–1904), vol. I, p. 393, vol. II, p. 58, vol. III, p. 114; *De veritate sacre scripture*, ed. R. Buddensieg (Wyclif Society, 1905–7), vol. I, p. 159, and elsewhere.

[28] See M. Aston, 'Wyclif and the vernacular', *SCH* Subsidia 5 (1987), 281–330, and A. Hudson, 'Wyclif and the English language' in A. Kenny (ed.), *Wyclif in his Times* (Oxford, 1986), pp. 85–103.

[29] See the material discussed by R. H. Rouse and M. A. Rouse, 'The Franciscans and books: Lollard accusations and the Franciscan response', *SCH* Subsidia 5 (1987), 369–84.

London.[30] Thirteen years later, in February 1395, twelve conclusions from the Lollard sect were in turn nailed to the doors of St Paul's and of Westminster Hall.[31] Concealment of views was obviously not in question in any of these episodes, since publicity was in all cases the aim; but the success of all gestures was postulated on the assumption of literacy, and the choice of the written rather than the spoken word reflects not only their perpetrators' fear of suppression but also a realistic apprehension of a wider audience (cf. frontispiece).

On the other side the dangers of written heresy were early apprehended, and the authorities tried to push the new troublemakers back into the stereotype of the *laicus illiteratus*. Already in the 1380s books and tracts written and disseminated by Wyclif and his followers were sought, scrutinised, confiscated and destroyed; Wyclif's writings, indeed, were persecuted when the heretic himself strangely escaped. The significance of the precise wording of these texts was plainly appreciated in the demand that they should be sent in 'absque correctione, corruptione, sive mutatione quacunque, quoad ejus sententiam vel verba' (without correction, deletion or alteration of any kind, whether to their meaning or to their words).[32] The later major legislation against Lollardy equally brings written materials under review: the 1401 *De heretico comburendo* identifies the making of books as a typical activity of the heretics, whilst Arundel's 1407 *Constitutions* notoriously forbade the dissemination or ownership of vernacular biblical texts unless they and their owners had received episcopal licence.[33] Paradigmatic of later ecclesiastical procedure is the model abjuration that probably originates from the pen of Thomas Brouns, Chichele's chancellor, in 1428: in this the suspect acknowledges that he has written, compiled, retained in his own possession and approved *libros, hereses et errores continentes* (books containing heresies and errors); following abjuration he promises to pass over to the bishop's officials all such *libros siue quaternos ac rotulos, hereses, errores siue erronea continentes* (books or pamphlets or rolls

---

[30] *Fasciculi Zizaniorum*, ed. W. W. Shirley (*RS* 1858), pp. 290, 329–31, Lambeth reg. Courtenay, fols. 29v–30 in Wilkins, vol. III, pp. 164–5, Knighton, vol. II, pp. 170–2 (see n. 17); see Aston, 'Wyclif and the vernacular', pp. 297–300, 328–30 and Hudson, p. 73.

[31] Johannis de Trokelowe *Chronicon et Annales*, ed. H. T. Riley (*RS* 1866), p. 174; Roger Dymmok *Liber contra duodecim errores et hereses Lollardorum*, ed. H. S. Cronin (Wyclif Society, 1922), p. 9.

[32] See Hudson, p. 177; the last is *Fasciculi Zizaniorum*, p. 314.

[33] *Stat. Realm* II.127, reprinted Wilkins, vol. III, p. 253; Wilkins, vol. III, pp. 314–19.

containing heresies, errors or erroneous matter) that he himself
owns, has written or knows to have been dictated, and to inform
those same officials of the whereabouts of such material in the
possession of others.[34] The procedural material that accompanies
this model abjuration equally makes constant reference to the
possession of books, especially *libri in Anglico reprobate leccionis* (books
of forbidden matter in English), as incriminating evidence.[35]

The procedure of the episcopal authorities here and elsewhere
implicitly acknowledges the obvious point: legislation by a dominant orthodox hierarchy can with constant vigilance and persecution produce public disavowal of former obstinately maintained
disobedience – it cannot enforce an individual's private assent.
Books are one of the most public and persistent means of proclaim-
ing and disseminating heresy; therefore written materials become
the object of official destruction as well as, or even in preference to,
the individual heretic. By 1410 Wyclif himself had passed beyond
the range of the human authorities in England to harm him (even if
in 1415 the fathers at the Council of Constance called for the
exhumation of his body, its burning and the scattering of his ashes –
a call that was not heeded until 1428), but that did not stop a
conflagration of his writings in the presence of the university's
chancellor at Carfax in Oxford, or three years later a similar bonfire
at St Paul's.[36] The late Lollard, John Phip, who between 1518 and
1521 preferred to burn his books lest his books burn him, was
testifying to the same status of the written word that had led to these,
and numerous similar earlier actions by the same authorities.[37]

This late testimony reveals also, of course, that the orthodox
hierarchy had been singularly unsuccessful in their drive to push
heresy back into illiteracy. The number of surviving Lollard books,
amazingly high in view of the persistent persecution, points to the
same failure. And despite their overt opposition to the use by the
heretics of writing, the proper medium of orthodoxy and obedience,
there are numerous signs that, consciously or unconsciously, the
ecclesiastical authorities realised that the battle of the books was one
that they could not win. As Margaret Aston has observed, the

---

[34] See 'The examination of Lollards', *BIHR* 46 (1973), 145–59, here p. 156.
[35] See sections IV, VI, IX, pp. 157–9.
[36] Thomas Gascoigne, *Loci e Libro Veritatum*, ed. J. E. Thorold Rogers (Oxford, 1881), p. 116;
Wilkins, vol. III, p. 351, dated January 1413.
[37] Foxe, *Acts and Monuments*, vol. IV, p. 237.

procedure followed by bishop Alnwick's officials in the series of
investigations between 1428 and 1431 in the Norwich diocese
involved the production of an indented duplicate of the suspect's
abjuration; one copy was to remain with the episcopal officers, the
other with the suspect – recognition that, despite the claimed
illiteracy of many of them, the heretics valued the written word and
might, for good or ill, be influenced by it when the bishop's official
was safely out of the way.[38] That this was not simply acknowledgement of the power of the talisman is shown by earlier episcopal
activities.

   It seems clear that by 1410 archbishop Arundel had realised that
orthodoxy must appropriate the tools of the heretics – that the
medium of the vernacular could not be allowed to become a dominant part of the message of heresy, but must be brought back for
legitimate use. That year Nicholas Love sent to him for archiepisco-
pal examination his translation into English of the pseudo-Bonaven-
turan *Speculum vite Christi*, with his own pious and polemical additions. Arundel was so impressed by his inspection that he not only
commended and approved it, but also 'auctoritate sua metropolitica
vtpote catholicum publice communicandum fore decreuit et man-
dauit ad fidelium edificacionem et hereticorum siue Lollardorum
confutacionem' (by his metropolitan authority he decreed and
ordered it to be made public to the edification of the faithful and to
the confounding of heretics or Lollards).[39] It seems clear that
Arundel was here recognising Love's polemical intention: not only
do various of the Carthusian's additions overtly refute Lollard
positions, but the text as a whole, in which the four gospels are
harmonised and where scriptural quotation is indivisibly assimilated
into a continuous narrative with apocryphal detail and pious meditation, stands in opposition to Lollard insistence upon the 'naked
text' of the bible. In one sense, then, Love's work was openly and
covertly a refutation of Lollardy. But in another sense Love's work
might be regarded as an alternative to the biblical translations that
Arundel's *Constitutions* had banned – like those translations, it provided religious reading for the newly literate, but with the orthodox
interpretation of scripture built in to the narrative. The text was an
acknowledgement of the success of the opposition, not only in setting

---

[38] 'William White's Lollard followers', *Catholic Historical Review* 68 (1982), 495.
[39] Cambridge UL Ms. Additional 6578, fol. 2v; see Hudson, pp. 437–8.

the intellectual agenda but also in determining the means by which that agenda was to be pursued.

Love's translation, with its polemical outbursts and its authorizing colophon, is a peculiarly explicit example of the effect of Lollard literacy. Other orthodox texts of the fifteenth century usually are less flagrant in their demonstration of their *raison d'être*, even if they are equally strident in their opposition to heresy. In the case of Reginald Pecock, however, is found again the explicit refutation of Lollard tenets in addition to the recognition that this can only be effected by appropriation not merely of the heretics' literary tools but also by acceptance of the concomitant dominance of reasoned argument. Ownership of scripture by the laity should be allowed, albeit only with episcopal approval; availability of other translations in books is desirable when those books would inculcate obedience to the authorities and other virtues. Pecock's instinctive dislike of widespread literacy comes through, despite his insistence upon the rule of reason in theology: Christ commanded his apostles to *preach* the gospel, not to write it down, since by preaching men should believe and appropriate the message whereas writing fosters over-ingenious intellectual speculation and self-advancement.[40] But he was realist enough to acknowledge that 'wiþout writing Y can not see as for now is þese daies eny sufficient suerte for feiþ'.[41] Pecock was, of course, in turn condemned for heresy like his opponents; his fault was in part theirs, the reliance upon reasoned argument in the vernacular and the writing of those views in books accessible to the laity. Pecock's reliance upon reason is interestingly an echo of Brut's insistence that the only source of doctrine must be 'ex auctoritate scripture sacre aut probabili racione in scriptura sacra fundata' (from the authority of sacred scripture, or deduced by probable reasoning founded in holy scripture).[42] At Pecock's condemnation, as at that of numerous Lollards, his books were burned.[43]

The Lollard heresy is, then, a peculiar case in regard to literacy: the two issues are entwined with a particular intricacy and resist

---

[40] *Repressor of overmuch Blaming of the Clergy*, ed. C. Babington (*RS*, 1860), pp. 61–4; see Hudson, pp. 440–3.

[41] *The Reule of Crysten Religioun*, ed. W. C. Greet (Early English Text Society, Original Series 171, 1927), p. 433.

[42] See *Repressor*, pp. 5–7, *Reule* pp. 460–6.

[43] See V. H. H. Green, *Bishop Reginald Pecock: a Study in Ecclesiastical History and Thought* (Cambridge, 1945), p. 61.

separation. Literacy in a sense certainly *did* give rise to Wyclif's heresy; and, as I have argued elsewhere, Lollardy was in origin a *trahison des clercs*, educated to a high degree not only in letters but specifically in Latin letters.[44] But equally it is arguable that, had Wyclif and his first disciples limited the dissemination of their speculations to the university lecture halls in the conventional academic language of Latin, there would have been no 'Lollard heresy' such as troubled the English ecclesiastical authorities for 150 years – even if Wyclif's speculations about the eucharist went dangerously beyond the limits that had by the 1370s been set to the doctrine, containment of the contagion and refutation, if not abjuration, of the heretic would perhaps have been feasible. But Wyclif's preaching in London in the 1370s, when 'he ran from church to church', had given him a notoriety, as well as in all probability involved him in the use of English; the missionary activities of Repingdon, Hereford, Aston and Bedeman before and immediately after Wyclif left Oxford in 1381 had certainly spread his views to a secular audience in the vernacular; the process by which heretical views were disseminated in writing equally began before Wyclif's death. The heresy therefore appealed to the literate, and in time gave impetus to the wider growth of literacy. In turn, however, acknowledgement of that growing literacy encouraged not only the provision of more *heretical* books, but also of more orthodox books – heresy, it might be said, through literacy begot in some cases orthodoxy. But equally, at least for the first thirty or fourty years of its existence, heresy did not relinquish its academic aspirations: the continued use of Latin, the persistent citation of numerous authorities with full panoply of verbal reference to author, work and subdivision, the appropriation of learned modes of argument – all these testify to the continued memory of Lollardy's university origins. Walter Brut may have been an extreme example of the Lollard *laicus litteratus*, but he was far from the only one.

[44] Hudson, p. 516.

CHAPTER 14

Literacy and heresy in Hussite Bohemia

František Šmahel

The first reports on the emergence of heresy in the kingdom of Bohemia bear out a simultaneous occurrence of intellectual and popular religious non-conformism as early as the beginning of the fourteenth century. In 1315–16, two inquisitors of the Prague episcopal see found sixteen theses conflicting with the official creed in a treatise entitled *Declaracio salutarium mandatorum*, the author of which was *magister Richardinus medicus Ytalicus de Papia*. This doctor from Lombardy, suspect of Averroistic errors, found adherents not only in circles close to the Prague cathedral school, in which he most probably taught, but even in the neighbouring areas of the Olomouc bishopric. Here and there, people even kept his writings and books (*quaternos et libros*) in hidden places.[1]

The wider political implications of the trial of Ricardino of Pavia resulted in the establishment of a permanent inquisitorial office of Bohemia persecuting, since 1318, Waldenses, beghards, beguines and perhaps also members of other sects. Among the 4,400 persons suspected of heresy who were investigated by the inquisition between 1335 and 1355, more than one half was represented by Waldenses of south and west Bohemia. Even if exceptional cases among them included persons who could read and perhaps even write – such as a school rector, a professional book scribe (*librarius*) or a scholar's daughter (*scolaris filia*)[2] – religious instruction is most likely to have reached a majority of them by means of family traditions and orally transmitted teachings of clandestine preachers. To my knowledge, no text of the modest quantity of the Waldensian literary corpus[3] has

---

[1] A. Patschovsky, *Die Anfänge einer ständigen Inquisition in Böhmen* (Berlin and New York, 1975), pp. 30–46, 185–190 and 228–231.
[2] See Patschovsky, *Quellen*, p. 47, n. 131 (*magister scole*), p. 63 n. 201 (*librarius*) and p. 233, n. 201 (*scolaris filia*).
[3] Gonnet and Molnar, ch. VIII.

survived in Middle High German, the language of most of the sectarians from the lands of Bohemia.[4]

This situation changed considerably in the first half of the fifteenth century, when, protected by the Hussite revolutionary movement, Waldenses could emerge from hiding. The Hall 'At the Black Rose' (U černé růže), a college belonging to the corporation of the Bohemian nation at the university of Prague,[5] became a temporary centre of some German Waldenses and other non-conformists. Later on, preachers of the Hussite–Waldensian 'Internationale' found support in all their needs in the radical municipal communities of Tábor and Žatec.[6] This was obviously the reason behind the penetration of Táborite (i.e. radical Hussite) religious teachings into new Waldensian literature, diffused in small-size books (about 11 × 8 cm).[7] Three hundred years later, booklets of this size, printed in the neighbouring Protestant lands, brought non-Catholic tidings to Bohemia.[8]

Unlike most of the heretical sects targeted by the Inquisition, the Bohemian religious movement spread freely in the second half of the fourteenth century, finding no obstacles in the employment of all the contemporary facilities of the mass-communication media. One of the trends towards spiritual amendment, which did not fail to affect Bohemia, was the *devotio moderna* movement, the programme of which, the *Malogranatum* dialogue, has survived in the incredible quantity of 150 manuscripts.[9] While this best-seller of the monastic

---

[4] See Patschovsky, *Quellen*, pp. 71–82.

[5] For the contrary views about the Waldensian doctrine of the Dresden School 'At the Black Rose' see H. Kaminsky, 'Master Nicholas of Dresden: the Old Color and the New', *Transactions of the American Philosophical Society* n.s. 55–1 (1965), 5–28; J. Nechutová, 'Místo Mikuláše z Drážďan v raném reformačním myšlení' [The place of Nicholas of Dresden in early reform thinking], *Rozpravy Československé Akademie věd*, Řada společenských věd 77–16 (Prague, 1967), ch. 1; and R. Cegna, 'La Scuola della Rosa Nera a Nicola detto da Dresda', *Mediaevalia Philosophica Polonorum* 30 (1990), 10–67. For the so-called German Hussites from the Dresden School see H. Heimpel, *Drei Inquisitions-Verfahren aus dem Jahre 1425* (Göttingen, 1969), pp. 43–51. On the later German translation of the New Testament in the Táborite–Waldensian milieu P. Freitinger 'Bible české reformace: Codex Teplensis' [The Bible of the Czech Reformation: Codex Teplensis], *Křesťanská revue* 55 (1988), 231–6.

[6] See A. Molnar, 'L'Internationale des Taborites et des Vaudois', *Bolletino della Società di Studi Valdesi* 122 (1967), 3–13, and G. Gonnet, 'L'Internationale Valdo-Hussite', *Heresis* 13–14 (1989), 235–53.

[7] See R. Cegna, *Fede ed etica Valdese nel Quattrocento* (Turin, 1982), pp. 32–64.

[8] See M.-E. Ducreux, 'Lire à en mourir. Livres et lecteurs en Bohême au XVIIIe siècle', in R. Chartier (ed.), *Les usages de l'imprimé (XVe–XIXe siècle)* (Paris, 1987), p. 300, n. 52.

[9] M. Gerwing, *Malogranatum oder der dreifache Weg zur Vollkommenheit* (Munich, 1986), pp. 121ff.

scriptoria of central Europe pointed the way towards individual perfection, the reform preachers addressed mostly the broad masses of the population. Of course, the primary means of propagation of the biblical ideals and, of the critique of the depraved Church was still the spoken word, but model written sermons of some preachers were amongst the most frequent literary creations of those times. The high esteem of the postils of Conrad Waldhauser (d. 1369) or of Milič of Kroměříž (d. 1374) is borne out not only by tens of surviving manuscripts but also by numerous entries in the catalogues of medieval libraries.[10]

The contemporary *Narrative* of Milič describes vividly how this preacher gave out his texts 'to be copied by a multitude of clerks, two or even three hundred, in a manner that whatever he wrote today, the scribes were copying in full tomorrow'.[11] Milič had been a notary of the royal chancellery, and it would not seem strange if he put his experience to practice in his missionary activities. However, the excessive number of copyists, not matched by the group of surviving manuscripts written at the same time and at the same place,[12] does raise some doubts. On grounds of the fact that Milič was an author of treatises in Latin, manifestos, epistles and prayers in both Czech and German,[13] all would seem to indicate that he assigned the same degree of significance to the written word as to the oral message. An error could also be the reduction of the collective mentality of the Bohemian reformation to its learned component. It must be kept in mind that all the above-mentioned genres of reform literature, as well as many others, were addressed to the *litterati*, representing mostly university graduates fluent in Latin.[14] To a considerable extent, the full impact of the learned reform ideology on municipal and rural strata of the population was hampered both by the contemporary state of literacy and by the hardly satisfactory level of the internal christianisation.

---

[10] See P. Spunar, *Repertorium auctorum Bohemorum provectum idearum post Universitatem Pragensem conditam illustrans I* (Wrocław, 1985), pp. 172–6, and I. Hlaváček, 'Bohemikale literatur in den mittelalterlichen Bibliotheken des Auslandes' *Historica* 13 (1966), 132–4.

[11] *Narratio de Milicio* is printed by V. Kybal, *Matthiae de Janov dicti Magister Parisiensis Regulae veteris et novi testamenti III* (Innsbruck, 1911), p. 367.

[12] See V. Herold and M. Mráz, *Iohannis Milicii de Cremsir Tres sermones synodales* (Prague, 1974), p. 36.

[13] See Spunar, *Repertorium I*, pp. 171–92.

[14] See Grundmann, 'Litteratus', and recently A. Wendehorst, 'Wer konnte im Mittelalter lesen und schreiben?', in J. Fried (ed.), *Schulen und Studium im sozialen Wandel des hohen und späten Mittelalters*, Vorträge und Forschungen 30 (Sigmaringen, 1986), pp. 19–25.

Around 1400, knowledge of reading and writing was still dependent first and foremost on the density of the parochial system. By the number of parishes (one per 28 sq. km.) and monasteries (one per 413 sq. km.), the territory of the Prague episcopal see approached the level of advanced regions of Europe. One ordained priest served approximately 200 people. Of course, the situation in Prague with twenty-eight lower and middle schools, where every twentieth inhabitant belonged to the spiritual estate, differed greatly from the level of out-of-the-way village communities.[15] Not even these, however, entirely lacked opportunities for at least elementary education; instruction was provided either by the local parishes or by a series of 'schools' of poor clerks which took in pupils from among the sons of parsons, local talented youth or offspring of the country gentry. The two most eminent authors of religious literature written in Czech, Thomas of Štítné and Peter of Chelčice, learned their first lessons of reading and writing in such schools.[16] An idea of the numbers of clerks preparing for the priesthood is provided by the *Liber ordinacionum cleri* of the Prague episcopal see of 1395–1416. This source gives the number of those who received the lower order of acolytes as 13,261, that is, 630 persons every year on average.[17] Rather revealingly, some 25–30 per cent of the students who graduated from Prague university between 1399 and 1418 came from the villages, although there were no schools in the true sense of the word there.[18] The lowest components of the educational system were thus still represented by parishes, though, of course, not all priests and vicars attended to the education of talented boys with the same attention.

Among the royal towns, thirty to forty had regular schools as early as the thirteenth century; in less important towns and boroughs, schools turn up in written sources only in the second half of the fourteenth century. Around 1400, some one-third of the sixty-four non-royal towns and of 262 boroughs were provided with schools.

---

[15] See the summary of the present state of research in F. Šmahel, *Husitská revoluce I* (Prague, 1993).

[16] See W. Iwanczak, 'Tomáš Štítný, Esquisse pour un portrait de la sociologie médiévale', *Revue historique* 113 (1989), 3–28; H. Kaminsky, 'Petr Chelčický's Place on the Hussite Left', *Studies in Medieval and Renaissance History* 1 (1964), 107–36; and M. L. Wagner, *Petr Chelčický. A Radical Separatist in Hussite Bohemia* (Scottdale and Kitchener, 1983).

[17] A. Podlaha, *Liber ordinationum cleri 1395–1416* (Prague, 1922), p. x.

[18] F. Šmahel, *Pražské universitní studentstvo v předrevolučním období 1399–1419* [The university students of Prague in the prerevolutionary period 1399–1419] (Prague, 1967), pp. 27–9.

Nevertheless, the limitation of school space, lack of teaching aids and, in general, a poor living standard among the teachers set limits to the numbers of pupils even in large towns. Some boys and girls acquired the essentials of reading and writing in the course of family or monastic education but, by and large, literacy was a rare phenomenon among members of the third estate. Be that as it may, Bohemia constituted no exception in this aspect. In England, Germany or Italy, literacy did not make any significant progress until the end of the fifteenth century.[19] A certain number of students of municipal schools found employment in service to the Church, municipal or other administrative offices and, last but not least, in the courts of high aristocracy.[20] A very coarse-grained estimate of the number of those who could read and write in Latin or at least in one of the national languages would thus amount to some fifteen to twenty-five thousand people.

It thus seems at first sight that authors of literary works could indeed turn to a rather numerous community of readers. In actual practice, things were probably not so simple. First and foremost, let us take into consideration the considerable cost of procuring hand-written books. Only well-to-do individuals could commission copying of books or buy them second-hand, rewriting of books by one's own hand required not only professional skills but also abundance of leisure time. The so-called *reportata*, moderately priced records dictated or taken down in the course of lectures, were, due to the burden of a great number of abbreviations, hardly comprehensible for those who were not university graduates.[21] Moreover, the readers were dispersed and maintained no mutual contacts outside Prague and several large towns. Not even in Prague, however, can

---

[19] See, for example, J. A. H. Moran, *The Growth of English Schooling 1340–1548* (Princeton, 1985), pp. 172–4; Hudson, pp. 511–12; R. Köhn, 'Schulbildung und Trivium im lateinischen Mittelalter und ihr möglicher praktischen Nutzen', in Fried (ed.), *Schulen und Studium*, 218–23; and A. Petrucci, 'Pouvoir de l'écriture, pouvoir sur l'écriture dans la Renaissance italienne', *Annales. Economie – Société – Civilisation* 43 (1988), 831–4.

[20] See F. Šmahel, 'Piśmienność warstw ludowych w Czechach w XIV i XV wieku' [Literacy of the popular strata in fourteenth- and fifteenth-century Bohemia], in B. Geremek (ed.), *Kultura elitarna a kultura masowa w Polsce późnego średniowiecza* (Wrocław, 1978), pp. 189–205, and 'Nižší školy na Podblanicku a Vltavsku do roku 1526' [Primary schools in the region Podblanicko and Vltavsko up to the year 1526], *Sborník vlastivědných prací Podblanicka* 19 (1979), 133–71.

[21] See J. Hamesse, 'Le vocabulaire de la transmission orale des textes', in O. Weijers (ed.), *Vocabulaire du livre et de l'écriture au moyen age* (Turnout 1989), pp. 184–8, and F. Šmahel, 'Ceny rukopisných knih v Čechách do roku 1500' [Prices of handwritten books in Bohemia up to 1500], *Sborník historický*, 14 (1966), 5–49.

literacy be assumed as a matter of course in most of the simple congregations. In spite of rather frequent bilingualism,[22] the language form of written texts constituted a limiting factor. Czech-speaking persons understood texts written in German only with difficulty and vice versa; in addition to that, few people could read everything. As far as the propagation of reform teaching from a learned centre towards the broad masses of the population is concerned, Hussitism remained untouched by the 'typographical age' and had to do with predominantly oral means of mass propaganda.

The other serious obstacle hindering the full use of the written word in fostering the trend towards reform was insufficient internal christianisation. If Jean Delumeau has raised the question of the precocity of sixteenth-century reformations *vis-à-vis* most of the population,[23] the more so does this caution apply in the case of Hussite Bohemia. The visitation protocol of archdeacon Pavel of Janovice of 1378–82 clearly indicates that among the popular strata of Prague and of its village hinterland, knowledge of Church doctrine was limited to the barest essentials, in most cases to familiarity with the *Credo* prayer and the ten commandments.[24] On their way towards the full acceptance of, and full identification with, the attitudes of the learned reform ideology to luxury, simony and superficial cult practices of the Roman Church, both well-born and commoner believers had to advance from formal piety towards a deeper self-identification with the biblical-christian code in their individual and collective conscience. In other words, the first thing the reformers of Bohemia had to carry out was the full explanation of the basic rules of the christian creed to their potential allies among the population and their inculcation in their souls and minds.

In contemporary conditions, this goal could best be achieved by means of sermons, exposing the listeners to the emotional colouring of the spoken word and to a personal approach of the speaker.[25] Milič of Kroměříž, who had originally had some difficulties in

---

[22] E. Skála, 'Der deutsch-tschechische Bilinguismus', in *Sprachgeschichte* 41 (1977), 260–79.

[23] J. Delumeau, *Un Chemin d'histoire, Chrétienté et christianisation* (Paris, 1981), pp. 72–9.

[24] See Z. Hledíková, 'K otázkám vztahu duchovní a světské moci v Čechách ve druhé polovině 14. století' [On the question of the relations between secular and spiritual power in Bohemia in the second half of the fourteenth century], *Československý časopis historický* 24 (1976), 264–8, and I. Hlaváček, 'Beiträge zum Alltagsleben im vorhussitischen Böhmen', *Jahrbuch für fränkische Landesforschung* 34–5 (1974–5), 874–82.

[25] See recently P. T. Dobrowolski, '"Fides ex auditu". Uwagi o funkcji kazania w późnym średniowieczu', *Przeglad Historyczny* 81 (1990), 27–58 with other references.

obtaining listeners, is reported to have preached two to three times on holy days and regularly at least once on weekdays.[26] The repetition of sermons both amplified their impact and expanded the range of advocates for the reform demands. Jan Hus mounted the lectern on Sundays and holidays no less often. In the course of the ten years that saw his activities in the Bethlehem chapel of Prague (1402–12), he delivered some 3,500 sermons.[27] The Bethlehem chapel, devoted expressly to the purpose of explaining the divine word in the Czech language, had an extraordinary importance for the propagation of the reform movement in the capital, as it was spacious enough to take in three to four thousand persons who would hear a single sermon.[28] On the one hand, this offered to the reform ideas the opportunity to overcome the borders of parishes, of which there were forty-four in the capital agglomeration; on the other hand, the monolingualism of the instruction pushed into opposition the ethnically sensitive German-speaking inhabitants of Prague.

The main disadvantages of sermons were their non-repeatability, the spatio-temporal limitations of their impact and especially the communication 'flaws' in the propagation of ideas, instructions and programme headlines of the reform centre. This was the reason why the leading reformers strove to put down their sermons in writing, to arrange them into collections and to provide their adherents with them as with manuals. We know what stress Milič of Kroměříž laid on the reproduction of his sermons. It is worth noticing that Milič submitted to students and other scribes even the first collection of his sermons for which he chose the eloquent title of *Abortivus*. Unlike the synodal sermons, which he wrote in advance, his postils lack the 'inflammatory' emotion with which he is reported to have carried off his listeners. But they abound even more in quotations of authorities borrowed from other sermon collections and manuals.[29]

Systematic investigations of Jan Hus's sermon collections have shown that, with the exception of the Latin discourses before a synodal or university assembly of his *Postil*, they do not give evidence of him as a preacher but as a writer and teacher. We search in vain

---

[26] See *Narratio de Milicio* (as n. 11), p. 363.
[27] See A. Vidmanová, 'Hus als Prediger', *Communio viatorum* 19 (1976), 65–81.
[28] See O. Odložilík, 'The Chapel of Bethlehem in Prague', in G. Stökl (ed.), *Studien zur älteren Geschichte Osteuropas* (Graz and Cologne, 1956), pp. 125–41.
[29] See M. Kaňák, *Milič aus Kremsier. Der Vater der böhmischen Reformation* (Berlin, 1981), ch. v.

in these records for the critical attacks and daring assessments mentioned in various denunciations and charges. Both in his model versions and in his sermon collections that were definitely edited, Hus had in mind first and foremost his students of the Bethlehem preaching school,[30] for whom he intended to provide assistance in Sunday sermons (*de tempore*), holiday sermons (*de sanctis*) or on fast days before Easter (*quadragesimalia*).[31] In most cases, Hus gave over to his students written versions of his sermons or university lessons which he had prepared before. His students copied them but also altered and completed them from memory. The base of the manuscript tradition is thus usually not Hus's original or a single archetype but a group of archetypes maintaining, by and large, the same relationship to the lost original.[32] A special case is constituted by his *Postil*, which he wrote during his retirement in the country in 1412–13 when he had enough free time. Though he had used for this text his own earlier postils in Latin, he departed from them in not limiting himself to mere guidelines for explication. His *Postil* in Czech was meant to be read and, perhaps for this very reason, it contains a number of personal thoughts and recollections.[33]

Up to now, it has been commonly assumed that both original and translated writings amongst Old Bohemian literature, including writings of Jan Hus, were addressed to lay readers from among the nobility and municipal elites. In view of the low level of school instruction mentioned above and of the insufficient knowledge of Latin in many candidates for ordination, it may rather be supposed that a number of explications, treatises and such texts written by the reform authors was first and foremost destined to improve the level of average country clerks and parsons and of teachers of lower schools. Periodical plague epidemics resulted in Bohemia, much as elsewhere, in a sharp increase in the mortality of parochial clergy. The availability of free offices and vacant posts lowered the demands for the instruction of candidates for the priesthood. A number of

---

[30] On this reform school F. M. Bartoš, 'Hus jako student a profesor Karlovy university' [Jan Hus as a student and professor of Charles University], *Acta Universitatis Carolinae – Philosophica et Historica* 2 (1958), 9–26.

[31] See F. M. Bartoš and P. Spunar, *Catalogus fontium M. Iohannis Hus et M. Hieronymi Pragensis opera exhibentium* (Prague, 1965), pp. 137–50.

[32] See A. Vidmanová, 'Stoupenci a protivníci mistra Jana Husi' [The adherents and opponents of Master Jan Hus], *Husitský Tábor* 4 (1981), 55–6.

[33] Printed in *Mistr Jan Hus Postila. Vyloženie svatých čtení nedělních* [Postil. Explication of Sunday Scripture readings] (Prague, 1952).

young clerks did not manage to acquire a command of Latin and gratefully accepted manuals written in Czech. The need for reform propaganda thus multiplied the literary production in one of the national languages.[34]

Jan Hus had in mind his preacher students and other priests with insufficient knowledge of Latin when he wrote in Czech his *Expositions* of the Faith (*Výklad na vieru*), the Decalogue (*Výklad na desatero přikázanie*) and of the Five divine commandments (*Výklad na páteř*). The wording 'my dear' or 'my faithful christian', in which he turns to the reader fairly often, should not deceive us because, first and foremost, Jan Hus was addressing the community of priests. He was thinking of them all the time, even subconsciously, and it was especially to them that his instructions on 'how to teach the divine commandments in a short time' to an illiterate audience were directed.[35] These texts were supposed to provide for simple, uneducated, but busy christians short admonitions according to the instructions for use contained within them. 'And as simple people have difficulties in remembering long speeches, it is up to the keeper of these books to teach them to understand the creed in all brevity.'[36] Among all the owners of Jan Hus's explications, this duty was undoubtedly best performed by priests.

A most peculiar position within the literary works of Jan Hus is occupied by his treatise *On Six Errors*. He composed this text, in which he submitted full arguments for his parting from the doctrine of the Roman Church, in Latin and this was also the language of its version inscribed on the walls of the Bethlehem chapel in the later year 1412.[37] The form of this inscription aroused the wrath of the opponents of the reform movement, one of whom reproached Hus for 'having introduced erroneous teachings among the people by it'.[38] This, however, was not all. A popular song of the period

---

[34] Compare B. I. Zaddach, *Die Folgen des schwarzen Todes (1347–51) für denKlerus Mitteleuropas* (Stuttart, 1971), pp. 85–9. On the confrontation between Latin and the vernacular in Hussite Bohemia F. Svejkovský, 'The conception of the "vernacular" in Czech literature and culture of the fifteenth century', in R. Picchio and H. Goldblatt (eds.), *Aspects of the Slavic Language Question* (New Haven, 1984), pp. 324–35.

[35] The shorter Exposition of the Decalogue, printed by J. Daňhelka in *Magistri Iohannis Hus Opera omnia*, vol. 1: *Expositiones bohemicae* (Prague, 1975), p. 327.

[36] The shorter Exposition of the Faith, cf. *Hus Opera omnia*, vol. 1, p. 105.

[37] *De sex erroribus*, printed by B. Ryba, *Betlemské texty* (Prague, 1951), pp. 39–63.

[38] See V. Novotný, *M. Jana Husi korespondence a dokumenty* [The correspondence and documents of M. Jan Hus] (Prague, 1920), p. 252, no. 116.

recommended to all those who wished for instruction in the Holy Scriptures to go to Bethlehem and there 'to learn what Master Jan of Husinec had commanded to be written on the walls'.[39] For the time being, let us put aside the question of the manner in which the people were to be instructed or infected by the Latin inscriptions of the Bethlehem chapel. The important things is that Jan Hus himself did not trust in Latin and that he translated the *De sex erroribus* treatise during the first half of 1413 into Czech as *O šesti bludiech*. He provided the manuscript with introductory and closing paragraphs for every chapter and with interlinear glosses. This time, he addressed his ordained readers directly by sentences of the type 'for this reason, priest, rest content with it [i.e. be satisfied with it]'.[40] At any rate, the purpose of the Czech translation remained the same as that of its Latin model, namely 'that priests and students should evade the simoniac heresy, from which God has protected them until now'.[41]

Of course, Jan Hus remembered his readers who were cultivated members of the nobility and townsfolk. He addressed to them short admonitions in Czech of which it is sufficient to recall *The Mirror of a Sinful Man* (*Zrcadlo hřiešníka*), *The Three-stranded Cord* (*Provázek Třípramenný*), *On Matrimony* (*O manželství*), *The Kernel of Christian Doctrine* (*Jádro učení křesťanského*) and others.[42] One of these treatises, bearing the eloquent title of *The Daughter* (*Dcerka*), was destined by Jan Hus for pious women. Its very *incipit* indicates that Hus meant this text to be heard, not read: 'Hark with thine ear, perceive with thy reason and listen with thine ear voluntarily and readily, so that hearing, thou wilt understand what will be written.[43] Nevertheless, some pious women around Bethlehem could read and perhaps even write. This certainly applies to queen Sophia and to an anonymous noblewoman to whom Jan Hus addressed his epistles written in Czech.[44] The cloak of anonymity veils to this day one of the first female authors of Bohemia who defended Jan Hus from contempo-

---

[39] *Výbor z české literatury doby husitské I* [Anthology from Czech literature of the Hussite period], ed. B. Havránek, J. Hrabák and J. Daňhelka (Prague, 1963), p. 272.

[40] *On Six Errors*, printed by J. Daňhelka, *Magistri Iohannis Hus Opera omnia*, vol. IV: *Opera bohemica minora* (Prague, 1985), p. 273.

[41] See Ryba, *Betlemské texty*, p. 62, and *Hus Opera omnia*, vol. IV, p. 296.

[42] All these short expositions are printed in *Hus Opera omnia*, vol. IV.

[43] *Hus Opera omnia*, vol. IV, p. 163.

[44] See Novotný, *M. Jan Husi korespondence*, pp. 15–18, no. 7, and pp. 195–6, no. 78.

rary 'antichrists' in her *Knížky*, written in Czech.[45] This case was not quite isolated, When Táborite priests were appointed for St Peter's church in the Nové-Město (New Town) of Prague in 1421, the offended women parishioners submitted an application in writing which one of them read verbatim before the councillors in the city hall. However, the councillors succumbed rather to female outcry than to written protests in this case.[46]

Much as the writings of Jan Hus, even the Bethlehem chapel inscriptions were aimed at different addressees. The reconstruction of original texts based on archaeological remains[47] has clearly demonstrated that only the *Credo* (*Věři v Buoh*) and the *Decalogue* (*Desatero*) were written in Czech on the chapel walls.[48] In addition to the previously mentioned treatise *De sex erroribus* by Jan Hus, most of the wall surfaces that could have been visible to the naked eye bore two lengthy texts by Master Jacobellus of Stříbro/Mies conceding to the laity and even to babes in arms the Holy Communion *sub utraque specie*.[49] In addition to this fact, the observation that even the Hussite parochial church of St Michael in the Staré-Město (Old Town) of Prague[50] displayed texts written exclusively in Latin makes fairly safe the assumption that inscriptions in vernacular languages constituted rather the exception than the rule. The Old Czech text of the Ten Commandments, written in the Glagolitic script at the Slavic Benedictine abbey of Prague-Emauzy in 1412, represented more or less a curiosity.[51] More weight might be given to some commemorative inscriptions on public buildings, such as the two surviving slabs of sandstone, perpetuating in the Corpus Christi

[45] F. M. Bartoš, 'První česká spisovatelka' [The first female literary author of Bohemia], *Křesťanská revue* 24 (1957), 119–22.
[46] See Chronicle of Lawrence of Březová, printed by J. Goll, *Fontes rerum Bohemicarum V.* (Prague, 1893), p. 497. Generally see on this J. M. Klassen, 'Women and religious reform in late medieval Bohemia', *Renaissance and Reformation* 5/4 (1981), 203–21.
[47] See B. Ryba, 'Rozluštění latinského nápisu na stěně kaple Betlemské' [Decipherment of the Latin inscription on the Bethlehem Chapel wall], *Věstník Královské české společnosti nauk, Třída pro filozofii, historii a filologii* 1 (1949).
[48] Edited by Ryba, *Betlemské texty*, pp. 37–8.
[49] Both these tracts by Jacobellus of Mies (*Salvator noster* and *De communione parvulorum*) are printed in Ryba, *Betlemské texty*, pp. 105–38. See also J. Kadlec, 'Neznámé nápisy v Betlemské kapli' [Unknown inscriptions in the Bethlehem Chapel], *Časopis Společnosti přátel starožitností českých* 64 (1956), 29–31.
[50] See P. Spunar, 'Neznámé pražské nápisy v kodexu ÖNB 4550' [Unknown Prague inscriptions in Cod. ÖNB 4550], *Studie o rukopisech* 12 (1973), 175–87.
[51] See F. V. Mareš, 'Emauzský hlaholský nápis – staročeský Dekalog' [The Glagolitic inscription of Emausy – a Decalogue in Old Czech], *Slavia* 31 (1962), 2–7.

chapel of the Prague Nové-Město the solemn declaration of the orthodoxy of the Hussite Holy Communion by the cup. Though the existence of both Czech and German renderings of these inscriptions is safely documented before 1462, the purportedly original slabs are, in fact, faithful copies from the beginning of seventeenth century.[52]

As a reform centre of the Czech-speaking community of Prague, the Bethlehem chapel thus remained a domain of the spoken word. Even if most of Jan Hus's adherents were literate, they would hardly understand the Latin clauses on the chapel walls. As the language of university graduates and as a neutral means of communication between the Czech- and German-speaking communities, however, the Latin language is likely to have played at Bethlehem the same role as it played in administrative practices of ethnically mixed towns. At any rate, remains of the Bethlehem inscriptions show clearly that in view of their graphical form, even a qualified Latin speaker had to read them aloud word by word. Of course, only a very short distance separated reading aloud from translating the text into Czech or German for the benefit of the audience standing by. When I suggested some time ago that perception of the message of frescoes or table paintings in churches required the assistance of a priest, a clerk or some other educated person, this idea seemed to be a little far-fetched. However, who but a learned interpreter could have explained to interested laymen and laywomen the barely visible and sometimes even reversed Latin inscriptions? Be that as it may, a man with a pointer is clearly present in some Italian and Bohemian fifteenth-century paintings.[53] In spite of that I could hardly believe my own eyes when, in 1991, I met an elderly gentleman who suddenly produced a pointer to show me interesting details of a late Gothic altar painting in the Holy Spirit church at the town of Hradec-Králové.

The antithetical treatise of Nicholas of Dresden, known under the titles of *Tabulae novi et veteris coloris* or *Cortina de Anticristo*, also required an interpreter. The original name of this text of 1412 is probably contained in its opening sentence: *Incipit conversacio Cristi*

---

[52] See J. Hejnic, 'Dvě nápisné památky z doby husitské' [Two inscriptions from the Hussite period], *Sborník Národního muzea v Praze* A 15 (1961), 238–56.
[53] On this see M. Baxandal, *Painting and Experience in Fifteenth Century Italy* (Oxford, 1972), pp. 54, 71–2, and F. Šmahel, 'Vom Mittelalter zur Reformation: Modi legendi et videndi', *Umění* 32 (1984), 318–30.

opposita conversacioni Anticristi.[54] As the pictorial cycles of two illuminated manuscripts of the second half of the fifteenth century[55] were obviously based on Nicholas's text, most specialists believed that his *Tabulae* could have been employed as a means of pictorial propaganda in the Bethlehem chapel as early as the time of their origin. However, doubts were cast on this hypothesis some time ago and the use of transferable wooden boards or paper placards was suggested.[56] The structure of the original Latin *Tabulae* does not correspond to the needs of book illumination, however, and thus it seems more acceptable to assume their painted versions were carried on the walls of a vestibule area (so-called *mázhaus*) of some building to which the public had access, such as, most probably, the Bohemian-nation college 'At the Black Rose', in which Nicholas of Dresden himself lived. However that may be, Latin texts, accompanying the individual scenes of the antithetical cycle, required an interpreter.[57] The perception of frescoes or transferable paintings carrying a propaganda message thus became a kind of an audio-visual performance. A later phenomenon of the same kind may be seen in marketplace shows of various street singers such as the 'cantimbanchi' of Italy, 'ballad-mongers' of England or 'Gassensänger' of Germany who expounded to their audience their sets of horror and other stories in words but also in series of home-made transferable paintings.[58]

The ideologists of Hussitism, caught in a perpetual struggle with their learned opponents, had naturally the best of reasons to convince their simple adherents of the biblical or patristic foundations of the reform demands. Jan Čapek, a radical partisan of Jacobellus of Stříbro, employed his poetic talents for reform didacticism. In the

---

[54] Printed in Kaminsky, 'Master Nicholas of Dresden', pp. 38–64.

[55] The Codex Theol. 182 of the Niedersächsische Staats- und Universitätsbibliothek Göttingen dates from the 1460s, the so-called Jena Codex in National Museum Library Prague IV. B. 24 was illuminated in the first part of the sixteenth century. Cf. Z. Drobná, *The Jena Codex* (Prague, 1970).

[56] On Hussite pictorial satires see K. Chytil, *Antikrist v naukách a umění středověku a husitské obrazové antiteze* [The antichrist in medieval doctrine and art and Hussite pictorial antitheses] (Prague, 1918); M. Vlk, 'Obrazy v Betlemské kapli' [Pictures in Bethlehem Chapel], *Časopis Národního Muzea* 130 (1961), 151–62; F. M. Bartoš, 'Po stopách obrazů v Betlemské kapli' [On the track of the pictures in Bethlehem Chapel], *Časopis Národního Muzea* 133 (1964), 129–42; and H. Bredekampf, *Kunst als Medium sozialer Konflikte. Bilderkämpfe von der Spätantike bis zur Hussitenrevolution* (Frankfurt on Main, 1975), pp. 304–29.

[57] See F. Šmahel, 'Die Tabule veteris et novi coloris als audiovisuelles Medium hussitischer Agitation', *Studie o rukopisech* 29 (1992), 95–105.

[58] See P. Burke, *Popular Culture in Early Modern Europe* (New York and London, 1978), pp. 94–100.

course of the year 1417, he converted quotations of Church authorities favourable to the cup for the laity in Holy Communion to a series of rhymed verses in Czech, making is thus easier to memorise the 'holy truths'. In addition to the introductory question, the rhymed translation in writing follows sentences in Latin so that this bilingual florilegium could have been employed more extensively. A similar concept is shown by the contemporary rhymed treatise *Against Pilgrimages (Proti poutím).*[59]

The increase in numbers of adherents that the reform movement won amongst the populace opened much wider opportunities for the use of songs as a means of Hussite catechising, as an emotional declaration of solidarity and as a mobilising appeal. A popular ditty against archbishop Zbyněk Zajíc of Házmburk/Hasenburg, who burned John Wyclif's books and 'wronged thus the Bohemians', was sung by students in the streets of Prague as early as 1410. There was almost no important event which would not have immediately become a theme for shorter or longer compositions in verse.[60] In addition to their propagandistic, mobilising and informative functions, Hussite songs also served for instruction and education. A special role is played by songs and rhymed compositions for children, which have a double educational purpose: children easily remembered the song texts and taught them to relatives and other adults. Indirect evidence for this is yielded by the verse version of the Decalogue for children by Jan Čapek of 1417, making reference to chants of the little ones which you constantly hear everywhere in the streets'.[61]

An example of the versatility of Hussite songs may be seen in the famed chorale *Ye who are the warriors of God (Ktož jsú boží bojovníci)*, the repeated singing of which drove home the ABC of the Hussite military code of conduct. According to the chorale, the first and

---

[59] Both versified tracts, *Otázka nynie taková běží* and *Proti poutím* were published by F. Svejkovský, *Veršované skladby doby husitské* [Rhymed compositions of the Hussite period] (Prague, 1963), pp. 90–8. On John Čapek see F. M. Bartoš, 'Z politické literatury doby husitské' [From political literature of the Hussite period], *Sborník historický* 5 (1957), 31–42, and F. Svejkovský, 'Z básnické činnosti Jana Čapka' [From the poetic activities of Jan Čapek], *Listy filologické* 85 (1962), 282–96.

[60] The fundamental work on Hussite song is still Z. Nejedlý, *Dějiny husitského zpěvu* [History of the Hussite chant], 6 vols. 2nd edn (Prague, 1954–6). For texts see also *Výbor z české literatury*, vol. I, pp. 256–341.

[61] Printed in *Výbor z české literatury*, vol. I, p. 301. On the songs for Hussite children, Nejedlý, *Dějiny*, vol. IV, pp. 230–1, and N. Rejchrtová, 'Hussitism and children', *Communio viatorum* 22 (1979), 201–4.

foremost duty of all the archers and lancers of knightly rank, as well as of all pikesmen and flailsmen of the common people, was to 'pray for God's help and believe in Him'. In view of the initially limited numbers of Hussite warriors, the song commanded them 'never fear the enemies / do not mind their great numbers'. All the troopers had to obey their captains, remember the password, stay with their own battalions and protect their brethren. It was expressly forbidden to everyone, including baggage boys and grooms, to kill enemies for booty. All without exception were to clutch their arms firmly and to attack the enemy with the joyful cry of 'God is our Lord'.[62]

Both Hussite sermons and songs or rhymed treatises had common religious and didactic goals. While, however, hearing sermons was more or less limited to a single passive reception, singing or memorisation of rhymed compositions represented simultaneous participation in and reproduction of literature passed on by oral tradition. This mode of diffusion was, of course, excluded for the basic work of reform fundamentalism, the bible translated into vernacular. In this aspect, Bohemia occupies a more than honourable position in both major languages. The beautifully illuminated bible of king Wenceslas IV of the 1380s contains in six volumes a nearly complete text of the Old Testament in German. A complete translation of all the books of the bible into Czech was available in 1385 at the very latest, while a unified and systematic translation of the so-called third redaction was finished in the twenties of the following century, that is, in the course of Hussite wars.[63]

The ownership of Czech versions of the bible by well-to-do lay-persons such as a Táborite captain[64] was not absolutely unique. Nevertheless, possession does not automatically presuppose reading. On the other hand, a number of lay readers could not afford their

[62] The Czech text in *Výbor*, vol. I, (as n. 39) pp. 324–5, English translation by F. G. Heymann, *John Žižka and the Hussite Revolution*, 2nd edn (New York, 1969), pp. 497–8. On its author see E. Pražák, 'Ktož jsú boží bojovníci', *Strahovská knihovna* 4 (1968), 5–17.

[63] See the comprehensive summary of the present state of research by V. Kyas, 'The fourteenth century Old Czech translation of the bible and its development in the fifteenth century', in R. Olesch and H. Rothe (eds.), *Biblia Slavica*, vol. I–2: *Kuttenberger Bibel* (Paderborn, Munich, Vienna and Zürich, 1989), pp. 49–52. On the German translation, F. M. Bartoš, 'Der Schöpfer der Rotlew-Bibel', in H. Gericke, M. Lemmer and W. Zöllner (eds.), *Orbis Mediaevalis. Festgabe für Anton Blaschke* (Weimar 1970), pp. 31–40 and the fascimile edition of the Wenceslas bible in *Akademischer Verlaganstalt Graz*.

[64] See for example A. Matějček, 'Bible Filipa z Padařova, hejtmana táborského' [Bible of the Tábor commander Filip of Padařov], in R. Urbánek (ed.), *Sborník Žižkův 1424–1924* (Prague, 1924), pp. 149–69.

own copies of the bible. Most of the adherents of the reform demands could not read and had thus to rely on their memory. Those who wanted to hear the divine word and meditate on it found ample opportunities to do so. A woman named Kačka (Kate), a maidservant of the noble lady of Šternberk/Sternberg, fell under suspicion in 1378 through too frequent participation in the Holy Communion. Having been questioned by the vicar general whether she preached herself, she denied it but admitted that together with other ladies and maidservants she frequently meditated on the sermons that they had heard. Moreover, she confessed to having composed a prayer, a written copy of which she promised to despatch to the consistory.[65]

A good memory, independent judgement and the gift of eloquence were far from being a privilege of the educated. Quite like Kate, various 'doctors' of the needle and cobbler's stool, clothmakers and bakers from the Hussite community of Sezimovo-Ústí, participants of the so-called mountain congregations, plebeian partisans of the radical Prague preacher Jan Želivský (John of Želiv), as well as the captains of Táborite troops, were digesting the sentences of the preachers.[66] Attentive and systematic listening to sermons over long years gave open-minded laypersons a certain sum of biblical facts and sentences on which they could build up their own opinions and attitudes even without school instruction. In the eyes of the popular masses, the biblical inspiration removed the difference between a preacher who studied theology and a lay missionary of the faith. Participation of the laity in biblical actualisation thus had its darker side in a unilateral, partial and tendentious command of the biblical message. The university masters of the Prague reform centre were well aware of this. Jacobellus of Stříbro, for instance, emphatically insisted on the fact that 'the common people are unable to grasp fully divine illumination' and that, for this reason, 'they do not need every truth at every time'. Pure truths were to be revealed to 'the more understanding and to the higher (i.e. educated), to the common people, then, only milk'.[67]

In spite of the fact that the Tábor community of brethren and

---

[65] See F. Tadra, *Acta judiciaria consistorii Pragensis I* (Prague, 1893), pp. 311–12, no. 398.

[66] See F. Šmahel, 'Husitští "doktoři" jehly a verpánku' [Hussite 'masters' of the needle and cobbler's stool], in N. Rejchrtová (ed.), *Smířování* (Prague, 1983), pp. 89–96, and *Dějiny Tábora I-2* (České Budějovice, 1990), pp. 598–605.

[67] See A. Molnár, 'Aktywność ludu w ruchu reformatorskim' [Reform activities of the people in the light of Hussite sermons], in Geremek (ed.), *Kultura elitarna*, (as n. 20) pp. 9–10 and 28–9.

sisters emerged in the peak period of Chiliasm refusing all worldly learning, literacy and heresy very soon joined hands even in this focal point of radicalism. The range of Táborite writing merits attention both by the extent of the genres represented and by the intentionally 'low' literary style, though only a part of these works was destined to oral transmission. The foremost preachers of Tábor thought in Latin and composed their treatises, manifestos and polemics in Latin. The language, scientific apparatus and variety of genres of the putative library of the Tábor authors all point to its location rather in a faculty of theology of some university than in a revolutionary stronghold bristling with life.[68] Of course, it must be constantly kept in mind that all the Tábor preachers acquired their basic and higher education thanks to the school facilities of the pre-Hussite regime. In consequence of the confiscation of ecclesiastical property, of the eviction of Roman clergy and of the absence of local candidates for the orders, both Tábor and all Hussite Bohemia restricted access to education and, because of this, also to the divine word – the free enunciation of which headed as number one the list of their common demands in the form of the four articles of Prague.[69]

Hussite Bohemia was purged of the ignominy of heresy as a sequel to its military victories resulting in the conclusion of agreements with emperor Sigismund and the Basel council. Legalised duality of the creed opened the way for propagation of the reform confession in churches and schools of the land, in contrast to the Lollardism of England which had grown, just like Hussitism, from Wycliffite roots.[70] In spite of the fact that Hussitism restricted rather than enlarged the base of literacy, the prevailing orientation of its oral and written propaganda contributed both directly and indirectly to the increased reception of literary works among the common people. In accordance with this, the genre system of the literature written in the Czech language underwent partial transformation. In spite of the limits in genre variety, imposed during the Hussite period, the actualisation and appeal of the texts increased.[71] This fate did not,

---

[68] See A. Molnár, 'Taboristisches Schriftum', *Communio viatorum* 22 (1979), 105–22.
[69] See F. Šmahel, 'Antytezy czeskiej kultury późnego średniowiecza' [Antitheses of the Czech culture of the late middle ages], *Kwartalnik Historyczny* 90 (1983), 714–21.
[70] Compare Hudson, esp. chs. 4–5.
[71] See J. Kolár, 'K transformaci středověkého žánrového systému v literatuře husitské doby' [On the transformation of the medieval genres in the literature of the Hussite period], *Husitský Tábor* 5 (1982), 135–51.

however, spare Hussite Bohemia from seeing apostates in its own ranks. The Unity of Czech Brethren, a heresy within a heresy, emerged as the first reformed Church in the history of Europe. Nevertheless, the pursuit of its ascendance towards the peaks of Bohemian literary culture lies beyond the temporal scope of this volume.[72]

[72] The best work on this topic is still R. Říčan, *Die Böhmischen Brüder. Ihr Ursprung und ihre Geschichte* (Berlin, 1961). See also P. Brock, *The Political and Social Doctrines of the Unity of Czech Brethren in the Fifteenth and Early Sixteenth Centuries* (The Hague, 1957).

CHAPTER 15

Heterodoxy, literacy and print in the early German Reformation

Bob Scribner

I

The major themes of this chapter are encapsulated in an auto-biographical passage in which Menno Simons described the process of his conversion to Anabaptism. In 1524, at the age of twenty-eight, Simons became a priest in his home village of Pingjum, working alongside the parish priest and another curate. The parish priest was fairly well educated, the fellow curate less so than Simons, but both had read more of the scriptures. Simons confessed: 'I had never touched them, for I feared if I should read them, I would be misled.' For two years he was 'an ignorant preacher' and spent his free time drinking, gambling and whiling away the hours with his fellow priests. In the third year of his ministry, he began to have doubts about the validity of the eucharist as he handled the bread and wine in the mass. However, according to Menno, whenever the three young priests discussed matters of scripture, 'I could not speak a word with them without being scoffed at, for I did not know what I was driving at.' He then decided to explore the New Testament for himself, although it is unclear whether this was in the vernacular or in Latin. 'I had not gone very far when I discovered that we were deceived, and my conscience, troubled on account of the aforementioned bread, was quickly relieved, even without any instruction. I was in so far helped by Luther, however, that human injunctions cannot bind unto eternal death.'[1]

---

[1] Menno Simons, 'Reply to Gellius Faber', in L. Verduin and J. C. Wenger (eds.), *Menno Simons, The Complete Writings* (Scottdale, 1956), pp. 668–72, cited in this and the following paragraph after the extract in Hans J. Hillerbrand, *The Reformation in its Own Words* (London, 1964), pp. 266–70. I should like to express a considerable intellectual debt to Klaus Schreiner, whose stimulating explorations in 'Laienbildung als Herausforderung für

He then heard of a God-fearing, pious man named Sicke Snijder who had been beheaded in Leeuwarden for being rebaptised. Struck by the oddity of the notion of a second baptism, he went diligently back to his New Testament, but could find no mention of infant baptism. He discussed the matter at length with his parish priest, who also conceded that there seemed to be no scriptural basis for infant baptism. Simons next turned to 'several ancient authors' who taught that children were cleansed from original sin by their baptism, although he concluded that this was at odds with the scriptures. He consulted in turn Luther, Martin Bucer and Heinrich Bullinger. They stated in turn that children were baptised on account of their own faith, so that they might be the more carefully nurtured in the way of the Lord, and in response to a divine covenant. Simons found all these replies to be incapable of scriptural proof. He concluded: 'When I noticed from all these that writers varied so greatly among themselves, each following his own wisdom, then I realised that we were deceived in regard to infant baptism.'

II

Although Menno Simons more strictly belongs to the history of Dutch heterodoxy, the active interchange between the Low Countries and Germany at that time excuses his appearance in a discussion focussed primarily on Germany. His case exemplifies many of the more general points I want to make about the relationship between literacy and heterodoxy in the age of the Reformation, and I shall return to it several times in the discussion that follows. The German Reformation undoubtedly provides an excellent testing ground for many ideas on the connections between literacy and heresy. It is conventional wisdom that there was a very low level of heretical or heterodox activity in Germany for most of the fifteenth century, a phenomenon that has been linked to low levels of literacy. However, the first age of printing enabled the spread of elementary education among the urban classes, creating a rising tide of functional literacy, which in turn enabled an expanding lay interest in printed works of piety, many of them recycled from the predominantly scribal and clerical cultures of the pre-print era. According to

Kirche und Gesellschaft', *Zeitschrift für historische Forschung* 11 (1984), 257–354, set me thinking along the lines taken by this chapter.

this view, the overwhelmingly religious nature of the printed works produced during the period up to 1520 attests that the generation immediately before the Reformation and the generation that made the Reformation itself were deeply preoccupied with matters religious. The 'Luther affair' of the years 1517–20 thus occurred within the context of a lay reading public with a growing thirst for religious knowledge, a thirst which was to be slaked by the accelerated output of the printing press in the 1520s. The printed word, and by implication lay literacy, were the enablers and bearers of the astonishing wave of religious heterodoxy that swept across Germany and which within a few years brought the entire ecclesiastical structure to the point of collapse.[2]

The roots of such developments lie deep in the fifteenth century, and we can the better appreciate this if we keep in mind the age profile of those who made the German Reformation during its decisive phase. We are speaking here of three generations: those like Erasmus born in the 1460s, who were well into middle age by 1520; those like Luther born in the 1480s, who were by 1520 in the bloom of mature adulthood (or, if you prefer, on the edge of middle age); and those like Menno Simons born around the turn of the century, who encountered the first surge of the Reformation movements in the full vigour of their young adulthood. Their formative educational experiences occurred, respectively, in the 1480s, the early 1500s and the 1520s, and they provide an essential generational framework for our understanding of the developments of the Reformation. I shall refer to them as the older, middle and younger generations respectively.[3]

What seems common to all three generations was the firm assumption that religious knowledge was linked to the ability to read, if not the scriptures, then at least the swelling mass of printed devotional literature. This assumption is not entirely unproblematic

---

[2] For a classic statement of this view that has influenced the modern generation of Reformation historians, see Otto Clemen, *Die lutherische Reformation und der Buchdruck* (Leipzig, 1939); and most recently Bernd Moeller, 'Das Berühmtwerden Luthers', in Leif Grane and Kai Hørby (eds.), *Die dänische Reformation vor ihrem internationalen Hintergrund* (Göttingen, 1990), pp. 187–210; for a succinct summary of the late-medieval situation, Ernst Schubert, *Einführung in die Grundprobleme der deutschen Geschichte im Spätmittelalter* (Darmstadt, 1992), pp. 264–88.

[3] The importance of generations has scarcely been mentioned in Reformation historiography. It was first brought to my attention as an important feature of the Counter-Reformation by R. Po-Chia Hsia, *Society and Religion in Münster 1535–1618* (New Haven and London, 1984), p. 68.

in its social historical aspects. We know very little about real levels of literacy for this period and all estimates of literacy rates are matters of the purest speculation. We are forced to deduce what we can from the presence (or absence) of schools, which at the beginning of the sixteenth century were an almost exclusively urban phenomenon. Yet most towns, however small, could boast of at least a Latin school and probably a German elementary school (a school teaching 'writing and reckoning'). A metropolis such as Nuremberg could even support four Latin schools teaching as many as 850 pupils at one time, while an unspecified number of informal German schools might have brought the total number of school pupils up to the 4,000 children of both sexes mentioned for 1487 in a local chronicle.[4] The late-medieval trend was for urban civic authorities to take charge of those Latin schools formerly under clerical control, so that they unmistakably served lay civic purposes. The clear intention of urban magistrates was to promote wider schooling at all levels, whether for reasons of social order, to stimulate economic advancement or even for purely altruistic reasons. However, there was a vast gulf between the instruction provided by the Latin schools intended to train an intellectual elite of clerics, officials and children of the urban patriciate, and the purely functional literacy offered by the German schools intended for artisans and most females. On the other hand, education was regarded as a mark of social status and a means of economic advancement, and the desire for social mobility attracted many artisan children to Latin schools and many children from the countryside to schools in the town, even if they had to live on their wits as 'poor students' and from time to time risk the wrath of the authorities. If this last group rose no higher than the status of ordained priests, they at least returned to their village in the same way as Menno Simons did in 1524, with the potential for further self-education.[5]

Some historians reviewing such evidence have recently argued

---

[4] Rudolf Endres, 'Die Bedeutung des lateinischen und deutschen Schulwesens für die entwicklung der fränkischen Reichsstädte des Spätmittelalters und der frühen Neuzeit', in Lenz Kriss-Rettenbeck and Max Leidtke (eds.), *Schulgeschichte im Zusammenhang der Kulturentwicklung* (Bad Heilbronn, 1983), pp. 144–65, esp. p. 150 for the estimate of 1487 numbers.

[5] Endres, 'Bedeutung', pp. 144–6, 148–51; see also R. Endres, 'Das Schulwesen in Franken im ausgehenden Mittelalter', in Bernd Moeller, Hans Patze and Karl Stackmann (eds.), *Studien zum städtischen Bildungswesen des späten Mittelalters und der frühen Neuzeit* (Göttingen, 1983), pp. 173–214; Klaus Wriedt, 'Schulen und bürgerliches Bildungswesen im Spätmittelalter, in the same volume, pp. 152–72.

that earlier assumptions of low levels of literacy in Germany at the beginning of the sixteenth century are incorrect, although no figures have been offered to replace earlier 'guesstimates'. It seems undoubted that literacy was a very unevenly distributed phenomenon. It was probably very widespread in a town such as Nuremberg, undoubtedly the richest and, alongside Cologne, the most populated town in Germany, which sent students to university in numbers vastly disproportional to its population. Literacy may have been very high in other major urban centres and in smaller towns, and would clearly have been greater in regions with a higher urban density. The same is possibly true of rural literacy, which was dependent on access to urban schools. We would certainly find at least some persons in each village able to read and write, although significant rural literacy – by this I mean habitual reading and the ability to write with some ease – may have depended on the nature of cultural relationships between town and country and on the density of the regional urban and marketing network. However, such speculation tells us little about the social status or stratification of literacy, nor about the different skills or levels of skill involved.

A more useful approach is to accept that there was some degree of literacy throughout Germany, but to try to appreciate its importance through an understanding of forms of communication and opinion formation at the time. This enables us to argue that it was not so much literacy as such that was important, but how literacy interacted with other forms of communication, especially oral forms, as well as the social context in which ideas were received and internalised.[6] Menno Simons offers a useful example, revealing that his own hesitant reading of scripture arose within the context of regular discussion with his fellow priests in Pingjum. From reading Luther he acquired one firm evangeligal principle ('that human injunctions cannot bind unto eternal death'), but could otherwise find no illumination to the question about infant baptism which troubled him – a question he seems to have set himself following an oral report of the martyrdom of Sicke Snijder. Significantly, he first

---

[6] For a preliminary statement of the problem, R. W. Scribner, 'Flugblatt und Analphabetentum. Wie kam der gemeine Mann zu reformatorischen Ideen?', in Hans-Joachim Köhler (ed.), *Flugschriften als Massenmedium der Reformationszeit* (Stuttgart, 1981), pp. 65–76, and in more detail, Scribner, 'Oral culture and the diffusion of Reformation ideas', in *Popular Culture and Popular movements in Reformation Germany* (London, 1987), pp. 49–69. For this

discussed his problem with his fellow priest before consulting authorities in print. He found no satisfaction from reading ancient authors, nor from consulting Luther, Bucer or Bullinger (we must assume in their printed works). It is not surprising that Simons believed that he had acquired his understanding of baptism and the Lord's Supper 'through the illumination of the Holy Ghost, through much reading and pondering of the scriptures'. In his socially restricted circumstances, he had little alternative, although we may notice that he eventually went on to preach his new-found beliefs, so moving from the private to the public sphere, and from literacy to complete orality.

It is important to realise that in the period under discussion literacy was not privileged over orality as a form of communication. Both were assumed to be equally authoritative, attested by the equivalence in many texts of reading and hearing (*lessen und lesen hören*). There is no space here properly to dicuss the problem of orality in any detail, but we can identify some of the forms in which it was expressed, forms which constituted different modes of oral communication whose context influenced receptivity, reception and internalisation of ideas. We can distinguish seven different kinds of orality, all of which I have found attested in sixteenth-century sources. First, there is *orality for dissemination of information*, seen in the public reading of mandates and statutes or the proclamation of information in church. The second involves *hieratic orality*, orality as a liturgical and sacramental act, exemplified in the hearing of evangelical sermons, which were probably far ahead of printing as the most important mass medium of the age. Third, there is *interrogative orality*, aroused by curiosity and eagerness for knowledge, exemplified by Menno Simons's discussions with his fellow priests. Fourth, there is *disputatious orality*, arguing about ideas and their implications – many Reformation discussions were of this kind. Fifth, there is *orality as gossip*, the casual communication of information while passing the time, but which also plays a part in opinion formation. Sixth, we can mention *domestic orality*, discussions conducted in the intimate sphere of the family or household, and which have a different character from matters discussed in public. Seventh, we could mention *orality as incitement*, verbal challenges to take action to

reason I find the notion of 'passive literacy' to be of limited value, since it privileges literacy, while paying little attention to other modes of communication.

exemplify or manifest one's convictions – many public incidents such as acts of iconoclasm were precipitated in this way.[7]

There is a further point to take into consideration: namely, that political context is as important as social context for appreciating the role of both literacy and orality in forming opinion. Authorities of different kinds were clearly aware of the political significance of choosing oral or written proceedings in many kinds of negotiation. The prince–abbots of Kempten, for example, were notorious throughout the fifteenth century for using every possible means of coercion to impose more servile forms of tenure on their subjects, which were then confirmed in writing by sealed attestations, produced in subsequent disputes as firm evidence that the subjects had been traditionally (*seit alters her*) servile. From 1423 this was further supported by the use of a forged charter from Charlemagne, which attested that fee-paying subjects were in effect serfs. On the other hand, the letters of privilege held by the peasants were systematically destroyed by the abbot, so that they were left to rely only on oral tradition. This strategy continued until the revolts of the early 1520s, by which time the abbot had introduced a new tactic of divide and rule, demanding that the oath of allegiance should not be taken by all subject communities simultaneously on the meadow at Kempten, where traditionally there were demands for charters and letters of privilege to be produced and read out, but individually, by each community swearing to an episcopal official at each local court. Here and in many other cases, both orality and literacy were weapons in a political struggle. It is not surprising that during the German Peasants' War, the rebels so often followed a double strategy, first of destroying all letters, charters and title deeds of their lords, so that the latter were also thrown back on oral memory; on the other hand, they insisted that all negotiations, concessions and agreements with their lords should be attested in writing with sealed letters.[8]

Literacy was no less part of the power plays inseparable from urban politics of the age, the more so since 'public opinion' in such small-scale societies was so heavily dependent on orality. Much has been written about the emergence of 'public opinion' in the age of the Reformation, although I suspect that when it is carefully

[7] Examples of all these forms in Scribner, 'Oral culture'.
[8] Günther Franz, *Der deutsche Bauernkrieg* (Darmstadt, 1975), pp. 11–13.

analysed, we will discover that it differed little in its essentials from 'public opinion' in the later middle ages. As I understand it, 'public opinion' was essentially local and was comprised of a dense network of information interchange and human interactions occurring within a local framework. Moreover, within a socio-political unit such as a German town, it was certainly no unitary phenomenon, but consisted of the interaction and additive effect of several partial forms of opinion, each of which might be seen as 'public opinion' in miniature. We can distinguish six such partial forms, three formal and three informal. Thus, we can speak first of an *official public opinion*, for example when a town council speaks publicly in the name of 'the mayor, council and commune'. Second, there was a *ritualised public opinion*, expressed in formal occasions of civic ritual intended to communicate a unified viewpoint to the entire city, such as in official assemblies of the commune or in annual oath-taking cere-monies. Third, there was a *sectional public opinion*, that expressed in corporations or bodies such as guilds, city quarters or parishes. Although this was itself a product of a chain of complex interactions, such opinion often had a decisive role in propelling a town towards a more unified collective opinion. Besides these three more formal forms of opinion, there were more informal manifestations. There was as a fourth category the *public opinion of sociability*, which devel-oped in inns and taverns, places on which shrewd politicians kept watch and whose emerging expressions of opinion they neglected to their peril. Fifth, there was a *public opinion of the streets and the market*, occasioned by chance encounters of a different kind from those of sociability, and which was often designated as 'common gossip' (*gemein gassenred*). Finally, there was a *private public opinion*, expres-sions of opinion formed at home, in the circle of the family or in the workplace, but which were none the less public knowledge.[9]

In another context, we might go on to analyse the nature and dynamics of each of these forms of opinion and to identify something about the processes of their interaction to create the overall phenomenon of 'urban public opinion'. Here I merely want to mention the importance of literacy and/or orality for the complex-

---

[9] The issues raised here discussed in more detail in Bob Scribner, 'Mündliche Kommunika-tion und Strategien der Macht in Deutschland im 16. Jahrhundert', in *Kommunikation und Alltag im Spätmittelalter und früher Neuzeit*, Veröffentlichungen des Instituts für Realienkunde des Mittelalters und der frühen Neuzeit, 15 = Sitzungsberichte der Österreichischen Akade-mie der Wissenschaften, philosophische-historische Klasse, 596 (Vienna, 1992), pp. 183–97.

ities of urban politics, as civic governments attempted to deal with the ebb and flow of opinion within their communities. There is no doubt that the introduction of written records, kept by a city secretary and preserved in a chancery or archive, made an enormous difference to civic politics and to autonomy, and represented both a pragmatic and an ideological leap forward – indeed, even in the sixteenth century, it became a point of pride for a small territorial town to demand its own city secretary and almost a point of sovereignty for the prince to refuse the request.[10] However, the balance between oral and written proceedings remained an important feature of sixteenth-century town politics. It mattered politically whether proceedings in the town council were recorded in detailed minutes or someone merely recorded decisions to be made public. It mattered that the control of official records remained firmly in the hands of town council officers, not least guild privileges and charters, agreements with the commune, and records of past transgressions by ruling elites. Urban revolts were often precipitated by discovery of such well-concealed documents, or by demands for the production of politically embarrassing documents which had been made to 'disappear' but which were preserved in oral tradition. The same principles applied to a city's dealings with its clergy, especially with powerful foundations or religious orders. The wider political importance of civic authorities taking control of Latin schools out of the hands of the clergy is clear, as was the desire to bring all forms of record-keeping into lay hands, not least the proving of wills, private contracts and pious foundations. On the other hand, the tactic of only converting oral transactions into writing when it suited and favoured civic interests was skilfully applied in dealings with the clergy right through to the upheavals of the Reformation.[11]

The impact of the printed word on this complex business of what we might call politicised opinion management still awaits careful analysis. Reformation historians have devoted a great deal of attention to studying the impact of the printed word on the spread of evangelical ideas, but have too often operated with naive methodo-

---

[10] Compare R. W. Scribner, *Popular Culture and Popular Movements in Reformation Germany* (London and Ronceverte, 1987), pp. 272–3.

[11] The classic case is found in Erfurt: see Bob Scribner, 'Die Eigentümlichkeit der Erfurter Reformation', in Ulman Weiß (ed.), *Erfurt 742–1992. Stadtgeschichte, Universitätsgeschichte* (Weimar, 1992), pp. 241–54, esp. 245.

logical assumptions and a limited understanding of 'public opinion' and the processes of its formation. It is clear from the outline sketched in so far that we need to go well beyond the classic but unilinear Laswell formula still cited with approval by early modern historians, 'who says what . . . in which channel . . . to whom . . . with what effect?'. This reduces the problem to something analogous to understanding the mechanics of levers, when what we should be looking for is something analogous to biological processes. I cannot hope to offer any more precise guidelines here other than pointing out where one might look and what elements should be taken into account. However, I am struck by a number of salient features in those case studies where I have been able to examine opinion formation under the appropriate microscope. Orality was as important as the printed word in the formation of opinion, both collective and individual, manifest in the important role of the sermon in arousing evangelical fervour. Scribal culture was no less important, especially given the essentially local nature of all forms of public opinion. The handwritten pasquillade could, under local conditions, work as effectively as the printed broadsheet to focus views and precipitate political action. The difficulty arises because we are dealing with little understood rules of collective opinion and collective action, which cannot be interpreted simply in terms of an additive effect, by merely focussing on the opinion formation of a single individual and extrapolating from there. We are grateful to find accounts as detailed as that offered by Menno Simons (although we should not forget that this is a retrospective construction, filtered through the screen of acquired convictions which the author seeks to justify). We cannot deduce from this rather restricted account (which is silent about so much social and personal context) anything meaningful about how or why wider collectivities were attracted to Anabaptist belief. Here my paradigmatic case reveals the limitations of analysis as well as some of its parameters.

III

So much for a preliminary discussion about the question of literacy and print. We should now introduce the matter of heterodoxy, in my period no less inseparable from broader social historical issues. The German Reformation is famous perhaps more than any other movement in European history for invoking the judgement of ordinary people, in the jargon of the time the 'common man' (note the gender coding!). The propaganda of all kinds, printed or otherwise, that became a potent weapon for the spread of heterodox ideas constantly invoked the notion that the 'common man' could judge the truth of religious issues better than the learned. Once the truth was put in their hands by the Reformation message, whether transmitted by sermon, public dispute, private conversation or the printed word, the common folk would exercise an unerring instinct in recognising and distinguishing true religious from false. The most condensed version of this view was found in the fictitious figure of Karsthans, the uneducated yet literate, preaching and bible-quoting peasant, able to confound the arguments of priests or scholars by his instinctive wisdom. It matters little, perhaps, that we can scarcely find a real life example of a Karsthans. Two figures who assumed the mantel were certainly neither peasants nor uneducated, while Diepold Peringer, the so-called 'peasant from Wöhrd', who could preach and cite scripture as well as a priest, was a fraud, a highly educated member of a religious order, who assumed the cloak of a real-life Karsthans to call attention to his preaching.[12] The importance of Karsthans is, perhaps, ideological and propagandist: he represented a symbol of the possibility of religious and social renewal encompassing all levels of society, even the lowly and despised peasant. He thus encouraged ordinary people to take charge of their own religious destiny, providing a stimulus not merely to lay reading but to direct action in support of reform.

There is something of a paradox here. The leaders of the Reformation movements were almost exclusively members of an intellectual elite, highly educated men of learning, drawn predominantly from the priesthood or the religious orders, many of them already in established positions of authority and in some cases well on the way to becoming important functionaries in the church.[13] It needs to be said repeatedly that the Reformation was not precipitated by laymen from outside the ecclesiastical and social establishment, but from within, by the clergy, and above all by those who

---

[12] Otto Clemen, *Beiträge zur Reformationsgeschichte* (Berlin 1902), vol. II, pp. 85–96.
[13] The same is true of the authors of Reformation pamphlets, fewer than a dozen of whom, from among many hundreds, have been identified as lay people, including only one woman: Paul A. Russell, *Lay Theology in the Reformation. Popular Pamphleteers in Southwest Germany 1521–1525* (Cambridge, 1986), identifies seven authors; Martin Arnold, *Handwerker*

were the best minds of the older and middle generation. It was only among the younger generation, among whom the status of the priesthood and of academic learning had been severely diminished, that we find the emergence of primarily lay leaders. But even here, as the case of Menno Simons reveals, the priesthood still provided a springboard into Reformation heterodoxy. There is clearly a vast difference between the propagandist image of the typical evangelical preacher and the social reality, and this warns us that we must look more carefully behind the polemical and propagandist facade of the early Reformation.

The idea that the true proponents of religious reform were the unlearned, while the learned were its real foes has a long tradition, stretching back into the middle ages. The Reformation merely brought an intensification of the notion within social and political circumstances more effectively suited to putting reform into action. From the beginning of the sixteenth century, there was a forceful tide of negative opinion directed at academic scholarship and professional scholars. The proverb *die Gelehrten, die Verkehrten* (literally 'twisted scribes', but the untranslatable pun best rendered as 'the learned are liars'), attested in common German usage during the fifteenth century and drawing on a long tradition that contrasted book learning with *sancta simplicitas* (holy simplicity) and *docta ignorantia* (learned ignorance), crystallised around the turn of the century into a direct attack on theologians and jurists. These professions were depicted both as the oppressors of the weak in the interests of the great and powerful and as sure guides along the highroad to hell.[14] The criticism was, therefore, both social and religious, and in 1512 was applied by Thomas Murner to those 'doctors of sacred scripture' who presumed to show the way to eternal life while despising divine law and straying far from the path of salvation.[15] It became a constant component of the popular propaganda for the

als theologische Schriftsteller. Studien zu Flugschriften der frühen Reformation (1523–1525) (Göttingen, 1990), identifies four further authors.

[14] Carlos Gilly, 'Das Sprichwort "die Gelehrten die Verkehrten" oder der Verrat der Intellektuellen im Zeitalter der Glaubensspaltung', in A. Rotondó (ed.), *Forme e destinazione del messaggio religioso: aspetti della propaganda religiosa nel Cinquecento*, Studi e testi per la storia religiosa del Cinquecento, 2 (Florence, 1991), pp. 229–375.

[15] 'Man nent uns meister der geschrifft / Die heilig ist und sele antrifft ... Wir achtendt nit das götlich recht / Es macht uns im haupt schwampellecht / Wir sindt die ersten under gelerten / Die bösen, valschen und verkehrten / Und zeigendt dir das ewig leben / So wir wyt louffen irr dar neben', in Thomas Murner, *Narrenbeschwörung*, in *Thomas Murners deutsche Schriften* (Berlin, 1926), vol.II, p. 120.

Reformation, and was put in the mouths of the laity as a reproach directed especially against the clerical supporters of the papacy. Indeed, in one pamphlet of 1525 it was even used to contrast the deceitful Latin learning of the monks and priests with the German learning of the laity: 'You twisted scribes have hidden everything from laypeople with Latin, as tricksters do ... For this reason the priests and monks are vexed that books are printed in German and their secrets are thereby revealed.'[16]

This quotation perhaps provides some clue to the actual thrust of the criticism, which would otherwise present us with a certain paradox, for many authors found using the proverb were, like Thomas Murner, not exactly unlearned. However, as a criticism of Latin-based learning by predominantly German-literate and Germanophone reformers (many by choice rather than by necessity), it arose out of some fundamental distinctions in the stratification of learning that emerged towards the end of the fifteenth century. Despite a fall in population over the course of the fifteenth century, the German universities witnessed a steady expansion in student numbers throughout that period. The last decade of the fifteenth century saw five times as many students enrolling for university study as a hundred years previously. The expansion was cyclical, with two phases of rapid development (1385–1428/34 and 1450–80) interspersed with two of stagnation (1428/34–1450 and 1480–c. 1500). The rate of increase of matriculations slowed appreciably after 1460 and the decade 1481–90 even witnessed a small negative increase. Most matriculands were of urban origin – only 17 per cent of matriculated students came from a rural background – and the bulk of student numbers was increasingly supplied by the small to medium town whose economy was dominated by agriculture or craft production. This possibly explains why the cycles evident in the rise and fall of matriculations, allowing for regional variations, so closely mirrored the cycles of agrarian conjuncture. Around 80–90 per cent of university students did not rise above a basic arts education, while the true elites of learning were the medics, the theologians and above all the jurists. Academic stratification

---

[16] 'Ir glerten oder verkerten haben uns leien alle ding mit dem latein verschlagen, wie die Gaukler thun ... Darumb verdrüss die pfaffen und münch, dass man teutsche büchlin druckt ind ir häle da durch fürhar bricht', in 'Ein Weggesprech zu Regensburg zu ins Concilium zwischen einem Bischoff, Huren wirt und Kuntzen sein Knecht' (1525), in O. Schade, *Satiren und Pasquillen aus der Reformationszeit* (Hannover, 1856), vol. III, p. 174.

mirrored social stratification, with only the richest and most socially eminent able to scale these peaks of learning, a group moreover whose university attendance was not so susceptible to the fluctuations of economic cycles.[17]

Leaving aside the complexities of conjunctural cycles, it seems undoubted that the German universities at the end of the fifteenth century experienced an 'overcrowding crisis', and that the supply of those with a basic university education far outstripped demand for officials, bureaucrats, secretaries, clerks and the like. Certainly, many may have found employment as priests, for the expansion of higher education played its part in raising the educational standards of the parish clergy and by the end of the fifteenth century it was increasingly common for even the rural clergy to have some minimal university education. However, the more important trend was the leavening of urban intellectual and cultural life by a growing number of lay arts graduates. The gulf between such men of liberal education and the representatives of higher learning, jurists and theologians, was social, political and cultural, and was more than enough to account for an animus against the *Gelehrten*. Seen in this light, the origin and appeal of the attack on academic scholarship embodied in the tag *die Gelehrten, die Verkehrten* is self-evident.[18]

This casts into a different light the polemical invocation of the 'common man' as the most effective critic of the established system of religion and the surest guide to evangelical truth. In an urban context the term 'common man', it has been pointed out, often designated not the vast body of the disenfranchised but the citizen–householder who was a legal member of the commune and was, we may surmise, most likely to have enjoyed elementary schooling and to have mastered at least some German book-learning, if only in terms of the literature of practical and technical knowledge that formed a major part of the non-religious output of the printing press. Here we should think of the urban reading public as comprised of two different kinds of reader, those who encountered their book learning of all kinds in German, including translations of Latin

---

[17] Rainer Christoph Schwinges, *Deutsche Universitätsbesucher im 14. und 15. Jahrhundert* (Stuttgart, 1986), pp. 23–60, 207–20, 487–96.

[18] Schwinges, *Deutsche Universitätsbesucher*, pp. 217–19 and 488 for the term *Überfüllungskrise*. On the educational standards of the parish clergy, A. Braun, *Der Klerus des Bistums Konstanz im Ausgang des Mittelalters* (Münster, 1938), pp. 97–9; R. Kiermayr, 'On the education of the pre-Reformation clergy', *Church History* 53 (1984), 7–16.

works; and those who may have been schooled in Latin, but who also read largely in German or German translation. A third, but smaller, group were those who read largely in Latin.[19]

During the later middle ages (and doubtless earlier) the distinction between the 'learned' and the 'unlearned' (*litteratus/illiteratus*) turned not so much on the simple issue of literacy versus illiteracy, as on the distinction between Latin literacy and literacy merely in the vernacular. The advent of printing certainly intensified the terms of the dispute, which covered religious issues, questions of social status and power, linguistic presuppositions (did the German language possess the necessary subtlety of expression for complex theological, scientific or aesthetic concepts?) and a high degree of downright snobbery. The turn of the century saw the debate intensify around the issue of technical knowledge, the lead being given by the medics and jurists, exactly those members of the higher university faculties to which most educated townsmen did not belong or ever aspire to belong.[20]

The threat perceived by jurists was somewhat different from that felt rather more keenly by the medical profession. Jurists seem to have been more concerned about lay judges and advocates squeezing the academically trained legal scholar out of legal practice, especially as legal proceedings moved increasingly in the direction of written rather than oral pleading. The hostility in some towns towards the disproportionate influence that could be wielded by the public servant equipped with a doctorate in both laws and with privileged access to knowledge of the law via his command of Latin may have contributed to the fears felt by the older and middle generation of jurists. Certainly, it was almost a commonplace of the grievance lists in the disturbances stirred up by the urban commons in the years 1470–1525 that no doctor of laws should be employed by or sit on a town council. However, such fears were groundless; the younger generation of jurists would doubtless have perceived that the trend was in the opposite direction and would favour the increasing employment of doctors of both laws in all areas of civic

[19] On the 'common man', Robert H. Lutz, *Wer war der gemeine Mann. Der dritte Stand in der Krise des Spätmittelalters* (Munich, 1979) and P. Böckmann, 'Der gemeine Mann in den Flugschriften der Reformation', *Deutsche Vierteljahrresschrift für Literaturwissenschaft und Geistesgeschichte* 22 (1944), 186–230; on urban reading publics, Schreiner, 'Laienbildung', p. 277.

[20] Schreiner, 'Laienbildung', pp. 279–87.

and princely administration. Medics found themselves in a different situation, fearing that translations of their textbooks would harm their incomes by encouraging self-help among common people. Moreover, they faced effective competition from the informal practice of medicine by cunning folk and folk healers.[21]

Such debates made patently clear to the older and middle generation that knowledge was indeed power, and that breaches in the monopoly of knowledge weakened the hierarchical position of social and political elites. They were conducted alongside discussions about the levels of knowledge appropriate to each estate, and the fear of social upheaval if those of low estate aspired to knowledge beyond their rank. This medieval *topos* was undoubtedly given new urgency by the undeniable evidence of social mobility that so troubled the ruling elites of the older and middle generation, and who struggled in vain to lock as many social groups as firmly as possible into place in the social hierarchy.[22] Yet there was downwards as well as upwards mobility, something that agitated many nobles who perceived a trend of declining educational standards among their own class. The turnaround may not have been as dramatic as was feared by Wilwolt von Schaumburg (1446–1510), who complained in his autobiography that the nobility's neglect of university study had opened the way for the children of mere peasants to climb into great bishoprics or the great offices of state at the courts of the emperor, imperial electors or sovereign princes. The underlying fear of social inversion was none the less neatly expressed when he cited in this context the common proverb 'that the chairs have leapt up upon the table'.[23] We must none the less recognise that the opposing positions in these debates about the dangers of making professional knowledge accessible to untrained common people often cut clean through group allegiance. It was doctors of medicine such as the Colmar city physician Lorenz Fries who upheld the utility of translating medical texts from the Latin

---

[21] On lawyers, Gerald Strauss, *Law, Resistance and the State. The Opposition to Roman Law in Reformation Germany* (Princeton, 1986), pp. 4–30. On medics, Joachim Telle, 'Wissenschaft und Öffentlichkeit im Spiegel der deutschen Arzneibuchliteratur', *Medizinhistorisches Journal* 14 (1979), 32–52.

[22] Schreiner, 'Laienbildung', p. 277; Schubert, *Einführung*, pp. 122–3.

[23] *Die Geschichten und Taten Wilwolts von Schaumburg*, ed. Adelbert von Keller (Stuttgart, 1859), p. 2.

and who accused their professional colleagues opposed to such a step of fearing that their ignorance would be thereby exposed.[24]

The same is true if we turn to the corresponding debate about religious knowledge; which revolved around the twin questions whether the laity should be allowed access to the bible in the vernacular and what kinds of religious literature should be offered to the laity, if at all. These were stock medieval controversies, given added urgency by the use of the vernacular scriptures by groups such as the Waldensians, Lollards or Hussites or by recourse to mystical writings such as those of Meister Eckhart that provided access to religious experience outside the controls exercised by the clergy. Such issues provide the backdrop for this volume as a whole and do not require any further elaboration, except to highlight the way in which the advent of printing intensified them at the end of the fifteenth century. The eighteen editions of the complete German bible that appeared between 1466 and 1522 certainly served to keep the controversy alive. On the one hand, there were those such as the author of the preface to a 1478/9 Cologne edition of the bible who held that all persons, learned and unlearned, clerical and lay, would find salvation and consolation through reading the vernacular bible.[25] On the other hand, there was the author of a memorandum possibly prepared for the Nuremberg printer Anton Koberger, who produced an edition of the German bible in 1483. The anonymous author listed eleven reasons why 'uneducated but curious' laypersons should not be allowed access to the bible in the vernacular, by means of which they might make their own exegesis and come to believe themselves more clever than their priests.[26]

That lay people would seek their own way to salvation independently of the priesthood was the openly expressed fear of the critics of the vernacular bible as well as the perception of its advocates. The author of the Koehlhoff Chronicle, published in Cologne in 1499, praised printing as a special gift of God which enabled every person to read for himself or have read out to him the way to

---

[24] Telle, 'Wissenschaft und Öffentlichkeit', pp. 34–6. As with the lawyers, this debate continued well into the seventeenth century.

[25] Cited in Schreiner, 'Laienbildung', p. 298, although the dating must be corrected from 1480, see Heimo Reinitzer, *Biblia deutsch. Luthers Bibelübersetzung und ihre Tradition* (Wolfenbüttel, 1983), p. 70.

[26] Reinitzer, *Biblia deutsch*, p. 58; F. Geldner, 'Ein in einem Sammelband Hartmann Schedels (Clm 901) überliefertes Gutachen über den Druck deutschsprachiger Bibeln', *Gutenberg Jahrbuch* (1972), pp. 86–9.

salvation.[27] The same point was made in 1515 by the anonymous author of a manuscript sermon, putting in the mouth of a lay christian the statement: 'We now have in our hands the holy scriptures, and cån know and expound for ourselves what is necessary for salvation, and need neither the church nor the pope'.[28] Geiler von Keysersberg came to the opposite conclusion, that it was an evil thing to print the bible in German, just as it was dangerous to give a child a knife to cut bread for itself. This reveals the complexity of the positions taken up in the debate, since Geiler expressly advocated the production in German of works of piety for the laity, translating Gerson's *Ars moriendi* for the Strasburg German-reading public who wished to follow up his sermons but were unable to do so in Latin. By contrast, the archbishop of Mainz, Berthold von Henneberg, in 1485 issued a formal mandate prohibiting the translation into German of any kind of theological work on the grounds that this would falsify sacred truth.[29]

It was this kind of thinking that led fifteenth-century catechetes to insist that the laity only needed to know as much about religion as was fitting to their estate, so that it was sufficient for a peasant to know the *Pater Noster*, the *Ave Maria*, the apostles' Creed and the ten commandments.[30] The advocates of this viewpoint must have been deeply shocked when the holiest of liturgical secrets, the canon of the Mass and its words of consecration, traditionally spoken silently so that the laity should not hear and misappropriate them, were betrayed to the common gaze by a German exposition of the Mass published around 1482, which included a translation of the canon and the words of consecration in both German and Latin. Indeed, the second edition of this work removed the words of consecration in both languages as something unsuitable for the laity.[31]

Klaus Schreiner has called attention to two contrasting mind-sets

---

[27] 'Dat ein ieder minsch mach den wech der selicheit selfs lesen of hoeren lesen', *Die Chroniken der deutschen Städte vom 14. bis ins 16. Jahrhundert* (Leipzig, 1977), vol. xiv, p. 792, lines 25–6.

[28] 'Wir hant ietz die heilig Geschrift selbs in Handen und können selbs wissen und ußlegen, was zur Seligkeit Not, und bedurffend nit dazu Kirche und Papst', cited in Johannes Janssen, *Geschichte des deutschen Volkes*, 7th edn (Freiburg i. Br. 1881), vol. I, p. 607; Schreiner, 'Laienbildung', p. 311 has misread this reference as applying to Geiler von Keyserberg.

[29] Schreiner, 'Laienbildung', p. 299.

[30] Egino Weidenhiller, *Untersuchungen zur deutschsprachigen katechetischen Literatur des späten Mittelalters* (Munich, 1965), pp. 16, 149, 169.

[31] Franz Rudolf Reichert (ed.), *Die älteste deutsche Gesamtauslegung der Messe* (Münster, 1967), esp. p. xxvii for the second edition.

in this conflict. On the one hand, there were those reformers who held that the vernacular translation of the bible involved no challenge to the magisterial authority of the Church but was certainly a necessity presupposition for a reform of the church; on the other, those who saw it as the thin end of the wedge, leading to loss of the authority and prestige of the clergy and directly to heresy. Of necessity, the logic of this latter position meant that the critics of the vernacular bible regarded reformers as little better than heretics or at best willing to collude with heresy. Lay reading of the bible was part of a syndrome that set itself up in opposition to the ordinances and principles of the Church.[32]

It is perhaps one of the ironies of the process that in the last quarter of the fifteenth century clerics of all persuasions did allow translations of works of piety for the use of the laity, whether in the conservative sense that permitted works that agreed with the healthy doctrines of the Church or in the reforming sense that the widest possible range of vernacular works of piety would strengthen lay piety and promote the cause of reform. Such works were directed at the broadest spectrum of lay readers, 'the young and the old, the lord and the servant, ladies and maids'.[33] They were designed to encourage lay reading and undoubtedly did so, but were also aided by a growing perception of a widespread desire to read. As one tract of 1498 put it, 'everyone today wants to read and write', a comment that cannot be separated from the perceived link between education and social mobility.[34] Yet the salient feature of the entire business of promoting pious lay reading is the role of the clergy, exhorting, debating, translating and publishing. Much of this peak of this activity occurred during the formative period of the older and middle generation of the reformers of the sixteenth century. It comes as no surprise that they took up the challenge of their fellow clerical reformers and carried it on with an even more passionate intensity.

---

[32] Schreiner, 'Laienbildung', pp. 294, 297, 321.

[33] The wider context of this passage from 'Tafel der christlichen Weisheit', a catechetical work composed in 1438/9 and extant only in two manuscripts of 1458 and 1471, is informative for a number of reasons, including the link of hearing and reading: 'Jungkfrauen, wittiben und eleuten will ich unterweysen, daz sie sich strafen, pessern und erkennen, dy jungen und di greysen, herrn, knecht, frauen auch meyden hort und lest sie stetiglich' (Weidenhiller, *Untersuchungen*, pp. 83–101, the passage cited on p. 90).

[34] 'Alles volck wil in yetziger zit lesen und schreiben', Schwinges, *Deutsche Universitätsbesucher*, p. 219; Schreiner, 'Laienbildung', p. 347, n. 318.

IV

Let us now turn to the Reformation itself, given the cumulative understanding that we have gleaned from the sketch so far. It is clear that the evangelical movements were not created *ex nihilo*, by a bolt from the blue. The features of opinion formation that are identified by the conventional view linking heterodoxy, literacy and print were all in place well before the 'Luther affair' became a matter of public debate. The interaction of these three elements in the 1520s shows remarkable continuity with the 1480s and 1500s. The debates over the vernacular bible, the religious role of the laity, especially the 'unlearned' lay person, the importance of lay reading were all so familiar to the older and middle generation of evangelical reformers that they were virtually recycling ideas imbibed in their formative years. The importance of upwardly mobile urban classes eager for education and the social advancement that it brought is a further common strand, as is the presence of an active reformist clergy working within a tradition of open debate and advocacy of a lay-led reform. Indeed, we can even see earlier traces of the idealisation of the 'simple layman' that found its most extreme exemplar in Karsthans. Of course we can understand from the perspective of the social historian how these things fitted into a complex pattern of opinion formation and the politics of power/knowledge. Thus, no-one from the educated older and middle generation who had perchance fallen into a magical sleep and slumbered away the years 1517–23 would have been surprised by the polemical assertion of Heinrich von Kettenbach in a pamphlet of 1523:

Nowadays one finds in Nuremberg, Augsburg, Ulm, along the Rhine, in Switzerland and in Saxony women, maidens, servants, poor students, artisans, tailors, cobblers, bakers, coopers, riders, knights, nobles, and lords such as the dukes of Saxony who know more of the bible (which is holy scripture) than all the universities such as Paris, Cologne and the rest, and than all the papists in the whole wide world. And they can prove it, and prove it every day.[35]

---

[35] 'Man fynt jetzunt zu Nornburg, Augsburg, Ulm, am Rheynstrom, in Schweyz, in Sachsen wyber, junckfrawen, knecht, bechanten, handwerksleut, schneider, schuster, becker, püttner, reyter, ritter, edeln, hern, als nemlich die hertzogen von Sachssenn, die mer wyssen in der bibel (welch die heylge schryfft ist) dann all hossen schuln, auch Paris, Coln etc. und all papisten, so wyt die welt ist. Und sie kunnens bewern und bewern es teglich', cited in Gilly, 'Sprichwort', p. 253.

None the less we cannot escape from the paradox to which I called attention earlier, that all these stereotypes were being invoked by men from the intellectual elites, themselves embedded in the body of that Church they so scathingly criticised and which they helped to shake to the foundations. The continuity with the last decades of the fifteenth century is found here in one other unexpected point, namely an ambivalence towards the very principles the reformers advocated, residual traces of the conservative mind set which, as we have observed in the case of Geiler von Keyserberg, could also infect the thought of someone of reforming instincts. Thus, scepticism towards book learning and the suspicion that printing may not have brought unqualified benefits to christians is found in both Erasmus and Luther. Away from the heady days of the early 1520s, Luther believed that a multitude of books could harm the Church, that true christians should stick to books approved by those of the right religious opinions and that the production of innumerable books was a sign of heretics and fanatics. Luther even applied this to his own writings, and thought that these could be a distraction from study of scripture itself.[36]

It was a prime principle of Protestant belief that the Word of God had a plain and evident sense accessible to the ordinary layperson, and this was certainly where the emphasis was placed in polemics against Catholic opponents, who were accused of obscuring the truth of Christ and repressing the biblical message of salvation. Yet it quickly became a dictum of the new evangelical church that ordinary lay people could not be relied upon to derive knowledge about the way of salvation directly from their own reading of scripture. The examples of those 'false brethren' who read scripture incorrectly began to mount, as early as 1522 and 1523, beginning with Karlstadt and Müntzer, encompassing those radical thinkers, such as Menno Simons, designated as Anabaptists and sacramentarians, as well as the peasants who in 1524–5 fell into 'fleshly' readings of the gospel. In the Lutheranism that emerged between the late 1520s into the 1540s, the ability to read and properly interpret the Bible became tied to professional exegetes, trained in the three biblical languages and most commonly in possession of a degree in

---

[36] This view appeared as early as 1526 in his lectures on the 'preacher Salomon', *D. Martin Luthers Werke. Kritische Gesamtausgabe* (Weimar 1883–1986), vol. **xx**, p. 201, and was repeated in the late 1530s, vol. **I**, pp. 657–8; see also his comments in *Tischreden*, vols. **III**, pp. 622–3, **IV**, pp. 84, 432–33, **V**, p. 661.

theology from a Protestant university. Lay reading of the scriptures was certainly not discouraged, but it took place in close co-ordination with the proper guidelines set down by the preacher of the Word, an ordained office which came to have many of the same marks of social status and distinction as the old priesthood. Indeed, the role of preacher was elevated about that mere task of reading the bible, for preaching was a 'special grace from God', which was to provide the right guidelines for reading scripture with a 'right understanding'.[37] The role of the bible in early modern Protestant-ism is a largely unexplored theme, especially at the popular level, although it seems certain that the most common Protestant experi-ence was not of an unmediated bible, but one increasingly filtered through marginal glosses, sermons, cathechisms and devotional literature.[38] Even the level of ownership of bibles is unexplored territory, as is the question of the uses to which the bible was put: we have fascinating evidence that Protestant bibles became talismanic objects of great magical potency, almost as a condensed replacement for the old saints' relics.[39]

Another aspect of this paradox helps partly to explain it. Throughout the first decade of the Reformation, the leadership roles of the older and middle generation were assured precisely because of their authoritative status as members of a clerical elite, as religious professionals to whom mere lay folk could turn for judgement on difficult matters of belief. A good deal of Luther's charismatic authority flowed from the popular view of him as a friar, as a doctor of theology, as someone authoritatively able to expound the sense of scripture. The same was true of other evangelical reformers, whose preaching and exposition of scripture induced the confidence to follow them and abandon the old religion. If their printed works

---

[37] Schreiner, 'Laienbildung', p. 319. The polemical insistence on the right of lay christians to read the bible for themselves can effectively be traced in the prefaces to the various editions of the bible (or its various parts) throughout the sixteenth century: Jürgen Quack, *Evangelische Bibelvorreden von der Reformation bis zur Aufklärung* (Gütersloh, 1975). The fear of the laity being misled appears as early as Zwingli's 1529 preface to the Prophets, and was strengthened later in the century with the growing disputes over Lutheran orthodoxy; Quack, *Evangelische Bibelvorreden*, pp. 57, 147.

[38] Richard Gawthrop and Gerald Strauss, 'Protestantism and literacy in early modern Germany', *Past and Present* 104 (1984), 36–43.

[39] R. W. Scribner, 'The impact of the Reformation on daily life', in *Mensch und Objekt im Mittelalter und in der frühen Neuzeit*, Veröffentlichungen des Instituts für Realienkunde des Mittelalters und der frühen Neuzeit, 13 = Sitzungsberichte der Österreichischen Akademie der Wissenschaften, philosophische-historische Klasse, 568 (Vienna, 1990), p. 328.

were bought and read, it was because of their authoritative religious voice.

The deferential attitude of the laity was an important factor here. If much of evangelical lay opinion was anti-clerical and constituted an unprecedented attack on the clergy, it was parallelled by respect for the 'good clerics', those who taught and inspired true religion and piety. Certainly, deference was socially stratified and was tied to the politics of discourse, as shown by those peasant rebels of 1525 who felt unable to engage directly in any form of dialogue with their social betters, despite the propagandist idealisation of evangelical common folk as those able to speak for themselves.[40] The German-literate urban laity may have displayed more self-confidence, attested by numerous street-corner confrontations in which lay people were willing and able to engage in a new evangelical form of discourse, although this was often only at a polemical or propagandist level. When it became a matter of theology and deciding theological issues (rather than religious feeling or piety), lay folk were still overwhelmingly deferential towards the learned. Indeed, among the non-fervent but broadly evangelical public we can often discern a good-natured puzzlement over many issues of the Reformation: an attitude that these are complex matters that even scholars cannot resolve, so how can we presume to do so? The main lay demands were pastoral not theological, and once a 'genuinely chrisitan' pastor was acquired, ordinary lay folk were often content; hence, the triumph of learned elites during the Reformation and in the long run.

Before, during and after the Reformation these learned elites acted both as middlemen and as gatekeepers. As middlemen they transmitted to non-elites their altruistic vision of a Church reformed by an emancipated laity. However, they also began to have second thoughts once the uneducated began to act on such idealised stereotypes. Once the peasant was 'in the know',[41] and presumed to steer the vehicle of reform, it could easily career off the rails, as the events of 1523–5 revealed. Thus, the elites were compelled to become

---

[40] The best example is found in the Baltringen peasants who 'saw no one among their number who was used to speaking to the authorities, who would know how to present their case as was necessary', in Tom Scott and Bob Scribner (eds.), *The German Peasants' War. A History in Documents* (New Jersey and London, 1991), p. 122.

[41] The phrase 'der bawr wirt witzig' coined in 1521 by Eberlin von Günzburg, *Ausgewählte Schriften* (Hallen 1896), vol. i, p. 65.

gatekeepers, attempting to regulate how much knowledge was good for the unlettered. They both realised and demonstrated the linkage between power and knowledge. Literacy was an important trigger of potentially dangerous knowledge – dangerous because it could get out of control. Heresy is knowledge become dangerous precisely because it has got out of control, especially when so persistently held that it challenges hierarchy and the ideological coherence that constitutes hegemony: the prime characteristic of a heretic is always stubbornness. This brings me back to Menno Simons and all the thousands like him who become Anabaptists. They presented by 1528 an enormous embarrassment for new Protestant authorities because of their claim to have discovered ideas not in the mainstream of evangelical doctrine. However, it was difficult to persecute them for conscientiously held beliefs without betraying a primary principle of the Reformation itself. In the end, therefore, Anabaptists were persecuted not for conscientiously held beliefs, but for stubbornly persisting in them once they had been shown to be 'false doctrine'.[42] What an irony for the evangelical reformers of the 1520s: the sometime heretics had by the end of that decade become the new inquisitors.[43]

[42] Such was the attitude in Augsburg in the 1530s, see *Urkundliche Quellen zur hessischen Reformationsgeschichte* (Marburg, 1951), vol. IV, pp. 104–5.

[43] Research for this article was carried out while holder of a British Academy Marc Fitch Readership, for which I should like to express my thanks for the time free from teaching and administrative duties.

CHAPTER 16

Literacy, heresy, history and orthodoxy: perspectives and permutations for the later Middle Ages

R. N. Swanson

Analyses of the relationship between heresy and literacy tend to concentrate on literacy's role in the history of individual heresies, focussing on the heretics and their literate remains. However, if heresy is approached not for itself, but as part of the development of christianity, and links with literacy pursued more tangentially, different emphases may emerge. If links between heresy and literacy are assessed in terms not of the literate heretics, but of the literate reactors to heresy, further shifts in perspective may occur. Hence this consideration of perspectives and permutations, widening beyond heresy and literacy to history and orthodoxy as well.

The question of perspective is a real one. To what extent must we equate 'heresy' with literacy, and how? Medieval christianity, from which the heresies of the contemporary Latin West necessarily derived, was a religion of a Book; but of a Book which lacked textual rigidity. Despite the Vulgate's ubiquity, corruptions and variations were not uncommon. Nor was the bible totally prescriptive: there was almost limitless scope for interpretation, and for expanding the religion by the accretions of tradition – themselves written down and commented on. The production of the various biblical glosses and the process of accumulative commentary was the work of the literate, the transmission of tradition alongside authority a process of historical growth. One tension among those which generated heresy was precisely that polarisation between the acceptance of tradition as a valid and validating force within the Church, and calls for repristination based on interpretation (and re-interpretation) of the bible as the prescriptive and sole foundation for christian action.[1]

As this chapter establishes parameters for discussion, footnotes are few. Many of the issues emerge in the other contributions. I am grateful to Peter Biller, John Edwards and Chris Wickham for comments on earlier drafts; and to the editors for letting me read the other essays before completing this final version.
[1] See Moore, chapter 2 above.

This is most evident with the biblicism of the Waldensians and Wyclif and, later, the first Reformers; but similar strands appear in the debates about the Spiritual Franciscans (even if tangentially), and in the way certain groups sought a precise *imitatio Christi*.

Because Western christianity developed, indeed was transformed, between 1100 and 1500, heresy was almost a necessary concomitant. Necessary, because the development reflected a succession of choices in terms of doctrine and acceptability, often with little real precision in formulation or interpretation. But we are also told, often, that heresy is a matter of choice: the wilful refusal to accept definitions offered by 'the Church'.

These ecclesiastical definitions were made by the literate. The authorities which defined the acceptable, whether specific doctrines or relatively minor practices, were those with access to the textual traditions of the theologians. This could operate in a variety of ways. At its crudest, and subject to considerable nuancing, the repetitive listing of sects and reproduction of the stereotype of heretical depravity was at root a literary and literate concoction, with little real meaning for those actually accused of heresy. Equally, as concern to define and identify heresy grew from 1100, and particularly with the distinction between heresy and error (even if the condemned doctrines were often categorised in terms of earlier heresies), the role of the learned in the process became increasingly important. The commissions which investigated particular texts, individuals or traditions, consisted of theologians and lawyers, the learned. This matters; for Western christianity's literate tradition changed considerably between 1100 and 1200, and developed further thereafter. It was transformations in the definitions of the faith – and of heresy – accepted among the literate which made other versions of christianity unacceptable. Why the changes occurred is not the issue, although those of the twelfth century may be linked with the growing prominence of the newly literate *clerici*. Their voluble concern about heresy may have originated in anxiety to establish their own status in the contemporary society which they hoped to remould (perhaps especially important given the criticism of the schools and their products at the time) and the uncertainties produced by their speculations about the nature of christianity. Possibly some clerics also doubted the basic validity of their stances: the claims of Latin theology against 'innate' interpretation by popular preachers were at their most confrontational just then.[2]

To some extent the literate brought these 'unacceptable' versions of christianity to public notice by deliberately challenging them, in speech or writing. Paradoxically, this could produce a situation where intended refutations were also repositories of heresy: to varying degrees, those responding to unorthodoxy offered vehicles for its dissemination. Differentiation may be needed between Latinate and vernacular vehicles, perhaps between oral and written, but that the ideas were reproduced is what really counts. Beyond this, the historiography of heresy contains a further strand which is influential in its own right: the dependence on the literate orthodox as recorders of the unorthodox, in inquisitors' manuals, court books of late medieval English bishops, and elsewhere. This again matters: historians are forced to use the language of the victors, and to label something as 'heresy' is to do just that. Tautologically, it could be claimed that unless something was condemned as heretical then it was not actually heretical. Lack of condemnation, although not evidence that unorthodoxy did not exist, does suggest that it did not cause concern (which need not mean that the orthodox were complacent). The evidence of the recording of heresy and the polemical reaction to it does not always offer precise indications of the actual extent or content of a heresy.

Additionally, the literate might become so obsessed by perceived threats that they would invent a heresy – like that of the 'Free Spirit' – from the ambiguities of 'popular' illiterate spirituality. Or they might be trapped by their own labels, as with the problems of distinguishing 'good' from 'bad' beguines in the Low Countries after the legislation of the Council of Vienne, complicated by the concurrent existence elsewhere of other *beghini* associated with the Spiritual Franciscans and attacked on that account.[3] Perhaps most important of all, the initial determinations of the learned provided the checklists for use in inquisitorial processes, questions on specific issues which would allow a label to be applied. The effect of that approach

---

[2] See Moore, chapter 2 above.
[3] Lerner; Lambert, pp. 178–81; E. W. McDonnell, *The Beguines and Beghards in Medieval Culture, with Special Emphasis on the Belgian Scene* (New Brunswick, N.J., 1954), pp. 521–58; D. Nimmo, *Reform and Division in the Medieval Franciscan Order, from Saint Francis to the Foundation of the Capuchins*, Biblioteca Seraphico-Capuccina, 33 (Rome, 1987), pp. 176–90; Lerner, chapter 11 above.

needs no underscoring: its imposition of coherence and similarity on beliefs which might be very different; its inability to convey nuances of belief by not asking questions on certain matters; its teasing out of statements which made people seem more extreme than they perhaps were in reality; and the traps which it posed for contemporary assessments of the prevalence of particular heresies, and for historians' attempts to interpret such material.

Beyond such general considerations the main focus of attention must be the links between heresy and literacy. Many issues require attention, bearing on the nature of heresy and the format of the historical record.

Given the fragmentation within medieval christianity, and the tensions and weaknesses of its doctrinal and ideological development, the frequent uncertainty about the boundaries between the orthodox and the unorthodox is unsurprising. In 1116, Henry of Lausanne's episcopally authorised preaching at Le Mans turned into a rejection of episcopal authority; while the later eccentricities of Margery Kempe in England incurred lay hostility, but bishops who questioned her found her orthodox.[4] Such cases could be multiplied, reflecting changes in spiritualities and the resulting tensions as those who were guardians of orthodoxy adjusted to the situation. Sometimes that did involve condemnation – in the thirteenth century to the extent of exhuming the Guido Lacha whom Brescia's contemporary laity had considered a saint, or in the attack on some of the cults of the host in fifteenth-century Germany. But reaction might be delayed, for whatever reasons, allowing ambiguity to persist. It was over thirty years before the authorities quashed the cult of Armanno Pungilupo at Ferrara: he died in 1269, but his tomb was not destroyed until 1301, despite considerable testimony to his Cathar connections.[5]

The heretication of many groups, and the nature of their condemnation, is known only through recording by the literate. There is clearly a problem here, of continuity and evidence. Many small

---

[4] Moore, chapter 2 above; C. W. Atkinson, *Mystic and Pilgrim: the Book and the World of Margery Kempe* (Ithaca and London, 1983), pp. 103–28.

[5] S. Wessley, 'The thirteenth-century Guglielmites: salvation through women', *SCH* Subsidia 1 (Oxford, 1978), p. 302 n. 68; C. Zika, 'Hosts, processions, and pilgrimages in fifteenth-century Germany', *Past and Present* 118 (February, 1989), 28–9, 48–50; M. da Alatri, 'L'eresia nella cronica di Salimbene', *Collectanea Franciscana* 137 (1967), 369–72.

groups are known only through material produced by their opponents: no records of their own survive. To be important to historians, heresies (as opposed to individual heretics) must have their literary remains (produced either by themselves or by their opponents), remains which can be tested to identify the heresy, and which by their survival can attest some degree of continuity. Exploitation of textual continuity and intellectual genealogies is certainly a feature of work on some of the less bizarre and more enduring and widespread heresies, notably the Waldensians and the Lollards.

But the problem of the continuity of heresy is then a real issue. Undeniably, the existence of literate heresy makes identification of heresy easier: texts provide concrete statements (even if they can be taken out of context) as well as precedents. In 1415 the illiterate John Claydon was tried in London for heresy; but it was his books (which had to be read to him) rather than his own statements of belief which were subjected to close examination.[6] As the heresies originated within mainstream christianity, they initially required no separate identification. Yet, like mainstream christianity, all heresies are, to an extent, text-based. The 'text', however, need not be a literary artefact: to adapt Brian Stock's notion of textual communities, the 'text' might be an individual life, or a group experience. Securing continuity in such circumstances would be an uncertain process: individuals die; groups split up. It is unlikely that several of the small twelfth-century groups, like those around Eon de l'Etoile or Peter of Bruys, could have continued long after the deaths of their leaders.

This notion of a living but illiterate textuality works in the long run against many heresies: lack of an independent canonical literate tradition seems eventually to produce disintegration. That seems to happen to the Cathars, possibly to the Spiritual Franciscans, and, eventually, to some of the Lollard groupings. These three strands, however, clearly had their literate traditions, which is why to ensure continuity the emphasis has to be on canonicity rather than simply literacy or textuality. Theoretically, such a tradition might take a variety of forms. One possibility would be for it simply to supersede the orthodox christian tradition. More likely would be a process of accretion – and, perhaps, excision – which by changing the canon

---

[6] A. Hudson, 'Lollard book production', in J. Griffiths and D. Pearsall (eds.), *Book Production and Publishing in Britain, 1375–1475* (Cambridge, 1989), pp. 25–6.

would alter the interpretations and prescriptions of the precedent tradition, much as the addition of the New Testament to the Old had defined christianity, and transformed the pre-existing Jewish tradition for the followers of the new faith. Such a transformation would lead to the creation of what rhetorical theorists might now label a 'discourse community', with language – governed by a particular written text or group of texts – providing 'a basis for sharing or holding in common: shared expectations, shared participation, commonly (or communally) held ways of expressing'.[7] Of course, orthodoxy itself was – or was defined by – one such community; but the 'heretical' forms provide an alternative, possibly explicitly competitive, identity.

Certainly the ecclesiastical authorities would appreciate the significance of the creation of the literate canonical tradition for the heretical groups; hence the attempted 'deliteralisation' of heresy – the ban on vernacular scriptures, the burning of books, and attempts to control interpretation by restricting access, increasingly insistent as printing made the threat more potent. The overall attitude to potentially heretical dissemination parallels the powers for ensuring an uncorrupt canonical tradition for Judaism which were assumed by the christian authorities as guardians of tradition and purity, as exemplified in the Talmud trials of the thirteenth century and the destruction of material which was considered as perverting 'true' (i.e. exclusively Old Testament based) Judaism. This similarity must be more than accidental. As the christian New Testament canon was seen as the ultimate and definitive development beyond the canon of the Jewish Old Testament tradition, it simply could not be supplanted or supplemented, whether by heretics, or, indeed, by the Qur'an. An alternative canon also implied an alternative structure, as manifested in Catharism, and implicit (but more insidious) in Joachite speculation after c. 1200. Ideas of an imminent Third Age to supersede the Age of Christ obviously challenged the status and authority of the existing ecclesiastical system, even if incorporated into a specifically christian teleology.

---

[7] B. A. Rafoth, 'The concept of discourse community: descriptive and explanatory adequacy', in G. Kirsch and D. H. Roen (eds.), *A Sense of Audience in Written Communication* Written Communication Annual, 5 (Newbury Park, London and New Delhi, 1990), pp. 140–53 (quotation at p. 140); B. A. Rafoth, 'A discourse community: where readers, writers, and texts come together', in B. A. Rafoth and D. L. Rubin (eds.), *The Social Construction of Written Communication* (Norwood, N.J., 1988), pp. 131–46.

The nature of any heretical canonical tradition may require more detailed definition. Given the range of biblical interpretations, the Vulgate could provide the required basis, but that would also require an independent exegetical tradition. Perhaps the required canon should be a non-Vulgate bible, since the authorities could use their interpretations of the Vulgate against its 'misusers'. The main difficulty arises with the issue of the independence of the exegetical tradition. The Church seemingly had no immediate objection to the straightforward translation of scriptural texts; but it did claim the right of supervision of their interpretation and utilisation. This is evident even from the turn of the twelfth and thirteenth centuries, with Innocent III's comments on the appearance of vernacular scriptures at Metz.[8] It often led, however, to ambivalence on the part of the Church: concern to prevent the appearance of purely 'literal' translations on one hand, and on the other the legitimisation of 'translations' which incorporated lengthy commentaries and explanations of the technicalities of the terms. In general (although with some notable regional exceptions, like northern France) what had to be translated was not *Scriptura sola*, but the orthodox theology which interpreted that scripture: appreciations had to be supervised alongside receipt of the simple text.

A similar problem arises with the Spiritual Franciscans. Their insistence on the 'gospel quality' of Francis's Rule and Testament provided a canonical focus; but as those texts were shared with the conventual branch of the Order, and so prey to ambiguity, they may not constitute an independent tradition. The apocalyptic writings of Peter Olivi did, however, attain something of that status.[9]

The failure to establish an enduring independent canon, because of either internal wrangling, or destruction by the orthodox, seems to result in a dual tradition. One strand consists of a living non-literate textuality which is the focus for the majority of the members of the groups, perhaps maintained chiefly by a process of family continuity. Alongside this exists a developing, but declining and disparate, literary tradition. The model does seem to apply to some of the major heretical strands. The vitality of the Cathar tradition virtually disappeared in the thirteenth century, to be replaced by

---

[8] L. E. Boyle, 'Innocent III and vernacular versions of scripture', *SCH* Subsidia 4 (Oxford, 1985), pp. 97–107; V. Coletti, *L'Eloquence de la chaire: victoires et défaites du latin entre Moyen Age et Renaissance* (Paris, 1987), pp. 42–3.

[9] Nimmo, *Reform and Division*, pp. 152–8; Lerner, chapter 11 above.

the situation at Montaillou (whose recording depends on the literate traditions of the champions of orthodoxy).[10] The Spiritual Franciscans became increasingly frantic, but with islands of literate textuality, centred for example around Olivi, Arnold of Villanova and the Neapolitan court.[11] Finally, the Lollards were still producing new works in the early fifteenth century, but from the late 1430s onwards were seemingly dependent more on the creation of islands of group experience centred on the incarnate textuality of people like William White, gradually developing into a series of distinct 'discourse communities'.[12] The division within the movements may be most obvious with the later Waldensians, which suggests a number of internal tensions. Their literate tradition is certainly disparate, even eclectic; yet their selective biblicism seems to avoid the requirement of a fixed canonical tradition, and so permitted their own exegetical divisions.[13] Their Latinate leadership and the activities of the wandering preachers suggest coherence in their overall structure, possibly providing continuity through lives-as-texts to compensate for the lack of exegetical continuity.[14] However, there is clearly an interpretative tension between the Latinity of the leaders and the vernacularism of the *credentes*, which may well provide the postulated 'double-track' tradition.[15] This does not deny the importance of literature and literacy for these groups, but it does suggest that the fact of literacy may have little to do with heresy.

And, indeed, need it have? Perhaps implicit in the examination of links between heresy and literacy is the idea that they are somehow

---

[10] Wakefield and Evans, pp. 64–7 (with extensive translation of Cathar works at pp. 447–630); E. Leroy Ladurie, *Montaillou: Cathars and Catholics in a French Village, 1294–1324* (Harmondsworth, 1980); A. Borst, 'La transmission de l'hérésie au moyen âge', in *Hérésies et sociétés dans l'Europe pré-industrielle, 11ᵉ–18ᵉ siècles* (Paris, 1968), pp. 275–6. Biller, chapter 4 above.

[11] Nimmo, *Reform and Division*, pp. 181–5 (and, for later Spiritual literature, pp. 279–309); R. G. Musto, 'Queen Sanchia of Naples (1286–1345) and the Spiritual Franciscans', in J. Kirschner and S. F. Wemple (eds.), *Women of the Medieval World: Essays in Honor of John H. Mundy* (Oxford, 1985), pp. 193–202. Lerner, chapter 11 above.

[12] M. Aston, *Lollards and Reformers: Images and Literacy in Late Medieval England* (London, 1984), pp. 71–100 (but cf. R. G. Davies, 'Lollardy and locality', *TRHS*, 6th ser., 1 (1991), 200–1); Hudson, 'Lollard book production', p. 127. See also A. Hudson, *Lollards and their Books* (London and Ronceverte, 1985), pp. 165–75.

[13] M. Deanesly, *The Lollard Bible and other Mediaeval Biblical Versions* (Cambridge, 1920), p. 28; Lambert, *Medieval Heresy*, p. 163.

[14] For the Brethren, P. Biller, '*Multum ieiunantes et se castigantes*: medieval Waldensian asceticism', *SCH* 22 (1985), 215–19, 222–7.

[15] Patschovsky, chapter 7 above.

symbiotic, and that it is the increase in heresy which needs to be considered. That claim can be inverted: except in rare instances heresy prior to the sixteenth century (and perhaps even then) remained a minority occupation. To stress connections of literacy and heresy is to overlook the connections between orthodoxy and literacy. Yet it is undeniable that, of the torrent of christian material produced in the later middle ages, the vast majority was perfectly orthodox. Moreover, the very acquisition of literacy was often part of the acquisition of orthodoxy – in so far as the primer was the fundamental book of instruction for those learning to read, then orthodoxy comes first.

This again opens up several possibilities. Implicit in much discussion of the relationship between heresy and literacy is the assumption that 'literacy' is literacy in the vernacular. In the technical vocabulary of the learned, however, this is still illiteracy; it was not a Latinate literacy, although it retained the possibility of Latinity. Latin literacy is, of course, vital, and it would be foolish to deny the extent to which Latin posed threats to orthodoxy as the language of 'intellectuals'. Here the 'philosophical' heresies stimulated by the expanding influence of the works of classical writers and the attempts to reconcile faith and 'reason' enter the picture. They are perhaps especially significant for the twelfth century, when Western christian theology was itself in the process of acquiring real definition; while the increasing influence of Aristotle and the Arabic commentators in the thirteenth century cannot be ignored. From 1400 a different Latinate literary strand also threatened orthodoxy, with the rise of humanism and the growth of historical linguistics capable of repristinating the scriptural texts and challenging some of the bases on which orthodoxy was constructed. This was in part a revival (or continuation) of old debates on the utility of the classics to the christian and the ways in which their study affected faith; but the humanist advances had further implications. Lorenzo Valla epitomised the new challenge, seeking renewal of the biblical text, undermining the Donation of Constantine, and challenging traditions on the origins of the apostles' Creed – this last as the catalyst for a series of heresy accusations culled from his works. The marriage of old philosophical debates and humanism was revealed in the process against Pico della Mirandola in 1487, when some of his philosophical theses were placed before a commission of inquiry and duly condemned. Here a further potentiality in the linkage of heresy and literacy became apparent, this being one of the first debates about heresy to be conducted in print (albeit in Latin), and therefore immediately addressed to an audience beyond the prime participants.[16]

Vernacular movements raise different issues. The vernacularity of late medieval literacy, increasingly evident from *c.* 1300 onwards, has its own ramifications for the connections, if any, between heresy and literacy and the processes for the transmission of the former. Among other things, the equations must incorporate developments in the vernacular languages, especially their permeation by Latinate theological terms which would affect a language's ability to address theological debates. However, in the context of pre-print medieval societies, the impact of vernacular heresy was almost unavoidably restricted: geographically regional or localised (a regionalisation and fragmentation akin to the localisation of the various manifestations of orthodox christianity), chronologically limited by linguistic and orthographic change. A merely vernacular heresy offered only a small-scale threat to the totality of christianity: it was Latinate heresy, heresy capable of transmission both transgenerationally and internationally, which contained the greatest threats. Before the sixteenth century the sheer process of translation between vernaculars – often into and then out of Latin – usually seems to have proved too great an obstacle to extensive transmission of vernacular heresy. Where books with heretical implications were transmitted, on closer examination that process was often dependent on their heresy not being fully appreciated: the books were translated not as vehicles for heresy, but because they were felt to validate a particular form of orthodoxy (even if one which had to be treated circumspectly). This certainly seems to apply to Margaret Porete's *Mirror for Simple Souls*, and to the 'Free Spirit' tract, *Schwester Katrei*.[17] Against this, a heresy's initial appearance in Latinate form did seemingly stimulate vernacularisation, with English and Czech versions of Wyclif's Latin works, the rendering of Spiritual Franciscan tracts into Italian or Provençal dialects and translation of Hussite works among the

---

[16] J. H. Bentley, *Politics and Culture in Renaissance Naples* (Princeton, N.J., 1987), pp. 116–17; G. di Napoli, *Lorenzo Valla: filosofia e religione nell'umanesimo italiano*, Uomini e dottrine, 17 (Rome, 1971), pp. 279–312; W. G. Craven, *Giovanni Pico della Mirandola, Symbol of his Age: Modern Interpretations of a Renaissance Philosopher*, Travaux d'humanisme et Renaissance (Geneva, 1981), pp. 2, 47–75.

[17] Lerner, pp. 72–5, 216; see also Nimmo, *Reform and Division*, pp. 305–6.

Vaudois of Piedmont.[18] (There was also some heresy which was bilingual from the start, as in the writings of Arnold of Villanova.[19])

What then follows is a different matter. The acquisition of literacy obviously opens up numerous possibilities, some of which are heretical. But were those possibilities necessarily not available without literacy? Here it becomes necessary to revert to first principles. 'Heresy' reflects a questioning based on perceptions of an apparent irreconcilability between the world as the Church proclaims it to be and the world as it is – tensions which can focus on purely practical matters, like the fact of transubstantiation, on the effectiveness of prayer to the saints, on the problem of where evil comes from and why. But awareness of those tensions is a purely cerebral event: literacy is unnecessary. On the other hand, literacy – regardless of the language – may help, if appropriate written texts become available, to encourage a further process of questioning; it may also resolve the doubts. The initial stage is the act of questioning; the response as conditioned by literacy reflects the intellectual acceptability of the various answers which become available. Several heresies stimulated by intellectual development obviously depended on a precedent literary tradition to evoke the conflict; but that does not mean that similar questions could not arise without the pre-existing literature: it is a matter of circumstances, not necessity. Nevertheless, the production of a literate response makes concrete the implicit challenge to authority in the act of questioning, which is otherwise ephemeral unless recorded by the literate (as in some of the late medieval heresy cases in England). The production of a literate consideration of doubts then clearly presents a challenge to the orthodox authorities, whose response may vary. It may be simple condemnation, as may be seen in the attacks on Peter Abelard and the reaction to many of the academic heresies of the twelfth and later centuries, including the treatment of Wyclif in the Blackfriars Council of 1382.[20] There may be perception of a deeper

---

[18] Nimmo, *Reform and Division*, pp. 301–3, 308–9; F. Šmahel, '"Doctor evangelicus super omnes evangelistas": Wyclif's fortunes in Hussite Bohemia', *BIHR* 43 (1970), 25–6; Brenon, chapter 8 above.

[19] Lerner, chapter 11 above.

[20] D. E. Luscombe, *The School of Peter Abelard: the Influence of Abelard's Thought in the Early Scholastic Period* (Cambridge, 1969), pp. 103–42; A. V. Murray, *Abelard and St Bernard; a Study in Twelfth-Century 'Modernism'* (Manchester and New York, 1967), pp. 39–44, 49–88; D. Knowles, 'The censured opinions of Uthred of Boldon', *Proceedings of the British Academy*

threat, requiring firmer and more wide-ranging action to test whether the literate statement is but the tip of an iceberg among the illiterate; apparently the stance adopted with the followers of Amaury of Bène at Paris in 1210, followed by the rounding up of others who probably would not otherwise have been investigated.[21] Seemingly much rarer were confrontations with heretics on their own terms, and in the vernacular, with formal written refutations of their proposals. That approach had its dangers, made painfully obvious to Reginald Pecock in fifteenth-century England when accused of heresy and deprived of his bishopric of Chichester for writing against Lollardy in English.[22] Equally two-edged might be the exploitation of awareness of a heretic's literacy by providing a vernacular indentured version of the abjuration or submission, as occurred with some Lollards. The documents were a constant reminder to the abjurer of his or her own precarious status, but might also provide a reminder and reinforcement of the abjured doctrines, possibly even a basis for further dissemination.[23]

The conclusion to be drawn is that literate heresy is but an offshoot of questioning which need not be connected with literacy. The attractiveness of heresy as a choice against orthodoxy is not necessarily conditioned by literacy, but it may be assisted by it. Certainly, the acquisition of reading skills increased the dissemination of literate heresy; that in itself may make visible and concrete less coherent but equally widespread uncertainties about the faith which had developed naturally anyway, perhaps allowing disparate notions to congeal into a 'discourse community'. Something like that can at least be postulated for Lollardy. But literacy *per se* does not demonstrate a particular propensity to heresy, even if evidence in some cases suggests that the connection was presupposed.[24] Literacy could also reinforce orthodoxy. The existence of literate heretics may be more important than the existence of literate heresy: the

37 (1951), 313–50; J. H. Dahmus, *The Prosecution of John Wyclyf* (New York and London, 1952), pp. 89–98.

21 H. S. Denifle and E. Chatelain, *Chartularium universitatis Parisiensis* (Paris, 1891–9), vol. I, pp. 70–2; H. F. Delaborde (ed.), *Oeuvres de Rigord et de Guillaume le Breton, historiens de Philippe-Auguste* (Paris, 1882–5), vol. I, pp. 232–3; G. Dickson, 'The burning of the Amalricians', *JEH* 40 (1989), 347–69. See also H. Grundmann, 'Hérésies savantes et hérésies populaires au moyen âge', in *Hérésies et sociétés dans l'Europe pré-industrielle, 11ᵉ–18ᵉ siècles* (Paris, 1968), p. 210.

22 R. M. Haines, 'Reginald Pecock: a tolerant man in an age of intolerance', *SCH* 21 (1984), 129–34.

23 Hudson, p. 187; Aston, *Lollards and Reformers*, pp. 97–8.   24 Biller, chapter 4 above.

people were a prerequisite for spreading heresy. Writing provided a means of transmission, geographically and temporally; but the heretics provided the means of communication. The audience for literature was always greater than the readership – for orthodox works as well as heretical writings.

The existence of texts which might be judged heretical could well dilute the border between orthodoxy and unorthodoxy, so that while literate individuals desired to be orthodox they unconsciously imbibed heretical teachings: again, Lollard interpolations of some late medieval English writings indicate such processes, as does the careful glossing of the English version of Margaret Porete's *Mirror for Simple Souls* to circumvent some of its more dubious statements.[25] Access to literacy might increase the questioning facility and thereby necessitate greater control of access to texts. This is exemplified in the drive to control access to the bible in English, whether by Arundel's Constitutions of 1407 or by the ominously entitled Act 'for thadvauncement of true religion and for thabbolisshment of the contrarie' in 1543.[26] This is a local revival of the earlier debates about the vernacular scriptures, although apparently with greater intensity than elsewhere. Debates continued after the Reformation: Luther's initial ardour for universal access to a vernacular bible cooled fairly swiftly, reverting to controlled interpretation which replaced unsupervised access by a preliminary process of catechisation which was considered sufficient access for the majority.[27] In these instances, and others, the access to literacy would stimulate and perhaps validate the questioning; but it would not originate it. The act of reception stimulates the questioning in the search for understanding; that reception might be via literacy, in reading, or might stimulate the acquisition of literacy. Yet literacy remained a minority qualification; and each type of literacy – each vernacular, as well as literacy in Latin – was a minority of that minority, with all

[25] Hudson, 'Lollard book production', p. 135; M. Doiron, 'The Middle English translation of "Le Mirouer des simples ames"', in A. Ampe (ed.), *Dr. L. Ruypens-Album: Oopstellen aangeboden aan Prof. Dr. L. Ruypens s.j. ter gelegenheid van zijn tachtigste verjeerdag op 25 februari 1964* Studien an Tekstuitgraven van Ons Geestelijk Erf, 16 (Antwerp, 1964), pp. 133–4, 141–6. See also Lerner, pp. 72–5, 200–8.

[26] P. McNiven, *Heresy and Politics in the Reign of Henry IV: the Burning of John Badby* (Woodbridge, 1987), pp. 114–16; *Statutes of the Realm*, vol. III (London, 1817), pp. 894–7 (esp. 896).

[27] G. Strauss, 'Lutheranism and literacy: a reassessment', in K. von Greyerz (ed.), *Religion and Society in Early Modern Europe, 1500–1800* (London, 1984), pp. 112–15, 117–18. See also Scribner, chapter 15 above.

the implications of that for transmission and communication. Most reception was auditory, making access to the written text a mediate, not immediate, experience. That is significant, for the receiver could misunderstand what was being conveyed: one strand of complaint against learned sermonisers in fourteenth-century England was that they confused their audiences, and thereby undermined their faith.[28]

Orality, auditory reception, and with both the use of memory for textual transmission (as well recorded among the Lollards), also have ramifications for a possibly crucial issue, that of 'passive literacy'. Certainly, the integration of heretics and heresy into an increasingly writing-orientated society would be influential, but its operation would vary, with pressures operating in different directions. The prominence of literate families and individuals among heretical groups, as foci for dissemination and authorisation or authentication of the text, is often notable.[29] On the other hand the expansion of 'passive literacy' in a specifically orthodox format was part of the programme for revivification of the Church advanced at Lateran IV; how that operated as encouragement or discouragement to heresy remains to be investigated.

Such a barrier between text and context is where this comment draws to a close. Historians depend on the literate to provide their evidence. They can then turn to the texts produced by the literate heretics, and to those produced by their equally literate opponents; indeed, often historians depend more on the latter than the former. But that dependence on literacy offers no real insight into the mental state of those who undramatically fail to appear in the evidence: can it automatically be assumed that they were totally orthodox? Guglielma of Milan might well have been considered an orthodox saint rather than a leader of heresy; there was concern in early-fourteenth-century Milan that heretics were intruding false saints into the calendar.[30] Equally, to emphasise the relatively large 'movements' of heretics, vocal through their literate remains

---

[28] R. N. Swanson, 'Chaucer's parson and other priests', *Studies in the Age of Chaucer* 13 (1991), 75–7. See also Coletti, *L'Eloquence*, p. 72.

[29] On 'passive literacy' see Moore, chapter 2 above. For the socially literate contexts of heresy see especially the essays by Biller and Paolini, above (chs. 4 and 5).

[30] S. E. Wessley, 'James of Milan and the Guglielmites; Franciscan spirituality and popular heresy in late thirteenth-century Milan', *Collectanea Franciscana* 54 (1984), 5.

(whoever produced them), may divert attention from the non-vocal, whose numbers might have been larger. Erroneous wandering preachers were probably more common than is usually recognised. Although their role has been extensively considered for the twelfth century, in later periods – perhaps particularly in pre-Wycliffite England, where they possibly provided some foretastes of what was later labelled as Lollardy – they receive little attention. In the English context, there is usually no detailed record of their errors, and as they did not establish secure successions they are generally ignored.

The ambiguity surrounding many such references to heresy may be characteristic. Armanno Pungilupo, Guglielma of Milan, Peter Olivi, all seem to fit into the pattern. An English parallel might be the cult of Richard Wyche, burnt for heresy in 1440, but whose ashes were treated as relics. A more extreme continental case would be the cult of the greyhound saint, St Guinefort.[31] Faced with such ambiguities and uncertainties, to deal with issues of literacy and heresy is also to raise questions about the history of heresy, and historians' awareness of it. Such investigation also throws into relief the problem of the links between literacy and the extent and spread of orthodoxy, of the response of the literate as orthodox to the heretics as literates or illiterates. The permutations are manifold, but each of them must be addressed to produce a full appreciation of the issues which arise.

[31] Above, n. 5; Wessley, 'Thirteenth-century Guglielmites', pp. 300–2; Lerner, chapter 11 above; J. A. F. Thomson, *The Later Lollards, 1414–1520* (Oxford, 1965), pp. 149–50; J. C. Schmitt, *The Holy Greyhound: Guinefort, Healer of Children since the Thirteenth Century* (Cambridge, 1983).

Index

Leading figures and authors of heterodox groups and religious movements are listed, or given cross-references, under them: *Anabaptists, Beguins, Bogomils, Cathars, Franciscans (Spiritual), Hussites, Lollards, Reformers, Taborites, Unity of Czech Brethren, Waldensians*. Authors of treatises describing or refuting heresies are listed under *Heresies, texts describing*; trials, inquisitors and authors of inquisitors' manuals under *Inquisition*; individual popes under *Papacy*. Modern authorities are not indexed. For the sake of clarity, any long entry is given an initial heading in capitals, and at the end of the entry a space is left before other headings resume in alphabetical order.

Lightning Source UK Ltd.
Milton Keynes UK
UKHW011958141118
332367UK00001B/100/P